ADMINISTRATIVE SECRECY IN DEVELOPED COUNTRIES

ADMINISTRATIVE SECRECY IN DEVELOPED COUNTRIES

Edited by
Donald C. Rowat

Professor of Political Science
Carleton University
Ottawa, Canada

A comparative study in the series *Studies in Administrative Procedures*
Sponsored by
International Institute of Administrative Sciences, Brussels
First published as *Le Secret Administratif dans les Pays Développés*
© Editions Cujas 1977
This edition© International Institute of Administrative Sciences 1979

Softcover reprint of the hardcover 1st edition 1979

First published 1979 by
THE MACMILLAN PRESS LTD
London and Basingstoke
Associated companies in Delhi
Dublin Hong Kong Johannesburg Lagos
Melbourne New York Singapore Tokyo

British Library Cataloguing in Publication Data

Administrative secrecy in developed countries
 – (Studies in administrative procedures)
 1. Official secrets
 I. Rowat, Donald Cameron   II. Series
 323.44´5   JC597

ISBN 978-1-349-04126-8   ISBN 978-1-349-04124-4 (eBook)
                            DOI 10.1007/978-1-349-04124-4

Contents

Preface

When the Committee of Studies in Administrative Procedures of the International Institute of Administrative Sciences decided, three years ago, to undertake a study of 'Public Access to Administrative Information', it was conscious of tackling a subject likely to appeal to many public law specialists. I think I may now safely state that the class of cultured readers to whom the book will be of interest has turned out to be much larger than we at first intended.

Credit for this is largely due to our general reporter, Professor Rowat, of Carleton University, Ottawa. With undeniable talent, he has vigorously and brilliantly summed up the national reports reproduced here. As a political scientist, he shows how the progress of democracy would be assisted if the Administration's filing cabinets were opened. Administrative documents, except for those clearly and precisely classified, should, in his opinion, be made available, under judicial control, to the public and to the press, which is its professional informant. The Scandinavian, especially Swedish, experience, to which he devotes more than half his report, appears to him to be convincing.

As Professor Rowat points out in his introduction, this study differs somewhat from the previous ones. The Committee originally intended to study administrative cases. The following surveys were thus launched: *Prevention of Cattle Diseases*, for which I was entrusted with the general report, *Control of River Pollution by Industry*, with a general report by the late Professor Litwin, and *Ascertaining Entitlement to Compensation for an Industrial Injury*, for which Judge Spielmeyer was responsible. My recollection of those first studies is closely linked with the memory of Professor van Poelje, the Netherlands Councillor of State who was then chairman of the Committee. Subsequently, attention was centred on *The Administration of Publicly-Aided Housing*, by Professor Ascher, and on *Building Permits: A Comparative Study*, by Professor Jacques Stassen, the present Director General of the International Institute of Adminis-

trative Sciences. The common feature of the studies is that they refer
to matters in which the Administration, for the sake of the general
interest, comes into conflict with the Citizen, who can claim to have
legitimate private interests; so that it is important to work out
methods of resolving or reducing the conflict. For instance, if sick
cattle are slaughtered, serious loss is incurred by the owners and an
award of compensation is one means of persuading them to agree to
a sacrifice required in the general interest.

When the Committee decided to deal with the subject of the
present volume, it doubtless changed its course, since the conflict
between public and private interests is here less apparent. Yet there
may be a conflict, particularly when an individual needs access to a
file kept by the Administration in order to obtain information for
establishing that an administrative decision was illegal. But, much
more often, public access to the files has no such implications.

The observations made by an official conducting an inquiry or
inspection may be of interest to a labour or employers' union, or to
an association wishing to promote certain reforms or to know the
results of laws in force or the conditions under which they are
applied. Moreover, access to administrative documents undeniably
facilitates the control of governmental action and helps to protect
the citizen against arbitrariness. The reasons for its refusal, though
often quite legitimate, may also be less convincing, e.g. a feeling that
the documents in question are like a private enterprise's papers and,
hence, are the service's property. Sometimes even, there are no
logical grounds for the refusal, which is simply prompted by
instinctive mistrust or by respect for tradition.

But this volume differs still more from the previous ones by the
general reporter's approach to his task, since Professor Rowat has
chosen to present a somewhat doctrinal report in which he does not
hesitate to take a firm line and, unlike his predecessors, has
deliberately avoided dwelling on side-issues which are, however,
not insignificant if the doctrine is meant to be put into application.
Practising administrators will perhaps regret this, but less specialised readers will certainly peruse the book with keener interest.

We do not share the opinion that the – by now very relative –
principle of administrative secrecy has really been tainted from the
start by being inherited from absolute monarchy. In the past, the
State's functions were very restricted and essentially limited to
government, war and peace, and taxation, i.e. to fields still looked

upon as warranting secrecy. And, as there were no typewriters or duplicators, documents were too valuable to be entrusted to outsiders. The connection between absolute monarchy and secrecy is perhaps therefore that they co-existed; not a cause and an effect.

On the other hand, there is no denying the extent to which historical traditions and, if one looks further, the multiple circumstances with which a nation has been confronted during the centuries, have affected its choice of administrative customs. The choice of the United States is accounted for, as Mr Singer calls to mind, by the country's bitter memories of Crown Privilege, which have led to a certain mistrust of the Administration, and by the balancing role assigned to the press under the First Amendment. But in other countries, the Administration has played an important part in cementing national unity and defending the people against the high and mighty, or in setting up the Nation as example of discipline and effectiveness which remains particularly close to its heart. In other countries again, the geographical – if not the strategic – position has come into play. Mr Rowat grants that this is true of Canada and the same may be assumed of Sweden, even though the origins of the country's liberalism go back to the eighteenth century. The progress of openness in the United States is to some extent a result of the reduction, whether lasting or not, in international tensions. The above factors may not be disregarded for the sake of adopting a perfectionist notion of Democracy.

While I thought I should question Professor Rowat's opinion about the origin of administrative secrecy, it also seemed to me that, in his eagerness to be convincing, the general reporter was presenting a rather gloomy picture of the position in the countries that still adhere to the principle of secrecy. When he goes into the consequences of secrecy there, he explains, for instance, that a citizen has no right of access to documents in his own case. This is a strange allegation, when it is observed that, among the countries – Belgium, the Federal Republic of Germany, France and the United Kingdom – whose systems are examined in the present volume, none actually deprives the citizen of the means for stating his case before the courts. The British House of Lords ruled, in 1968, that the courts could weigh a minister's statement that a file was secret and should not be disclosed to the interested parties. A similar rule appears to prevail in Germany, where the parties in a case are entitled to inspect the documents in their files. M. Boulard's report

for France also shows that, since 1905, public servants who are liable
to punishment have had the right of access to their files and that
access is similarly granted in other cases. Moreover, the administrative courts dismiss from consideration any documents which
cannot be discussed by both sides; and, should a litigant have been
denied access to the file, the facts he alleges are presumed to be true.
M. Boulard also refers to the famous *Trompier Gravier* case of 1944.

When each country begins to compare the advantages of the two
contrasting systems described by Professor Rowat, it will, besides,
have to take into account not only its own historical background but
also the significance, considering the characteristics of its administrative organisation, of the decision to be taken. As the national
reports show, there are profound differences from country to
country.

In Sweden, the only function assigned to the ministries themselves, each in its sphere of activity, is to issue the essential
regulations and supervise their application, which is entrusted to
agencies that attend to the day-to-day management of the services
and make rules to implement the regulations. There is no freedom of
access to the internal documents of ministries. Moreover, we are
told that there is a tendency to form certain services into companies
with commercial objects, in which case their documents are not
open to scrutiny. At all events, if the principle of administrative
openness were adopted in France, for example, its implications
would be much wider than in Sweden.

Mr Wraith points out that in the United Kingdom the central
government's responsibilities are comparatively limited. Education, housing, town planning and other equally essential public
utilities are administered by local authorities. A change of system
would have a different impact there too.

Professor Bullinger, in his report presented on behalf of the
German National Section, is of the opinion that public access to
administrative records is basically an essential feature of direct
democracy in small-scale countries. This seems to be confirmed in
the parts of M. Boulard's and Mr Wraith's reports, on behalf of the
French and United Kingdom National Sections respectively, where
they observe that access to administrative files is much more freely
authorised at the local government level. It may therefore perhaps
be concluded that, in states whose inhabitants are reckoned by the
million, free access to administrative records cannot reasonably be

upon as warranting secrecy. And, as there were no typewriters or duplicators, documents were too valuable to be entrusted to outsiders. The connection between absolute monarchy and secrecy is perhaps therefore that they co-existed; not a cause and an effect.

On the other hand, there is no denying the extent to which historical traditions and, if one looks further, the multiple circumstances with which a nation has been confronted during the centuries, have affected its choice of administrative customs. The choice of the United States is accounted for, as Mr Singer calls to mind, by the country's bitter memories of Crown Privilege, which have led to a certain mistrust of the Administration, and by the balancing role assigned to the press under the First Amendment. But in other countries, the Administration has played an important part in cementing national unity and defending the people against the high and mighty, or in setting up the Nation as example of discipline and effectiveness which remains particularly close to its heart. In other countries again, the geographical – if not the strategic – position has come into play. Mr Rowat grants that this is true of Canada and the same may be assumed of Sweden, even though the origins of the country's liberalism go back to the eighteenth century. The progress of openness in the United States is to some extent a result of the reduction, whether lasting or not, in international tensions. The above factors may not be disregarded for the sake of adopting a perfectionist notion of Democracy.

While I thought I should question Professor Rowat's opinion about the origin of administrative secrecy, it also seemed to me that, in his eagerness to be convincing, the general reporter was presenting a rather gloomy picture of the position in the countries that still adhere to the principle of secrecy. When he goes into the consequences of secrecy there, he explains, for instance, that a citizen has no right of access to documents in his own case. This is a strange allegation, when it is observed that, among the countries – Belgium, the Federal Republic of Germany, France and the United Kingdom – whose systems are examined in the present volume, none actually deprives the citizen of the means for stating his case before the courts. The British House of Lords ruled, in 1968, that the courts could weigh a minister's statement that a file was secret and should not be disclosed to the interested parties. A similar rule appears to prevail in Germany, where the parties in a case are entitled to inspect the documents in their files. M. Boulard's report a court be exercising a right to control, it would rather hesitate to overrule an opinion expressed on such a point. The Administration is also in the best position, if not the only position, to sort out which documents or parts of them refer to individuals and must be kept secret and which, on the other hand, may be disclosed. Besides, the existence of documents obviously has to be indicated, since the public will otherwise be unaware of them and unable to identify them and ask to see them. Leviathan will thus always be present, and the devil must be given his due!

As was to be expected, the reports clearly show that, everywhere, practice does not exactly keep to the rules of written law. As stated by the Yugoslav reporter, Mr Petrovič, 'although most of these rights [of access to information] are realised in practice, the practice is not always in conformity with constitutional principles.' Where the right of access to information is acknowledged, the Administration reacts in self-defence to restrict it. Pressure in the opposite direction is exercised in countries where the right is refused. Close attention should therefore be paid to the seemingly unimportant, but really vital, question of the procedure for obtaining the information. If the procedure is red-tapist, if the inquirer has to establish a strictly interpreted 'legitimate interest', or if there is a somewhat heavy scale of fees, the liberal provisions defining freedom of access may become mere window-dressing.

The truth is that, whatever the starting-point, a compromise is necessarily reached, so that the differences between countries where files are secret and those where access to them is a right end up by being less glaring than people think.

Pressure has undoubtedly been exercised, in the last few years, by public opinion to strip the Administration of its mystery, and it may well happen that the trend will lead a number of governments to share Professor Rowat's views.

But the national reports show that, almost everywhere, efforts are being made to give greater publicity to administrative work. States have become large publishing houses. Regulations often provide that the general public or directly interested persons should be consulted before certain decisions are taken and that a file should be placed at their disposal containing background information, including the documents relating to the preparation of a case. Without legislative provision to that effect, the courts have ensured the protection of public servants or other individuals by ruling that the relevant papers should be made available to them (see the United Kingdom and French reports). Some countries have even moved towards indirect freedom of access through an Ombudsman as in the Scandinavian countries, a Parliamentary Commissioner for Administration as in the United Kingdom, or a mediator as in France.

Compromises that are, of course, still open to improvement have thus been worked out in the countries still adhering to the traditional rule of secrecy.

At the same time, however, public opinion has, during the last few years, been getting uneasy. Since the Administration is the data bank with the largest amount of stored or storable materials, information about a person's age, family, health, income, property, offences, convictions, etc., might be divulged. The campaign in favour of greater openness of public administration is thus accompanied and partly contradicted by a counter-movement. Nothing more clearly shows that there is no simple answer in any particular case. Still, I could not dispute that progress towards a greater openness of administrative work is required or that there is something attractive, at least intellectually, about the assertion of a right of access to administrative records. We all live by symbols as much as by bread.

To conclude these observations that have been suggested by a series of first-rate reports, I should like to express the gratitude of the International Institute of Administrative Sciences to Electricité de France and to the Paris Chamber of Commerce and Industry for the aid kindly granted for the preparation of these reports and the publication of the French edition of this volume.

ANDRÉ HEILBRONNER

Introduction

DONALD C. ROWAT

CHOICE OF SUBJECT

The subject of this study, which was chosen by the *ad hoc* committee of the International Institute of Administrative Sciences as the seventh in its series of comparative studies in administrative procedures, differs somewhat from the previous ones. Like them it deals with a current problem of public administration common to many countries, and focuses on the area where the administration comes into contact with the public and the ordinary citizen. Like them, too, it aims to examine not only laws and regulations but also administrative practices and their consequences. It differs, however, in that, instead of dealing with a specific administrative activity, such as issuing building permits or preventing cattle diseases, it focuses on a problem which affects the whole of public administration and its relationship to the public in a democracy. It is therefore not a 'case study' in the same sense as the previous ones. It did not require the same detailed collection of facts about a particular programme, and thus called for a somewhat different approach.

The choice of subject by the *ad hoc* committee was a wise one because of its importance and the increasing attention being given to it in many countries. Some countries, such as Denmark, Norway and the United States, have recently made important changes in their law and practice on the subject, while others, such as Canada, France and the United Kingdom, are now making or considering such changes. Because the traditional law and practice are currently being questioned in several countries, the time seemed opportune to make a comparative study of the current situation, including recent changes and proposals, in a number of countries. Because of my own interest in the subject, I was pleased to be invited by the *ad hoc* committee to be the general reporter, and to be the first Canadian so honoured.

COUNTRIES INCLUDED

In the choice of countries to be included in its series of comparative studies, the International Institute has tended to be limited to those countries in which it has active national sections to advise on the selection of suitable experts as reporters. This has tended to give a concentration on developed countries. One could argue that this is desirable because it is in such countries that the law and practice on the chosen subjects have tended to be most fully developed, and most carefully examined by competent scholars. The present study is no exception. Although an effort was made to include some developing countries, this effort was eventually abandoned because of the difficulty of finding suitable reporters, perhaps because the subject is mainly of current concern in the developed countries.

As the title indicates, then, this comparative study of administrative secrecy and the public's right of access to information is restricted to developed countries. Under such a title, it would have been desirable to include other important developed countries, but it is hoped that the countries included constitute a representative sample of the range of approaches to the problem. In this respect we were fortunate in being able to include two socialist countries, Hungary and Yugoslavia. To have included additional developed countries would have made the book too long and the problems of translation and editing too great. It was considered worth while to have a separate essay on each of the Nordic countries, because recent legislative changes have moved Denmark and Norway closer to the tradition of openness in Sweden and Finland, and because the situation in all four countries is now so different from that in most other countries.

The inclusion of Canada and the United States presented some difficulty because the Institute had no section in Canada to advise on the choice of a reporter, and because both countries are decentralised federations with a clear division of constitutional, legislative and administrative powers between the central and provincial or state governments. The latter have their own laws

which regulate their own administrations, and also local governments. These laws may vary considerably, especially in the United
States. For instance, some states have so-called 'sunshine laws',
which may require an even greater degree of openness than is
provided at the federal level by the Freedom of Information Act. A
notable example is Florida.

The problem of obtaining a reporter for Canada was easily solved
by my agreeing to prepare the report on Canada myself. I was also
asked to participate in the choice of a reporter for the United States,
and we were fortunate in obtaining the agreement of the chairman
of the Administrative Conference of the United States, Antonin
Scalia, to be the reporter for that country. He attended the country
reporters' meeting, discussed below, and made many useful suggestions, for which we thank him. Unfortunately, however, he
resigned as chairman of the Conference before the report on the
United States could be undertaken, but the task was taken over and
ably executed by M. J. Singer, staff attorney of the Administrative
Conference. Although the situation at the provincial and state level
in Canada and the U.S. is similar to that at the federal level, readers
are warned that our essays deal mainly with the central government, since it is difficult for a single scholar to gather detailed
information on the laws and practices of all units of government in a
decentralised federation.

NATURE OF THE STUDY

The general aim of this study, as set forth by the *ad hoc* committee, is
'(*a*) to define the boundary between warranted and unwarranted
secrecy, and (*b*) to inquire into the lines on which a satisfactory
boundary may be struck between (i) the legitimate requirements of
science, industry and the general public, and (ii) the need, for quite
specific and justifiable reasons, to keep certain information confidential or even strictly secret.' The committee also outlined several
main points that ought to be covered in such a study, and requested
me to prepare a more detailed outline and questionnaire as a guide
to the country reporters.

It seemed to me that, with minor revisions, the points set forth by
the committee covered the main aspects of the subject and would
form suitable main headings for the outline. I therefore prepared an
outline proposing that the content of the country studies should be

organised under the following main headings: a general introduction on background factors; the general rights of public access to administrative information, including provisions regarding the types of information to be kept secret; the holders of administrative information, including the political executive and other administrative authorities; the recipients of administrative information, including official bodies, such as parliament and the courts, and special segments of the outside public, such as the press, scholars and citizens with a personal interest in their own case; information procedures, including the holding and transmission of information, the security classification of documents, and the refusal and release of information; and a conclusion discussing general trends and recent or proposed changes. A detailed outline was sent to all of the reporters for their critical comments, revised in the light of these comments, and presented as a basis for discussion to a meeting of the reporters, held in Brussels in June 1974.

At that meeting the outline was further refined, and it was agreed that, because of the breadth of the subject, the study should be limited to: (i) the problem of public access to information, and should exclude government information services and efforts to keep the public informed; (ii) administrative authorities, excluding access to information held by the legislature or its committees, even though it was agreed that this was an important topic. Also, the study should concentrate on access to documents, and only secondarily extend to information given orally.

The meeting also agreed that, because of the great differences in law and practice among the countries to be included in the study, especially between those which provided a legal right of public access and those which did not, a detailed questionnaire would be inappropriate. Instead, the reporters should write integrated essays of a reasonably uniform length based on the main headings of the outline, but should not feel constrained to follow the outline in every detail. These essays would then form the body of a book which I would edit, and for which I would write a comparative report. This approach, it was thought, would result in more readable country reports, less repetition in the editor's general report, and a shorter final volume. We also agreed that we should try to add in an appendix the most important laws and regulations for each country, but unfortunately difficulties of translation and the length they would have added to the book precluded their inclusion.

CONTENTS OF THE BOOK

The resulting book, then, contains essays on the extent of public access to administrative information in twelve countries: four in Scandinavia (Sweden, Finland, Denmark and Norway), four in Western Europe (Belgium, France, the United Kingdom and Western Germany), two in Eastern Europe (Hungary and Yugoslavia), and two in North America (Canada and the United States). In their order of presentation the countries are arranged under geographical headings by region, and alphabetically within each region, except for Sweden and Finland. Scandinavia appears first because the laws on public access in the Scandinavian countries are now so different from those in most other countries; and Sweden is presented first because the other Scandinavian authors refer to its unique and long-standing system of openness. Finland is next because it was strongly influenced by the Swedish system at an early date. Within their essays, the authors have followed the main headings of my outline, so that there is a reasonable uniformity in the presentation of their material, thus making comparison easier.

A difficulty in conducting a study of this kind is that the very nature of the subject makes it hard to collect information on actual procedures and practices, especially in those countries where the traditional emphasis has been on administrative secrecy and where there is no public right of access to information. In such countries it may be difficult to discover, for example, what types of security classification are used for documents, and the procedures used for classifying them. On the other hand, the practices used in countries which have a more open administrative system are likely to be of most interest to readers. For this reason, in my comparative survey I have taken the opportunity to add information about the practices in the Scandinavian countries. This is derived from a research tour I made in 1973 to Sweden, Finland and Denmark, specifically to gather information on this subject. To avoid repeating information given by the country authors in the body of the book, I have tried to restrict my survey to comparative statements and a discussion of the general nature of the problem. I have therefore organised the survey so as to place the countries in two broad categories for purposes of comparison: those which have a specific law on rights of access, and those which adhere mainly to the principle of discretionary secrecy.

An international multi-authored study of this kind inevitably runs into problems of translation and delay, and is necessarily very much a co-operative project, requiring much generous help and advice from scholars in many countries. I should like to thank all who have given such help and advice. In particular should be mentioned André Heilbronner, the chairman of the *ad hoc* committee which originated the project; Yves Chapel, Director of Research for the IIAS, without whose prompt and full replies to my letters asking for help this project would have been left unfinished; Peter Moore, officer of the IIAS secretariat, whose expertise at translation made life much easier for me; Janice Tyrwhitt, my assistant editor, whose help in making translations more readable was invaluable; Walter Gellhorn, Distinguished University Professor at Columbia University, whose advice on an author for the U.S. and on a publisher for the English edition enabled the study to proceed and be published more quickly; and of course all of the authors, who patiently endured the editor's whip and cheerfully agreed to suggested revisions, even though they might require another retyping of their manuscript.

A French edition of this book was published by Editions Cujas, Paris, in 1977. In the English edition, updating information has been added to the end of 1977. I am pleased to acknowledge that the English edition has been published with the help of a grant from the Social Science Federation of Canada, using funds provided by the Canada Council.

DONALD C. ROWAT

July 1978

Notes on the Contributors

S. BERENYI is Professor of Administrative Law and Administrative Sciences and head of the Institute of Administrative Sciences at Eötvös Loránd University, Budapest.

J. C. BOULARD is a *Maître des requêtes* of the Council of State, Paris.

M. M. BULLINGER is Professor of Public Law at the University of Freiburg-im-Breisgau.

N. EILSCHOU HOLM is head of a Division of the Danish Ministry of Justice, chairman of the committee appointed to review the Danish Act of 1970 on Access of the Public to Documents in Administrative Files, and author of *Offentlighedsloven* (Copenhagen: Juristforbundets Forlag, 1971), a commentary on that Act.

A. FRIHAGEN is Professor of Law at the Institute of Public Law, University of Bergen and author of several books on administrative law including *Offentlighetsloven med kommentarer* ('The Norwegian Public Access Act [1970] with Commentaries', 2nd ed., 1974).

ANDRÉ HEILBRONNER is a Councillor of State in France and chairman of the IAAS Committee of Studies in Administrative Procedures.

S. HOLSTAD is head of a Division of the Swedish Ministry of Justice.

E. JORION, a Belgian civil servant from 1945 to 1970, is a professor at the University of Brussels, chairman of the Political Science Branch of the Faculty of Social, Political and Economic Sciences, and Director of Research at the Institute of Sociólogy.

T. MODEEN is a professor in the School of Law at the University of Helsinki, having previously been Professor of Public and International Law and Dean of the Faculty of Political Science at Åbo Akademi, Åbo (Turku).

T. G. NAGY is an associate professor in the Institute of Administrative Sciences, Eötvös Loránd University, Budapest.

MIODRAG PETROVIĆ is Assistant Director of the Republican Institute of Public Administration of the Socialist Republic of Serbia.

DONALD C. ROWAT is Professor of Political Science, Carleton University, Ottawa. He is editor of *Basic Issues in Public Adminis-*

tration (New York: Macmillan, 1961) and *The Ombudsman: Citizen's Defender* (London: Allen & Unwin; Toronto: University of Toronto Press; Stockholm: Norstedt & Sons, 2nd ed., 1968); and author of *The Ombudsman Plan* (Toronto: McClelland & Stewart, 1973).

M. J. SINGER was Articles Editor of the *Columbia Law Review*, 1973–74, and became *Juris Doctor* of Columbia University in 1974. He was subsequently staff attorney in the Office of the Chairman, Administrative Conference of the United States: the views expressed in his chapter are his own and do not necessarily reflect those of the Conference or its Chairman. He is now practising law in Washington, D.C.

R. E. WRAITH, formerly Research Officer of the Institute of Local Government Studies at the University of Birmingham, is now Research Officer at the Royal Institute of Public Administration.

Comparative Survey

DONALD C. ROWAT

A comparison of the twelve developed countries covered in this survey reveals that they may be divided into two main categories: those which have a constitutional or other law providing for a public right to administrative information, and those which do not. Seven countries are in the first category, while only five are in the second. Countries of the first type are the four in Scandinavia, the United States and the two East European countries. Those without such a right are the four other countries in Western Europe, and Canada.

It should be noted that the proportion in each category is not representative of all developed countries because the vast majority still adhere to the traditional principle of discretionary secrecy. As mentioned in the Introduction, the four Scandinavian countries were included in the survey specifically because they provide a right of public access to documents, and it was thought that their laws and practices would be of interest to readers in countries that have not yet established such a right. For this reason, too, I will give a more detailed comparison of the laws and practices in Scandinavia, based partly on information gathered during my research tour on the subject in 1973.[1] In doing so, I have organised the material under the same headings as the main headings used in the country studies, for easier comparative reference.

PUBLIC ACCESS IN SCANDINAVIA

The country which has enjoyed public access to administrative information for the longest period of time is Sweden. The principle of public access was adopted there as early as 1766, as part of the provisions of the Freedom of the Press Act, one of the country's basic constitutional laws. These provisions arose out of the intense struggle in the last half of the eighteenth century between the two main political parties, the Hats and the Caps. When the Hats were defeated in 1765 after a long term of office, the Caps inserted the principle of public access in the Freedom of the Press Act because of their frustration over administrative secrecy as well as press censorship under the previous regime. After a period of absolutism between 1772 and 1809, the Freedom of the Press Act was re-established, and the principle was soon fully accepted as part of the normal political life of Sweden.

It is curious that Sweden's example was not followed by other democratic countries until well into the twentieth century. Finland, which had been part of Sweden before 1809, was strongly influenced by the Swedish tradition of administrative openness, but did not have a specific law on the subject until 1951. And it was not until a very recent year, 1970, that Denmark and Norway adopted comprehensive laws of this kind.

Despite the long tradition of administrative openness in Sweden, even in that country there is interesting evidence to show that the proper balance between openness and secrecy is not an easy one to maintain, and that changes in technology cause new problems to arise. For instance, the introduction of computers, and a court decision, later confirmed by a legislative amendment, that computer records are to be classed as documents for purposes of public access, have raised new problems. On the one hand, the easy availability of computer information may be regarded as a danger to personal privacy, while, on the other, its centralisation and difficulty of access by the average citizen makes it easier to withhold. Because of this, in recent years a parliamentary committee was established on the subject, and its recommendations resulted in a new Data Act, which went into effect in 1973. Also, the increasing importance of broadcasting as a medium of communication, especially of television, has resulted in the appointment of a parliamentary committee to study the relationship of broadcasting and films to the press, and this is likely to result in either a revised Freedom of the Press Act or a separate new Media Act.

COMPARISON OF RIGHTS OF ACCESS

In all four countries there is a specific, enforceable right of public access to administrative documents, provided by law. In Sweden the relevant law, the Freedom of the Press Act, is part of the constitution, which means that it can be amended only if the amendment is re-passed after an intervening election. The Secrecy Act, on the other hand, which spells out the types of documents that are to be kept secret in accordance with the general categories listed in the Freedom of the Press Act, is an ordinary law. Except for the categories of foreign affairs and national defence, it lists these exceptions in narrow and limiting detail. In Finland, though the Public Access Act of 1951 is an ordinary law, the more detailed secrecy provisions are in the form of a decree, which has a lower legal status. These provisions are much briefer and more general than in Sweden, and hence leave more discretion to officials and less specific grounds for appeal. The Public Access Acts in Denmark and Norway also contain exemptions from access, but these too are much broader than Sweden's exemptions in the Secrecy Act.

The Danish and Norwegian Acts do not provide as full a right of access as do the laws for the other two countries. The first Danish law on the subject, passed in 1964, limited the right of access to citizens with a personal interest in the documents of a particular case, and it was not until 1970 that the right was extended to the public generally. In Denmark and Norway reporters or citizens must identify and request specific documents. This means that they must know that a document exists before they can ask for it. In Denmark, since they do not have access to departmental registers, they may not even know that a document exists. These are serious limitations on public access.[2] They help to explain why the Danish national press bureau does not consider it worth while to send reporters on daily visits to the ministries. An official in the Danish Ministry of Justice told me in 1973 that, since the adoption of the Danish and Norwegian Acts in 1970, his Ministry had received only about ten requests for documents from the press and the public, while in Norway every morning a reporter would call at the Norwegian Ministry of Justice and ask to see several documents. However, the Danish Act is to be reviewed by a parliamentary committee, and the limitations may be removed.

In general, then, Sweden still remains the most open of the Scandinavian countries. Nevertheless, when the new laws were adopted in Denmark and Norway, a serious attempt was made to implement them liberally. For example, officials in the Danish and Norwegian Ministries of Justice conducted training sessions for public servants in other ministries and agencies, and gave them guidelines on the changes in practice needed to give a liberal interpretation of the new law. And both Ministries have placed advertisements in all daily newspapers to inform citizens of their right of access to official documents. A Norwegian advertisement in 1975 featured a cartoon of four citizens poking into a bureaucrat's files, and gave a simplified explanation of the Act. It pointed out that a citizen does not have to give a reason for wanting to see a particular document; 'pure curiosity is a satisfactory ground', it said, and added that if his request is refused he can appeal to the Ombudsman or a court.

Regarding documents which may be kept secret, all four Scandinavian countries follow the basic principle of spelling out specific types of exempt documents or information, and the public has a right of access to all others. This right is enforceable through an appeal to the courts or an Ombudsman (or in Finland and Sweden to the Chancellor of Justice). Although the specification of documents which may be kept secret is much more limited in Sweden, in all four countries the general areas of secrecy are basically the same: foreign affairs and national security, the prevention and prosecution of crime, the invasion of personal privacy, internal working papers, and some government and business economic matters.

THE HOLDERS OF INFORMATION

Perhaps the most significant differences among the Scandinavian countries are found in the types of authorities which hold administrative information. In this respect, Sweden shows the greatest difference from the others. In Sweden governmental departments are separated from the ministries under boards, and have much the same degree of independence as public corporations or regulatory bodies in other countries. As a result, when a department wishes to communicate formally with any ministry, it must produce a document which is then sent through the mail to the ministry, and this makes it publicly accessible. This means that even policy advice at a high level from a department to its relevant minister becomes public knowledge, whereas in other countries such advice is normally passed from a department to its minister as an internal document. This fact is of great importance in contributing to the openness of the Swedish administrative system.

On the other hand, as in other countries, since the ministers (and their attached secretariats) as the political executive (the council of ministers) are considered to be a single unit, documents passing from one ministry to another before decisions are taken are regarded as internal working documents and therefore not accessible. In fact, because of their separation from the departments, the ministries act more as a single unit than in most other countries. For this reason, certain high-level types of policy document are kept confidential *before* a Cabinet decision is made that might be released at an earlier stage in the other Scandinavian countries.

The separation of departments from ministries may help to explain why so few documents on diplomatic relations are made publicly available. The Ministry of Foreign Affairs has no corresponding department to send it completed policy documents. Also, in the Secrecy Act documents on foreign relations are given a broad exemption. Even so, some Swedish scholars have told me that the withholding of such documents is based partly on tradition and practice, and that a more vigorous enforcement of the Freedom of the Press Act by the press and the public could make the Ministry of Foreign Affairs much more open to public scrutiny. This situation is evidence that, even in a country which has a liberal tradition of openness, there is a constant pressure from the Government to withhold information for its own convenience, and that the press and public must be continuously vigilant in enforcing the law.

Other types of authorities that hold information are public corporations and local governments. In Sweden there is an important legal distinction between ordinary public corporations and share companies in which the government holds the majority of the shares. Since the latter are more like private companies, they need not adhere to the access provisions of the Freedom of the Press Act. Several Swedish informants told me that one of the main reasons the Government has been setting up public corporations as share companies is to prevent public access to their documents. Local governments, too, have been areas of controversy in Sweden. There has been a tendency for local officials to withhold information, and in some city governments the executive committee has refused to release the reports of committees until they have been reviewed by the executive committee itself. In Denmark, too, local government presents a problem. Under the new Danish law, a whole city government is regarded as a single authority, and therefore reports passing from one part to another are regarded as internal papers. In the case of a huge city government such as Copenhagen, this can cause much administrative information to be withheld from the public. However, the dealings of local governments with the Ministry of Interior must now be released. Local governments in Finland have a stronger tradition of openness, especially the government of Helsinki, where the person who was mayor for many years was a former newspaper man.

THE RECIPIENTS OF INFORMATION

Among the important recipients of administrative information are of course the courts and parliament. Under a system of general public access, these official bodies do not have as much need for special privileges of access. Also, the question period in parliament tends to be less important for this purpose, simply because administrative information is so freely available. In Sweden, if a parliamentary question requires the preparation of documents by a department, as it often does, as soon as the documents are sent to the relevant minister they become public. If the answer is thus known before it gets to parliament, this tends to lower the prestige of parliament. A solution to this problem would be to have the answer prepared within the minister's office by getting the information by telephone from the department, but in practice it is easier to ask the department to do the work of preparation. The newspapers have largely solved the problem by adopting an unwritten rule of not revealing the answer before it is presented to parliament. As agents of parliament, the Ombudsmen in Scandinavia have special access to secret information in investigating complaints against the administration, as do members of their staffs, but of course are bound by any statutory provisions forbidding the release of secret information.

In all four Scandinavian countries, perhaps the most controversial group among the receivers of information are persons who wish to see the documents in their own cases. The courts and the Ombudsmen have often been involved in interpreting the law in such cases, especially regarding medical records and the records of persons accused before the courts. In Sweden, for instance, the Supreme Administrative Court decided that the records of the health insurance organisation, which used to be considered private, must be made publicly available. As a result, a private citizen could then find out what illness his neighbour had. A parliamentary committee on computers and privacy has since proposed an amendment to the Freedom of the Press Act to prevent such invasions of privacy. A similar problem dealt with by the court has been whether patients should have access to their own medical records held by doctors in public hospitals. This is a particularly delicate problem in the case of mental patients. In a series of cases the Court has mainly supported the doctors, who favour confidentiality, but in cases where doctors were keeping medical records secret for their own convenience, it has decided against them in order to preserve greater openness. Doctors may not keep private notes, and all their information must be on the record. However, they may destroy patients' records after ten years, a fact which may be unfortunate for medical research. The openness of medical records to employers also presents a problem, since an employee's previous medical (especially mental) history may influence an employer's decision. Some people feel that this is an invasion of privacy, while others regard it as relevant information in hiring.

In Finland, the Supreme Administrative Court has similarly decided that a doctor can refuse medical documents to a patient, or to a relation if the patient has died. A case in 1966 concerned the right of a man to get information on his wife and dead son. The decision was that he could get it regarding the son, but not his wife without her consent. Another case, decided by the Ombudsman in 1970, concerned the rights of the parents of a boy killed in a robbery to get information regarding the cause of death. The doctor in the hospital had refused this information, but the Ombudsman concluded that they should have the right to get it. Two decisions of the Supreme Administrative Court in 1971, however, indicated that doctors could refuse such information, with the result that the law is now uncertain on the subject. The question of whether suspects of a crime should have access to the documents in their own case has also required legal interpretation. Similar problems of interpretation exist in Denmark and Norway. In such cases, the courts have had to try to balance the true interests of the requester of the documents against the harm that might be done to the public interest.

Probably the most important group in the outside public who receive governmental information are the news reporters. The effectiveness of an access law depends heavily on the organisation, traditions and practices of the press. This is revealed by the differences in this respect among the four countries. In Sweden, the national press bureau sends reporters on daily rounds of the ministries and most important departments and agencies. It has about fifteen reporters who cover about seventy ministries and departments. As a result, the press bureau sends out annually about 5000 government stories on the national wire and about 40,000 to local newspapers. Reporters in Norway and Finland (but not Denmark) also do daily rounds of ministries but there the coverage is not so thorough. In Finland, for instance, during my visit in 1973 reporters from the national press bureau were making daily rounds to only three ministries: Interior, Transport, and Social and Health. Reporters do not call daily at the Ombudsman's office, and rely mainly on his press releases and annual report for news stories on cases. Some of my informants stated that the main reason the press bureau had not extended the system to other ministries was the cost of extra staff and of photocopying documents, while others argued that it was simply a matter of tradition and inertia on the part of the press bureau. Another factor, however, may be the reluctance of the Government to provide facilities for the press in each ministry. In Sweden, most ministries and departments provide a press room with a typewriter, where all incoming documents and mail, even from private citizens, are laid out for an hour each morning for inspection by reporters. If a reporter wants additional information on a case, he has free access to the department's documentary files.

Since the media are interested in current news, they of course rely heavily on oral information obtained quickly from officials by personal interview or telephone. The easy accessibility of oral information is therefore of prime importance to the press. Even before the new access Acts were passed in Denmark and Norway, press relations with officials were very good. Partly for this reason, reporters and news organisations have not had to appeal in many cases under the new laws. A more important reason, however, may be that the very existence of the access laws has given reporters a lever with which to press for information. The ability to threaten to ask for documents in a case (or even twenty copies of the same document) no doubt forces officials to be freer in offering information orally and to be surer that their information is accurate.

An interesting question taken up by the Danish Ombudsman soon after the Act of 1970 came into effect was whether an official must respond to a reporter's oral request by telephone to see a particular document, or whether he could instead insist that the request be made in writing. Since a reporter is likely to need immediate access to a document for a news story written the same day, the Ombudsman concluded that, to reporters, a delay of information amounts to a denial of information, and that therefore a request by telephone should be sufficient, as had already been stated in the guidelines issued by the Ministry of Justice.

This example of a Danish official stalling on a press request for documents is unusual, however. Generally Danish officials have been co-operative in responding to press requests for documents under the new Act, though some reporters still complain that they cannot get copies in time for deadlines. Two outstanding examples may be given of information revealed through the press soon after the Danish Act went into effect. In the first case, the press demanded and got documents containing proposals made to the Government by the SAS airline, a Scandinavian government corporation. Formerly, these documents would have been secret. The other was a case in which a newspaper published accusations against local public welfare homes. The Government asked the homes for reports in response to these accusations, and the newspaper successfully requested and published these reports. Since the reports showed many of the accusations to be false, their publication helped to clear the air, and may be regarded as a desirable public service. Most Danish reporters have copies of the Act and know its contents, but one of my informants felt that they need a more detailed guide to the meaning of the provisions regarding what may be kept secret.

In Sweden and Finland an important buttress to press access is the legal requirement regarding the non-revelation of news sources. News reporters cannot be compelled by the courts to reveal the name of a person who gave them information, even if this person was a public employee. In Sweden, if there is a 'leak' of information, a senior official is not even allowed to ask a reporter from whom he got his information, and the official may not conduct a search for the name of the offending junior official, unless the information was clearly in the secret category under the law. This constitutes a powerful protection against governmental withholding of information. It is in marked contrast to the ambivalence of court decisions on this subject in the common-law countries, though several American states have similar 'shield' laws for reporters, as Mr Singer's Chapter 12 reveals.

An important reason why the extensiveness of public access in Sweden does not create serious problems regarding the invasion of personal privacy is that Sweden has a very responsible press. The main press organisations are members of a press council, which has developed a code of ethics and has appointed a 'press Ombudsman' to receive complaints against the press. As a result, the news media voluntarily refrain from printing or broadcasting the names of accused persons who might be innocent, or of citizens when this would invade their privacy.

Readers may find the following example enlightening. The names of people who complain to the Swedish parliamentary Ombudsmen are not ordinarily given in news stories. For instance, the day I visited the Ombudsmen's press office in 1973, a reporter from the national press bureau was typing up a story based on a letter of complaint that had been opened that morning. A young man who lived in a small town had been struck by a motor car while riding his bicycle. He wrote in to complain that the policeman investigating the case had demanded to see his licence to drive an automobile. This was such an odd case that the reporter was writing a brief story to be sent back to the newspaper in the young man's home town. The reporter explained to me that neither the policeman's nor the young man's name would be given in the story, so as not to embarrass them, even though there is no legal prohibition against giving the names. On the other hand, the press obtains from the tax department and publishes the names of movie stars, businessmen and officials who have the highest incomes in Sweden, as a matter of public interest.

INFORMATION PROCEDURES

An important limitation on public access to administrative information in the Scandinavian countries has been created by the distinction between documents and internal working papers. An understanding of this distinction is vital because of the false arguments used in other countries by some opponents of access. They claim that public access would seriously interfere with the day-to-day work of administration, and would inhibit public servants from giving frank advice to their superiors for fear it would be made public. It is important to realise that there is no right of access to internal notes, drafts and tentative working papers. The right applies only to completed documents or documents sent from one authority to another. Thus normally the right of access exposes to public view only an official's fully considered advice in the form of a finished document. This is not likely to inhibit his frank opinions, which can still be given to his superior confidentially if necessary. Instead, knowing that his written advice on an important matter may be made public, he is likely to think it out more carefully and to present a view that is not only more clearly argued and more fully supported but also more objective. In short, his advice will be better.

Since the distinction between a document and a working paper cannot always be drawn easily, no doubt officials in Scandinavia sometimes take advantage of this fact to keep information confidential in the form of an exempt working paper which, if defined as a releasable document, would be publicly available. Much administrative information at the policy-making level within ministries is thus kept confidential, although readers in other countries would probably be surprised at the number of policy documents that are released which in order countries would be considered internal documents. In Sweden, for instance, although ordinarily ministry documents on a policy matter are not publicly released until a decision has been made by the Cabinet, at that time all of the supporting documents, including those containing the views of senior officials, are released with the decision.

In countries having a right of access, as in other countries, the originator of a document may indicate its security classification by placing a secrecy stamp on it. But the difference is that neither he nor his superiors may make the final decision as to its secrecy. It must fall in the category of matters which are listed as secret according to law, and if a reporter or a private citizen disputes the classification he may appeal to an independent authority for a decision on whether the document should be released.

In the Scandinavian countries there is more than one such authority to which an appeal can be made. In Finland and Sweden the appeal can be taken to the Supreme Administrative Court, to the Ombudsmen, or to the Chancellor of Justice, while in Denmark and Norway it can be taken to the ordinary courts or the

Ombudsman. The difference between the types of appeals that go to a court and to an Ombudsman (or to a Chancellor of Justice) usually depends on the seriousness of the case. For instance, a newspaper or business firm would usually take a case to court, while a reporter or a private citizen would usually complain to an Ombudsman. There are far more appeals in Sweden than in the other Scandinavian countries, and most of them are made in the form of complaints to the four parliamentary Ombudsmen. For instance, in 1972 the Swedish Supreme Administrative Court heard twenty-five appeals against the withholding of documents, while the Ombudsmen received over 100 such complaints. Probably the main reason for the greater number of appeals in Sweden is the longer tradition of openness and hence the greater awareness by the press and the public of their rights.

CONCLUSIONS

Although the experience of three of the Scandinavian countries with a right of public access to official documents is too recent to reach any firm conclusions, Sweden's long experience with it indicates that it changes the whole spirit in which public business is conducted. It gives public debate a more solid foundation, causes a decline in public suspicion and distrust of officials, and this in turn gives them a greater feeling of confidence. Professor Nils Herlitz, an eminent Swedish scholar, has described the effect of public access in Sweden as follows:

Our judgement on public affairs is facilitated; public debate is given a firmer basis, whether we judge what the authorities think, or what they have done, or what they should do . . .
In every step an authority takes, it feels that it is under public control, under the imminent danger of having its steps discussed and criticized. The publicity is always in the minds of the officials and makes them anxious to act in such a way that they will not be exposed to criticism . . . But on the other hand, they will feel a certain amount of confidence. They need not be exposed to vague suspicions, since there is always an opportunity to control their work . . .
It would be an understatement to say that in Sweden publicity [of documents] is generally and highly estimated. It would be more

exact to say that it is regarded as indispensable. Whilst, in the eyes
of other nations, [it] may look impossible and incredible, most
Swedes, including many high lawyers, regard access to official
documents as something like a natural right and believe that it
has a counterpart in all civilized countries.[3]

Readers in other countries who fear that public access to documents
will create too much administrative openness should keep in mind
that even in countries with such access there is still considerable
administrative secrecy. In the first place, the law provides that
certain matters may be kept secret, to protect the public interest and
personal privacy. Second, the important distinction between
documents and working papers ensures that the administration will
not become immobilised by premature access or publicity. Third,
there is a constant pressure by the Government and officials to keep
matters confidential for their own convenience. As we have seen,
even in Sweden several areas of administration, such as the Ministry
of Foreign Affairs, publicly owned share companies and local
government, are not as open to the public as some observers think
they should be, and the propensity of officials to withhold
information still requires many appeals each year to enforce access.
Hence there has been little danger of too much administrative
openness.

   The only area in which this has been a problem in Sweden in
recent years has been the threat to privacy caused by the
centralisation of public and private computer information held on
individuals, which resulted in the Swedish Data Act of 1973. Before
its adoption, for instance, anyone could get from the courts, through
the use of a computer, a list of all divorced women in Sweden. It was
then possible for a commercial firm to send such women an
advertisement for a new husband. Such invasions of privacy were
prohibited by the Act of 1973, which restricts the use of personal
data held in all computers, both public and private, and provides
for the enforcement of the Act through a supervisory board.

   One of the favourite claims advanced by those who oppose access
in other countries is that Swedish officials evade the access law on a
large scale by passing information to one another orally instead of
committing it to paper. This claim, of course, is impossible to
document, but unfortunately it is similarly difficult to disprove. My
own view is that it is mainly a myth based on false fears of
administrative openness and on two serious misconceptions. The

first is a lack of understanding that there is no right of access to working papers. This means that it is quite possible to transfer confidential information in written form within a department or the ministries. The second misconception is the assumption that there is a great desire on the part of Swedish officials to withhold non-secret information. My interviews with Swedish officials have led me to believe that, on the contrary, they are so imbued with the tradition of openness that-they automatically expect as much information as possible to be released. It is true that a few matters of a delicate nature, such as personal recommendations, are dealt with orally or by telephone rather than committed to paper, as they would be in any country. But my Swedish informants felt that in this respect the administrative practices in Sweden were not much different from those in other countries. In fact, one of my informants, a line administrator, insisted that the tradition of documenting every-thing is so strong in Sweden that officials do not transfer information by telephone or interview as much as they do in other countries.

Those who argue that the attitude of openness with which Swedish officials are imbued cannot be created quickly are probably right. A long-standing tradition of secrecy cannot be reversed overnight simply by passing an access law. The law must be accompanied by a thorough programme of administrative training in the new practices it requires. Such programmes were conducted in Denmark and Norway, and this goes far toward explaining the successful implementation of the new access laws in these countries. At the same time, because of the natural tendency for officials to withhold information for their own convenience, the public and the press must be constantly vigilant to enforce their rights of access. This vigilance must be supported by a thorough knowledge of their rights. Hence the provisions of the law and the key decisions interpreting these provisions must be widely known among not only officials but also reporters and the general public. To meet this need in Sweden, Mr B. Wennergren, later one of the Ombudsmen, produced a short book on the provisions and key interpretations of the Freedom of the Press Act regarding public access. In an excellent comparative article, his conclusion regarding the Swedish experience is that the right of access is very seldom abused, and that it does not impede the daily work of administration 'to any degree worth mentioning'.[4]

OTHER COUNTRIES WITH A RIGHT
TO INFORMATION

ACCESS TO RECORDS IN THE UNITED STATES

In the United States, as in Sweden, the constitution protects the freedom of the press. The first amendment of the American constitution expressly forbids laws 'abridging the . . . freedom of the press'. This has contributed to a stronger tradition of administrative openness than that enjoyed by most other countries. Unlike the constitutional law in Sweden, however, this amendment does not contain specific provisions for access to administrative documents. As a result, the release of such documents has been largely at the discretion of the President and the heads of departments and agencies.

It was not until 1946 that provisions were included in a congressional law, the Administrative Procedure Act, which attempted to require the routine disclosure of government-held information. It stated as a general principle that there should be free access to documents except for those that must be kept secret. However, as the author for the United States points out, 'the attempt failed . . . because the statute's vague language and broad exceptions enabled recalcitrant government officials easily to find reasons for withholding information, notwithstanding the clear congressional intent to the contrary.' Thus the Act exempted from disclosure records involving 'any function of the United States requiring secrecy in the public interest' as well as 'information held confidential for a good cause found'. Moreover, only 'persons properly and directly concerned' were entitled to procure certain public records, and there was no provision for judicial remedy.

The attempt also failed because the Act was soon followed by the period of the Cold War in the 1950s, in which the desire to protect national security caused almost a mania among government officials for keeping information secret. The result was an unnecessary over-classification of millions of government documents. This finally caused an opposing reaction by the press, the public and Congress. As a result, in 1961 President Kennedy instituted a system for automatically de-classifying most secret documents at the end of twelve years, and in a famous letter to his secretaries stated that 'any official should have a clear and precise case involving the national interest before seeking to withhold from publication documents or papers fifteen or more years old.'[5] Even before that, the period during which most classified documents were held before being accessible to historians and others was only twenty years, while the period required by most other countries was fifty years.

The most important change, however, came with the adoption of the Freedom of Information Act of 1966. This Act, replacing the provisions of 1946, stated unequivocally that public access to most documents was to be the general rule. More significantly, it listed what types of documents could be kept secret, in nine general categories of exemption, and provided for a means of public appeal against withholding. These provisions finally established the Swedish principle of openness: disclosure is the general rule, and documents may not be withheld unless they fall under one of the exemptions specified by law. The categories of exemption, however, are fewer and broader than those of Sweden and hence leave more room for official discretion and less room for appeal.

The Act required many more records to be either published or indexed and made available for inspection and copying, such as those containing final decisions. Other records, as in Denmark and Norway, are made available only by a specific request for particular records. This is a serious limitation because it puts the onus on the public to identify and request specific records. Also, as in Norway, inter-agency memoranda are considered to be internal records. In other ways, however, the Act is more liberal than the laws in Denmark and Norway.

As Mr Singer indicates in his chapter, the Freedom of Information Act has brought about a radical change in the public's right of access, and in the attitudes and practices of officials. This is no doubt partly due to the public's vigorous enforcement of the Act in the courts, which have spelled out in greater detail the types of document which may legitimately be withheld under the nine exemptions. As he notes, certain difficulties arose in applying the Act, especially in interpreting the meaning of some of the exemptions. For this reason it was amended in 1974, with the amendments becoming effective in February 1975. Among the important changes was expanding the scope of the Act to include the Executive Office of the President. Difficulties of interpretation still remain, however, notably regarding the meaning of 'reasonably described' requested records and of 'internal agency memoranda'. A more precise meaning for many of the provisions, especially the new amendments, still remains to be spelled out by the courts.

Obviously, the much greater degree of public access provided by the Freedom of Information Act has not brought the American federal administration grinding to a halt. Indeed, it appears to have been well accepted by most administrators, who are attempting to implement it in good faith. Many of them even admit that its effect on the administration has been salutory, and results in the writing of better reports. It has also been emulated in many of the states. Mr Singer reveals that 39 of the 50 states had passed open records laws by the end of 1974. As Professor Anderson notes, open records laws exert 'a pervasive preventive effect by virtue of the sobering influence of prospective public scrutiny'.[6]

Considering the failure of the Act of 1946, the lesson of American experience is that a comprehensive right of public access cannot be successfully established unless the matters which may be kept secret are spelled out by statute in limiting detail and there is provision for appeal against the withholding of documents, in order to ensure that the right can be enforced. If the words stating what matters may be kept secret are too vague, this gives officials too much discretion to withhold information and does not provide sufficient grounds for appeal.

THE RIGHT TO INFORMATION IN HUNGARY AND YUGOSLAVIA

Both of the socialist countries included in this survey, as the authors of the chapters on them point out, provide in their constitutions for a general right of all citizens to information that is necessary for participation in the socialist state, and this implies a right to administrative information. The constitutions do not specifically state, however, that citizens have a general right of access to administrative documents, nor do they specify what types of matters must not be disclosed, as does the Swedish constitutional Act. Moreover, these countries do not have a single general law that declares and spells out the right of public access as the normal rule, and specifies in detail the exceptional documents which may be kept secret.

On the other hand, they do have a general law on administrative procedure which grants a right of access by citizens to administrative documents in cases in which they have a specific personal interest, and this right is enforceable in the courts. Furthermore, the representatives in assemblies at all levels have powers of access to administrative information and documents on behalf of their constituents. In Hungary, as the authors point out, Members of Parliament even have the power to see secret documents, though the information in them may not be passed on to other persons.

Two powerful types of institution in Hungary which can enforce the right of citizens to administrative information, in addition to the ordinary courts, are the Public Prosecutor's Office and the People's Control Commissions. These institutions, which are designed to control administrative action in general, also include within their purview the withholding of information. The Public Prosecutor's Office can act on complaints from the citizens, while the People's Control Commissions are general investigating bodies acting on behalf of the citizens at all levels of government.

According to the authors, representatives of the media have a right to administrative information which is not secret, but it is difficult to say how this right works in practice. The fact that there is not a comprehensive law declaring specifically that any citizen has a right of access to administrative documents, and specifying the particular exempted matters that must be kept secret, appears to give the political and administrative authorities considerable discretion to withhold documents by declaring them to be state or public service secrets; and administrators have no clear guidelines for releasing or withholding information. As the authors for Hungary point out (p. 260):

> A number of problems arise . . . from one central fact: the head of an organ and his staff must withhold information in some cases and release it in others. On the one hand, they are bound by an oath to keep state and public service secrets. Moreover, they may not communicate to unauthorised persons any information obtained as part of their work, and which may produce disadvantages for the organ or some other person. On the other hand, wherever a legal norm declares that information may be given, the staff of the organ must supply it. The only guidance they get is the rule stating that they must carry out their duties in accordance with the appropriate rules and regulations and the instructions of superior officers.

This leads to the conclusion that a general right to information is not the same thing as a specific right of public access to documents. The former still leaves considerable room for discretion to withhold documents and information.

COUNTRIES WITHOUT A RIGHT TO INFORMATION

The remaining countries included in this survey (Canada, Belgium, France, the United Kingdom and Western Germany), like most countries of the world, have neither a constitutional nor an ordinary law providing a public right to administrative information. It is true that all of their governments have elaborate publicity programmes to inform the public and that recently some of them have made significant moves in the direction of greater public access to documents. But they still adhere to what I call the principle of discretionary secrecy.

THE PRINCIPLE OF DISCRETIONARY SECRECY

This means that the decision to withhold administrative information or to refuse access to documents is at the discretion of the executive Government. It is free to withhold not only for legitimate reasons, such as the protection of national security or personal privacy, but also to protect itself from public criticism against wrongdoing, or even to avoid a minor embarrassment or inconvenience. Instead of the general principle that all administrative information is open to the public except for those matters which are specifically required by law to be kept secret, the principle is that all administrative information is considered to be secret unless the Government decides to release it; and the Government has control over the timing and form of its release. Thus in Canada every public servant employed by the federal government must swear an oath that he will not 'without due authority . . ., disclose or make known any matter that comes to [his or her] knowledge by reason of such employment.' And Canada's Official Secrets Act contains severe penalties for any public servant who dares to give information without permission. In Commonwealth countries, which have inherited the British parliamentary system, Governments even flaunt the principle in the face of parliament. For instance, the Government leader in the Canadian House of Commons said recently in his evidence before a parliamentary committee, 'I think members of parliament have the right to ask, and the Government has the right to decide what it will answer.'[7]

How did this principle come to be established in modern democracies, and why has it been maintained? It became established simply by inheritance from the past, from earlier undemocratic times. In the long history of mankind, modern democracy is very young. One could say that it dates only from the European revolutions of 1848. It has been only gradually unfolding since that time, and its evolution is not yet complete. Governments inherited the principle of administrative secrecy from the period of absolute monarchy in Europe, when the king was in control of all information released about the government. Though executive Governments later became responsible to parliament, they preserved the tradition of discretionary secrecy for their own convenience. Parliament and the public have not questioned the principle until recently because it has been a strong inherited tradition. We have imbibed it with our mother's milk, so to speak. Another reason we have not questioned the principle is that in modern democracies much administrative information is made freely available. In fact, a torrent of information pours out of government offices every day – millions of words a year. Modern Governments make a genuine effort to inform the public about their administrative programmes and activities. As a result, the general public are not fully aware that much administrative information is purposely withheld, or that the information released is slanted in favour of the Government and its bureaucracy.

ITS UNDESIRABLE EFFECTS

The reason several developed countries have either recently abandoned the principle of discretionary secrecy or are now seriously questioning it is the realisation that it is preventing the full development of democracy. It inhibits the free exchange of information and prevents Governments from being fully accountable to parliament and the public. Let us now consider its undesirable effects in more detail.

First of all, it creates confusion and uncertainty within the administration itself. On the one hand, most officials have a genuine desire to keep the public informed. But on the other, their oath of

secrecy and the requirement of permission from higher authority
cause them to fear releasing information. When in doubt they play
safe by withholding it. Also, they have no clear guide regarding
what types of information should be kept secret, or for how long.
Hence, they tend to suffer schizophrenic mental conflicts caused by
doubt about whether to release or withhold information. Timid
officials withhold it unnecessarily, while bold ones leak confidential
information that they think should be made public.

The effects of the principle on the outside public are even more
serious. A citizen does not even have a right of access to documents
in his own case. If an administrative decision has had an adverse
effect on him, he may be given no information on why or how the
decision was made. Without any right of access to the documents, he
has no way of questioning it, and may not even know that it should
be questioned. To the average citizen the public service is
anonymous, faceless and impervious. He may get so little information about an administrative decision against him that he has no
way of knowing whether it was made by unfair procedures or for
improper reasons. Such a situation is an undeniable temptation to
arbitrary action by government officials.

It is partly for this reason that I have been a strong advocate of the
Ombudsman plan.[8] One of the great values of an Ombudsman is
that, as an official of parliament, he acts as an agent for the citizen in
getting at information on a particular case. The citizen may
complain about his treatment by officials to the Ombudsman, who
then has the legal power to investigate and find out what went on
behind the wall of administrative secrecy. However, the limited
access to documents provided by an Ombudsman is not enough. The
former Swedish parliamentary Ombudsman for civil affairs, Mr
Alfred Bexelius, has said, 'I have always maintained that free access
to official documents is of far more importance for the legal security
of citizens than is the office of Ombudsman.'[9]

There are also key professional groups in society who feel the
undesirable effects of the secrecy system. But unfortunately their
interests are so different that they do not complain with a common
voice. Among these groups are news reporters, lawyers and judges,
natural and social scientists, and historians.

Reporters and broadcasters complain that they must depend on
either tailor-made handouts or oral information that is often slanted
and inaccurate. Because of the anonymity of civil servants, they
must work in a weird world of illicit information, where officials give

them a story orally and then insist that they must not give its source. Many reporters, however, are not fully aware of the seriousness of not having access to documents. Under the pressure of deadlines, they find it easier to depend on the telephone or personal interviews, and on news summaries prepared by information officers. They are thus spared the trouble of reading the original documents and do not worry about having no access to them. Yet, without access to these documents, they must accept an official's interpretation of them, and cannot check the truth or accuracy of the information they received.

Lawyers and judges complain that the tradition of executive or crown privilege is so extreme that the government can use it to withhold essential evidence in court cases. Natural scientists complain that the walls of military security are so impenetrable as to prevent the free flow of information that is essential to scientific development, while social scientists are hampered in their investigations of serious social problems by the unnecessary withholding of documents. Historians are prevented from giving a full account of recent events because they have no right of access to the relevant public records. Often rules regarding the types or ages of documents that they may see are conflicting, and granting access is at the whim of the official or department concerned. Though some countries have recently reduced their fifty-year rule for secret diplomatic documents, most countries still require them to be locked away for a ridiculously long period of years.

With so many indications of the undesirable effects of discretionary secrecy, it is small wonder that in modern democracies the public are now questioning the whole principle. We are beginning to realise that it is a tradition preserved by Governments and administrative officials for their own benefit. Knowledge is power, and they hate to give up exclusive control over it. Governments can doctor and time news releases to favour the party in power, and can even use publicity campaigns to cover mistakes. We are told only what the Government wants us to know, and a 'paper curtain of secrecy' is drawn across the rest.

Governments must face the fact that the principle of discretionary secrecy is incompatible with democracy, for it leads to distrust and fear on the part of the public. If the decisions at the very apex of our political system are made secretly in administrative offices and executive cabinets, much of the political process is hidden from the people, and they can hardly be blamed if they imagine the worst.

Yet the means available to the public and parliament for obtaining access to official information are woefully inadequate. Often Opposition Members of Parliament try unsuccessfully to dig vital information out of a reluctant Government. And just as often, they do not even know what to ask for because they do not know what is really going on behind the clouds surrounding Mount Olympus. Such a system is based on the premise that we must trust the Government and hope for the best. This is entirely too paternalist a concept for a democracy. Parliament and the public cannot hope to call the Government to account if they do not know what is going on. Nor can they hope to contribute their talents to the process of framing new policy and legislation if that process is hidden from view.

Under pressure for freer access to documents, some executive governments have adopted the principle of their 'obligation to inform' the public. But even if this principle is adopted whole-heartedly, a government will still have ultimate control over the release of information. All too often this information turns into propaganda through the inevitable selection of favourable information, and through the Government's power to give it wide distribution and frequent repetition in the media. Opposing viewpoints cannot be presented with equal opportunity and vigour. Under a system of discretionary secrecy, the 'obligation to inform' can easily become the freedom to propagandise, and the public has no easy way of finding out whether there has been any maladminis-tration. This is an important reason why the press and public need a clear and specific right of access to administrative documents. Only in this way can they check on the objectivity and accuracy of the information being released.

CONCLUDING COMMENTS

More than a decade ago I came to the following conclusion:

The principle of open access to administrative information is essential to the full development of democracy. In spite of the enhanced need for secrecy in certain areas resulting from the Cold War, the logic of democracy demands that the long-term trend be in the direction of the principle of publicity. This trend may be seen in the growth of vast public information services for modern democracies, in the relaxation of the fifty-year rule, and in the steady development of legislation in the United States towards the Swedish principle of open access. For when essential information is withheld from the public, there is a grave danger that the discussion of public policy will be shallow and that the people will be unable to control their government. My recommendation, then, is that other democracies should prepare to abandon the principle of secrecy.[10]

By the time the survey was made for this book, three countries – Denmark, Norway and the United States – had adopted comprehensive open records laws on the Swedish-Finnish model, and several of the other countries in our survey were moving in this direction, notably Britain, France and Canada. An important development in France has been the creation, by a decree issued on 11 February 1977, of an official commission charged with promoting greater public access to administrative documents and with proposing desirable changes in the laws or regulations. Significant recent changes in Canada have been the Government's directive of 1973 on the release of documents to Parliament, and its approval in February 1976 of the principle of an access law, followed by its Green Paper on the subject in June 1977.

Like most other countries, however, Canada is still far from reaching the stage described in the words attributed to Mr Kissinger in a cartoon that appeared in Toronto's *Globe and Mail* on 18 October 1975. During Mr Kissinger's visit to Canada and while attending a state dinner, he made certain derogatory remarks about well-known American politicians, in private conversation with his dinner companions. Unfortunately, the microphone at his table was accidentally connected to a loud-speaker system, so that his remarks were easily overheard by reporters and were printed in the press. The cartoon shows him back in Washington reporting to a worried-looking President Ford and saying, 'It's a beautiful open society. Why even their bugging system is amplified and played live in all the corridors!'

As long as the present state of international tension continues, no nation can hope to achieve the sort of 'beautiful open society' that the cartoonist has Mr Kissinger describing. But the passing of the period of the Cold War, with its passion for secrecy, provides a better opportunity than ever for democratic countries to move in the direction of greater openness. Among the developed countries not included in this survey, three which have recently adopted or are in the process of adopting access to information laws are Austria, the Netherlands and Australia.[11] I venture to predict that within the next decade many more countries, both developed and developing, will adopt such laws.

The full establishment of the principle of public access, however, will require a complete abandonment of the tradition of discretionary secrecy. There must be a radical change in law, practices and attitudes. Although practices and attitudes may not be changed sufficiently by the passing of a law, this is a necessary condition for the change. The adoption of a law has great symbolic and dramatic value in altering both public and official attitudes. However, as the failure of the American provisions of 1946 shows, a law on the subject will not succeed unless it contains three key provisions. It must: (1) unequivocally declare that the general principle is to be open public access to documents; (2) list narrowly and specifically the types of matter which may legitimately be kept secret; and (3) provide a right of appeal to an independent authority such as the courts or an Ombudsman or preferably both. It should also require all documents to be listed in registers, so that their existence will be known and so that they can be easily identified and requested.

Governments rarely surrender any of their own power voluntarily. Since a monopoly over information gives them power, such a law will not be adopted without strong pressure from all segments of society that suffer under the traditional system of discretionary secrecy.

NOTES

1. There is not much comparative literature on the subject. What does exist is mainly a comparison of the laws, and gives little information on actual practices. The three main articles, which compare the four Scandinavian countries and the United States, are: John McMillan, 'Making Government Accountable – A Comparative Analysis of Freedom of Information Statutes', *New Zealand Law Journal* (1977), 248–56, 275–80, 286–96; Stanley V. Anderson, 'Public Access to Government Files in Sweden', *American Journal of Comparative Law* xxi, 3 (summer 1973), 419–73, which includes translations of the Scandinavian laws and regulations; and Bertil Wennergren, 'Civic Information – Administrative Publicity', *International Review of Administrative Sciences* xxxvi, 24 (1970), 243–50. Readers may also be interested in my earlier article, 'The Problem of Administrative Secrecy', *International Review of Administrative Sciences* xxxii, 2 (1966), 99–106, which contrasts public access in Sweden and Finland with discretionary

secrecy elsewhere. See also Itzbak Galnoor (ed.), *Government Secrecy in Democracies* (New York: Harper and Row, 1977), which has chapters on the United States, Canada, Britain, Israel, Netherlands, West Germany, France and Scandinavia, and a comparative conclusion; F. E. Rourke (ed.), 'Symposium: Administrative Secrecy, A Comparative Perspective', *Public Administration Review*, 35 (January 1975), 1–42, which has five short articles on the U.S. and Britain; and Thomas M. Franck and E. Weisband (eds.), *Secrecy and Foreign Policy* (New York: Oxford, 1974), on the U. S., Britain and Canada.

2. These and other limitations led Professor Stanley V. Anderson to make, in his otherwise excellent comparison, the following exaggerated statement: 'In Denmark the public right of access is illusory.' (op. cit., 440).

3. 'Publicity of Official Documents in Sweden', *Public Law* 50 (spring 1958), 55, 56, and 58. Unfortunately, the Swedish principle of public access is often translated as 'the principle of publicity'. Hence, to get a more accurate meaning from the passage quoted, the reader must substitute 'public access to' for 'publicity of'.

4. Op. cit., 249.

5. For further details see my 'The Problem of Administrative Secrecy', op. cit., 101–2.

6. Op. cit., 447.

7. Mitchell Sharp, in answer to a question during a hearing before the Standing Joint Committee of the Senate and House of Commons on Regulations and other Statutory Instruments; see *Minutes of Proceedings and Evidence*, Issue No. 13 (18 February 1975), 17.

8. See my *The Ombudsman Plan* (Toronto: McClelland & Stewart, 1973) or the earlier volume which I edited, *The Ombudsman: Citizen's Defender* (London and Toronto: Allen & Unwin, and The University of Toronto Press, 2nd ed., 1968).

9. Letter to the author, 3 January 1966.

10. 'The Problem of Administrative Secrecy', op. cit., 105.

11. In Austria a section of the Federal Ministries Act of 1973 requires departments to provide information in response to inquiries by citizens. In the Netherlands an Openness of Administration Bill was approved by the lower house of the legislature in February 1977 but approval by the upper house was delayed by the resignation of the Government. In Australia the Government was preparing legislation based on the reports of two interdepartmental committees but had not yet introduced it by the end of 1977, and the state of South Australia was also planning to introduce legislation. On Austria see: Committee of Exports on Human Rights, *Proceedings of the Colloquy of the Council of Europe on Freedom of Information and the Duty for Public Authorities to Make Available Information* (Strasbourg: Council of Europe, 1977). On Australia see: Royal Commission on Australian Government Administration. Appendixes to Report, Volume Two, *Appendix 2.A: Freedom of Information* (1976), containing a fully drafted freedom of information bill annotated in great detail; Attorney General's Department, *Proposed Freedom of Information Legislation: Report of an Interdepartmental Committee* (1974) and *Policy Proposals for Freedom of Information Legislation: Report of an Interdepartmental Committee* (1976): all three reports published by the Australian Government Publishing Service in Canberra; also, John McMillan, 'Freedom of Information in Australia: Issue Closed' *Federal Law Review* 8 (1977), 379–434.

1 Scandinavia

1 Sweden

SIGVARD HOLSTAD

Right of Access to Official Documents

The public character of the administration of justice and of the state and municipal administration is of long standing in Sweden. The right of every citizen to have access to official documents was laid down in law as early as the latter half of the eighteenth century. The Freedom of the Press Act of 1766 gave citizens the right freely to print publications on their own responsibility. The purpose of this was to guarantee a free interchange of opinions and the enlighten-ment of the public. In this connection the right to reproduce official documents in print was considered to be of great importance. Access to the documents that were to be reproduced was obviously a prerequisite for the reproduction. For this reason every citizen was given the right to have access to official documents and to reproduce them in print.

This right has been maintained since 1766, with only a short interval, as an important integral part of the freedom of the press. Today the basic provisions are to be found in the Freedom of the Press Act of 1949. This act is a fundamental or constitutional law; it cannot be repealed or changed, unless the parliament (*Riksdag*) makes two identical decisions separated by general elections. The legislators have tried in this way to prevent a temporary change in public opinion from resulting in citizens being deprived of their right freely to express their opinions in print.

The public character of official documents makes it possible for the public to examine how the state and municipal authorities deal with matters and how they make their decisions. This aspect was probably paramount when the principle was first laid down. Those who have a primary interest in examining the documents in a matter are naturally the parties concerned. But it has not been considered sufficient that official documents are available to the parties in a matter. The public at large is also considered to have such an interest.

Another factor underlying the principle of public access to official documents is the assumption that there will be greater confidence in the authorities if the latter are working in full view of the public. The question of information is a third reason for the principle. It is obvious that free access to official documents facilitates the distribution among the public of information concerning the affairs of the state and of the municipalities. The fourth motive bears close relationship to the third. Thanks to the principle of public access to official documents, the public discussion of the aims and means of governmental activities – a discussion that is of vital importance to a democratic society – can be founded on a more solid basis.

In chapter 2 of the Freedom of the Press Act the principle of public access finds expression in the stating of a right for every Swedish citizen to have access to official documents. The more precise meaning of this right will be discussed below. It should be mentioned in this context, however, that the provisions in the Act are applicable only to the relationship between an authority which keeps a certain document and a private person who wants to have access to the document in question. The right of a public authority to have access to documents which are in the keeping of other authorities is not regulated in the Act.[1] Nor are provisions of such a kind, with a few exceptions,[2] to be found elsewhere. It should also be mentioned that all public bodies – Parliament and the Government, as well as the courts and the state and municipal administration authorities – are subject to the principle of public access (chapter 2, sections 3 and 5 of the Act). The principle also applies to all kinds of bearers of information (ch. 2, sect. 3 of the Act). It is thus of no significance whether a certain piece of information is to be found in a document in the traditional sense of the world or is recorded on magnetic tape.

The Decree on Service to the Public
The principle of public access, as expressed in the Act, means that an authority which holds a certain official document is obliged either to make the document available on request, in order to make

it possible for the person who asks for the document to read it on the premises, or to give him a copy of the document. On the other hand, the Act does not put the authorities under any obligation to give verbal information as to the contents of a document. There are, however, provisions in this respect outside the Act. These provisions, which have been issued by the Government, are to be found in the Decree on Service to the Public.

Duty not to Divulge Secret Information
It is obvious that there must be exceptions to the principle of public access. The regulations in the Act and the Decree on Service to the Public mean that the authorities are under an obligation to give information to private persons. But this obligation is limited to such information as is public. It will be seen below that the Act makes a distinction between public and secret documents. There is no public access to secret documents.

There are no provisions in the Freedom of the Press Act concerning the right of an official to pass on secret information by word of mouth. Provisions imposing an obligation on public officials to keep certain information secret are to be found, however, in several statutes and decrees. A breach of duty to observe secrecy is usually punishable. A special question is to what extent it is possible, by means of provisions of this kind, to prevent information from being passed on to the mass media. Because of provisions in the Act, in most cases an official who gives information to the mass media cannot be punished even when his action implies a breach of duty to observe secrecy (ch. 2, sects. 1 and 3, and ch. 7, sect. 3).

RECENT CHANGES OR PROPOSALS

The Provisions on Recordings
When the present Freedom of the Press Act was instituted in 1949, it stated that documents, including maps, drawings and pictorial representations, should be available to the public. There was no definition of the term 'document'. From the wording and contents of the provisions, however, it is possible to draw the conclusion that the term 'document' denoted a source of information that was immediately available. But technological developments soon gave rise to difficulties as to the practical application of the provisions. It was questioned whether, e.g., gramophone records and magnetic

tapes were subject to the same rules as documents in the traditional sense of the word. These problems grew as the use of computers became more frequent.[3]

In 1969 the Minister of Justice appointed a special commission which was given the task of examining questions concerning the public or secret character of different kinds of sources of information. Among other things the commission was to consider the problems connected with new forms for the storing of information, such as phonetic recordings and recordings on magnetic tape or on punched cards or tapes as part of automated data processing (ADP). The commission accounted for this part of its task in 1972 in a special report.[4] The deliberations of the commission resulted in certain changes in chapter 2 of the Freedom of the Press Act. In the main these changes meant that the provisions concerning documents should also apply to recordings for ADP and to other recordings (ch. 2, sect. 2).

By amendments the Freedom of the Press Act, which entered into force as from January 1978, a definition was inserted in the Act. According to this definition a document is a presentation in writing or in picture form or a recording which can be read, listened to or in any other way understood only by technical means.

Further Revision of the Legislation

In the task of the above-mentioned commission were included not only the principle of public access to official documents and the exceptions from this principle, but also the question concerning the duty of public officials not to pass on the information contained in secret documents by word of mouth. The commission delivered its final report in April 1975.[5] In many respects the proposals of the commission come very close to the regulations now in force. In fact they amount mainly to a purely technical revision of the existing law on the subject. A novelty, however, is that the draft Act on Official Documents – the counterpart of the present Official Secrets Act (see below) – contains some provisions concerning the release of official documents by one authority to another. On the basis of the proposals of the commission, the Riksdag has passed a law (prop. 1975/76: 160) concerning a revision of the provisions in the Freedom of the Press Act on the right of access to official documents. The revision, which does not signify any fundamental changes in the existing system, became effective as from 1 January 1978.

Another government commission was entrusted with the task of revising the legislation that protects the freedom of the press and the freedom of expression, i.e., the Freedom of the Press Act and the Act on Freedom of Expression in Radio and Television. The commission brought in its main report (SOU 1975: 49) in the summer of 1975. This report formed the basis for a Government Bill (prop. 1975/76: 204) concerning a partial revision of the Freedom of the Press Act. In the Bill the Government presented proposals for extending the right of members of the public, including public officials, to procure and forward information for publication in the mass media. This Bill has now been passed by the Riksdag and came into force on 1 January 1978. In the summer of 1977 the Ministry of Justice published a draft of a new Official Secrecy Act (Ds Ju 1977: 1 och 11). The draft contains a joint regulation of secrecy concerning both the release of documents and the duty not to divulge information. It sets the rules for the relations between the authorities and private citizens as well as the relations between different authorities. A Riksdag decision on the draft is not expected until 1979, at the earliest.

GENERAL RIGHTS OF PUBLIC ACCESS

THE GENERAL SITUATION

The Principle of Public Access
The principle of public access, as laid down in chapter 2 of the Freedom of the Press Act, means that every Swedish citizen has free access to official documents. The term 'Swedish citizen' denotes not only natural persons enjoying Swedish citizenship but also Swedish legal persons under civil law.[6] Also, as will be set forth in some detail below, foreigners are for all practical purposes on a par with Swedish citizens (ch. 14, sect. 5 of the Act).

The principle of public access does not mean that all the information that is kept by, or stored within, an authority is available to everybody. The authorities are under no obligation to give the public access to anything but official documents. Nor is this obligation without exceptions. In some cases the interests of publicity must give way to opposing interests. The Act thus allows certain restrictions on the right of access to documents (ch. 2, sect. 2). One finds provisions stating the purposes that must be served by such restrictions in order to make them permissible, and a provision stating that the specific restrictions on the right of access must in principle be laid down in a special Act. The provisions imposing these restrictions are to be found in the Official Secrets Act. It should be mentioned that in most cases the provisions of this Act do not apply to persons who are parties in the matter with which a document is connected.[7]

Official Documents
Since the principle of public access applies only to official documents it is important to know what is meant by such a document. In the Freedom of the Press Act the term 'official document' is defined as any document that is in ˙ e keeping of an authority and that has been received or drawn u by authority. As mentioned above the term 'document' is defined as a presentation in writing or in picture form or a recording which can be read, listened to or in any other way understood only by technical means.

The meaning of the term 'authority' is not made clear in the Act. In principle, however, every state or municipal body that can be seen as a tolerably well-defined unit is an authority under the Act. This is true even in those cases where the business of a state or municipal body is to carry on economic or consultative activities, etc. A corporation under civil law, however, is not an authority, even if it is owned in its entirety by the state or by a municipality.[8]

The requirement that a document must be *in the keeping of an authority* in order to be considered an official document must not be taken to mean that an official document loses its official status by being temporarily brought to the home of a civil servant. Nor does a private document become official by being brought on to the premises of an authority. It can be taken as a general rule that a document that is normally to be in the keeping of an authority shall be regarded as an official document.[9]

Recordings for ADP and other technical recordings are deemed to be in the keeping of an authority if the recordings are at the disposal of the authority. This means that an authority can entrust recordings for ADP, etc., to the care of a corporation under civil law without the recordings losing their official character (ch. 2, sect. 3 of the Act).

According to the Act, documents that have been received by an authority are considered official whether finished or in the form of rough drafts, whereas documents that are drawn up within an authority are deemed to be official only when they have been finished. The reason for this latter provision is the opinion that an authority should be able to finish a decision or a report without being disturbed by undue interference from outside.

The Decree on Service to the Public

The provisions in the Decree on Service to the Public requiring an authority to offer advice and information apply only to state authorities but they are followed also by the municipal authorities. According to the Decree, the courts and other state authorities are under an obligation to give verbal or written information regarding the contents of files, records, registers and other documents that are available to the public. It goes without saying that this does not include the contents of secret documents. In other respects, too, an authority is supposed to assist the public with information concerning its activities, to the extent that is expedient.

Prohibitions on the Release of Secret Documents

The authorities are under no obligation to hand over to a member of the public a document that is not official or an official document that is secret because of its contents. Moreover, the Official Secrets Act contains a provision prescribing criminal liability for persons who hand over secret documents contrary to the provisions in the Act.

Duty not to Divulge Secret Information

The provisions in the Official Secrets Act apply only to the handing over of documents. But it goes almost without saying that civil servants cannot be allowed to give verbal information concerning the contents of secret documents, thereby evading the Act. This has been considered to follow from the provisions in the Act. In addition, one can find provisions enjoining secrecy in several laws and regulations, the majority of these having been issued by the Government. According to the new Instrument of Government, which became effective as from 1 January 1975, such unwritten rules as the one prohibiting verbal release of the contents of secret documents are not valid any more. As already mentioned, the Ministry of Justice has published a draft of a joint regulation of secrecy of documents and information in other forms.

TYPES OF INFORMATION KEPT SECRET

Unfinished Documents

Since there is no right of access to documents that have not been received or drawn up by an authority, the provisions on when a document is to be regarded as drawn up are of great importance. Distinctions are made in the Freedom of the Press Act between different categories of documents (ch. 2, sect. 7). The main rule, as regards documents in general, is that they are to be considered as drawn up when they have been dispatched, or, if they are to be used only within the authority, when the case or matter to which the documents belong has been finally settled. As a rule, *minutes* are considered to be drawn up when they have been approved. *Records, registers, diaries* and *similar lists* are deemed to be drawn up and thus to be official as soon as they are ready for use; this means that a new entry immediately becomes part of the official document and available to the public, if not otherwise provided for in the Official Secrets Act.

The Freedom of the Press Act also contains special provisions concerning *memoranda*, i.e. notes that have been made within a authority exclusively for the presentation or preparation of a case or matter (ch. 2, sect. 9). As instances of this one can mention notes used for the verbal presentation of a report, and preliminary or other drafts of letters or decisions. According to the Act such memoranda acquire the character of official documents only if they are filed together with the other documents in a case or matter. The same principle applies to recordings for ADP and to other types of recording, if they have been made only for the presentation or preparation of a case or matter.

One must distinguish between memoranda of the aforementioned kind and notes that contain factual information of importance for a decision, e.g., notes of what somebody has said during a conversation with an official of an authority. Such notes must be kept and filed with the other documents in a matter.[10]

The practical application of the provisions on when a document is to be considered as received or drawn up has sometimes given rise to intricate problems. If, for example, an official of a certain authority sends an unfinished document to an official of another authority for consultations or discussions, is this document then available to the public? Before the new chapter 2 of the Freedom of the Press Act went into force in 1978 there had been some doubts whether there was a certain margin for unofficial consultations in writing between officials of separate authorities, without the documents exchanged becoming public. As an instance of this can be mentioned a case tried by the Supreme Administrative Court (RÅ 1963 ref. 16) which concerned an authority that had undertaken to draw up a proposal on behalf of another authority. Before the proposal was formally dispatched, a draft was sent over to some officials of the latter authority. The Court found that this action did not mean that the document had been dispatched in the sense of the Freedom of the Press Act. Thus, although the draft had in fact been sent over to persons outside the former authority, it was not an official document as far as that authority was concerned. The question remained, however, whether the draft, after having reached these persons, was to be regarded as having been received by the authority with which they were connected and thus as an official document from the point of view of this latter authority.[11] The two questions mentioned above were answered in the new art. 9 of chapter 2. According to this provision, documents are not be regarded as 'official' in the situations indicated.

The Exceptions to Public Access
According to the Freedom of the Press Act, the following restrictions on the right of public access to official documents are allowed: restrictions that are necessary on account of

1. the security of the state or its relations to other states or international organisations;
2. the state's central financial, monetary or currency policy;
3. the activities of public authorities for inspection, control or supervision in other cases;
4. the activities to prevent or suppress crime;
5. the economic interests in public activities;
6. the protection of the personal or economic circumstances of the individual; or
7. the protection of species of animals or plants.

The Official Secrets Act
As already mentioned, the types of documents that were to be kept secret were to be specified in detail in a special Act, and this was done in the Official Secrets Act. In more than 40 sections this Act enumerates the documents that are to be kept secret on the grounds

stated in the Freedom of the Press Act, as set forth above. Though space does not permit a comprehensive account of the Official Secrets Act, some explanation of its main provisions can be given.

The provisions in the first four sections are motivated by regard to the safety of the realm and its relations to foreign powers (*inter alia* a provision on documents concerning national defence).

Documents concerning the activities of public authorities for inspection or for the combating of crime are secret to a certain extent because of the provisions in sections 7 and 10. Section 10, which refers to the documents of the police and of the public prosecutors, is also intended to protect the privacy of persons.

The provisions on the business of the Bank of Sweden (sect. 31), on borrowing (sect. 33), purchasing, selling, contracts by tender (sect. 34), and the business and operating conditions of government enterprises (sect. 34a), serve to protect the economic interests of the state and of communities.

The economic interests of private persons and corporations are protected by provisions *inter alia* on documents concerning guardianship (sect. 15), documents containing basic data for statistics (sect. 16), tax returns (sect. 17), documents relating to government investigation, control and support of industry and commerce (sect. 21), documents on labour exchange (sect. 25), communications (sect. 28), post, telegraph and telephone (sect. 29) and on lending (sect. 32).

The privacy of individuals is protected by the provisions in sections 11–14. Those in section 14 are of special importance, since they refer to the majority of documents concerning the public health, care of the sick, and social welfare services. Section 14 contains an extensive enumeration of matters concerning, e.g., public health, medical care, social assistance, child welfare, treatment of alcoholics, social insurance and some types of psychological examinations. As a rule documents on such matters are secret regarding the personal circumstances of private individuals. This rule, however, does not normally apply to decisions. Thus, if information on an individual is included in a decision, this information is released with the decision.

According to the provision in chapter 2 of the Freedom of the Press Act, the types of documents to be kept secret shall be specified in a special enactment. However, the provisions allow the Government to issue prescriptions concerning the secret character of certain groups of documents. As a result, there are several decrees on secrecy in existence, concerning *inter alia* documents relating to national defence and to Government investigation, control and support of industry and commerce.

The provisions on secrecy must be seen as exceptions from the principle of public access to official documents. This means that the provisions of the Official Secrets Act must be applied in a restrictive spirit. If an official document is not described in a statutory or other legally valid provision enjoining secrecy it cannot be kept secret.

Information not in an Official Document

The provisions of the Official Secrets Act do not apply to information that has not been incorporated in an official document, i.e., information that either has not been incorporated in any document whatsoever or has been incorporated in a document that is not official. It has already been mentioned that the authorities are under no obligation to hand over documents that must be regarded as drafts or that otherwise concern matters that have not yet been finally settled. On the other hand, there is no express prohibition against releasing such documents. When deciding on access to a document that is not official, an authority must *inter alia* take into consideration whether the release of the document is well-advised at that point of time. Of course interests of secrecy may also be of importance in this connection. If the document in question contains such information that the document would have been regarded as secret, had it been finished and thus official, the authority cannot be expected to release the document.[12] In some cases the unwarranted release of an unfinished document may be regarded as a punishable service irregularity.

THE HOLDERS OF INFORMATION

ADMINISTRATIVE AUTHORITIES

As a rule a document referred to in the secrecy provisions is secret irrespective of by which authority the document is being kept at a given moment. Though the secrecy provisions do no prohibit one authority from lending a secret document to another, a document which was secret when it was drawn up retains its secret character after it has been lent to another authority. If a person wants to have access to a document and there are copies in the keeping of several authorities, he may approach any one of the authorities with a request. The authority that is thus approached has to decide the question of access to the document on its own responsibility, irrespective of where the document was originally drawn up (ch. 2, sect. 14 of the Freedom of the Press Act).

There are two main types of provision on the secrecy of documents: provisions that make secrecy the rule but allow certain exceptions from this rule, and provisions where the principle is that the document is public and secrecy the exception. Secrecy prevails either until the matter to which a document is related is finally settled, or until a certain space of time – two, five, 20, 50 or 70 years – has elapsed.

In the same way a private person can suspend secrecy that is exclusively in the interests of that person. This is true of documents concerning his personal as well as his economic circumstances (see e.g. sects 14 and 17 in the Official Secrets Act). This means that as a rule a document of this kind can be released if the person who is protected by the secrecy of the document gives his consent. In some cases, however, documents that are secret for the protection of individuals can be handed over without the consent of the persons concerned. It is thus possible for an authority to make such documents available for scientific research, if this will cause no risk of abuse (see e.g. sect. 14 of the Official Secrets Act). In cases of this kind the authority can make access subject to conditions concerning the use of the document and its contents. Ignoring such conditions is punishable by law.

PUBLIC CORPORATION, POLITICAL EXECUTIVES AND PARLIAMENT

As mentioned earlier, the principle of public access does not apply to corporations under civil law that are wholly or partially owned or otherwise dominated by the state or a municipality. It is to be noted, however, that a document that is dispatched from such a corporation to an authority becomes official as soon as it has been received by the authority.

The Government, Parliament and its committees are regarded as authorities and are thus subject to the principle of public access. The political parties, on the other hand, are not authorities. This state of affairs may give rise to intricate problems, for example when a document is received by a minister. If he receives the document in his capacity as party functionary, the document does not become official. But if the document has been sent to him in his capacity as a minister and official of the state, the document must be treated as official. The same principles apply to documents that are drawn up by a minister or within a ministry. An explicit provision to this effect went into force on 1 January 1978.

THE RECIPIENTS OF INFORMATION

GENERAL ACCESS

It is laid down in the Freedom of the Press Act that foreigners have the same rights as Swedish citizens, unless otherwise provided in the Act or other statutes. As far as the right of access to official documents is concerned, the Act does not contain any such special provisions with regard to foreigners. Nor are such provisions to be found elsewhere.

In general, then, an authority that has to decide on a request for access by a private person – physical or legal – has to examine only whether the document in question is official and, if this proves to be the case, whether it is public or secret. It is of no interest to the authority to know the identity or nationality of the applicant or the reasons for the request; nor has the authority any right to investigate these circumstances.[13] In the same way the obligation of authorities to give information under the Decree on Service to the Public is in no way related to the identity of the person who wants the information or his reasons for wanting it.

It has been seen above that some provisions on the secrecy of documents make it possible for an authority to hand over a secrect document if there is no risk of the document being abused. In such cases the authority concerned must have access to information on the applicant and the reasons for the request, in order to be able to form an opinion as to the risk of abuse.

Neither the Official Secrets Act nor the Decree on Service to the Public grants any special privileges to the mass media. In practice, however, many authorities give more service to the mass media than they are obliged to do. Thus the ministries and several other authorities put special rooms at the disposal of the representatives of the press where they have daily access to the incoming mail, unless it is secret under the Official Secrets Act.

Though the Freedom of the Press Act does not put authorities under any greater obligation to release documents or pass information to the mass media, this Act and the Act on Freedom of Expression in Radio and Television do contain provisions to the effect that a person who passes on information with the intention that it shall be published in print or broadcast by radio or television cannot be punished even though the information passed on is secret. According to the main rule in the Freedom of the Press Act it is the editor who has sole responsibility for the contents of a printed periodical (ch. 8, sect. 1). Rules to the same effect are to be found in the Act on Freedom of Expression in Radio and Television. This protection of the informant is not complete, however. A public official who, by passing on information to be published or broadcast, thereby commits high treason, espionage or some other crime against the security of the realm that is specially mentioned in the Freedom of the Press Act, can be punished under ordinary criminal law (ch. 7, sect. 3). The same is true of a public official who passes on information by an illicit release of a secret document or, in cases stated in a special Act, deliberately sets aside a duty to observe secrecy. Moreover, in the provisions on the protection of the informant it is stated that, in cases where an informant cannot be punished, authorities are not allowed to investigate the source of the information that has been passed on for publication or broadcast (ch. 3, sects. 4 and 5).

ACCESS BY PARTICULAR BODIES AND GROUPS

It is laid down in the Instrument of Government that one of the parliamentary committees – the Committee on the Constitution – is to examine the activities of the ministers and the management of matters incumbent on the Government. The Committee has a right, in the process of this examination, to have access to all documents relating to Government matters, irrespective of the documents being secret or public. Also, the Parliamentary Ombudsmen and the Chancellor of Justice have a right to be present at the deliberations of the courts and other public authorities and to have access to their documents, even if they are secret. The authorities are also under an obligation to give the ombudsmen or the Chancellor of Justice all the information that they may request.

The Official Secrets Act contains a provision (sect. 38, para. 2) that makes it possible for a court to have access to secret documents in the keeping of other authorities, if the documents in question can be presumed to contain information of importance as evidence in a case before the court or in pre-judicial inquiries. There are, however, certain exceptions to this rule. According to another provision (sect. 38, para. 1), the Government has a general right to grant access to a secret document if it considers this necessary for the protection of public or private interests.

RESTRICTIONS ON USE BY RECIPIENTS

An authority cannot make the handing over of a public document subject to any restrictions or conditions as to the use of the document. In some cases, however, it is possible for an authority to make such restrictions or conditions when making a secret document available. These may be to the effect that the recipient of a document must not pass the document on to anybody else, or that the information contained in the document must not be used in certain ways (see e.g. sect. 14 or the Official Secrets Act). The setting aside of such conditions is punishable (sect. 41).

INFORMATION PROCEDURES

THE HOLDING OF INFORMATION

The practical usefulness of the principle of public access to official documents is obviously dependent on to what extent the activities of the authorities are *substantiated in documents*. The Freedom of the Press Act has nothing to say on this matter, but in several other legal instruments there are provisions on the duty of the authorities to make records of the proceedings that take place before them, of their decisions and of the facts that form the basis for these decisions. The principle of public access furthermore presupposes that *documents are being kept for the future* to a rather large extent. There are no provisions in the Act, however, on the duty of the authorities to keep documents for the future.[14] Such provisions are to be found only in decrees issued by the Government. They allow for the weeding out of unimportant documents.

The question of *registration of official documents* is also of importance for the realisation of the principle of public access. If such documents were not entered in journals or registered in some other way, it would often be impossible for a person who wants to have access to a certain document to know if the document exists and where it can be found. There are no general provisions on the registration of documents in the Act, [15] but such provisions are laid down in several other legal instruments. Registers normally are public even though they contain entries concerning secret documents. If this were not the case the public would not be aware of the existence of secret documents and would thus be unable to submit the question of access to such documents to the decision of the competent authorities.

If an authority finds that special measures are necessary to prevent the unauthorised release of a secret document, it can make a note on the document stating its secret nature. The provisions on this subject are to be found in the Freedom of the Press Act (ch. 2, sect. 16) and in the Official Secrets Act (sect. 40c).

THE TRANSMISSION OF INFORMATION

Making a Document Available
When access to a document is requested, authorities are under an obligation to make the document available immediately or as soon as possible.[16] A request for access can be made verbally or in writing. Before access is granted, the authority has to decide whether the document is official and, if this proves to be the case, whether the document also is public. The request must be submitted to the authority that keeps the document and this authority then decides the question.

It would be impracticable for the authority itself to decide every question concerning access. If the care of documents has been entrusted to a special official, such as a registrar, this person can decide to release the document. In doubtful cases he can leave the decision to the authority if the latter can decide the question immediately (sect. 40a of the Official Secrets Act). If he finds that the document in question is not a public official document, he will refuse to hand it over to the applicant. If the applicant is dissatisfied with this refusal, he can have the question submitted to the authority, which then has to decide the question without delay. A request for such a submission can be made orally or in writing.[17]

On request a public document must be made available on the premises free of charge for reading and copying. A person who wants access to a document also has the right to order a copy of it, but must pay a certain fee – at present a few crowns a page. In most cases the applicant can choose between reading the document on the premises and ordering a copy. In other cases, however, only one of these alternatives is possible. For instance, if the release of a document would expose it to being damaged, the applicant is only entitled to a copy of it.[18]

The Freedom of the Press Act contains some special provisions with regard to access to technical recordings. A technical recording – i.e., a recording that cannot be read or listened to without technical aids – must be made available in such a form that it can be read or listened to. The authority must either provide the applicant with a transcript of the recording or put the necessary technical equipment at his disposal. As a rule this is done free of charge.[19]

The fact that part of a document is secret does not give an authority the right to refuse to release all of the document. According to express provisions in the Freedom of Press Act, those parts of the document that do not contain secret information must be made available on request. If this cannot be done in any other way, the authority is under an obligation to make a copy of the document with the secret part excluded (ch. 2, sect. 12).[20]

Making Information Available
According to the Decree on Service to the Public, the courts and other authorities must, on request, give information as to the contents of files, journals, registers and other documents available to the public. This obligation is not unlimited, however. The fulfilment of the primary tasks of the authorities must not be interfered with. A person who wants certain information can ask for it orally either by visit or by telephone, or in writing. The answer to a question is normally given by the same medium as that of the question itself. As a rule information is given free of charge. In some cases, however, a small fee is charged for written information.

CLASSIFICATION AND DECLASSIFICATION

The Freedom of the Press Act distinguishes only between secret and public documents. In principle there are no grades of secrecy. If a document is secret it must not be handed over to anyone. However, different types of documents must be kept secret for different periods of time. As a rule a maximum period of secrecy is laid down. Documents concerning the personal circumstances of individuals are to be kept secret for 70 years (see e.g. sects. 13 and 14 of the Official Secrets Act). As regards the national defence and the relations to foreign powers a secrecy period of 50 years is the rule. For documents kept secret on account of public or private economic interests the period is much shorter, usually 20 years. In some cases there is no maximum period of secrecy at all. Thus for example reports and notes that have been recorded in the general register of criminals or in a police register are secret for an unlimited period (sect.11).

In one respect the Act makes a distinction between different types of secret documents. Regarding documents the secrecy of which is of special importance to the safety of the realm, the Government can provide that the question of access must be decided by a special authority (ch. 2, sect. 14). The Government has issued such provisions in several decrees on, *inter alia*, documents concerning the police and national defence. In these decrees the competence to decide questions of access has been given to heads of ministries. Since 1 January 1978 it is possible to appeal against such a decision by a minister. The appeal must be lodged with the Government. On a document of this kind a note must be made stating that the document is secret according to a cited provision in the Official Secrets Act, and stating who shall decide questions of access to the document. Hence the principle that the question of access is to be decided by the authority holding the document does not apply to such documents.

As regards other secret documents, if an authority finds that special measures are necessary to prevent their unauthorised release, it can make a note on a document stating its secret nature. Such a note must contain information as to the relevant provision on secrecy, the name of the authority that has made the note, and its date. Such a note is binding neither on the authority that made it nor on any other authority. A document carrying such a note might be a public one in spite of the note, while, on the other hand, a document might be secret although it is without a note on secrecy. When access is asked for, the competent authority must decide the question without regard to the existence of such a special note, which thus serves only as a 'danger signal'.[21] The main reason for this is practical. With this system it is not necessary to make a thorough scrutiny of every document as to its possible secrecy until it is asked for.

Non-official Documents

An authority is under no obligation to release a document that is not official. On the other hand there are no provisions expressly prohibiting the authorities from granting access to such documents. On documents of this kind one can sometimes find the word 'confidential' or some similar expression, which is used to indicate that the document is intended for a limited circle.

THE REFUSAL AND RELEASE OF INFORMATION

Official Documents

It is possible to appeal against a decision of an authority not to grant access to a document or to release a document with restrictions as to its use, but one cannot lodge an appeal against a decision to make a document available. Thus if a private person considers himself harmed by the release of a document, he cannot have the decision altered. If he is of the opinion, however, that access to the document was granted unlawfully, he can make a complaint to the Ombudsmen or to the Chancellor of Justice.[22]

According to the provisions in the Freedom of the Press Act and in the Official Secrets Act an appeal shall be lodged with the competent Administrative Court of Appeal and, as regards decisions by such a court, the Supreme Administrative Court. Regarding documents kept by the courts of general jurisdiction, however, the appeals shall be lodged with those courts. Appeals must always be heard without delay. There are no provisions limiting the right to bring an appeal to the court of highest instance.

There are a few exceptions to the principal rule that all refusals to release documents can be appealed against. Thus decisions made by the Government, Parliament, parliamentary commissions or the Ombudsmen are final.

As mentioned earlier, in some cases the Government can grant access to secret documents without the question having been first decided by a subordinate authority.

Refusal to Give Verbal Information

It is not possible to appeal against a refusal to give verbal information. If the information in question is to be found in a document, however, the person who wants the information can ask for the document instead. He can also complain to the Ombudsmen or to the Chancellor of Justice.

SPECIAL STATUS OF INTERESTED PARTIES

To a large extent the provisions on the secrecy of documents do not apply to interested parties in cases or matters being dealt with by the courts or other authorities (sect. 39, para. 1 of the Official Secrets Act). It is obvious that a party, in order to look after his interests properly, must have access even to secret documents concerning his case.

There is one exception to the rule that a party in a case or matter has access to secret documents (sect. 39, para. 2 of the Official Secrets Act). An authority can refuse to give access if it is of very great importance to public or private interests that the contents of a document be not made known. This exception does not, however, apply to judgments and other decisions.

The exception has been put to practical use regarding case records at hospitals. In principle a patient has access to his own case sheet. Sometimes, however, it can be harmful for the patient to know the contents of his case sheet. For this reason the Official Secrets Act makes it possible to keep case records secret even from patients themselves, if there is well-founded reason to believe that making them available would be detrimental to the treatment. The same rule applies *mutatis mutandis* if access to a document would endanger somebody's personal safety.

CONCLUSION

As was mentioned in the introduction, the principle of public access to official documents dates back as far as the latter part of the eighteenth century, and the principle has not undergone any radical changes since then. The provisions on the subject in the Freedom of the Press Act and the Official Secrets Act primarily concern documents in the traditional sense of the word, i.e., sheets of paper bearing written information. Apart from the purely technical aspects of the methods of access, these provisions do not take into consideration the special problems connected with the emergence of ADP techniques, for instance those caused by the fact that such techniques make it possible to put together and store great amounts of information concerning private individuals. It is therefore not unlikely that the increasing use of ADP will influence the future framing of the principle of public access.

Some of the problems connected with the use of ADP have been solved in an Act on the use of personal registers based on ADP techniques, the Data Act of 1973. The provisions of this Act are being enforced by a special authority. These measures probably constitute only a beginning, however. There remain many problems to be solved, and some of these may not yet have come within sight.

NOTES

ABBREVIATIONS USED IN NOTES

JO   Justitieombudsmännens ämbetsberättelse (The Annual Report of the Parliamentary Ombudsmen)
prop.   Government Bill
RA   Regeringsrättens årsbok (The Annual Report of the Supreme Administrative Court)
SOU   Statens Offentliga Utredningar (The Swedish Government Official Reports)

1. See prop. 1948:230, p. 122.
2. See e.g. the Act on the General Register of Criminals.
3. See e.g. RÅ 1969 ref. 11; and 1971 ref. 15.
4. SOU 1972:47.
5. SOU 1975:22.
6. See P. E. Elsin, *Allmänna handlingars offenlighet och sekretess* (Stockholm, 1966), p. 9; and RÅ 1956 ref. 39.
7. See below, Special Status of Interested Parties.
8. See e.g. S -H. Ryman and E. Holmberg, *Offenlighetsprincipen och myndigheterna, sjunde uppl.* (Lund, 1975), and Håkan Strömberg, *Tryckfrihetsrätt, fjärde uppl.* (Malmö, 1973), p. 66.

9. See Strömberg, op. cit., p. 69.
10. See RÅ 1971 ref. 23.
11. See JO 1974, p. 412; and SOU 1966:60, p. 138.
12. See Elsin, op. cit., p. 20.
13. JO 1971, p. 348; and Ryman – Holmberg, op. cit., p. 17.
14. See prop. 1948:230, p. 125.
15. See e.g. JO 1971, p. 341.
16. See Carl Norström and Tor Sverne, *Social sekretess* (Kristianstad, 1974), p. 23.
17. See Ryman-Holmberg, op. cit., p. 19.
18. See e.g. JO 1966, p.362.
19. See prop, 1973:33, p. 81; and Ryman-Holmberg, op. cit., p. 17.
20. JO 1971, p. 333.
21. See Norström-Sverne, op. cit., p. 24.
22. See Ryman-Holmberg, op. cit., p. 22.

2 Finland

TORE MODEEN

Finland was part of Sweden until 1809. In Swedish law the question of public access to administrative and other official information has traditionally been connected with the principle of freedom of the press. Freedom of the press means that everybody has the right not only to study official documents, but also to receive copies of the documents and to reproduce them in large numbers without any censorship. In earlier times official documents were asked for by citizens mainly for the right to reproduce them, as today newspapers distribute information taken from official documents and thus serve the purpose of closely watching public administration and the administration of justice.

Since Finland was then a part of Sweden, the Swedish Freedom of the Press Act of 1766 (repealed by the Constitution of 1772) also applied to the Finnish part of the Kingdom. A decree of 1774 permitted only a restricted freedom of the press. This became more restricted toward the end of the Swedish period in Finnish history.

THE RUSSIAN PERIOD

In 1809, when Finland became an autonomous Grand Duchy under the Russian Czar, Swedish law as of 1809 continued to apply in Finland. All of the old Swedish law remained valid in Finland: constitutional law, civil law, criminal law, procedural law and administrative law, even when the administrative and judicial organisation of the autonomous Grand Duchy of Finland (which under Sweden had not enjoyed autonomy) had to be adapted to the changed circumstances. The law of freedom of the press in Finland, immediately after 1809, was therefore the same restrictive one that was effective in Sweden during the last decades before 1809.

Even less freedom was permitted under a decree of 1829, influenced by Russian authoritarian thinking. In 1847, however, an Imperial Ordinance stated that all public ordinances, orders and documents could be printed by anyone, though formerly unpublished documents could be printed only after due permission. Nevertheless, public access to official information continued to be very restricted in Finland.

An era of liberalisation began when Czar Alexander II ascended the throne. A decree of 1865 declared the principle of freedom of the press. This decree also contained provisions concerning public access to official documents, and commanded civil servants to give out such documents to the public without delay. But freedom of the press was soon restricted again in 1867, though the provisions concerning public access to official documents remained unchanged. Because newspapers were censored, these provisions were not of much significance.

The Constitutional Act of 1906, proclaiming Civil Rights for the Finnish subjects of the Czar, was therefore received with great expectations by the people. Freedom of the press was mentioned among the rights. But this very liberal Act was only a temporary concession of the Czar, drawn up when Russia had been weakened by losing the war with Japan, and was not put into effect. The oppressive Russian rule, typical of the turn of the century, continued until the disintegration of the Russian Empire in 1917.

Finland's situation was much less favourable than that of Sweden, where public access to administrative and judicial information was firmly established in the Constitution Act of 1809 and the more specific Freedom of the Press Decree of 1812, and was developed into a very real civil right. Despite repeated statutes proclaiming freedom of the press and even public access to official documents, the Russian trait of secrecy, typical of any authoritarian regime, was very much apparent even in autonomous Finland.

THE CONSTITUTION ACT OF 1919

The Constitution Act (in Finnish 'Hallitusmuoto', in Swedish

'Regeringsform') of the independent Republic of Finland (1919) proclaimed freedom of the press as a civil right for every Finnish citizen. The same year a Freedom of the Press Act was issued. The Act contains five articles concerning the right to publish official documents (paras 26–30). However, the right of access to official documents was not included in the list of civil rights given Finnish citizens under the Constitution Act. Nor did the Freedom of the Press Act contain any reference to this matter, despite the 1865 decree, which, although of minor real importance, had been the law in force up to 1919.

THE LEGAL SITUATION 1919–1951

The omission from the Constitution and the Freedom of the Press Act of any references to public access to official documents had the predictable effect that public authorities took a very cautious, even restrictive, attitude to demands for access. In spite of the principle of public access – which was never officially denied – the practice was quite secretive in cases where no provisions proclaiming access in a particular statute could be found. In some cases there were explicit rules concerning the right of the public to receive copies of public records (for example in the Local Government Act). Most court cases in the period 1919–51 concerned the interpretation of these rules. Finnish public servants were, and still are, less inclined to pay attention to general principles of the law than to specific provisions in statutes.

Of particular interest is a decision of the Supreme Court of Justice (Reports 1941: II 8) which confirms the validity of the general rule of public access to official documents without specific provisions in a statute. The case concerned a citizen's right of access to the archives of a lower court of justice. The dispute arose from the judge's demand that the citizen should restrict himself to ordering (paid) copies of the records, whereas the citizen claimed he should be able to study the records himself, and to make notes and copy those he needed. This claim, which was granted by the court, relied clearly upon the general principle of public access to official documents, since the statute presupposed only paid copies of the records.

Under the 1919 legislation, the situation was unsatisfactory. The lack of explicit rules on public access to official documents failed to clarify this right. There was even a risk that the right might fall into desuetude and disappear from Finnish law, if no measures such as an appropriate statute were taken within a reasonable time.

THE 1951 PUBLICITY OF DOCUMENTS ACT

PREPARATORY WORKS

In the 1930s the Draft Legislation Board of the Ministry of Justice prepared a report which was published just before the war (Publications of the Draft Legislation Board 1939:4, issued in separate Finnish and Swedish editions). The report was drafted under the leadership of the former President of the Republic, K. J. Ståhlberg, the grand old man of Finnish administrative law, and C. G. Möller, later Chancellor of Justice.

Further work was postponed by the war but quickly resumed, and a new report was published (1945:6). The Government's Bill proposing a Publicity of Documents Act was given to Parliament four years later (1949:105).

There was a discussion in Parliament whether the Bill's proposed rights of access were sufficiently broad. Nevertheless, the Bill was accepted by the majority of the House and the enacted statute is thus chiefly based upon the wordings of the Government's Bill. The Publicity of Documents Act (in Finnish: 'Laki yleisten asiakirjain julkisuudesta'; in Swedish: 'Lag om allmänna handlingars offentlighet') was issued on 9 February 1951 (Statutes Series 1951:83). Like all other legislation, the Act is available in both languages used in Finland: Finnish and Swedish. A Publicity of Documents Decree was issued by the Government in accordance with the Act and in the same year (1951:650). Since the Act has not been subject to any amendments, its original version is still the present law on the matter in Finland.

THE INFLUENCE OF SWEDISH LAW ON THE 1951 ACT

During the first fifty years of Finnish autonomy under Russian supremacy, Swedish law remained in force almost unchanged in Finland because the Russian Czar refused to convene the Finnish Diet, without which no law-making could take place. The Russian attitude changed, however, when Alexander II ascended the throne. As new legislative work then began in the 1860s, Finland was determined not to break with its old Swedish legal traditions. Finland's new legislation was entirely based on the old system and, in many cases, was clearly influenced by more recent Swedish legislative measures. When Finland became independent in 1917–18 its legal system was thus still very similar to Sweden's; for instance the same code of 1734 was partly in force in both countries. After gaining independence, Finland was able to take an active part in Scandinavian co-operation in the field of legislation. This had not been possible while Finland lacked sovereignty. Quite naturally Finland's relationship to Sweden became a special one because of their common legal history. Finland continued to look to Sweden, and in many cases to follow Sweden's example, when new legislation was to be introduced. But Sweden was not always the giving party; sometimes Finnish law served as a model for new Swedish legislation.

In Sweden public access to official documents is based on historic legal rules. In this respect the development during the nineteenth century was especially important. Finland therefore had good reason to study Swedish law carefully when it decided to enact its own legislation in this field. How much has Finnish legislation been influenced by Swedish law?

The drafters of the Finnish Act knew Swedish law. Many facts in their report prove this knowledge. But the Finnish Act appears, in many respects, a distinctive piece of legislation, not a copy of the corresponding Swedish Act. The constitutional guarantee for public access to official documents in Finland and Sweden differs completely and the Acts are drafted along quite different lines. Since public access to official documents in Sweden is linked to the constitutionally protected right of the citizen to enjoy freedom of the press, and since the right of access is based on more detailed provisions in Swedish law, fundamental differences between the two countries in this field can be observed.

On the other hand, Finnish citizens have traditionally regarded the right of access as stemming from the common legal heritage of Finland and Sweden. The existence of the 1951 Finnish Publicity of Documents Act must thus be seen against this background.

THE CONSTITUTIONAL AND LEGISLATIVE BACKGROUND

As stated before, public access to official documents is not a constitutionally protected civil right for the citizen, since it is not included in the catalogue of rights in the Finnish Constitution Act. Since this right is based on ordinary statutory law, exceptions from the right can be made by means of ordinary Acts approved by Parliament. An explicit statement to this effect can be found in the Publicity of Documents Act (para. 9(1)).

This Act also provides for restricting the general rule of accessibility by governmental decree (or regulation), which may prescribe that matters or documents shall be kept secret if this is required by: the security of the State or its relations with foreign powers; in the interest of defence, prevention or prosecution of crime; management of the government's or self-governing societies' or private business enterprises or legal proceedings; or the individual's significant personal interest in the area of religious guidance, health and medical service, prison detention or public control activity (para. 9(2)). In individual cases the President of the Republic and the Government may prescribe that matters and documents which are under consideration by them or by subordinate authorities shall be kept secret (para. 9(3), 11-12).

Thus the Government has powers to restrict the citizen's right of access to official documents either by general decrees or by decisions made in individual cases. It is thus obvious that the enjoyment of this right is by no means subject to parliamentary control.

In reality, however, the general rule of public access to official documents has not been seriously restricted by executive measures. Though the Publicity of Documents Decree contains a number of exceptions to the general rule, these exceptions mainly concern matters where secrecy may be considered desirable. Only on very rare occasions have decisions concerning secrecy been made in individual cases.

Even if not protected by the Constitution and Parliament, public access to official documents thus appears in Finland as materially satisfying, since the Government has not misused its powers to restrict this right but, on the contrary, has pursued a very restrained policy.

FREEDOM OF THE PRESS AND ACCESS TO OFFICIAL DOCUMENTS

The 1951 Publicity of Documents Act meant a breach in the traditional concept according to which public access to official documents was a part of the freedom of the press law. Although the 1919 Freedom of the Press Act had not mentioned the citizen's right to have access to official documents for other purposes than to have them printed, the existence of the general right of access had been based on the freedom of the press idea. When the Publicity of Documents Act came into force, the two concepts – the right of access to official documents and the right to print such documents (without censorship) – became formally separated and hence must be treated as two different questions.

But it is obvious that these two questions are still connected in many ways. For example, when the Freedom of the Press Act restricts the right to print public documents to those 'which are not to be kept secret by law', this means that documents to be kept secret under the Publicity of Documents Act, the Publicity of Documents Decree or any other statute cannot be given out to be printed.

INDIVIDUAL AND PUBLIC ACCESS

A clear distinction must be made between two different situations in which a citizen may want to study official documents. He may have a direct personal interest in the case and therefore want to study the authorities' records in that particular case in order to defend his interest. Only with a complete knowledge of the authorities' view on the case as it appears from the records can he satisfactorily pursue his case. A quite different situation arises when a citizen, usually a curious journalist, wants to look into the files and records of authorities for the purpose of distributing information to the general public. The Publicity of Documents Act contains clear provisions only regarding the second situation. This does not mean, however, that the legal rights of an interested party are less than those of an ordinary citizen.

According to an opinion given by the Parliamentary Ombudsman in 1970, a concerned person shall have an absolute right of access to documents related to his own case, compiled by or in the possession of administrative authorities, even if these documents, because they concern personal matters, otherwise should be kept secret. The Ombudsman's opinion concerned a case where a patient had died at a public hospital and his parents wanted to read his medical records kept by the hospital's personnel in order to ascertain that he had been properly treated. An earlier opinion by the Chancellor of Justice (1965) had also declared the right of a patient to have access to his doctor's opinions of his health, as stated in writing to the Central Board of Health. And three recent (1971) decisions of the Supreme Administrative Court clearly confirm the opinion that concerned persons should have the right of privileged treatment in obtaining information from otherwise secret documents. A concerned person cannot base his claim on any general rule in a written statute in such cases. The question of his right to information must be answered according to rather vague principles in customary law, as expounded in legal decisions and opinions of the Ombudsmen and the Chancellor of Justice.

GENERAL RIGHTS OF PUBLIC ACCESS

THE GENERAL SITUATION

According to para. 2(1) of the Publicity of Documents Act, official documents are those made up and issued by an authority as well as documents sent in or submitted to an authority and in its possession. (The term 'official document' includes all categories of documents covered by the publicity rules, even documents issued by private persons which are in the possession of authorities but which cannot exactly be regarded as 'official'.)

Documents *made up by public authorities* are ones prepared by the administration for interior use, i.e., not to be delivered outside the authority. Examples are records kept by a body, minutes of its meetings, or reports concerning the interior functioning of an authority. Documents *issued by public authorities* are, on the other hand, to be sent out of the authority, either to another authority or public body, or to a private citizen or private body. Documents *in the possession of public authorities* are those sent in or submitted to an authority, for instance applications, complaints or letters.

The general rule under the Publicity of Documents Act is stated in para. 1, according to which *official* documents are public. The definition of the concept 'official document' as given in para. 2 is very broad and gives little information on the content of the concept.

More precise dispositions as to the accessibility of official documents are to be found in paras 3–5. Para. 6(1, 3) concerns the categories of persons who benefit from the right of access to official documents. Para. 6(2) gives the authorities discretionary powers to reveal information from documents not yet public.

The law thus guarantees the accessibility of official documents as a general rule. If a document meets the requirements stated in the law for official documents it is automatically accessible. The citizen may thus presume that a (final) official document is accessible, if there are no explicit provisions in the law which declare the document secret. These exceptions from the general rule may be of a general nature and concern all information of a certain category. In this case they are to be found in the Publicity of Documents Act, with the Publicity of Documents Decree giving a more detailed specification of the different fields of public activity in which the documents are to be kept secret. Furthermore, a number of secrecy rules concerning particular kinds of documents and information can be found in special legislation.

The exceptions are by no means so numerous that the general rule can be said to have been seriously restricted. The general rule of publicity thus appears as an important guarantee of control over public administration and the administration of justice in Finland. Cases in which documents have been individually declared secret by decision of the Government have been very rare.

The concept 'authority' refers to national, communal and church, as well as other autonomous public authorities, including also their meetings as public entities, representative assemblies, boards, commissions and committees, together with their civil servants and officeholders (para. 2(2)). The distinction between public and private law thus influences the field of application of the Publicity of Documents Act. Only bodies governed by public law fall under the publicity rules.

In Finland a considerable portion of public administration has traditionally been run by private institutions, although in later years usually with State financial support. This has been especially true in education, but private institutions have also taken part in social and medical administration. This part of public administration has not been considered open for public scrutiny under the Publicity of Documents Act, since the act strictly confines its sphere of application to 'public authorities'. This gap in the law is becoming less serious, however, since the State and the local governments are gradually taking over the direct administration of services which used to be run by private organisations in the fields of education, welfare and health.

The question whether a body is to be classified as a public-law or a private-law body is usually not answered in the statutes, but left open. But the public-law status of a body usually appears clearly in its organisation and powers and, in some cases, in the legal situation of its employees. It is thus possible, by examining the body more closely, to find out if it should be regarded as a public authority under the Publicity of Documents Act. For instance, according to an opinion of the Chancellor of Justice, published in 1956, the National Pension Institute, an independent body governed by public law, is to be considered as a public authority under the Publicity of Documents Act.

WHEN DO OFFICIAL DOCUMENTS BECOME PUBLIC?

According to para. 3 of the Act notations in official registers become public as soon as entered; minutes, when approved; official action, including that pertaining to written communication between authorities, when signed. If decision is given after notice by the authority, it shall be released accordingly. Private documents which come into an authority become public as soon as these are received by the authority.

An important restriction, therefore, is that minutes of public bodies are not accessible before they have been signed and approved. Only then is a decision final and the document ready to be given to the public, after its wording has been checked by the official responsible for the final drafting of the record. In reality this means that the public must wait a few days after the meeting of a corporate board or a city council before its records become public, a delay that news media sometimes find hard to accept.

A document sent to an authority is considered to be in its possession when the document has been registered as received. Usually it will also be given a number or other designation and then filed.

An exception to the rule that information received by the authorities immediately becomes public, and that minutes become public when approved, is stated in para. 4 with regard to the police and public prosecution. Information concerning criminal cases is not public before the case has been brought to court or discontinued. The reason for this exception is obviously that criminal investigation must be conducted without too much publicity.

DOCUMENTS UNDER PREPARATION AND WORKING PAPERS

Official documents can only be considered as 'public' when they are in final form, e.g. as decisions, communications and decrees. Proposals for and drafts of these, drawn up within an authority, are not accessible under para. 5. This statute reflects the idea that preparatory work and records should be excepted from the general publicity rule. Another category of non-accessible information mentioned in para. 5 is any memoranda, reports or interior studies written in preparation for a decision. Before a decision is made much paperwork usually has to be done. It is often done in a very informal way and may contain personal opinions and unchecked information.

The law has been interpreted in such a way that interior working documents, such as memoranda, reports and non-official correspondence, do not later become public after the case has been finally decided. When the law, on the other hand, says that documents under preparation are not *yet* public, this refers to final drafts of decisions or other documents waiting to be approved. As long as a decision is under preparation it is not public, but once approved by the legally competent authority the decision is accessible information.

Since a draft is not the same thing as a final document, it is improper to state that a draft is not *yet* public. A rough draft or outline of a decision will not later become public, because it is an internal working document.

Some examples taken from the Supreme Administrative Court's decisions illustrate the application of para. 5. The Government had to examine a particular case concerning a commune. The official in charge of preparing the case had written a memorandum explaining the background. This memorandum was added to the agenda of the meeting. The memorandum as well as the agenda were considered public documents (Reports 1966:A I 6). An expert's written opinion concerning the legal ownership of a piece of land, ordered by a City Board, was considered an interior document and thus not accessible (Reports 1959: II 213). A memorandum prepared by a working group within a Ministry was considered an interior document and therefore did not have to be given out (9 February 1972, No. 402). A memorandum written either by a court member or a court reporter, containing a proposal for the decision and the reasons for this proposal, meant to be read by the court members, is not accessible information (Reports 1969:A II 222). (See also Supreme Court of Justice, Reports 1965:II 84.)

In practice para. 5 has caused many problems of interpretation. The most important are mentioned here. Official correspondence between authorities is accessible, even if related to a case still under preparation. If a central governmental board, for example, sends a letter to a ministry, it will be accessible as soon as issued by the sender and as soon as received by the receiver. The problem is, however, whether a 'private' letter sent by one official to another in official mail and concerning an administrative case shall also be considered as accessible information.

Local government authorities usually send the agendas of their meetings some days in advance to their members. Sometimes an agenda also contains a proposed decision. An agenda is not a public document, since it clearly falls under para. 5 of the Act, and the citizen has no right to obtain such information. Yet often such agendas are also sent to the press.

In some cases a decision is the result of two (a superior and an inferior) authorities' joint decisions. The usual procedure in such cases will be that the inferior authority makes a proposal to be finally decided by the superior authority. Is then the inferior authority's proposal accessible or is it to be considered only a preparatory document to be kept secret?

An example will illustrate this question. The Central Board of Postal Administration makes proposals to the Ministry of Communications for changed postal rates. The final decision is made by the President of the Republic by decree, the Minister of Communications presenting the case. The Board was once reluctant to release such a proposal, but the Chancellor of Justice found it to be an accessible document, issued by the Board. This example shows that the question of whether a decision is to be considered final must be answered for each authority separately, and that even if an authority does not make final decisions, its proposals to higher authorities, once sent, should be considered as final for it, and therefore as public documents.

Another example confirms this interpretation. A city board made a general decision according to which all decisions made by subordinate local boards to be reviewed by the city board should be kept secret until reviewed. Under Finnish municipal law a city board has the right to demand that a decision made by a lower local authority be submitted to it for review, if the board suspects it to be illegal or undesirable. The Supreme Administrative Court, however, annulled the board's decision and declared the lower authorities' decisions to be accessible (Reports, 1954: I 5). It has been clearly established, moreover, that a decision made by a local authority which has to be submitted to a central authority for approval before it can be executed is to be regarded as final and accessible within the meaning of the Publicity of Documents Act when submitted by the local authority.

Under the rule that documents in the possession of an authority shall be considered as public, application papers concerning vacancies in the public service are accessible documents. Sometimes applicants for posts declared vacant wish to remain anonymous in the press and other news media. But, when asked, the authority that has received the written application must give it out and thus reveal the name of the applicant. This last rule is not contrary to the provision declaring as public only matters finally decided by the authorities, because the provision does not affect the publicity of documents *received* by the authority preparing a case. Only internal preparatory documents made up by the authority itself are secret. Under the same rule, appeals and complaints sent to an authority and related to a case under the authority's consideration are considered accessible information.

One more problem should be mentioned. Does preparation of a case mean the same thing as planning? A great deal of the administrative work in our days concerns planning: economic and physical. These plans attract much interest. One important purpose of planning is to stimulate public discussion about the future development of a community, about schools or health services, about roads and communications but also about the necessary administrative organisation. Modern views about citizens' participation demand that such information be given to the citizen before decisions are made.

In some cases, for instance in urban planning, the law requires that plans be available to the public before they are finally approved. But when there are no such statutory rules, the question must be answered according to the Publicity of Documents Act. This means that planning must be regarded as not necessarily accessible information, since it means preparation, not conclusive measures.

ABSOLUTE OR DISCRETIONARY RIGHTS OF ACCESS

When an official document is considered accessible under the Publicity of Documents Act, the citizen has an absolute right of access to this document. When denied this right, the citizen may bring the case to a higher authority for review, in the last instance to the Supreme Administrative Court. Because the rules concerning the accessibility of official documents are by no means easy to interpret, due to their very general wording, practices may vary somewhat in different branches of public administration. But these differences cannot be accepted, since the law should not be interpreted in more than one way: only one solution can be regarded as the right one. Even if there might be different interpretations of the general rules, this does not change the fact that these rules are to be considered absolute ones, not subject to the discretion of the authorities concerned.

INFORMATION TO BE KEPT SECRET

The other side of the coin is that official documents and other information, which clearly under the Act are not to be accessible, must be kept secret by the authorities. But there are three kinds of secret documents: those to be kept absolutely secret under the Act (para. 9 (2), and the Decree, para. 1, already discussed earlier); documents which are secret under paras 3–5 of the Act, regarding which the authorities have been given a discretionary right to reveal information; and those concerning private individuals' personal matters (Act, para. 17–18), which may be given out if the person concerned gives his permission, but which otherwise are to be kept absolutely secret.

When para. 6 (2) states that information from documents which are not yet public as provided in paras 3, 4 and 5 may not be furnished without the permission of the authority, this unclear statement has been interpreted so as to give the authorities a discretionary power regarding the release of such documents or information about them. For instance drafts or memoranda may be given out, but only if the authorities find this appropriate. The citizen has no legal right of access to these documents.

An official is never obliged to give any oral information, even about otherwise accessible documents. He is, on the other hand, entitled to do so, and even, in the cases mentioned in paras 3,4 and 5, about information otherwise not automatically accessible. In such cases he must have the permission of the authority in possession of this information, if he is not himself alone the competent authority. In this connection may also be mentioned para. 20 (2), according to which special reasons in certain cases can be found for revealing the contents of all kinds of secret documents (not only the cases mentioned in paras 3, 4 and 5). In such cases permission must be secured from the ministry to which the authority in possession of the document is subordinate.

Under para. 10 of that Act, it may be prescribed by statute or decree that a document will become public only after the lapse of a certain time; or after the consideration of the matter to which it pertains has been concluded either finally or in the government department where it is currently pending; or that permission for its being made public should be obtained either from the authority that is considering or has considered the matter, or from a higher authority, or from the person the documents concern. The authority that has the right to decide that a matter shall be secret may also prescribe that it shall be treated as secret by a lower authority (para. 11). An authority which is not authorised in a particular case to order that a matter or document under its consideration be kept secret, may apply for such an order from a higher authority (para. 12).

The Decree mentions four cases (para. 1, 6–9) when the secrecy of documents depends on the will of the authority concerned. For instance, a prisoner's records at a prison are to be kept secret if the chief director of the prison does not agree to have them given out or to have information from the records given to a citizen demanding this information. Thus the responsible authority decides as to the accessibility of records about persons under suspended sentences, under guardianship or on probation. Documents concerning commercial or industrial activities of the State or other public bodies may also be given out only with the permission of the authority or body concerned. And a private firm decides about the accessibility of documentation in the possession of authorities concerning it.

In a case decided by the Supreme Administrative Court, however, a municipality was obliged to give out information about a business deal already decided. A bookseller who had made an offer of school material to the local executive board wanted to study his competitors' offers after the board had decided which offer to accept. The bookseller's demand was accepted by the Court against the board's refusal (Reports, 1962 II 190). (See also decision of 25 October 1965, No. 4180.)

Under paras 17–18 of the Act two categories of documents made up by or in the possession of authorities about individuals shall be kept secret. The first type concerns notations on spiritual guidance or church discipline, memoranda entered at prisons, reformatories, custodial institutions or hospitals, medical certificates, and other comparable records. The second type concerns personal letters in the possession of authorities which do not pertain to court proceedings. The Act states that neither type may be given out without the consent of the person concerned.

These provisions, together with similar ones in particular legislation, aim at the protection of the personal integrity of the individual, and the law on this is interpreted very strictly. For instance, an opinion of the Parliamentary Ombudsman, given in 1966, supported an authority's refusal to let a husband look into his wife's personal records, and said he should have only the right to see the records concerning his new-born child. The provision concerning private letters is an expression of the principle that mail must be secret, which is stated in the Constitution Act.

In the above cases the consent of the person concerned changes the publicity rules. For example, if a wife consents to her husband's access to her personal records in a hospital, the hospital must give them out to him. She can give the same right to her attorney or any other person who enjoys her confidence.

DOCUMENTS TO BE KEPT SECRET
UNDER PARTICULAR LEGISLATION

Several particular Acts contain provisions declaring certain official documents to be secret. In some cases the regulations concerning the accessibility of these documents are rather elaborate, and cover different situations. Examples of such cases are census rolls, the central criminal register and the register of vagrants, documents and records concerning court proceedings, the tax officers' registers and archives, and documents held by the secret service.

The authorities' right to give out information in such cases depends on the particular matter. When the information concerns private individuals, it may usually be given out to the public only with the consent of the person concerned. If the documents concern governmental matters, the secrecy depends on the importance of the matter in question. In less important matters the authority may be considered to have a discretionary right to give out some information. In other cases such information cannot be given. At any rate, there exists no right of public access to such documents.

Some of these provisions may be especially mentioned because of their particular interest. Under the Parliament Act (para. 56) and the Rules of Procedure of Parliament 1927 (para. 58), the speaker has the right to declare a session of the Parliament non-public. In this case the accessibility of the minutes depends on the discretion of Parliament. In practice the minutes of such secret sessions have always been published later. A municipal council may also, under para. 28 of the Communal Code, declare a meeting of the council as non-public, in which case the minutes may also be declared secret, except for the decision itself.

Parliamentary sessions are very seldom held secretly. This has happened only when extremely important political questions, usually concerning foreign affairs, have been discussed. Secret meetings of a local council usually occur when business deals are discussed and when the interest of the municipality demands that such discussions should not be made known.

In the Census Registration Act of 1969, everybody is given the right to receive information from such registers. However, an exception is made for notes concerning crime, vagrancy and disease or registered persons' confinement in prisons, hospitals or other institutions (para. 12 (1)). Such information is only given to authorities that need the information.

Under the Obligation to Provide Official Statistics with Information Act of 1954, information gathered by the Central Board for Statistics shall not be used for purposes other than statistics. The officials of the Board are forbidden to reveal any information concerning business matters or a private individual's economic situation (para. 6). Also, the Taxation Act of 1958 declares all information as secret which is to be found in tax returns or in appendixes to the returns (para. 133, see also para. 132).

POLITICAL PARTIES

Under the Political Parties Act of 1969 certain conditions are required for the registration of a society as a political party. The right of parties to receive financial aid from the State depends upon their representation in Parliament (decree of 1973). Until the law was amended in 1975, the registered political parties enjoyed a monopoly regarding the nomination of candidates for parliamentary elections and elections related to the election of the President of the Republic (Parliamentary Election Act 1969). In spite of their important powers, they cannot be considered as public authorities in the meaning of the Publicity of Documents Act. Documents made up or issued by or in the possession of the political parties and their executives thus fall outside the sphere of this Act.

THE RECIPIENTS OF INFORMATION

It is Finnish citizens who are given the right to claim access to official documents in the law (para. 6 (1)). The Supreme Administrative Court has interpreted this provision literally so as to grant only to physical persons the right of access. A request by an association of retired military officers for access to official documents in the possession of the General Staff was thus rejected, because the claimant was not a Finnish citizen (Reports 1956 II 578). Since the person representing an association or any other body (for example a newspaper) always has the right to claim access in his own name, this restrictive interpretation is of very little importance.

There are thus no provisions regarding the right of private bodies or groups to administrative information. The only exception concerns researchers 'or others who need' official documents containing information concerning private individuals (para. 17 (2)). Researchers and others who have been given permission to study otherwise secret documents must undertake not to misuse them with the aim of damaging or disparaging the person a document concerns, or those close to him. Another condition is that the documents must have been transferred to a public archive. This indicates that a certain time must have passed after the closing of the case treated in the document, since the general time limit before documents are transferred to public archives is ten years (Public Archives Act, 1939, para. 6 (2)).

An alien's access to official documents depends on the discretion of the authority (para. 6(3)). In this case there is no right of access, only the possibility.

The Code of Procedure gives an editor of a newspaper or a journalist the right, if heard as a witness in court, to refuse to reveal his source of information (17:24(2)). Finnish law thus protects the journalist's right to keep his sources secret.

INFORMATION PROCEDURES

THE HOLDING OF INFORMATION

The Finnish legislation concerning accessibility concerns *documents*. It is presupposed that citizens want to have access to written documentation as the most reliable form of information. But the Act contains no definition of the concept 'document' ('asiakirja/ handling'). In the Decree, however, there is a provision (para. 1 (2)) according to which the same rules applying to written documents shall apply to maps, drawings, pictures, films, tapes 'and other such things'. From this provision, which could be interpreted as giving the legislator's view of the question, it may be concluded that the concept 'document' should be given a broader content than just printed, typed or handwritten documents.

In recent years the administration has begun to collect facts in data-processing electronic computers. The question has arisen whether this kind of information should be made available to the public according to the rules given in the Publicity of Documents Act. This question must be answered in the negative. The legislators of a 1951 Act, prepared mainly in the 1930s, could not foresee computerised data banks and the problems to which public accessibility to such information might lead. Particular legislation should be enacted for this field. So long as we lack such legislation, the public will have no clear legal right to demand access to the data-processed information held by State or other public bodies.

The State's Data Bank Act of 1964 and Decree of 1975 are based on the principle that the Bank shall not give out information to others than those who have called upon its services. This means that when State authorities (or in some cases private subjects) give the Bank information to be computerised, only the client will be given the results of the process and the right to use this information, except for a few instances in which the law may require information to be given to others (for example, under the rules concerning the courts' right to obtain information).

A peculiarity regarding the organisation of the State's Data Bank is that only its governing board and its manager are responsible according to the law regarding public servants' penal liability. The personnel are hired under private law contracts. As long as the State's Data Bank is organised in this unusual way, it cannot serve as a source of information for the press and other citizens comparable to that of a public authority under the Publicity of Documents Act.

THE TRANSFER OF DOCUMENTS TO THE ARCHIVES

According to the Public Archives Act of 1939, the National Archive may decide that authorities' documents, once they are more than ten years old, shall be transferred to it. Local State authorities must transfer all documents older than forty years to the provincial archives; also municipal documents more than ten years old may be transferred to provincial archives. These archives function according to an Act of 1970.

THE TRANSMISSION OF INFORMATION

When a person wishes to obtain access to an official document, he must orally or in writing ask for it from the authority that has the original document in its keeping. According to para. 7 of the Act, the authority must, if requested, present to the citizen a formal copy of the document. This means that the citizen must pay copying charges and also the tax prescribed for copying official documents. It is up to the authority to decide whether the citizen may be permitted instead to read the document himself and to copy it, depending on how much this will interfere with the daily work of the authority. If a document is to be kept partly secret, the official responsible for it must see that no secret information is given out. In each department there is a civil servant responsible for supervising this kind of information. In practice these provisions do not seem to have been misused by officials to restrict the citizens' need for quick information, even if the authorities do not necessarily provide photocopying machines for the public.

THE CLASSIFICATION OF INFORMATION

The Act specifies (para. 24) that all secret documents are to be recorded in special journals and kept where they will not be accessible to unauthorised persons. Secret documents must be marked 'secret'. If an authority transfers a secret document to another authority, it is particularly important that the document be marked 'secret' (para. 15), especially when it is transferred to a public archive (Decree I, para. 4).

TIME LIMITS FOR SECRECY OF DOCUMENTS

Unless otherwise provided by law, secret official documents become public 25 years from the day the document is dated. Documents concerning private individuals' matters become public 20 years after the death of the person whom a document concerns (para. 21). When there is reason for it, the Government may provide that a document shall be kept secret even later, but not longer than 50 years from the expiration of the time limits just mentioned.

Secrecy of a document ceases when the time specified in law or other provision by an authority has expired or when the authority or a co-ordinate or superior authority to which the document has come for consideration, revokes the provision (para. 20(1)).

THE REFUSAL OF INFORMATION

If a demand for access to an official document is denied by the competent official, the demander may ask for a decision on the matter by the authority concerned. If the authority confirms the official's refusal, the citizen has a right of appeal to a superior authority. In the last resort the Supreme Administrative Court is competent to decide on the matter. The authorities and the Court are under an obligation to deal with such matters without delay (para. 8).

'Justice delayed is justice denied.' This is certainly true of cases concerning access to official documents. Since the press is usually the demander of such information, it is clear that every delay will be considered an obstacle to the press's work. In some cases the news media will not press the authorities for decisions, or make appeals, since the subject has interest only if it is current. But in other cases the press or other persons interested in obtaining access to documents will persist in their demands for information. This has happened even in cases of only minor general interest, when the demander has wanted to get a decision as a matter of principle, in order to have an interpretation of the law.

The number of appeals on such cases to the Supreme Administrative Court is very small. Some of the Court's published cases even concern situations where access should have been given without hesitation. They show that the authorities sometimes lack knowledge of the law. This is not very surprising, since the authorities were never efficiently informed about the provision of the 1951 Act. Only gradually have the authorities become more and more aware of their obligations to give out documents. Even today the law on this matter has still not completely penetrated the minds of all officials. The reports of the Chancellor of Justice and the Ombudsman thus still contain many clear cases of violations of the publicity rules (see, for example, Chancellor's Report, 1969 and 1971).

One may perhaps venture to observe that it takes a considerable time before a new method of control becomes efficient. This was true of the functioning of the Parliamentary Ombudsman, which did not become really efficient until recent years although the institution was founded in 1920.

Officials who disobey their obligations under the Publicity of Documents Acts are to be punished by ordinary courts, with fines or even prison confinement (para. 27). This provision also covers cases where an official violates his obligation to keep information secret. Each public officer must swear an oath not to reveal information that has to be kept secret under the law (Decrees of 1964 and 1919).

As an example may be mentioned the famous Zavidovo Case, where top secret information given by the President of the Republic in a memorandum to a small number of members of Government and high State officials in August 1972 leaked out and was published in October the same year in three newspapers: one Finnish, one Swedish and one Norwegian. The Chancellor of Justice, who was in charge of the case, found out that three men on the distribution list of the memorandum had breached the rules of secrecy. The leak could consequently be ascribed to them, even though the question of responsibility for the leak, for lack of proof, was not raised by the Chancellor. These three men were: a former member of the Government who had received the document when still a minister; a member of the Government; and the head of the President's office. The first and the last man were prosecuted in court, found guilty of violation of the secrecy obligation and punished by fines (Supreme Court of Justice decisions, 1975 and 1977). The second man, who was still a member of the Government when he gave out secret information, could because of this not be prosecuted in an ordinary court, but only in the High Court of Impeachment (Constitution Act, paras 47, 59). Since his irregularity was not, according to the investigation, serious enough to justify such strong action, the Chancellor decided not to prosecute him. He was, however, removed by the President from the Government (Chancellor's Report, 1973, 1975).

A citizen who has been denied access to official administrative documents may thus not only process the matter within the administration and, in the last resort, appeal to the Supreme Administrative Court. He may also, if he finds that the official in charge of the case has clearly violated the law in refusing him access, prosecute the officer in an ordinary court, or report him to a public prosecutor or to the Chancellor of Justice or the Parliamentary Ombudsman, who may take such action. Since the ordinary courts lack competence to deal with administrative matters, they cannot declare a document accessible, even if the law is clear on this point. Only the Supreme Administrative Court may do that. But even the ordinary courts may pronounce their views about the interpretation of the law in cases where an officer is being prosecuted for having refused.

The Parliamentary Ombudsman and the Chancellor of Justice play an important role in ensuring that public officials observe the Publicity of Documents Act. In several cases of refusal of access, the citizens have preferred complaining to the Ombudsman or to the Chancellor, rather than making appeals. The Ombudsman or the Chancellor cannot command an authority to give out information –

only its superior body or the Supreme Administrative Court can do that – but they can state their opinions and even prosecute the guilty officer, if his negligence or fault have been serious. These opinions, especially when published in the Chancellor's or the Ombudsman's Annual Reports, are observed by the administrative authorities and serve as guidelines for future similar cases.

CONCLUSION

This short survey of Finnish law and practice concerning public access to administrative information has shown that even if the problem is regulated by a general statute, many questions have been left without answer in the written law. A new version is needed, and one is now under preparation in the Ministry of Justice.

A modern view thus demands that citizens should also have the right to ask for information by telephone. Today no officer is under an obligation to give oral information, either personally or by phone. The public would also like to have the right to ask the officials for help in finding the documents they need. This kind of service now depends on the goodwill of an officer. From the client's point of view, it would also be more convenient, if they could first be given the opportunity to read and copy a document and only then have to ask for an official copy for which they must pay. The present law makes paid copies the main rule.

The concept of 'preparatory documents' has also been interpreted in a way that obstructs the accessibility of administrative information of such general interest as planning measures. The law should be changed so as to make it possible for the press and others interested in public administration to obtain more information about plans. Even the State's activities should perhaps be given more publicity.

A study group within the Ministry of Justice has suggested that all preparatory material be made accessible when a case is decided, as a means of increasing the available information about public administration.

The Zavidovo Case, on the other hand, has made it necessary to strengthen the rules concerning the secrecy of delicate documents and other information concerning the State's foreign relations. A recent government report (1974:70) has proposed more precise rules on the filing and copying of top secret documents.

Even if the trend goes in the direction of more openness and less secrecy in public administration, there will still be reluctance to give out all kinds of preparatory information. In answers given to a governmental commission proposing new rules on the publicity of documents, for example, the Ministry of Public Finances stressed the importance of secrecy in preparing the State budget.

The protection of the citizen's right of personal integrity has also been discussed recently, when the legislation concerning public data banks was studied by a governmental commission. It seems obvious that this kind of information should be handled with caution and not be given out to others than those directly concerned.

3 Denmark

NIELS EILSCHOU HOLM

HISTORY OF THE DANISH ACT OF 1970

In 1970 the Danish legislature passed an Act on Access of the Public to Documents in Administrative Files.[1] This enactment marked the consummation of official considerations of this matter over a rather long period of time.

The principle of publicity is regarded as a fundamental element in the procedural rules governing the work of the legislature and of the judiciary. Ever since the first democratic constitution of Denmark (1849) it has been provided that the legislative assembly shall meet in public. The constitution of 1849 also envisaged that the principle of publicity should govern the judicial process, and this was laid down by the Administration of Justice Act (1916), under which the law courts as a general rule sit in public. In both fields the principle of publicity is regarded as an important means of securing and maintaining public interest in legislative and judicial matters and public confidence in these branches of government.

In most areas of public administration a similar system of publicity – publicity in the sense of public sessions or meetings – would not be feasible, for the simple reason that the great majority of administrative decisions are taken without a preceding oral hearing or conference. Consequently, rules on publicity must be given a different form, designed to meet the peculiarities of the administrative process, if publicity is to be adopted as a general principle governing also the executive branch of government.

When Denmark was considering how to adapt the principle of publicity to the administrative process, Swedish legislation on open files presented itself as an obvious source of inspiration. As is well

76

known, legislation on open files is deeply rooted in Swedish constitutional law. The Swedish rules at present governing these questions depend in the main on provisions of 1937 and 1976, but the fundamental principles go back more than 200 years, to the first Act on Freedom of the Press of 1766, and they have been in force in Sweden without interruption since 1812.

It seems, however, that the Swedish system for a long time was completely unnoticed in Denmark. Interest in these matters was not aroused until the question of more publicity in public administration was entered as an item on the agenda for the 4th General Meeting of the Nordic Association for Public Administration (*Nordisk Administrativt Forbund*) in Helsinki in 1929. The subject was introduced by the Swedish professor C. A. Reuterskiöld, and among the Danish participants in the subsequent discussion were two prominent civil servants, who expressed themselves in favour of more openness in public administration.

This discussion had no immediate impact on public debate in Denmark. But it was recorded, and the idea commented upon favourably, by the leading treatise on Danish administrative law, appearing in its first edition in 1936. The discussion was restored to life when, after the end of the Second World War, the question of legislation on access of the public to documents in administrative files was accorded high priority in the general debate on the need for better protection of the individual against the acts of administrative authorities. In this general context the case for open files in public administration was argued in legal writings and discussed at a number of Nordic conferences over the first five to six post-war years.

However, as early as 1946 the question had been taken up for consideration on the official level in Denmark. That year a committee was appointed by the Government to make an overall review of the executive branch of government (*Forvaltningskommissionen*), and the terms of reference of the committee expressly included the question of the feasibility of introducing in some form or other the principle of publicity in public administration.

The committee reported on the question in 1950, and a majority of eight members, out of the committee's membership of fifteen, expressed the view.

> . . . that the Danish system of parliamentary government, with its inherent responsibility before parliament of the appropriate

Minister for any administrative decision made a general extension of the right of the public to obtain knowledge of administrative matters unnecessary, even undesirable, and that the introduction of such a system would entail decisive disadvantages and doubtful advantages.

The majority did, however, add, that

> . . . it would seem that a satisfactory solution might be found by revising the Act of 1866 [which, with a number of limitations, provided for access of parties to an administrative proceeding to the documents in the file of their own case] so that an applicant whose application has been refused is given the right to request information on the particular circumstances of apparently corresponding cases, including cases in which the application has been complied with. By this means, an unsuccessful applicant would be able to acquaint himself with the administrative authorities' manner of handling applications, administrative practices governing the issuance of licences, etc., and thus be in a position to judge whether arbitrariness has been committed in the decision of matters which should be governed by uniform considerations.

The minority of the committee recommended that the whole question be submitted to a more thorough examination by a broadly composed committee.

At about the same time, publicity in public administration was also included in the terms of reference of a sub-committee under a committee appointed, also in 1946, to review the Danish constitution (*Forfatningskommissionen*). The recommendation of the sub-committee on this item followed quite closely the views expressed in the report of the Committee on the Executive Branch of Government. The sub-committee found it

> . . . desirable that this question be submitted to a thorough examination, which might also include the question of a revision of the Act of 2 February 1866 on Communication of Documents to Applicants and Complainants, as well as the question of requiring administrative authorities to give reasons for their decisions.

Several years were to elapse before these recommendations were acted upon, but on 25 February 1956 the Prime Minister appointed a committee to carry out the thorough examination previously called for.[2]

The Committee on Publicity in Public Administration, *Offentlighedskommissionen*, was chaired by a justice of the Supreme Court and composed of representatives of the major political parties, central and local government services, the mass media, the bar association, and the union for higher civil servants. The Ombudsman, Professor Stephan Hurwitz, and the leading legal expert on administrative law, Professor Poul Andersen, were also appointed members of the committee.

The terms of reference of the committee were

... to consider and make recommendations on the question whether, and if so to what extent and in what manner publicity may be introduced in central and local government, including the question of a revision of the Act of 2 February 1866 on Communication of Documents to Applicants and Complainants.

The Committee submitted its report in December of 1962 (*Betænkning om offentlighed i forvaltningen*, No. 325/1963).

Once again, opinions on the principal question were evenly divided. A majority of eleven members found that the reasons put forward in favour of introducing such a sweeping reform were not persuasive, and that the disadvantages inherent in adopting and administering such a system were greater than the advantages which it might entail. A minority of nine members found that the considerations advanced in favour of introducing the principle of open files in public administration as a general rule were so decisive that the hesitations voiced by the majority would have to yield. One member of the minority, however, expressed the view that it would seem to be the most expedient solution to pass, as a first step so to speak, legislation entitling a party to an administrative proceeding to request access to the documents pertaining to that particular case (i.e., general rules on discovery in administrative proceedings), and then at a later stage to reconsider, on the basis of experience gained under such legislation, the question of giving the public at large access to documents in administrative files. On the contingency that the legislature might follow the advice of the minority, the report contained a Draft Bill on Access of the Public to Documents in

Administrative Files, elaborated by the committee as a whole.

As regards the second element of its terms of reference – revision of the Act of 1866 – the committee was unanimously of the opinion that the Act was deficient in several respects. Thus, under that Act only applicants and persons who had filed a complaint with an administrative authority, not other (e.g., third) parties to an administrative proceeding, were entitled to acquaint themselves with the documents concerning that particular case and this right did not cover all the materials on which the decision was based. Furthermore, the party was only entitled to peruse the file *after* a decision had been made, and only if the decision had come out against the party concerned. Accordingly, the committee also elaborated a Draft Bill on Access of Parties to Documents in Administrative Files.

The Government, after having considered the report of the Committee on Publicity, decided to follow the advice of the majority and submitted to Parliament only a Bill on Access of Parties to Documents in Administrative Files. This Bill, which in most respects followed the lines of the committee's draft, was enacted (as Act No. 141) on 13 May 1964, and came into force on 1 October of that year.

However, in his speech when introducing the Bill in Parliament, the Minister of Justice expressed the view that the recommendations of the minority of the Committee on Publicity deserved consideration, and he pointed out, following the reasoning of the single member of that minority, that the experience gained under the Bill now proposed, if enacted, would provide a better basis for such further considerations. This indication was followed up by the parliamentary committee appointed to examine the Bill, and on the proposal of that committee there was inserted in the Bill a provision under which the Act should be taken up for reconsideration in the parliamentary year 1969/70, at the latest.

Under the Act of 1964, applicants and complainants as well as any other party to an administrative proceeding were as a general rule entitled – at any stage during the proceedings or after a decision had been made – to request that they may examine the documents relating to the matter. If the request was put forward while the case was under consideration, a decision on the case should be postponed until the party had been given the opportunity to study the documents. And a party might at any stage of the proceedings request (further) postponement with a view to allowing him time to submit his observations on the matter, orally or in writing.

These provisions are now – with minor amendments which are irrelevant in this context – included in the Act on Access of the Public to Documents in Administrative Files (see in particular chapter 2 of that Act). The Act of 1964 has therefore been repealed by the latter Act.

In compliance with the revision clause of the Act of 1964, the Government in autumn 1969 submitted to Parliament a Bill on Access of the Public to Documents in Administrative Files.[3] The Bill was drafted on the joint basis of the Act of 1964 and the draft Bill contained in the committee's report of 1963. With a few minor amendments the Bill was enacted in June 1970, and it came into force at the beginning of 1971.

One of the amendments to the Bill was the insertion of a new revision clause, under which the Act should be taken up for reconsideration in the parliamentary year 1974/75. The principal aim of this amendment was to make sure that the question of a further rapprochement to the Swedish system would be considered later, on the basis of experience gained under the Act of 1970 (for particulars see below).

In order to provide an appropriate basis for such a reconsideration of the Act in general, the Ministry of Justice in the spring of 1973 appointed a new committee to consider and make recommendations on amendments to the Act. The committee is expected to report in 1978.[4] For this reason, and in order to allow for a subsequent co-ordination of the result of the work of this committee with departmental work on the drafting of an administrative procedure Act, the time limit laid down in the revision clause has been extended to 1978/79.

SOME RECENT TRENDS

After the passage of the Act of 1970 there may be discerned two major trends within the general field of public access to administrative information. One trend has been aimed at limiting the access of the public to documents in administrative files out of consideration for the right of the individual to have his privacy respected. This trend has been perceptible particularly as regards access to information stored in the various public registers.

The problems arising from registration of information are, of course, not new. Even before the age of computerisation, registration of personal information might represent an intrusion on the privacy of the individual. Information may leak out from a manual file, it may be used for other purposes than those for which it was collected, and the contents of the data may be of such a character that the very registration must be regarded as a threat to privacy. As a consequence of modern technology, however, above all in the computer field, it is now to a much higher degree than earlier feasible in a very short time to store, process and disseminate information on private citizens, companies, etc. Although collection and dissemination of such information in the large majority of cases serves a legitimate interest, it must be borne in mind that the ever-expanding storing of information on individuals and companies in modern society, combined with the rapid spread of computer technology, has created a general distrust of the various forms of data-collecting and has made the public more aware of the problems in regard to protection of privacy.

In 1970 the Minister of Justice appointed a committee to consider the problems concerning protection of privacy which are related to the establishment and use of public and private registers. One of these problems is, of course, the question of access –access of the public as well as access of the person or entity whom the information concerns – to the registered information. Following a recommendation of this committee, an Act of 1978 on the establishment and operation of electronic data banks by administrative authorities provides *inter alia* that the right to obtain access to information stored in electronic data banks is not governed by the general provisions of the Act of 1970. On this point the Act of 1970 has been superseded by specific provisions on access in the Act of 1978. As regards the right of *the public* to obtain access to such information, these provisions are much narrower in scope than what would follow from applying the Act of 1970. It should be added, however, that even before the Act of 1978 it remained an open question whether the Act of 1970 was applicable to registers operated by administrative authorities.

The other major trend discernible within the general field of public access to administrative information has been towards more openness in public administration. This trend has been particularly noteworthy in the field of land-use planning. Under the Act of 1970 (section 2, subsection 2, no. 2), a request for access to documents in administrative files may be refused '. . . if it is found that the right to examine the documents in the matter should be subordinated to important considerations involving . . . the execution of official activities for . . . planning . . .'. It appears very clearly from the preparatory work that this provision was aimed, *inter alia*, at allowing for secrecy of documents, particularly in the preparatory stages of the planning process, when necessary in order to avoid economic speculation in real estate.

However, in recent years it has been a much-debated question whether serious problems in this regard are in fact inherent in premature publicity, and, if so, whether such problems should not rather be counteracted by other means than secrecy. And it has been pointed out that secrecy in the preparatory stages is inconsistent with the desire to meet the demand for a genuine public participation in the planning process.

This debate has brought about some very interesting experiments, particularly on the level of local government, with more publicity and public participation in the planning process,[5] and this experience is reflected in a new Act on land-use planning passed in 1975.

GENERAL RIGHTS OF PUBLIC ACCESS

THE GENERAL SITUATION

The general principle of the Act of 1970 is laid down in section 1, subsection 1, where it is provided that 'everyone shall have the right to request that he may examine documents in matters which are or have been under consideration by the public administration'.

This provision implies, on the one hand, that the Act covers administrative authorities only. Thus Parliament and its committees and other organs (e.g., the Ombudsman) are exempted from the coverage of the Act, as is the judiciary. But the Act covers all administrative authorities. The exemption of the judiciary covers only courts of law in the strict sense. The majority of administrative tribunals are covered by the Act, and this is, of course, also the case for government departments, directorates and other services, the various kinds of administrative boards, and central as well as local government bodies.

On the other hand, access may be requested to documents pertaining to any and all matters which are or have been considered or otherwise handled by an administrative authority, regardless of whether the documents serve or have served as the basis for the exercise of administrative, quasi-judicial, or quasi-legislative functions of the administrative authority in question, or whether they concern central or local government contracts, or activities of a purely practical nature.

As to the scope of the right to request access to administrative information, section 3 provides that this right includes '. . . all documents relating to the matter in question, including copies of communications sent by the authority concerned when these may be presumed to have reached the addressee'. The word 'documents' has not been interpreted restrictively, but should be read as covering, apart from written and printed materials, photographs, pictures, maps, sketches, ground plans, etc.

This provision is supplemented by section 4 on factual information received orally. In the daily work of administrative authorities it frequently happens that oral information, supplementary to that contained in the file of a particular case, is received, indeed solicited. This often facilitates a more speedy and flexible processing of pending cases than would be possible if all information were required to be submitted in writing, and it would be unfortunate if the Act were to exclude or to impede seriously such informal procedures. On the other hand, it is of obvious importance to ensure that the Act is not circumscribed or even evaded by this means. Section 4, therefore, provides that if an authority receives factual information of considerable importance for a decision, orally, this information must be recorded in such a way that it can be made available in accordance with the rules laid down in the Act.

Of course, the principle of open files cannot be adopted without some limitations, and the Act contains a number of exceptions to the general rules, outlined above, on what documents are accessible to the public. Before going into these provisions of the Act in detail, two important elements of the general framework of the Act should be underlined.

Under the Swedish legislation the contents of a document that is exempted from the general rules on access must be kept secret. In contrast, the Danish Act does not regulate the question of which matters should be kept secret. The Danish Act only stipulates the extent to which administrative authorities are *legally bound* to open their files, and administrative authorities are free to make documents available to members of the public, even if not required to do so under the Act. This has happened quite often in administrative practice, e.g., as regards documents which are not accessible under the Act, because filed before the Act entered into force (cf. section 13 (2) of the Act). This power to afford more publicity than required by the Act is discretionary, and it is limited by a number of provisions in other legislation on secrecy which bind persons engaged in public service and activities.

In another respect as well the Act of 1970 only contains a minimum standard. Before the Act, it was a quite generally prevailing practice for administrative authorities, when so requested, to give interested parties, as well as journalists and others, oral information on matters which were or had been under consideration by that authority. The Act, of course, does not impose upon administrative authorities a duty to extend this service, but the Act certainly does entail that as a general rule an administrative authority should not hesitate to give information over the telephone, when the information asked for is contained in documents accessible to the public at large under the Act. In accordance with this view, the Ministry of Justice in a circular letter to all administrative authorities, issued shortly before the Act entered into force, pointed out that an administrative authority, when receiving requests, particularly from representatives of the mass media, for oral information on pending or finished matters, should have regard to this means of gaining a more flexible execution of the Act.

EXEMPTED MATTERS

The provisions of the Act warranting exceptions from the general rule on public access may be divided into three different groups.

(1) Categories of Cases

One group of provisions exempts *certain categories of cases* from the coverage of the Act. These provisions imply that any and all documents pertaining to such matters are exempted. Thus, under section 6, subsection 1, the right of access shall not include *matters involving the prosecution of criminal offences*. This provision has been given a rather wide interpretation in practice. It includes, of course, documents received or produced by the police or by the public prosecution in the course of a criminal investigation, regardless of whether the case is actually brought to trial. But it also includes cases handled by the prison administration, e.g. documents concerning applications for pardon or for release on probation or parole, cases concerning extradition of criminal offenders, and criminal cases handled in the administrative process (in practice almost exclusively documents concerning violations of the tax and customs legislation, which in certain circumstances may be settled out of court by an administrative fine).

The reasoning underlying this exception is very complex. It is based partly on considerations for securing efficiency in the prevention, investigation and prosecution of crimes, and partly on a desire to respect the right to privacy of the individuals involved in such matters. And the exception should be seen against the background of a number of provisions in the Administration of Justice Act on public hearings, on discovery, and on access of parties and other interested persons to documents which have been produced in court during a trial. Following a recommendation from the Ombudsman, the committee appointed to review the Act has been asked particularly to reconsider this provision.

Under the same subsection, the right of access shall not include *matters relating to either appointment or promotion in the public service*. This provision has been interpreted narrowly in practice. It includes only documents relating to the matters underlined above, whereas documents relating to other personnel matters are governed by the general rules of the Act. This holds true also for documents on disciplinary proceedings against civil servants. Nor are these cases included under the provision exempting matters involving the prosecution of criminal offences. However, the general rules of the Act are to some extent superseded by special provisions in the Civil Service Act on disciplinary proceedings.

The exemption for matters relating to appointment and promotion in the public service has caused a great deal of debate at every stage of the legislative history of the Act. The reasons underlying the provision are, in the main, partly consideration for the right of applicants to have their privacy respected, partly a fear that public access to information on the identity of applicants might deter potential candidates, in particular – but not exclusively – persons working in the private sector, from applying for vacant posts in the public service. The terms of reference of the committee appointed to review the Act also expressly includes a reconsideration of this provision.

Other categories of cases under conditions specified in section 2, subsection 4, may be *exempted by administrative regulation* (see further below under (3)). However, until the end of 1976 this latter provision had only been utilised once, in order to exempt documents pertaining to certain government contracts.

Until recently it was the prevailing opinion that – apart from the exemption clauses mentioned above[6] – access might be requested to documents pertaining to any and all matters which are or have been considered or otherwise handled by an administrative authority, regardless of whether the documents serve or have served as the basis for the exercise of administrative, quasi-judicial, or quasi-legislative functions, or concern central or local government contracts or activities of a purely practical nature. However, a judgment delivered in 1975 by the Supreme Court has called in question this scope of the Act's coverage. The judgment dealt with the scope of the right of parties to have access to documents, but the pertinent provisions of the Act on this point are the same as those governing public access. The court held that the Act should be interpreted so as not to cover relations between a patient and a government-run hospital: hence the patient could not under the Act request copies of the case-sheets pertaining to his treatment.

(2) Types of Document
A second group of provisions, contained in section 5 of the Act, make exceptions for *certain types of document.* Some of these provisions, covering *documents underlying the policy-making process at cabinet level,* will be dealt with below.

Most of the provisions, however, cover *various types of internal working document* and the key provision is section 5, no. 3, of the Act,[7] which makes exception for '. . . an authority's working materials for internal use, e.g. memoranda, drafts, outlines, proposals and plans'. This provision is supplemented by no. 4 of section 5, which exempts 'letters exchanged within the same authority'. In administrative practice this is interpreted very narrowly as covering almost exclusively letters exchanged between sections or divisions within the same administrative authority.[8] No. 3 is also further elaborated by no. 5, covering 'letters exchanged between a local government council and its departments, committees or other administrative branches, or internally between these branches'.

The prototype of documents covered by section 5, no. 3, is the internal report-sheet (*referatark*), which traditionally has been the basis for the internal consideration of pending matters, particularly in the ministerial departments. Until fairly recently, the generally prevailing procedure for handling matters brought before a department would be that a junior civil servant started by drawing up an internal report on the case. This report would contain a summary of the facts as presented by the documents in the file, supplemented, if necessary, by information received orally from other authorities or from private parties, other persons, organisations, etc. Then would follow an exposition of the legal problems involved, which might include a statement on judicial or administrative precedents which would seem to be applicable. And the conclusion of the report would be a recommendation in the form either of a draft decision or of a proposal for further procedural steps to be taken. This internal report would follow the case – often as a cover to the file – through all stages of the internal decision-making process, and every civil servant participating in the decision up through the internal hierarchy would make his comments in writing on the report-sheet.

The working methods of the ministerial departments have changed considerably over the last twenty to thirty years. The function of the internal report-sheets as a means of communication between the different levels of the internal hierarchy has in a number of areas been rendered superfluous by a trend to delegate decision-making power to lower levels of the hierarchy. In other areas, more informal oral exchanges of views and ideas, more elaborate draft decisions, or notes and memoranda on particularly doubtful or important questions have replaced the report-sheets as the basis for departmental decisions. But even if these and other developments have changed the internal procedures for handling matters pending before departments, section 5, no. 3, has been drafted against the background of the traditional working methods outlined above.

As a consequence, in administrative practice the exception in no. 3 and its elaboration in nos 4 and 5 have been interpreted restrictively in two major respects.

The starting point for one of these limitations has been the provision in section 4 of the Act. Under this provision any administrative authority which orally receives factual information of considerable importance for a decision is under an obligation to record that information in such a way that it can be made available in accordance with the general rules laid down in the Act. This provision does not require that the information be recorded in any specific form, and the Act does not prohibit the information from being recorded in the internal report-sheets (as was, indeed, the usual practice before the passage of the Act). However, if the information received orally is recorded only in the internal report-sheets or in other internal working documents, the Act requires that those elements of the internal working document be extracted if access to the file of that particular case is requested under the Act. Furthermore, section 4 has been interpreted to imply that no 'factual information of considerable importance for a decision in a matter', whether received orally or by other means (e.g. by an inspection carried out by members of the staff or by perusing the files of other matters handled by the authority in question), may be exempted by virtue solely of the provisions making exceptions for internal working documents, but only if the contents of the information call for exception under one of the other exception clauses of the Act (i.e., the provisions mentioned below under (3)).

Under this interpretation, the exceptions for internal working documents in nos 3 to 5 cover only what one might characterise as decision-making documents, not fact-finding documents prepared by an administrative authority.

The other limitation placed upon the exceptions for internal working documents is that the exception clauses are interpreted so as to cover only (1) documents prepared by the administrative authority in question and (2) only such documents utilised exclusively as a basis for the internal consideration of pending matters by that authority. This implies that notes and memoranda which have been elaborated from the outset as internal working documents are no longer covered by the exception if forwarded to another administrative authority (e.g. another ministerial department). By virtue of this restrictive interpretation, administrative authorities cannot evade the general rule on public access to administrative information by exchanging 'internal working documents' instead of utilising more formal means of inter-departmental communication.

(3) Types of information
The third group of provisions exempt *certain types of information*. These provisions may lead in some cases to the exemption of one or more complete documents in a file or even of the entire file pertaining

to a particular case. But the underlying principle is that exceptions under these provisions require an individual examination of each document in the file, and if the documents or some of the documents are only in part covered by the provisions, the remaining documents or parts of documents must be produced for inspection upon request (see section 2, subsection 3, of the Act).

The most important provisions in this group are those contained in section 2 of the Act. Subsection 1 warrants exceptions out of consideration for business and personal privacy. Thus, under no. 1 of this provision the right of access to information shall not include documents containing ' . . . information relating to a private individual's personal or economic circumstances'; and no. 2 makes exceptions for '. . . information relating to technical devices or processes or to work or business conditions, to the extent that it is of considerable economic importance for the person or company with which the information is concerned, that the request should not be granted'.

Information covered by these provisions may be excepted even if the person or company with which the information is concerned consents to the production of the information or some of it. However, this type of information will in most cases be available to the person or company concerned under the special rules governing access of the parties to the file of their own case, and parties to a case may, as a general rule, use documents obtained under those rules as they see fit (see further below). Furthermore, as mentioned previously, administrative authorities have a discretionary power to afford more publicity than required by the Act. This power is limited by statutory provisions in other legislation on secrecy binding persons engaged in public service or activities. But these statutory provisions will rarely apply when the person or company concerned has consented to a request for public access to the documents in question. Consequently, the consent by the person or company concerned will often result in the administrative authority complying with such a request even if not required to do so under the Act.

Subsection 2 of section 2 warrants exceptions when required by consideration for the security of the State or for its international relations; *or* when necessary in order to ensure the execution of official activities for inspection, planning, control or other super-vision, or to protect the legitimate economic interests of central or local government; *or* if required in order to protect ' . . . other interests where the special circumstances of the matter make secrecy necessary'. This latter general clause has only been most sparingly used in administrative practice.

Subsection 4 empowers the appropriate minister to lay down by administrative regulation that certain types of matters or kinds of documents, for which the rules contained in subsection 1 and 2 would normally lead to refusal of a request for access, shall be exempted from the general rules of the Act. As mentioned previously, until the end of 1976 this provision had been utilised only once in order to exempt documents pertaining to certain government contracts.

The group of provisions dealt with under this heading also includes section 7 of the Act, which regulates the conflicts which might arise between the general rules of the Act and statutory provisions in other legislation on secrecy binding persons engaged in public service or activities. The existing statutory provisions on secrecy fall, broadly speaking, into two groups. The Penal Code and the Civil Service Act each contain rather generally phrased provisions prescribing secrecy for information which has been acquired in an official capacity and which in the nature of the case should be kept secret. These general clauses are in some areas supplemented by provisions in other legislation which, each within its own field, specify types of information which must be kept secret. Under section 7 of the Act only information covered by these specific provisions on secrecy is automatically exempted from the general rules on public access to administrative information, whereas the general clauses on secrecy do not in and of themselves exclude access. The types of information covered by this exception are primarily information concerned with business and personal privacy.

THE HOLDERS OF INFORMATION

ADMINISTRATIVE AUTHORITIES

As previously mentioned, the Act of 1970 covers administrative authorities only. Thus Parliament and its committees and other organs (e.g. the Ombudsman) are exempted from the coverage of the Act, as is the judiciary. But the Act covers all administrative authorities. The exemption for the judiciary covers only courts of law in the strict sense. All administrative tribunals are covered by the Act, as are government departments, directorates, and other services, the various kinds of administrative board, and central as well as local government bodies.

In some instances activities comparable to those undertaken by administrative authorities are carried out by entities established on a private law basis. Thus, to take an example, some major power plants are operated by joint stock companies, where most of the shares are held by a number of local governments. Similarly, a number of local governments operate public baths and sports grounds through limited companies controlled by the local government or governments concerned. Such (public) limited companies are not covered by the Act. The same holds true for private enterprises on government contracts or subsidised out of public funds (e.g., private schools, hospitals and institutions for children).

This does not imply, however, that information on such activities when held by administrative authorities is *ipso facto* exempted from the Act. On the contrary, even letters or other documents exchanged between such 'private' entities and an administrative authority participating in, subsidising or supervising its activities may only be excepted if the document or information concerned is covered by one of the exception-clauses of the Act.

POLITICAL EXECUTIVES

The Act contains no provision exempting letters or other documents held by a political minister. However, the general right of access to administrative information under the Act does not cover all letters or documents received or prepared by an administrative authority. Generally speaking, the Act covers only documents which concern the official business of the authority in question. Thus, for instance, invitations addressed to individual civil servants, asking them to make a speech or to prepare an article for a law review, and replies to such requests, will – at least in most cases – not be covered by the Act. Similarly, letters addressed to a political minister and not handed over to the department for official consideration are regarded as belonging to the personal files of the minister and are not covered by the provisions of the Act. However, letters or other documents received by a political minister may not be exempted if they concern pending matters or other official business of the ministry.

The restriction just mentioned is subject to one important limitation. Minutes of proceedings of the full Cabinet and records of other meetings between political ministers have traditionally been regarded as the private property of the individual members of the Cabinet. This tradition was confirmed in the report of the parliamentary committee appointed to examine the Bill on Access of the Public to Documents in Administrative Files. As a consequence, such minutes and records should be considered as covered by the Act only in so far as they, or excerpts therefrom, are handed over to a ministerial department for further considerations or processing.

This general limitation on the applicability of the Act is supplemented by a number of other provisions aimed at protecting the policy-making process at a high level. The most important of these is section 5, no. 1, which makes exceptions for '. . . minutes of meetings of the Council of State, records of meetings between ministers, and documents drawn up by an authority for use at such meetings'. This provision should be seen against the background outlined above. Furthermore, section 5, no. 2, exempts '. . . letters exchanged by ministries with regard to legislation, including appropriation Acts'. This provision has been interpreted restrictively in administrative practice. It covers only letters exchanged between ministerial departments, not letters exchanged between a ministerial department and subordinate administrative authorities, not even if letters from subordinate administrative authorities are forwarded as enclosures to letters exchanged between ministerial departments. And letters exchanged between ministerial departments are covered only if they concern the preparation of legislation, including the question whether legislation should be prepared at all. Consequently, letters exchanged between ministerial departments after an Act has been passed, e.g., on the interpretation or the execution of the Act, including comments on draft administrative regulations, will not be covered by this exception.

In this context, mention should also be made of section 5, no. 6, which excepts '. . . documents concerning questions of foreign policy or foreign trade'. This provision is supplemented by section 2, subsection 2, no. 1, which allows exceptions if required by important considerations involving *inter alia* '. . . relations with foreign powers or international institutions'.

Finally, section 6, subsection 2, provides that as far as legislation, including appropriation Acts, is concerned, a request for access to information shall only be granted when the Bill has been introduced in Parliament. The general rule of the Act is that access to information may be requested at any stage during the consideration of the underlying matter or after a decision has been taken (see further below). The aim of subsection 2 is only to deviate from this general rule by allowing the execution of requests for access to be postponed until consideration of the matter has been concluded by the submission of a Bill to Parliament. But, even after this time, documents covered by section 5, nos 1 and 2, as mentioned above, may be excepted from the right to access. As regards letters exchanged between ministerial departments (section 5, no. 2 of the Act), this exception is, however, somewhat restricted by virtue of a practice developed under the parliamentary rules of procedure (see further below).

THE RECIPIENTS OF INFORMATION

GENERAL ACCESS

Under section 1 of the Act 'everyone' has the right to request access to information covered by the Act. It is immaterial whether the person is a citizen of or resident in Denmark.

Under section 8, subsection 1, a request to examine the documents in a particular case must be put before the administrative authority that is authorised to decide on the substantive issues of that case. If a request is submitted to an administrative authority which is not authorised to grant the request, that authority should immediately forward the request to the appropriate authority.

The Act does not expressly regulate what uses the public may make of information obtained under it. The philosophy underlying it, however, does imply that everybody should be free to publish such information, and the silence of the Act on this point means that this freedom should be regarded as limited only by virtue of particular statutory provisions to this effect in other legislation. In actual practice, the most important, even if not the only, example of such limitations is the provisions of the Penal Code on the protection of privacy.

As mentioned previously, chapter 2 of the Act contains some special rules applicable to parties to an administrative proceeding. These rules are in all essentials carried over from the Act of 1964 on Access of Parties to Documents in Administrative Files.

Under these provisions the right of parties to obtain access to documents pertaining to their own case is more extensive than the right of the public at large under chapter 1 of the Act. In particular, the exceptions contained in section 2 of the Act are inapplicable when access to a file is requested by a party to the administrative proceeding in question (cf. section 10, subsection 1). Under this provision a request from a party to the proceeding may only be rejected to the extent '. . . it is found that the party's interest in using knowledge of the documents in the matter for the protection of his interests should be subordinated to vital considerations involving official or private interests'. Mention should also be made of section 10, subsection 3, which makes the provision in section 7 (referring to other statutory provisions on secrecy) inapplicable when a request for access is put forward by a party to the administrative proceeding.

Just as the Act does not regulate the uses the public may make of information obtained under chapter 1 of the Act, it does not regulate what uses parties to an administrative proceeding may make of information obtained under the special rules on access of parties. Similarly, the silence of the Act on this point entails that a party is free to publish such information, provided, however, that the publication does not constitute an infringement of other statutory provisions, in particular of the provisions in the Penal Code on the protection of privacy. A party is also free to empower other persons to exercise his rights under section 10 of the Act. This, of course, happens most frequently with respect to lawyers, accountants, surveyors or members of other professions regularly engaged to attend to the interests of parties. But in practice it also happens that persons complaining about administrative decisions give journalists, in particular journalists working for complaint columns in the newspapers, a power of attorney to peruse the file of the matter complained about on their behalf.

Access to administrative information may also be obtained under the provisions in the Administration of Justice Act on discovery in court proceedings. However, these provisions will rarely lead to production of documents which would not be obtainable also under the special rules pertaining to parties to an administrative proceeding in chapter 2 of the Access Act.

As a general rule the filing of complaints with the Ombudsman will not lead to an extension of public access to administrative information. As mentioned before, the institution of the Ombudsman is not itself covered by the Act of 1970, but access to letters and documents exchanged between the Ombudsman and an administrative authority may be requested under the Act by addressing the administrative authority in question. This may under some circumstances result in the production of internal working documents, if these have been forwarded to the Ombudsman as enclosures to replies submitted by the respondent administrative authority, but in most cases complaints to the Ombudsman will lead to more elaborate statements of facts or reasons for decisions, rather than to a widening of the scope of public access to administrative information.

Under Danish constitutional law Parliament and its committees may, as a general rule, only request access to documents or other information held by an administrative authority through the appropriate political minister, but the scope of this right has not been defined in either the constitution or statutory provisions. Under the parliamentary rules of procedure any Member of Parliament may pose questions to a political minister during weekly question-periods. However, in most cases the aim of such questions will be to obtain statements on governmental policies rather than administrative information in the narrow sense of the term. Of greater interest in this context is that, during the year, parliamentary committees forward a number of written questions pertaining to pending Bills or other matters within the jurisdiction of the committee, to the appropriate political minister, just as the minister is often invited to appear in person before the committee. While conferences with the minister are always held in closed committee sessions, copies of written questions and of the minister's replies to such questions along with enclosures are, unless otherwise expressly stated, immediately handed over by the secretariat of the committee to representatives of the news media covering parliamentary business. This practice, established in 1969 under a ruling of the parliamentary committee on the rules of procedure, also covers documents exempted from access under section 5 of the Act, if such documents – e.g., letters exchanged between ministerial departments with regard to a Bill pending before Parliament – are forwarded to the committee. As a consequence, documents forwarded to a parliamentary committee in reply to a written question and covered by the practice outlined above will often be available to other interested persons by addressing the ministerial department concerned, even if covered by one of the exception clauses of the Act.

The Act of 1970 does not apply to documents drawn up by an authority, or having come into an authority's possession, before the Act came into force on 1 January 1971. Public access to such documents cannot be requested as of right, but may be afforded at the discretion of the authority in charge of the documents. There are no general rules governing access of scholars to such documents, and there does not appear to be any uniform administrative practice in dealing with applications from scholars for access to information not covered by the Act. The official attitude seems to be fairly liberal, in particular regarding applications for access to documents dealing with conditions under the German occupation of Denmark (1940–45). Thus, in a recent case which was brought before the Ombudsman by an unsuccessful applicant, the Ministry of Justice stated that it was its general practice to grant applications for access to the files of criminal cases from scholars who wished to undertake advanced legal or historical research dealing with this period, and particularly research aimed at qualifying the applicant for an academic doctorate. Practice might be somewhat more restrictive when applications concerned information on more recent events.

INFORMATION PROCEDURES

THE TRANSMISSION OF INFORMATION

The preparatory work underlying the Act of 1970 makes it very clear that access to administrative information may be requested under the Act not only after a decision on the substantive matter has been taken, but also at any stage during the consideration of the matter by the administrative authority concerned. Section 6, subsection 2, of the Act, concerning legislation (see above) constitutes the only exception to this general rule.

Section 8, subsection 2, of the Act should be read against this background. Under this provision the authority receiving a request for access to documents ' . . . shall decide, with due regard to the dispatch of the matter in question, whether [the] request . . . can be granted immediately or at some later date . . . ' This provision does not warrant a postponement of the execution of a request for access to documents pertaining to pending matters only because the administrative authority finds the granting of the request at that particular time inexpedient (e.g., because the documents claimed would in the judgement of the authority present an incomplete picture of the matter). The subsection refers exclusively to obstacles of a practical nature to an immediate execution of a request. For instance, the documents at the time of the request may not be actually in the possession of the authority in question, or the question of whether the request should be granted gives rise to such doubts as to require more thorough considerations just as more urgent matters every now and then require consideration with a higher priority.

As a general rule the manner in which an administrative authority has filed its documents should not influence the accessibility of the information under the Act. However, in some cases the means of storing administrative information may undoubtedly justify a certain postponement of the execution of requests for access to such information. For example, documents stored in the form of microfilms must be reprinted, and if the information is available only in a computerised form, allowance must be made for such deferments as are necessary in order to process the information asked for without unreasonable cost.

Subsection 2 also provides that the administrative authority receiving a request for access to documents shall decide ' . . . whether the person who has made the request should be given access to the documents by allowing him to examine the documents on the spot or by providing him with a copy or photocopy of them'. In administrative practice, however, requests for transcripts or photocopies are usually granted, but under an administrative regulation (issued under section 8, subsection 3, of the Act) a certain fee is collected for this service (5 Danish Kroner per page), except for a party to a particular case, who may request copies of the documents free of charge.

THE DECISION-MAKING PROCESS

A request to examine the documents on a particular case must (under section 8, subsection 1) be put before the administrative authority which is legally authorised to decide on the substantive issues of that case. This authority is authorised to decide whether a request for access should be granted in respect of all documents pertaining to the matter in question, including documents prepared by and/or forwarded to that authority by other administrative authorities. It is also the responsibility of this authority to decide on the applicability of exception clauses primarily aimed at protecting interests attended to by other administrative authorities.

If an administrative authority is in doubt about whether a request for access should be granted, it may of course ask the advice of other administrative authorities concerned. Thus, in administrative practice the Ministry of Justice has in a number of cases advised other authorities on the interpretation of the Act. But the power to decide whether a request should be granted always lies with the authority which is authorised to decide on the underlying sub-stantive matter, and opinions on this question rendered by other authorities are only advisory.

An administrative authority cannot restrict the power and responsibility that under section 8, subsection 1, of the Act lies with another authority to decide on requests for access, by classifying documents forwarded to it as 'confidential', 'secret', etc. These and similar classifications of documents are without any legally binding effect under the Act, and should be regarded only as advisory opinions from the authority making the classification.

The general principles outlined in the two preceding paragraphs are subject to one important reservation. Under Danish adminis-trative law a superior administrative authority may ordinarily instruct subordinate authorities on the decision of individual cases. This power of instruction also covers whether to grant or refuse requests for access to documents under the Act of 1970. As a consequence, with respect to letters or documents exchanged between a superior and a subordinate authority, classification of documents made by the superior authority may be interpreted as an order to the subordinate authority not to grant requests for access to such documents.

A decision of an administrative authority on a request for access to documents under the Act of 1970 may be the subject of appeal to the superior administrative authority, if any, or submitted to the Ombudsman for consideration, or brought before the courts for judicial review, in accordance with the ordinary rules governing the exercise of these legal remedies.

CONCLUSION

When the Act on Access of the Public to Documents in Administrative Files was passed in 1970, there was general agreement that its predecessor, the Act of 1964 on Access of Parties to Documents in Administrative Files, had not given rise to any difficulty in administrative practice. But it was also the general feeling that the Act had not in fact been utilised to the extent envisaged in 1964, and that the main reason for this was that the public had been insufficiently informed of their rights under the Act.

From the point of view of principle, this lack of awareness on the part of the public was unsatisfactory. The Act of 1964 was aimed at enhancing the protection of the individual against acts of administrative authorities, and in order to fulfil this purpose, it should be inscribed, so to speak, on the mind of the man in the street as an element in his general concepts of justice. Just as any Danish citizen, at least broadly speaking, knows that he may file a complaint with the Ombudsman, everyone should also be familiar with his right to examine documents underlying administrative decisions likely to encroach on his interests.

This is the reason why the Ministry of Justice, in advertisements appearing in a great number of newspapers just before and after 1 January 1971, when the new Act came into force, called attention to this new piece of legislation, and in particular to its provisions on the rights of parties to administrative proceedings, carried over from the Act of 1964. These provisions were also the subject of a number of broadcasts over the radio at that time, examining and illustrating by way of concrete examples the uses which might be made of them. And in a circular letter issued by the Ministry of Justice to all administrative authorities it was emphasised that administrative authorities should, whenever appropriate, inform and advise members of the public – parties as well as other interested persons, including representatives of the mass media – on the contents of the provisions of the new Act.

It is, of course, difficult to prove the effects of such measures. But the fact is that the provisions of the Act of 1970 on the rights of parties to an administrative proceeding are now utilised to a considerably greater extent than under the Act of 1964, even if not to the extent one might wish for.

As regards the provisions on access of the public to documents in administrative files, the same pattern as that experienced with the Act of 1964 stands out: the provisions have not given rise to any difficulty, in the main owing to the fact that they are only sparingly utilised. The explanation for this is not – as with the Act of 1964 – ignorance of these provisions. From a realistic point of view, the principal beneficiaries of these provisions are the representatives of the mass media, and journalists generally covering administrative matters may be presumed to know of the Act. At least part of the explanation is, rather, that journalists prefer the more informal means of gathering information, which were improved indirectly by the Act as explained below. In most cases journalists are more interested in obtaining a particular piece of information orally, because they can get it more easily in this way and can also get some official or semi-official oral comments on it. The task of going through the complete file of a case is frequently much more tedious and time-consuming.

However, the main reason underlying the very limited uses made of the Act in all probability lies with the Act itself. Thus, under section 1, subsection 2, a request for access to documents must specify the case to which the documents pertain. And under section 3, no. 2, the right of access includes entries in journals, registers and other lists of documents kept by the administrative authority, but only entries relating to the case thus specified. The effect of these provisions is that the Act does not give access to peruse the bulk of incoming and outgoing mail, and also does not entitle journalists or others to carry out 'fishing expeditions' in the journals or registers of administrative authorities. An authority is not obliged under the Act to comply with a request to examine all cases of a particular kind, or all cases registered over a certain period of time. Those who wish to avail themselves of their rights under the Act must specify the particular case or cases, the documents of which they want to examine. Thus the provisions in fact imply that they must have obtained knowledge of the existence of such cases before addressing the administrative authority in question.

On this point the Danish Act differs from the Norwegian Act as well as from Swedish legislation, under both of which the journals or registers of all incoming mail kept by authorities covered by the Acts are as a general rule open for inspection.

This difference has been greatly increased by some trends in Swedish administrative practice. Thus, a number of central government authorities in Stockholm have established a general practice under which the incoming mail – and in some cases copies of outgoing mail as well – is exhibited for public inspection each day, usually from 10 a.m. to 3 p.m., after the registrar has sorted out documents excepted from the general rules governing publicity, but before the documents are distributed to the various divisions, sections, etc., for processing. The heaps of documents are placed in special anterooms and put at the disposal of those who want to inspect the documents. In actual practice a systematic inspection has been organised by a private news agency, *Tidningernes Telegrambureau*, which on the basis of reports prepared by its staff distributes the materials to the press enterprises associated with the agency. This procedure, however, covers in the main only the major departments and directorates of the central government in Stockholm. For instance, it is not followed by local government authorities.

This difference was of course examined and considered at great length in the report of the Committee on Publicity (1963), when preparing the Danish Bill on Access of the Public to Documents in Administrative Files, and in the parliamentary debates on that Bill. And the reasons for preferring the more limited Danish version were mainly of a practical and technical nature. The traditional system for registration of incoming and outgoing mail by Danish administrative authorities differs considerably from that prevailing in Sweden and Norway, and does not lend itself easily to serve as a basis for 'fishing expeditions' aimed at obtaining knowledge of what cases are pending before administrative authorities. Furthermore, the very advanced Swedish practice outlined above would seem to require a much more elaborate and detailed catalogue of exceptions than that envisaged by the Committee's draft,[9] and it was felt that the drafting of such a catalogue would give rise to almost insurmountable difficulties, when such an exercise could not draw on any previous experience.

The parliamentary committee appointed to examine the Bill agreed, that it was most expedient to set out with the somewhat limited version of the principle of open files proposed in the Bill, but it was provided, by an amendment to the Bill, that this question should be reconsidered in the parliamentary year 1974/75 (later postponed until 1978/79) on the basis of experience gained under the Act. Probably the most important item in the terms of reference of the committee appointed to review the Act is, accordingly, the question whether the Danish Act on this point should be put in line with the Swedish (and Norwegian) legislation.

Even if the provisions of the Act of 1970 have only been utilised sparingly in practice, this does not mean that the Act has had no impact on the administrative process. One of the aims underlying the Act was to bring about a change of attitude on the part of administrative authorities and to make civil servants more inclined towards openness, towards better relations with representatives of the mass media, and towards accepting the public's right to know what is going on in central and local government. In this respect, the Act has undoubtedly provided a firmer basis for the more informal seeking of information by journalists, which of course was extensively employed even before the Act. Before the enactment of the new provisions, individual civil servants, in particular junior civil servants, might often be in doubt as to the scope of their obligation to keep official matters secret. Now, they need not hesitate, when so requested, to give information – either orally or over the telephone – which is contained in documents accessible to the public at large under the Act. Information supplied orally is also apt to be more accurate and complete than before the Act, because the very fact that the recipients of such information may at any time choose to check the documents themselves calls for greater care in the handling of such informal requests.

Furthermore, there is no doubt that the Act and the public debate preceding and following its enactment have been contributory factors in bringing about a number of extremely interesting experiments, mainly at the local government level, with the better informing of and increased participation by the population preceding administrative decisions, particularly on matters of town and country planning and environmental protection.[10]

Finally, the experience gained under the two Acts on access to documents in administrative files will doubtless prove very helpful in the work recently undertaken by the Ministry of Justice on drafting an administrative procedure Act. In this context it will suffice to point to the clarification of concepts obtained under the execution of the two Acts. One of the criticisms frequently levelled against the Acts has been that key provisions of the texts used wordings and concepts of a rather vague and obscure meaning, and left too much freedom in the application of the Acts to the administrative authorities that they were supposed to control. The fears underlying this criticism have not materialised, however. In administrative practice the provisions of the Acts have been applied and interpreted in a very liberal spirit, fortified by opinions delivered by the Ombudsman on individual cases. And the considerable body of case law now available, clarifying a number of concepts fundamental to any statutory regulation of administrative procedures, constitutes an important contribution to the general body of Danish administrative law.

NOTES

1. Act no. 280, 10 June 1970, which came into force on 1 January 1971. For a more detailed survey of the legislative history of the Act, see Eilschou Holm, 'The Danish System of Open Files in Public Administration', *Scandinavian Studies in Law* 19 (1975), 155 *et seq.*

2. The question of requiring administrative authorities to give reasons for their decisions was, however, not included in the terms of reference of the Committee on Publicity. This question was not submitted for a thorough examination until the autumn of 1963, when the Ministry of Justice appointed a committee to study that matter. This committee reported in 1972, *Betænkning om Begrundelse af Forvaltningsafgørelser og Administrativ Rekurs* (No. 657/1972). This report is at present under consideration in the Ministry of Justice in the broader context of drafting a Bill for an administrative procedure Act.

3. In the autumn of 1967, members of the Conservative Party, the Liberal Party, and the Radical Liberal Party, then in opposition, jointly submitted a Private Member's Bill on Access of the Public to Documents in Administrative Files, closely similar to the committee's draft of 1963. This Bill lapsed along with other unterminated business before Parliament, when a general election was called in January 1968. At the election the three parties won a majority of the seats in Parliament and formed a coalition Cabinet. The Government Bill submitted to Parliament in 1969 was prepared by this Government. The question did not, however, give rise to much political controversy, and the Bill was adopted unanimously by Parliament with some minor amendments.

4. The report will be an extensive one, with a long summary in English which may be published separately. *Ed.*

5. See a series of four reports on public participation and secrecy in planning prepared by Georg Gottschalk and Jens Chr. Tonboe. The first report of the series was published in 1974, *Offentlighed, Hemmelighed og Medindflydelse i Planlægningen* with a summary in English (Copenhagen: Teknisk Forlag, 1974).

6. A few additional provisions exempting certain categories of cases from the coverage of the Act have been passed over, e.g. section 14 exempting matters involving the Faroe Islands.

7. This description does not quite cover the provisions contained in section 5, nos 7 and 8. No. 7 makes exception for 'letters exchanged between authorities and experts for use in court proceedings or when considering whether such proceedings should be instituted'; and no. 8 makes exception for 'material furnished as a basis for drawing up official statistics'. These provisions are passed over in the text.

8. The provision in section 5, no. 6, should, at least in part, be seen against this background. Under the restrictive interpretation of no. 4, it would be open to considerable doubt whether letters or documents exchanged between the Ministry for Foreign Affairs and the Danish embassies could be regarded as covered by that provision. It was therefore considered necessary to insert a provision expressly excepting 'documents concerning questions of foreign policy or foreign trade'.

9. As pointed out by Bertil Wennergren, 'Civic Information – Administrative Publicity', 36, *International Review of Administrative Sciences* (1970), 243 *et seq.*, at page 248, there is, as a matter of drafting technique, theoretically a choice between the general-clause technique and the technique of enumeration. The Nordic Acts all use techniques that include elements of both. However, as appears from the foregoing, the emphasis in the Danish Act is on the former alternative. By way of contrast it may be mentioned that the very comprehensive body of regulations governing exceptions from the general rule in Swedish law contains a catalogue with hundreds of items covering different categories of document.

10. See note 5.

4 Norway

ARVID FRIHAGEN

The Public Access Act of 1970 was passed by the Norwegian Parliament in the spring of 1970 and sanctioned by the Cabinet (King in Council) on 19 June the same year. It gives to any person who may be interested a general right of access to any document in the possession of any state or municipal body. At the same time, it contains a number of exceptions, and exceptions can also follow from other statutes. Among the exceptions in the Act itself should especially be noted 'internal, administrative working documents' and documents concerning 'the personal affairs' of the individual.

The system whereby the public has a statutory right of access to a document in public keeping is often called *the principle of public access*. The Act of 1970 introduces this as the rule in Norwegian administrative law.[1]

ACCESS FOR ALL

The Public Access Act was mainly intended to facilitate access to public documents for the press. However, it can be used by any interested persons or bodies who wish to obtain access to documents in an administrative case. It is not a condition under the Act that the person wishing to see the documents must be party to the case. Nor is there any requirement that he must have a special interest in or connection with the case.

It is especially for those who are not parties to the case in question that the right of access is of importance. Under the Administrative Procedure Act, parties to individual cases and interest groups concerned with proposed regulations normally already have a more extensive right of access to the documents of the case in question.

SECRECY RULES

To understand the Norwegian Public Access Act one must keep in mind that it only regulates the duty – the legal obligation – of public servants to comply with requests for access to administrative documents. The Act does not regulate obligations to keep documents secret, and does not prohibit anyone from making a document public. Thus a document which is not accessible under the Public Access Act is not necessarily subject to any rule requiring official secrecy so as to hinder the agency or the public servant from giving access to it. The Act only states which documents *must* be made available to the public, not which documents otherwise *may* be made available. At the same time, there are a number of secrecy provisions in various special statutes. Documents covered by a statutory secrecy provision are exempted from public access under a specific provision in the Public Access Act (sect. 5, subsect. 3).

Under Norwegian law there are thus three categories of document:

(1) Documents which under the Public Access Act must be available to the public. Here public servants have a legal obligation to make the documents available on request.

(2) Documents which do not by the Public Access Act have to be made publicly available, but which are not covered by secrecy provisions in any statute or by administrative orders. These documents may or may not be made publicly available at the discretion of the agency or the public servant.

(3) Documents which are either covered by secrecy provisions in statutes, or fall outside the Public Access Act but are covered by administrative secrecy rules without basis in a statute. This third group covers documents that the agency and the public servants are obliged to keep secret.

THE LEGISLATIVE BACKGROUND

THE SITUATION BEFORE 1970

Before the passing of the Public Access Act in 1970 there were no general rules giving reporters or other interested persons a right of access to government documents in Norway. Such rules are limited to the parties in individual cases and to the making of administrative regulations.

In addition there were – and still are – a number of narrowly defined specific regulations and statutory rules concerning the availability of records, etc. Thus the official records of land ownership are to be open to public inspection. As in most other countries, the laws on patents and trademarks and on limited companies require the registrations, etc., to be publicly available.

THE INFLUENCE OF SWEDISH AND DANISH LAW

The reforms in Norway can be traced back to the Swedish constitutional provisions of 1766. These rules, as now amended in 1949, give the press and interested individuals a general right of access to public documents.

The system and details in the Norwegian Act are in many respects rather different from Swedish law, however. This is, at least in part, probably due to the fact that administrative law and the administrative systems in Sweden and Norway are different in major respects.

Denmark passed a public access Act at practically the same time as Norway. As administrative law and organisation in general are very similar in Norway and Denmark, it is not unexpected that Norwegian and Danish law are generally speaking similar, even though the details differ. It seems, however, that this was only to a small degree due to direct co-operation or mutual influence.

THE ADMINISTRATIVE PROCEDURE ACT

The Norwegian Administrative Procedure Act was passed in 1967.

Sect. 18 of this Act gives the parties to an individual administrative case a right of access to its documents. Certain limitations are set out in sect. 18, para. 2, and in sect. 19. The Act also specifies in sect. 33 that in appeal proceedings the parties are automatically to be sent copies of relevant documents before the case is decided. Otherwise, the main rule under the Act is that there are no specifically adverse proceedings beyond the parties being given advance notice and a right of access to the documents and of expressing their views on the case. In addition, sect. 37 gives organisations and interested groups of persons a limited right of access to documents in cases regarding general regulations.

DIFFERENCES BETWEEN THE ACCESS ACT AND THE PROCEDURE ACT

There are several differences between the Public Access Act and the Administrative Procedure Act regarding access to administrative documents. Thus there are differences regarding *who* may require access, *in which cases* the rules apply, and *which types of document* can be requested. There are also some differences between the frameworks of the Acts.

The main point is that the Administrative Procedure Act can only be used by the parties to the case, except for the limited provisions giving organisations and interested groups access to documents regarding regulations. Under the Public Access Act, documents are to be made available to any interested person. This latter Act does not require that the person be a party or have any specific reason for being interested.

The Procedure Act only gives a right of access to documents in an individual case where one or several private persons are parties and the case concerns official governmental decrees as opposed to commercial issues or internal aspects such as public tenders and departmental reorganisation. The rules of access under the Access Act on the other hand cover all types of cases except those regarding government commercial matters. Important here is that the Access Act also covers cases of major public interests such as general regulations, proposed legislation, etc.

The exemptions from access in the Access Act and the Procedure Act are generally differently worded. They are, however, built up roughly over the same framework. Thus internal documents are exempted from access both to parties under the Procedure Act and to the general public under the Access Act. Otherwise, the more specific exemptions are worded differently in the two Acts. The exemptions from access are, as a rule, given a wider scope in the Access Act than in the Procedure Act.

Only the Access Act has a general exemption for documents covered by statutory secrecy. Rules in the various statutes requiring secrecy for specific types of information or specific types of document thus lead to automatic exemptions from access under the Access Act.

PUBLIC HEARINGS AND ADMINISTRATIVE MEETINGS

Neither the Public Access Act nor the Administrative Procedure Act obliges administrative bodies to hold hearings in public or to give the public or even the interested parties access to their meetings. Both Acts thus limit themselves to giving access to documents – not to information as such.

The Procedure Act does, however, have rules requiring that certain types of factual information and proposals must be written down or otherwise communicated to the party in question. The Access Act does not have any rules requiring information to be written down so as to be made available through documents. The tradition, however, is that all types of information of relevance to a case is written down in formal notes or memos. These become available to some degree.

There are some rules in more specific administrative areas requiring public meetings and public hearings. Otherwise, the general rule is assumed to be that meetings of administrative agencies are closed to the public.

Rules requiring meetings to be held in public are mainly found at the municipal level. Thus municipal councils must hold their meetings open to the press and the interested public. Exceptions apply where the council in question decides that a part of the meeting shall be in closed session due to the nature of the information that will be given or discussed. Similar rules apply to school boards and harbour authorities.

The Prices and Monopolies Act expressly gives authority to hold public hearings and agency meetings. Otherwise there are no rules regarding these matters outside municipal administration.

There has been criticism lately of the limited use of public hearings in Norwegian administrative law. It is argued that this is not in accordance with the ideas behind the Public Access Act. Proposals are now before Parliament for extending the scope of the rules requiring open meetings in municipal and regional administration.

THE RIGHT OF ACCESS TO DOCUMENTS

THE MAIN PRINCIPLE

The main principle of the Public Access Act is stated in sect. 2:

> Documents in administrative cases are public, unless exception is made by, or pursuant to, statutory law. Anyone may demand of the pertinent public institution to be apprised of the contents of a public document in a particular case.

The first paragraph of sect. 2 sets up as a main principle that the documents in administration are to be publicly available. In the second paragraph this is specified somewhat more directly: anyone – regardless of interest or special connection with the case – has a right by law to make himself familiar with the documents in specific cases at his request to the relevant administrative body.

The Access Act changes earlier law and gives government bodies and public servants not only the right to make documents available, but a direct legal duty to comply with requests from the public for access to administrative documents. The rule is so worded that it is the exceptions from access that will have to be shown. Thus the Act places upon the relevant government agency or government body the burden of showing that it should not be obliged to comply with a request for a specific document, if it wishes to refuse the request.

Sect. 2 states specifically that the Act only applies where exceptions are not made in other statutes. This means that any statute can give a wider or more limited access than otherwise would follow from the Act. There are, however, few such special provisions.

WHEN DOCUMENTS BECOME AVAILABLE

By defining at what time documents become 'documents in administrative cases', sect. 3 also sets up the main rule about at what time a document is to be made available to the public. Sect. 3 reads:

> Documents in administrative cases are documents which are drawn up by a public institution as well as documents which have come into, or have been submitted to, such an Institution.
>
> A document is considered to be drawn up when it is dispatched, or if this does not occur, when the public institution has concluded its handling of the case.

The main principle under sect. 3 is that public documents are to be held available even before the case is decided. The idea is to permit newspapers and interested organisations to discuss and influence decisions to be taken by the Government and the public administration.

Documents sent to a government agency or organisation are as a general rule to be held public from the instant the document is received. Thus an application for a permit or a statement sent from an interest group on proposed planning is to be held available as soon as it is received by the administrative authority. The same applies as a general rule to letters, memoranda, etc., sent from one public agency or body to another.

Documents sent from an administrative agency to a private organisation, a private person or company or to another public body are as a general rule to be held accessible to the public from the time the document is sent. This means that the copy the administration has of its letter is to be made accessible from the time the original letter is mailed or otherwise passed on to its recipient.

A document made or drawn up by an administrative body, but which is not sent out of the organisation, is to be made accessible to the public when the case is concluded. Viewed in the light of the exception in sect. 5 (subsect. 1) for 'internal, working documents', this means that documents drawn up by the administration which are not sent out will only be available to the public where the document itself represents or is a part of the formal, final decision of the case. The records of an administrative board or council will thus be public from the time the formal protocol or records are signed or otherwise become official.

SUSPENDED ACCESS

There was much discussion at the time the Public Access Act was drafted about whether it would be detrimental to the administrative process to give access to documents before the case was closed or at least ready for decision. It was feared by many that public opinion expressed through the press would put unwanted pressure on the administration and government. There was also a fear that interest groups and the press would take a stand on cases and issues on incomplete and thus misleading data if the documents were to be available before sufficient information had been gathered to give a complete picture.

As already stated, the main principle of the Act is that the documents are to be available as soon as they are either received by an administrative body or sent out by it. To limit the problems, sect. 4 sets out some limitations on the obligation to make documents available at this early stage. Sect. 4 reads:

> The pertinent public institution may decide in a particular case that public accessibility shall first take effect at a later stage in the preparation of the case than that provided for in Section 3, provided that the documents then available are assumed to give an obviously misleading picture of the case and public accessibility might be detrimental to public or private interests.
> In addition, the King may issue administrative provisions which provide that for certain kinds of cases or documents, or certain sectors of administration, public accessibility shall take effect at a later stage than that provided for in Section 3.

Sect. 4 contains two different types of power to delay the time of access to government documents.

The first paragraph gives to the agency holding the documents the power to delay the time of access, but only under very strict conditions. The first is that the documents available at the time of the request would give an obviously misleading picture of the case. In addition, public access must be detrimental to public or private interests.

The legislative background shows that these conditions were to be very strictly observed and that the wording was meant only to permit an agency to delay the time of access where it would be fairly obvious to outsiders also that accessibility at an early stage would be both misleading and harmful. Nearly any document presented by an interested party or interested group in a case could be said to give a misleading or slanted picture of the case. However, this certainly would not provide a basis for withholding the document from public access. In practice this paragraph of sect. 4 is rarely used, and there have been very few recorded instances where the agency has delayed accessibility by referring to this provision.

Of considerably more practical importance is the second paragraph of sect. 4. Here there are no specific limitations as to when or in which instances the Cabinet (King in Council) may grant exceptions from the time of accessibility as set up in sect. 3. On the other hand, this paragraph may only be used as a basis for delayed access when the Cabinet (King in Council) has made a formal order to this effect. Thus there can only be delayed access under this provision when a formal order has been promulgated in advance permitting delayed access and covering certain types of document or a specific part of government operations.

Rules delaying the time of access under sect. 4, para. 2, are set out in the decree of 11 June 1970. The main ones are as follows.

In cases of complaints against public servants or persons in activities requiring an official permit, public access to the documents may be delayed until the person complained of has had the opportunity to reply to the complaint.

In cases regarding questions of dismissal or suspension of public servants, public access to the documents may be delayed until the investigating body has made its final report or the case is otherwise concluded. Similar rules apply to the investigation of accidents where accessibility could be detrimental to the investigation.

There are also some limited provisions delaying the time of access in cases of refusal to deal under the Price Council, and in cases where the government has consultations with private companies in order to obtain a reduction of prices or to make necessary provisions against restraint of trade under the Prices and Monopolies Act. An exemption is also made for cases involving smoke damage. The applications for a permit to emit industrial smoke may be held confidential until they have been published.

As a whole, it must be said that the Cabinet (King in Council) has shown great restraint in permitting exemptions under paragraph 2. The exemption in the decree are all of a quite limited scope.

SPECIAL PROVISIONS REQUIRING SECRECY

Under sect. 5, subsect. 3, documents which are graded confidential by or in accordance with statutory law are exempted from public access, and there are more than one hundred statutes with provisions for confidential treatment of information or documents. A recent Department of Jusitice survey lists a total of some 130 statutory secrecy provisions. In addition there are a number of statutes giving an agency or the Cabinet power to make rules providing for the confidential treatment of specific documents or types of information.

These provisions vary considerably in scope, wording and importance. Many of the provisions are old and are not in accordance with the principles underlying the Public Access Act. It seems, however, that the provisions are not of such a scope and importance as to thwart the main principle set up in the Act. Thus press organisations and the newspapers generally do not seem to have major complaints as to the scope and application of the secrecy provisions.

The Department of Justice in several circulars has stressed that the older secrecy provisions with broad scope and general wordings must be interpreted considerably more narrowly than the wording might indicate, in view of the new principles set down in the Public Access Act. Also the Department has recently proposed that some of the statutes should be amended to give the secrecy provisions a more limited scope.

GENERAL EXCEPTIONS

According to sect. 1, the Public Access Act does not apply to documents that are part of the government's business activity. Thus documents on tenders or on buying and selling fall outside the Act. It could be said that, as a general rule, there is no required public access to documents regarding the government's commercial activities.

Furthermore, there are a number of specific exemptions set up in sect. 6 of the Act. Sect. 6 thus excepts:

(1) Documents which contain information on matters of significance for the security of the realm, for relations with foreign

powers and international organisations, or for the country's defence.

(2) Documents where exceptions are essential

(*a*) out of consideration for the proper execution of the state and local governments' financial, pay and personnel administration;

(*b*) because public accessibility will thwart public regulating and control measures or other necessary administrative orders or prohibitions, or endanger their execution.

(3) Documents which relate to or affect an individual's personal affairs of whatever kind, unless the person concerned consents to the release of such documents.

(4) Documents which contain information about technical devices and procedures as well as production or business matters, which it will be important from a competitive point of view to keep secret out of consideration for the person whom the information concerns.

(5) Documents in cases concerning appointments or promotions in the civil service. This exception does not apply to applicant lists.

(6) Reports on infringements, as well as general reports and other documents in connection with violations, of existing legislation.

(7) Examination papers and papers in similar tests, as well as responses submitted in connection with competitions and the like.

(8) The documents prepared in connection with the national budgets, both annual and long-term.

When a document in a case is excepted from public accessibility, the entire case may be excepted from public accessibility if the remaining documents in the case would give an obviously misleading picture of the case and public accessibility might be detrimental to public or private interests.

One should note that the last part of sect. 6 authorises any agency or government body holding a document to except the entire case from public access if the documents ordinarily subject to release would give an obviously misleading picture. This provision by the legislature, however, is intended only to be applied in very special instances. This gives the rule only a very limited scope in practice, and it is very rare that it is used as a basis to except a document from public access. The press organisations have so far not found one single instance where a case has been exempted by reference to the provision in the last paragraph of sect. 6.

Many of the exemptions in sect. 6, subsects 1–8, are, however, of a great practical importance. Most important is the exemption in subsection 3 relating to documents which affect or relate to an individual's private affairs, and the one in subsection 4 regarding documents which contain information which it will be of importance from a competitive point of view to keep secret out of consideration for the person or company whom the information concerns.

THE HOLDERS OF INFORMATION

THE GENERAL SCOPE OF THE ACT

The Act of 1970 applies to all administrative activities where a public institution acts on behalf of national or local government apart from business activity. But it does not cover private organisations or companies even when these occasionally have power by statute or by delegation to act on behalf of the government – e.g. in classifying ships or in controlling seaworthiness.

The Act covers all types of government agencies and bodies regardless of whether they are part of the regular national, regional or municipal government or are set up as more independent agencies under special statutes.

Public corporations are not covered by the Act even when they are completely owned by municipal agencies or by the national government itself. This is regardless of whether it is a corporation under the Limited Companies Act or is set up as a public corporation under a special Act of Parliament. In some instances, however, corporations completely owned by the government have been held to have such clear-cut characteristics as being part of the government that they must follow the rules laid down in the Act.

PARLIAMENTARY BODIES

The Public Access Act does not cover Parliament nor parliamentary bodies. This is not directly stated in the Act, but has been accepted as its intention in view of its legislative history. Nor does the Act cover the Ombudsman, who is formally organised as an agency acting on behalf of Parliament. Thus neither Parliament nor parliamentary bodies nor the Ombudsman are obliged to comply with a request for access to documents.

It must be noted, however, that documents sent from Parliament or a parliamentary body to the administration will be accessible under the Act when requests for access are made to the administration. Copies of documents sent from the administration to a parliamentary body will also be accessible when a request is directed to the administration.

THE COURTS

In principle the Public Access Act also covers the courts. Sect.1, however, indicates that it is only the courts' administrative activities that are covered by the Act. It has been assumed that the courts' traditional activities fall outside the scope of the Public Access Act, both because they are not administrative activities and because the regular criminal and civil procedure Acts exclusively cover the extent of public access.

The Act's coverage of the courts' administrative activity means that an interested person has a right of access to documents in the courts pertaining to registration of ownership, registration of companies, etc., and also correspondence with regard to the administrative organisation of the court – e.g. statistics on cases pending.

THE POLITICAL EXECUTIVE

There are no special exemptions for political ministers or proceedings in the Cabinet (King in Council) except the provision in sect. 5, subsect. 2, which excludes minutes of Cabinet meetings. It has been assumed, however, that a document from a minister to the Cabinet will as a general rule fall outside public access, as 'an internal document'. The exemption for internal documents in sect. 5, subsect. 1, is thus held to include correspondence and exchange of documents between the Cabinet and the ministries.

THE RECIPIENTS OF INFORMATION

GENERAL RIGHT OF ACCESS

Section 2 specifies that requests for documents may be made by 'any person'. This means that the person demanding access need not have any special interest or relationship to the case. The term 'any person' includes individual persons regardless of whether they are Norwegian or foreign citizens, and also companies, firms and interest groups.

The Act has no direct age limitations as to its use. In practice it has been assumed, however, that the person in question must be at least old enough to understand the importance of the documents and the responsibility for their handling – preferably at least fifteen years old. It is also thought that there may be a limitation as to the mental status of the person in question. Neither of these questions seems to have caused any problem in practice.

The Act is used to some degree by organisations – e.g. political parties and special interest groups. Thus organisations for the protection of natural resources and for the reform of prisons have used the Act in a number of cases. There are also instances where the Act has been used by individual persons acting in their own interest. This is rare, however.

The importance of the Act in practice is its extensive use by the press – including radio and other mass media. Thus Norsk Telegrambyrå – the main Norwegian news agency – has a special division with permanent personnel in all government departments. Incoming and outgoing mail is checked as a matter of routine. Of special importance here is the use by the press of the governmental 'journals', which list all incoming and outgoing correspondence, to find cases and documents of interest. In addition, the major newspapers make more selective requests for documents. Most regional government offices are also visited fairly regularly.

At the municipal level there are great variations in the use of the Act by the press. In many small municipal governments it is apparently little used by the local newspapers. Perhaps this is because they already have good access to information from municipal organisations, since local editors are often members of municipal councils, school boards, etc.

It might be added that there have been instances where administrative bodies have used the Act to get copies of documents from other administrative bodies. It has for example happened that a regional agency has used the Act to get information on state projects which it wished to hinder because of the local and special interests it represented.

THE USE OF INFORMATION OBTAINED

The Public Access Act does not in itself authorise the use or the publishing of documents to which a person has the right to get access. Yet it may be said that in principle, and as long as there is no other specific prohibition, documents accessible under the Public Access Act may also be published. Limitations will follow from the Penal Code. In addition, there are some limitations under the general rules of the Copyright Act. Thus it has been assumed that the author of a book sent into the authorities to be authorised for use in a specific school still has the copyright in the book. He can therefore, under the copyright rules, prohibit a journalist from publishing parts of the book, even though a public servant cannot refuse the journalist access to the book under the Public Access Act.

TYPES OF INFORMATION AVAILABLE

RESTRICTION OF ACT TO DOCUMENTS

The Public Access Act applies only to documents. This information cannot be required if it is not in the form of a *document*. This includes films, pictures, models and maps. Tapes and media from which information can only be produced by special instruments are, however, held to fall outside the scope of the Act. This means that material for the use of electronic computers is not accessible under the Act, except to the extent that information is contained in print-outs.

EXEMPTION OF INTERNAL DOCUMENTS

An important exemption under the Act is given in sect. 5, subsect. 1. Exempted from public access are:

> Proposals, drafts, opinions, and other similar working papers, explanatory notes or reports which the public institution itself prepares or, without being so required by law, procures for use in its internal proceedings with a case.

INFORMATION PROCEDURES

THE TRANSMISSION OF INFORMATION

Rules on how the public can get access to documents are given in sect. 8 of the Act:

> The public institution shall decide, out of consideration for the proper conduct of public business, how a document shall be made known to the person who asked for it, and so far as possible provide upon request a copy or transcript of the document. Section 20, paragraph 3 of the Act concerning Administrative Procedure applies correspondingly.

Under sect. 8 interested persons have a right to read documents which are to be made available. In addition, the Act obliges the administration to provide copies 'so far as possible'.

It is assumed that one can only refuse to supply copies where there are great practical problems. In practice copies have been denied in some instances, when a person has demanded copies of a large number of unspecified documents in a case. Copies of large maps have also been denied in a few cases. A recent survey by the Department of Municipal Government and Labour shows that requests for copies are very rarely denied, and that there seem to be very few problems in practice for the regional and municipal bodies to supply copies when requested.

The Act requires access to documents to be given without the paying of any charge. Sect. 8 does, however, give the government and municipal councils power to make rules charging a fee for making copies. In practice it is not usual for fees to be paid for copies and there are very few rules which permit the state or local government to charge a fee.

REFUSALS OF ACCESS

Some rules on the procedure for classification of documents are given in sect. 9 of the Act. In the first paragraph it is stated that any refusal of access to a document under the Act must be accompanied by a written reference to the legal basis for refusing – e.g., a reference to the relevant section and subsection in the Act.

It has been assumed that any refusal of access to a document must also include a written reference to the rules for appealing against the refusal. This is in accordance with the general principles laid down by the Administrative Procedure Act, sect. 27.

ADMINISTRATIVE APPEAL

Paragraph 2 of sect. 9 gives the rules on administrative appeal:

> The person who made the request may appeal against the refusal to the administrative instance immediately superior to the public institution which has made the decision. If the refusal is made by a municipal body established pursuant to the Act of 12 November 1954 concerning Local Government in the Urban District and in the Rural District Municipalities, or to the Act of 16 June, 1961, concerning the County Administration, the appeal is determined by the County Governor.

In practice there have been few appeals under sect. 9. By the end of 1973 there had been fewer than twenty formal appeals for refusal of access. Half of these appeals were directed to government departments and half to the county governors. It must be added, however, that the departments and other government bodies have issued a number of circulars and rendered advisory opinions on the general and individual application of the Public Access Act – often relating to a specific case. Thus the Department of Justice alone has given more than fifty formal advisory opinions regarding application of the Access Act, in response to specific requests for access to a document.

The Ombudsman has had a number of cases arising from the Act – not only individual ones, but also regarding how the general principles of the Act are to be applied and how practical problems should be solved on a more general basis. By the end of 1973 he had received some fifteen specific complaints alleging violations of the Act. Somewhat more than half the complaints were held by the Ombudsman to be warranted. All requests from the Ombudsman for changes in the application of the Act or to amend a refusal of access to specific documents have been followed by the administrative body in question. There have also been some questions in Parliament regarding the application of the Act – a few of which resulted in criticism of the government for not complying with the Act.

The legality of refusing to make a document accessible can be brought before the regular courts by the person who has been refused access. As of 1 July 1976 there had been no such case before the courts. It may be safely assumed that such cases will be very rare in the future also. It could well be, however, that cases will be brought by private companies or persons against the administration for making information or documents available unnecessarily when they should have been kept confidential as affecting commercial interests.

CONCLUSION

There have been few complaints from the newspaper organisations or otherwise that the Public Access Act is violated or not followed through in good faith. The press organisations, however, have made complaints that there are problems with rural areas and small municipalities not following through with the principle in the Act.

The general view both in the government and on the part of the press seems to be that the Act has not caused any major problems or excessive work load, and that many of the problems envisaged by the critics of the proposed Act were unfounded. There have been proposals for minor adjustments of the rules delaying the time of access and also proposals for adjusting the borderline as to what is to be exempted as 'commercial activities' under sect. 1 and 'internal documents' under sect. 5. Otherwise there do not seem to be any pending changes in the Public Access Act.

Perhaps the most important effects of the Public Access Act have been the change of attitude by government officials towards giving out information and the increased discussion in the press of issues before government agencies. It seems clear that the atmosphere between the press and government officials has changed considerably. Today the press has a much readier access to all types of governmental information than it had a few years ago.

NOTES

1. The Public Access Act of 1970 is discussed in A. Frihagen, *Offenlighetsloven med kommentarer* (Oslo: Eget forlag, 2nd ed., 1974), 467 pages. It includes summaries and comments on the rules, circulars, cases reviewed on appeal, advisory opinions, and surveys of the actual use of the Act in practice.

II Western Europe

5 Belgium

EDMOND JORION

HISTORICAL AND LEGAL FACTORS

Belgium is among the countries in which no legislation expressly establishes the general principle of freedom of information and ensures its application. In other words, it has no statutes comparable to those in force, for instance, in the United States and the Scandinavian countries. This does not imply, however, that a general principle of non-publicity prevails in the Belgian administration. On the contrary, the Belgian system of administrative publicity is directly derived from the inner meaning of its liberal and democratic 'Fundamental Charter'.

The large number of fundamental rights and freedoms recognised by the Constitution bears witness to its 'liberal' nature, viz.: individual freedom, freedom of opinion, of assembly, of association, of the press, of teaching, of worship, and of the use of languages; equality before the law; inviolability of home and property; secrecy of correspondence; the right to prosecute public servants; and the right of petition. The founding fathers intended to protect the Belgian state against any recurrence of the excesses committed by its previous rulers. The only primacy of power is that of the sovereign people.[1] The Belgian Constitution is thus imbued with both the liberal and the democratic spirit.

Article 25, by stating that all powers stem from the nation and are exercised in the manner prescribed by the Constitution, implies that every citizen, in order to be able to exercise his 'sovereign' prerogatives, should be informed of everything affecting the interests of the nation. Any principle or general regulation whose effect would be to deprive Belgian citizens of any access to information, even if the data were held by the government authorities themselves, would therefore be contrary to the spirit of the Constitution. That the right to information cannot be exercised without conditions – i.e. within certain limits, with certain formalities, and according to certain procedures – is a matter of common sense but also results from the distribution of powers under the Constitution. The right to address petitions to the public authorities, as governed by Articles 21 and 43, confirms, at one and the same time, that those authorities may not take refuge in a system of generalised reticence, and that access to information – as in this case, through petitions – is subject to certain conditions.

Publicity is and remains the rule. The only acceptable exceptions are those specified by law, and it is not by chance that the exceptions recognised by Belgian law, such as the defence and security of the state, the repression of crime, and diplomacy, are much the same as those allowed in the United States and the Scandinavian and other countries which are 'liberal' as regards information.

The principle of freedom of the press provides a final argument derived from the Constitution in support of the contention that the authorities may not systematically elude the citizen's legitimate curiosity. The Belgian writers on the subject look upon the press as an essential means of democratic control since, without its co-operation, the citizen could not obtain all the information he hopes for. By protecting the freedom of the press, the Constitution has deprived the authorities of the right to deny journalists the facilities they need to provide information in a democratic society.[2] The direct link between freedom of information and that of the press is confirmed by the fact that in the Swedish Constitution – reputed to be, at least in this field, the most liberal in the world – the principles concerning the publicity of official documents are the subject of a chapter of the Freedom of the Press Act (which is one of the Constitution's four constituent Acts). According to Nils Herlitz, 'the publicity of documents is still regarded as an ingredient in the freedom of the press.'[3] Likewise, Stanley V. Anderson writes that the main beneficiary, though not the principal instigator, of the legislation on free access to official documents is the press.[4]

OTHER BACKGROUND FACTORS

Two other essential factors should be taken into consideration. One is that the Belgian public authorities and administration, in accordance with the spirit of the Constitution, and pursuant to the relevant statutes and regulations, give wide publicity to their decisions and activity. In the Belgian context, the fields in which there is a demand for information cannot be dealt with without paying some attention to those in which there is little or no demand because the information supplied spontaneously by the authorities and their agencies wholly or partly satisfies the needs.

The second factor is the special meaning that should be attached, in Belgium, to 'public administration'. This chapter uses the term in a very wide sense, taking account of an important political development – the constant extension of full participation by private persons in administrative action. A question which cannot be overlooked is that of the ethical obligations as regards secrecy incumbent on the host of private persons involved in the work of the ministers' personal offices (*cabinets*), councils, committees, and other public services in such capacities as experts, technicians, specialists, and representatives of parties and interest or pressure groups. There can be no serious question of absolute secrecy in a political and administrative system where specific organs for openness and access – both inwards and outwards – are not only tolerated but also deliberately established.

GENERAL RIGHTS OF PUBLIC ACCESS

THE GENERAL SITUATION

The Legal Position of Public Authorities
Owing to the liberal spirit of the Belgian Constitution, it must be considered that, unless disclosure is expressly forbidden, public access to political and administrative information is free – though by no means unorganised and uncontrolled. The question therefore arises whether Belgian law contains prohibitory provisions of a kind amounting, in another form, to a system of secrecy. The legislation concerning professional secrecy, on the one hand, and the regulations enjoining secrecy on state officials, on the other, have helped to spread the idea that the Belgian administration is surrounded with a double barrier of secrecy. They seem to have led to the fairly frequent conclusion, abroad as well as in Belgium, that

ours is among the countries whose administration is legally secret and where publicity is therefore the exception. The following analysis is intended to show why that idea is largely unfounded and how it ought to be rectified.

In accordance with the spirit of the Constitution, administration information in Belgium is largely provided through the co-operation of the public authorities and of the citizens concerned. But that co-operation is not always equally shared. In certain circumstances, the initiative of the public authorities predominates and the receivers of information take a rather small part in the joint effort of dissemination. This applies, for instance, to purchasing and reading official publications, switching on radio and television programmes, and attending information lectures and meetings, perhaps followed by discussions. Conversely, the receivers of information play the leading part when they ask for particulars they desire. The Belgian system implies that action by the public authorities and by the public should not be dissociated, since they are two hardly distinguishable sides of the same process and two convergent trends of a common desire for information as regards the activity of the public services.

Official Publications
The official publications of public agencies are extremely numerous and are either compulsory or discretionary. A first group of compulsory official publications is made up by those connected with rules and decisions required by the Constitution, the Provinces Act, the Communes Act, or other statutes. The media are the *Moniteur Belge*, the *Mémorial administratif des provinces*, posters, proclamations, and personal notifications.

In many cases, legislation provides for suitable publicity for its subject-matter. A few examples of this are the notices in the *Moniteur Belge* concerning mining concessions, changes of surname, and patented inventions; and the posting of bills about compulsory education, drunkenness in public places, and prices.

A second group of such compulsory publications comprises those concerned with the preparation of legislation and decisions. As to statutes, the preparatory documents that are published are well known: the parliamentary annals, summary report, and papers. In the narrow sense, the papers are government and private members' Bills, amendments, and reports on the Bills. As to the preparation of orders and other administrative acts, innumerable publications are mandatory. Examples are found in the procedure for starting and carrying on dangerous, unhealthy, noisy or noxious trades; the examination of applications for mining concessions; the economic regulation of production and distribution under a Royal Order of 13 January 1935; the technical and commercial qualifications required for carrying on certain trades, as specified by the Act of 15 December 1970; public tenders; and the preparation of development plans under the Town and Development Planning Act of 20 March 1962 and its amendments.

There is a greater quantity of discretionary than of mandatory official publications. They are issued at such a rate that it has never been possible to make a complete list of them. Only a few typical examples will be mentioned here, chiefly to show the nature and importance of their contents, which, as might be expected, are infinitely varied. The following may be mentioned among the principal subjects dealt with: governmental or ministerial policy; the organisation and powers of the ministries; the creation, authority and organisation of their decentralised institutions; and regulations also published in the *Moniteur Belge* and in the compendia, such as the *Recueil Général des Lois et Arrêtés, Pasinomie*, or *Lex Belgica*, but which are conveniently issued in the form of brochures fully covering a given subject. Examples of this are the periodical *Codification-Personnel-Affaires Générales* published by the Ministry of Finance, the texts and documents of the Ministry of Foreign Affairs published by the Institut belge d'Information et de Documentation (INBEL), the Ministry of Economic Affairs publications concerning legislation as applied to commercial practices and to industrial and commercial enterprises in Belgium, and the Ministry of Communications *Code de l'Air* for civilian air pilots.

INBEL, just mentioned, is responsible for systematically publishing information about the most varied administrative institutions, including ministries, the Council of State, radio and television, planning, and state research establishments.

The discretionary publications issued by the provinces and the communes are also very numerous. The range and quality of the many publications issued by the Union des Villes et Communes Belges are noteworthy – for instance on the accounting, finance and civil liability of communes, funerals and cemeteries, and the regulation of advertisements. It should be stressed, however, that the above examples can only convey a vague idea of the enormous amount of publications voluntarily issued by the public services.

If the administration may be accused of secrecy, it is certainly not in this field. On the contrary, the administration may be said to strive hard to keep the citizen very fully informed of all its activities and of everything which concerns him.

Other media

Nobody is unaware that governments and public services use media other than their own publications for informing the citizen. They make extensive use of the services of the press, which they brief or inform by means of conferences, communiqués and various notices; they also use the cinema and, within the scope of the monopoly they hold, radio and television. Photographs and various kinds of sound-recording are also amply turned to account. Public hearings and meetings give direct information to those who attend them. The sessions of both Houses of Parliament are public, though each House may go into secret committee under the conditions specified in Article 33 of the Constitution. It should be noted that the debates of the Sections of the Houses are also open. The House of Representatives has six Sections and the Senate has four; they were formed in 1974 and combine the Committees – e.g. Justice, National Defence, Foreign Affairs – which are much more numerous but whose sessions are not open. The establishment of the Sections has therefore led to wider public access to parliamentary debates.

Law court sessions are open, unless openness would be dangerous for law and order or morality, in which case the court so rules. In matters connected with political or press offences, a session *in camera* can only be ordered on a unanimous basis, under Article 96 of the Constitution. Under Article 97, every judgment must be reasoned and be pronounced in open court. Similar public access, with the possibility of holding closed meetings, applies to the cultural, provincial, and communal councils, and to some other bodies.

In addition to meetings and hearings that must be open, there are of course also interviews by personal appointment and access to meetings of councils, committees, and commissions where information is supplied on paper, verbally or by any other means.

Lectures and exhibitions are also used for administrative communication. There are, moreover, information services which may obviously resort to means of communication other than official publications. Here again, an exhaustive survey of the data available is practically impossible. Only a thorough large-scale investigation could provide a sufficiently accurate picture of these aspects of public information. But it is well known that the information offices, meetings, radio, television and so on, open widely the doors and windows of public administration. Even that, however, is not enough, and the citizen has many other opportunities of requesting and obtaining a wealth of additional documents and other information, as will be shown further on in connection with the recipients of administrative information.

TYPES OF INFORMATION KEPT SECRET

Professional Secrecy
The rule for professional secrecy is stated as follows in Article 458 of the Penal Code:

> Any physician, surgeon, health officer, pharmacist, midwife, or other person who, on account of his status or profession, is the repository of secrets entrusted to him and who, except in the event of having been called upon to give evidence at law and of having been obliged by law to make known such secrets, has disclosed them shall be punished by from eight days' to six months' imprisonment and a fine of from one hundred to five hundred francs.

Evidently, public servants, with whom alone we are concerned here, are referred to by the words 'person who, on account of his status or profession, is the repository of secrets entrusted to him'. But as they may be entrusted with either administrative or personal secrets, one should ask which kinds of secrets are referred to in Article 458. As the article comes under Title VIII, 'Offences against persons', of the Code, one should infer that it only applies to public servants, regarding personal secrets entrusted to them. This first limitation of the scope of professional secrecy that applies to civil servants and other public servants needs to be pointed out, since, as mentioned above, public opinion has overestimated the role of secrecy in Belgian administration. Moreover, this professional secrecy is far from being general, so as to affect all administrative information; it relates only to certain particulars concerning persons, such as identity, religious denomination, income, health, racial origin and private life. To that extent only are public service officials bound by professional secrecy, which is quite distinct from the duty of discretion dealt with further on in this chapter. Besides this first important restriction, there are other exceptions to the principle which further reduce its real impact.

Article 458 of the Penal Code, quoted above, specifies two exceptions: one when evidence is given at law and the other when the law requires disclosure of the secret. Reference should particularly be made here to the Criminal Procedure Code which provides, in Article 29, that:

> Any constituted authority, civil servant, or public officer who, in the performance of his duties, obtains knowledge of a crime or other offence shall be bound immediately to notify the Public Prosecutor [*Procureur du Roi*] attached to the court of the district in which the offence has been committed or in which the accused might be found, and to transmit to the Public Prosecutor any particulars, reports and records related thereto.

It will be noted that the removal of secrecy is then for the sake of justice but, nevertheless, the public indirectly becomes to some extent informed.

The Public Servant's Duty of Discretion

Under Article 9 of the State Officials (Regulations) Act (Royal Order of 2 October 1937 and amendments, and particularly Royal Orders of 16 March 1964 and 17 September 1969), public servants have a duty of discretion regarding administrative information:

> *Article 9.* A state official must not reveal any facts that have come to his knowledge on account of his duties and are secret either by nature or by his superiors' instructions. This prohibition shall also apply after he has ceased to hold office.

The same Regulations lay down the punishments for breach of secrecy in such cases:

> *Article 13.* Any breach of the preceding articles shall be punished, as the case may require, by one of the disciplinary measures decreed in Article 77, without prejudice to the application of criminal law.

Owing to its general character, Article 9 refers both to the 'personal' or 'private' secrets mentioned above in connection with Article 458 of the Penal Code and the secrets we shall describe as 'administrative'. But Article 13, when referring to criminal law and therefore particularly to its Article 458, refers only, in our opinion, to its application in the event of the violation of personal secrets. It may be inferred that the violation of administrative secrets only gives rise to the punishments decreed by Article 77 of the Regulations. It rests with the administrative authorities to determine whether the latter should be added to the former, since the Regulations state:

> *Article 81.* A criminal proceeding shall suspend the procedure and the disciplinary decision. Whatever the result of such proceeding, the imposition of disciplinary measures shall remain for the administrative authority to decide upon.

Article 9 of the Regulations is difficult to interpret for various reasons, the chief of which, surprisingly, may be found in certain ministerial circulars or service instructions concerning it, since they are imprecise and even confused and contradictory. They are, of course, not helpful when they fail to mention obvious difficulties of interpretation. As briefly as possible, it may tentatively be stated that:

> Towards certain persons, officials are bound to secrecy concerning everything that occurs, is said, is written, etc., within the scope of administrative duties;
> Data in the form of personal secrets that are covered by Article 458 of the Penal Code, the contents of letters that are protected by the Constitution, as also telegraph and telephone communications, are secret by nature;
> When an official is dealing with superiors or with any 'competent' authorities or officials—those 'whose duties and responsibilities entitle them to take cognizance of the particulars in question'—there is no 'secrecy' but 'confidentiality', and he gives them the particulars under the seal of secrecy;
> Secrecy is therefore only compulsory when dealing with all other persons;
> Moreover, the duty of secrecy and confidentiality referred to in Article 9 is only binding on officials and not on authorities, such as

ministers, governors, and burgomasters, who have the privilege of what legal writers have called the *droit au secret*, which is the right to decide whether information should be kept secret or not. This essential point needs dwelling on at length.

To mention only the ministers, who are the supreme heads of the central government, it should be observed that they alone are answerable to the Houses of Parliament and, indirectly, to the 'sovereign people' for their management and for the carrying out of their political mandate.

As to the officials (*agents*), Article 9 of the Regulations reasonably binds them to discretion, in the sense of respect for secrecy towards any unauthorised person because they are no more than 'agents' of the state. It should be noted that, with equally good reason, the legislation concerning labour and employment contracts provides that workers and office staff must keep their employers' trade and/or business secrets.

State officials are unquestionably the ministers' 'subordinates' and may therefore not replace them by deciding, in what might be called the 'residual field of information', what should remain confidential and what should be made public in one form or another. The residual field of information thus at the ministers' disposal is constituted by what is left of the openness generally intended by the Constitution after the following have been excluded: (i) everything the ministers are obliged to publish or communicate, namely mandatory publications and the files, documents, information, and other materials prescribed by the rules of administrative procedure governing contentious and non-contentious matters; and (ii) whatever must remain secret, both to the ministers and their officials, either pursuant to Article 458 of the Penal Code or to other statutes or regulations specifically prescribing secrecy concerning persons (statistics, public health, certain records, taxation, etc.) or the state (national defence and security, diplomacy, certain records, etc.).

The residual field of information having thus been delimited, the ministers will make use of their corresponding powers, at their discretion but under their full responsibility, by issuing any additional publications they consider expedient and by communicating, either personally or by delegation of powers to their assistants, any files, documents or other information concerning their management (intentions, plans in various stages of preparation, the making and implementation of decisions, opinions on particular questions, etc.).

It is well known that the ministers make very full use of their publicity and information prerogatives. Nevertheless, the section which deals with these matters further on attempts to recall the principal ways in which they do so. When inquiring into the actual quantity and quality of governmental and administrative information, it should be stressed that:

> The ministers and the staffs of their personal offices make wide use of their responsibilities in this field through the innumerable interviews they grant to citizens and the mass of correspondence they exchange with them. There are no restrictions to the information thus publicly communicated other than the notion which the persons concerned have of their own responsibility. More explicitly, few items of information in this area of the ministerial 'residual field' are considered secret.

> The administration acts in practically the same way except for the slight – sometimes very slight – adjustments due to its both taking into account the limits of its powers in this matter, according to whether they are attributed or delegated, and going beyond those powers, though not without a certain caution influenced by the medium of deterrent force which Regulation 13, quoted above, contains.

Internal or Working Documents

As these documents are not specially provided for in any general regulations, their position can only be decided by referring to ordinary law as applied to administrative information. Making use of the powers which belong to them in their 'residual field of information', the ministers freely determine whether it is advisable or not to publish or communicate on request the documentation, results of surveys, research, inquiries, consultations, experts' and other reports, notes, opinions, projects, etc., which are the normal and plentiful instruments and products of their departments and administrative units. Administrative documents of this kind, however, are not usually intended for publication or for communication outside the competent services. In any case, this principle is borne out by the facts without there being any question of any violation whatever of the freedom of information. Like any other persons, public authorities and their officials are entitled to a degree of independence in the performance of their duties, whether professional or 'quasi-professional'. The latter word has been coined with the terms of office of ministers and other political-administrative authorities in mind.

It would be unthinkable that, as part of the normal right to perform their duties, the public authorities should not have the means and actual possibility of thinking, inquiring and deciding without being constantly pestered for information. In any case, the Belgian authorities and public servants in the wider sense cannot be suspected of systematically hiding their cards and of concealing their files from the legitimate curiosity of the electors and the public. The remarks further on about the recipients of information and the transmission of information will provide suitable opportunities for showing that this statement is well founded. But, at all events, as pointed out in the paragraph which follows, administrative documents must be lodged with the General Archives of the Kingdom, i.e. the Record Office, when they have no further administrative use, and may be inspected when they are fifty years old.

The Secrecy of Records

There are two categories of document. The first is documents over one hundred years old, which the departments and agencies concerned must deposit in the archives. Article 3 of an Act passed in 1955 declares that they are public.[5] More often than not, however, access to such information is only of interest to historians. The other category comprises documents less than one hundred years old that are no longer of any administrative use and whose deposit in the archives may be requested by the public authorities holding them. As the Act does not refer to access to these documents, one should infer that they may only be inspected if the ministers responsible for the keeping of the records consider it expedient. They have done so by deciding that the documents may be inspected when fifty years old. The reason for the delay is supposed to be that records have to be listed, classified, studied and so on, which takes a long time. As this has given rise to a good many complaints, especially by writers on modern history, the competent authorities are thinking of reducing the period to thirty years.

In this connection, it is worth noting that Belgian ministers consider that they ought to keep certain documents secret. These are the fairly recent instruments and evidence of their management. Being empowered to do so by the Act, they therefore have them kept in the ministries beyond the period of their administrative usefulness instead of depositing them in the archives; or else, if they are deposited, they can forbid their inspection.

One of the reasons put forward to justify that attitude is to avoid rekindling certain political quarrels which the authorities had only too much trouble in smoothing over or solving at the time. Certain files and cases ought allegedly to be allowed to fall into oblivion or at least be toned down by the passage of time. The reasoning is therefore of a political nature and the Belgian authorities' practice in this field sufficiently proves, in our opinion, that they think that their residual powers, when there is no statutory or regulatory obligation, entitle them to decide whether they should publish or communicate administrative information or keep it secret. This behaviour on the part of our rulers fully confirms, as might have been expected, that they do not feel bound by a principle of administrative secrecy which only affects their agents, state officials, and the like.

Defence and National Security
The relevant legislation is, first, the Penal Code, Articles 116, 118, and following, which deal with a series of offences against the rule of secrecy adopted for national defence or security, involving the disclosure of information or documents to or for an enemy, a foreign power or any unauthorised person. The penalties laid down are heavier when the person convicted holds a public office.[6] Articles 120 and following of the Penal Code deal with a long series of other cases related to military secrets and the security of the state. The provisions cannot all be mentioned here, but they chiefly deal with offences such as receiving secrets, obtaining them by certain means, including disguise, telecommunication and house-breaking, and subsequently disseminating them, for instance by sale, distribution or publication. The offences are described with a remarkable attention to detail, which is necessary and apparently effective.

Second, the Act of 4 August 1955 concerning national security in the field of nuclear energy (*Moniteur Belge*, 19 August 1955) authorises the Head of State to take measures about the research carried out and the nuclear materials and methods of production used by the establishments and legal or natural persons who have information, documents, or materials at their disposal that have been obtained directly from the Government or through its intervention. These security measures apply to the installation, protection, and preservation of the places, documents and materials, and to the determination of the conditions to be fulfilled for entering the premises assigned to the work and research referred to by the Act or for carrying on any activity there.

Third, there is the Royal Order of 14 March 1956 for the implementation of the above Act. Among other things, it organises the classification of information and other materials that call for security measures as 'top secret', 'secret' or 'confidential', and their keeping in suitable premises, cabinets, safes, etc.[7]

Fourth, the Act of 10 January 1955 relating to the disclosure and utilisation of inventions and manufacturing secrets affecting defence or national security forbids, under penalties which it prescribes without prejudice to those provided for by the Penal Code, any disclosure of manufacturing secrets and inventions, contrary to the interests of national defence or security.

The Protection of Personal Secrecy

This refers to secrecy concerning letters and telegraph and telephone communications; personal means and income, etc.; personal information in the statistics prepared by the state; and particulars held, for instance, in the communal registers of inhabitants and in the national register. In spite of the amount of legislation concerning the protection of these 'personal' secrets, they are merely mentioned here because, obviously, breaking open sealed envelopes entrusted to the post office, tapping telephone calls, or perusing statistics containing data concerning given legal or natural persons will hardly enable the public to obtain, from the public services, the desired 'political' and 'administrative' information to which it is entitled.

Letters and Telegraph and Telephone Communications

Only the 'secrecy of letters' has the honour of being mentioned in the Constitution, in Article 22. The Penal Code and various statutes effectively protect the secrecy of sealed envelopes entrusted to the post office, as also the latter's more modern forms of service: telegraph and telephone communications. The contents of letters, telegrams, or telephone messages which are held or circulate in administrative services come under the system of protection of professional secrecy (Penal Code, Article 458) to which is added, if necessary, the duty of discretion incumbent on state officials, Article 9 of whose Regulations refers to 'secrecy by nature'.

Information on Means, Income, etc.

The specific protection of secrets of this kind is provided in Belgium by the Income Tax Code, Article 244 and following, which makes various articles of the Penal Code enforceable, including Article 458 which establishes professional secrecy. Under these provisions, secrecy concerning income tax returns is incumbent on public servants, process-servers, solicitors, and any other persons involved in the application of the tax legislation. Secrecy is ensured either by keeping the information confidential within the administration or by the prohibition of any disclosure. The taxpayers' incomes are therefore preserved from the curiosity of the press, the Conseil d'Etat and other bodies. This even includes Members of Parliament unless a parliamentary inquiry is instituted, the state counsel's office (*Parquet*), and, except in the event of a flagrant offence or of denunciation by the administration, the criminal police. But it does not include the express orders or requisitions of examining magistrates and of authorities vested with the same examining powers as theirs.

It should be noted that, in the Belgian public service, the personnel, pay or other offices holding personal particulars concerning, for instance, remuneration, domicile and marital status, generally receive instructions concerning the publicity or secrecy to be observed, particularly when dealing with particular persons such as the wives or children of the public servants concerned.

The Secrecy of Statistics

Like the other forms of personal secrecy, this does not require much attention here, since it only covers the identity of citizens when a census is taken. That is why the statistics are anonymous; should the circumstances and methods of the investigation nevertheless make the identity apparent, i.e., if given persons can be recognised owing to the small number of informants, secrecy is in any case ensured by three safeguards due to the census officials coming under article 458 of the Penal Code, article 9 of the Regulations, and article 18 of the Statistics Act of 4 July 1962. Moreover, when the government is able to use the results of surveys for issuing regulations, it is expressly provided that the particulars obtained may not be communicated to the taxation authorities.

REGISTERS OF BIRTHS, MARRIAGES AND DEATHS

In the above three fields special provisions determine which particulars are divulged to whom and which are secret. Since 1969, the theoretical publicity of birth, marriages, divorces and deaths has been restricted in order better to protect personal privacy and to ensure the 'peace of families'. Specified authorities, as also persons who produce evidence of a family, scientific or other legitimate interest, may obtain copies of the certificates. Abridged certificates may be issued to any applicant, without mentioning the relationship of the persons to whom they refer.[8]

The Belgian national register, chiefly intended to centralise and redistribute the data, e.g. condition, addresses, occupations and qualifications of natural and legal persons, has so far only formed the subject of a government bill. According to the bill, access to the particulars registered would be withheld from any person not expressly entitled to it. The persons registered would be able to verify the entries concerning them, and public services and third parties would be able to obtain data under the conditions laid down by the statute or its implementing regulations.

THE HOLDERS OF INFORMATION

As there are no official provisions which stipulate how political executives should use their residuary power in the field of information, this point is hardly applicable to Belgium. Public access to the information held by political executives and by their administrative assistants, as also to their proceedings, reports and other documents concerning policy-making, is dealt with below. Further details about the holders of information are found in other parts of this chapter, including what has already been stated about the information issued by the public authorities.

THE RECIPIENTS OF INFORMATION

GENERAL ACCESS

This refers to data which the persons concerned may obtain on request. There are three main groups of such persons: the public, or legal and natural private persons; professional journalists, film operators, and other representatives of information media; and public institutions including public servants, dealt with further on under 'Access by particular Bodies and Groups'. The requirements and means of access to information of each group differ so much that we shall deal with them separately.

The means of access to information on request vary considerably. First, for private persons, they include petitions, requests and applications for unpublished information. These are addressed to every level of public authority, in accordance with articles 21 and 43 of the Constitution.[9] These means of access are well known to be widely used, and private persons have become so accustomed to making inquiries of members of Parliament, ministers, burgomasters, etc., and their services that it would be no exaggeration to speak of congestion. It is equally well known that the authorities and persons approached try to satisfy their correspondents or visitors. The vast number of interviews granted and the enormous increase in outward mail are evidence of this. State officials even tend to display great generosity and openness in their written – and still more in their verbal – exchanges with the outside, though they cannot be said to be seriously lacking in discretion. The causes and conditions of the process would have to be very closely studied before a final opinion could be expressed on the subject. This again shows that spontaneous disclosure on request, on one hand, and secrecy, on the other, can neither be separated nor studied in isolation. Unless care is taken to avoid doing so, the aggregate of the facts considered would be inaccurately interpreted. In legal matters, access to the documents is ensured by what are known as the rights of the defence, and a generally effective role is played by certain proceedings being void if the required formalities are not complied with.

Secondly, as regards the representatives of information media, such as professional journalists and radio and television newsmen, it has been stressed above that the press should, when carrying out its duty of democratic control, be looked upon as a valuable as well as legitimate helper of the information-seeker. That role is recognised by the authorities, and journalists are therefore normally allowed to apply to political circles and to the administration to obtain the fullest possible information. The word 'possible' has to be specified because the reasons why the authorities and the administration may or must withold certain information are well known.

When faced with justified or unjustified reticence or resolute silence, the press in Belgium makes a strong onslaught on the political-administrative stronghold with the help of all the most up-to-date scientific and technical means, even those used for military, scientific or industrial espionage. The contest between the administration and the press is then all the keener in that the journalists entertain a more intensive spirit of competition amongst themselves than that which prevails in commercial circles. The scoop is essential to the journalist, and its quest arouses his inventive genius and a truly uncommon perseverance. It should also be remembered that the information divulged by certain public servants and even their accusations, whether anonymous or not, supplement the press harvest of news. The question of the protection of journalists' sources of information thus arises.

In Belgium, journalists are considered to be neither referred to nor covered by article 458 of the Penal Code. This interpretation is reasonable as regards the obligation of secrecy, which could hardly be a condition of working for a news medium! It is much less so as regards the right of secrecy towards the administration of justice and, more particularly, divulging the sources of the information collected. In other words journalists may not, at law, claim professional secrecy for refusing to reveal their informants when a given case or fact forms the subject-matter of legal proceedings. In practice, however, the judicial machinery does not exercise over-much pressure, though this could go as far as conviction for contempt of court.

For the time being at least, this state of affairs is beneficial for political and administrative news, since the unlawful informants of the press know that they run no risk of being betrayed by their clients and are not scared into withholding information or even documents. But it is doubtful whether any legal solution that might be found for protecting press sources would ever include the supplying of information obtained through an offence against the law.

It should also be mentioned under this heading that the Act of 30 December 1963, by which the title of professional journalist is officially recognised and protected has strengthened the registered press, since the holders of a professional journalist card are now as a rule able to carry on their work without being obstructed, and under conditions of prestige in keeping with the importance of the press as an agent of democratic control.

ACCESS BY PARTICULAR BODIES AND GROUPS

Access by Parliament

Parliament has recourse to requests for information from the ministers, to interpellations at public sittings, to 'parliamentary' questions (cf. *Bulletin des Questions et Réponses*), to all the sources of information provided by the work of parliamentary committees and, when Parliament's attitude is more in the nature of control than information, to the parliamentary investigations which each House has the right to conduct under article 40 of the Constitution. Though volumes have been written about this, much seems to remain to be said and written as a prelude to likely reforms, since Parliament is complaining more than ever that the executive and the administration do not enable it normally to carry out its constitutional duty. The recent revival of select committees is also very significant in that respect. The research and studies to be conducted would, in any case, have to beware of appearances. Though the channels which connect Parliament with the personal offices and services of the ministers have a large flow, it remains to be ascertained whether they convey a sufficient wealth of sensible questions and of complete and sincere answers. To inform the citizen, Parliament must first be duly informed by the executive.

The Executive vis-à-vis Parliament

The executive has less difficulties in being informed, owing to its contacts with the deputies and senators through the work of the parliamentary committees. Moreover, Parliament's publications provide it with a very full and fairly reliable basis of written information. The Constitution has ensured, in article 88, that the ministers are entitled to be received in Parliament and be heard there when they so request.

Communications between the Ministers and their Departments
This type of communication also requires study because it determines whether Parliament, the press, and the public are properly informed. Such communications are innumerable, but their quality, expediency and regularity should be looked into. The bureaucracy has been taken to task, often unfairly, on countless occasions. For our part we think that a real, constant and consequently serious shortcoming is the total or partial ignorance of many public servants as to what is done, said, and, above all, decided 'higher up'. For various reasons which are more often than not political, but also through more or less conscious and tolerated defective organisation, the supervisors on the various levels have to run their services and attend meetings without having the most recent information from the top. This refers more particularly to the difficulty of being informed in good time of the decisions taken in the Council of Ministers or in the smaller interdepartmental committees. There of course remains the eternal, because probably insoluble, problem of the communications between the ministers' personal offices and the departments. That is where, in our opinion, the real crux of the problem of information and secrecy in public administration may be found. The nerve centre of our political-administrative community is today situated not in parliament but in the Government, at the summit of the real executive, on the level of the ministers and their personal offices. The latter are forums where the parties, the trade unions and other pressure groups – of which the least often mentioned and yet most influential is 'high finance' – meet to differ, discuss and decide. Everything depends on these political-administrative brains trusts to which the principal responsibilities have to be referred, whether it is a matter of deciding what should be released or of ensuring that certain news items should be kept secret.

Access through the Courts or an Ombudsman
So far, Belgium has not considered that any institution along the lines of an Ombudsman ought to be set up. Private members' Bills to that effect have been brought in, but nearly ten years have already elapsed without the first of them having yet been voted upon. In our opinion, public opinion is not pressing for an innovation of this kind because the present organisation of information is generally satisfactory to those concerned and, in any case, the kinds of defect observed would not be eliminated by an Ombudsman. Similarly, it

has not been thought advisable to give the courts any special powers of access to information in dealing with the public services on behalf of the citizen. The latter sometimes indirectly obtains particulars from the administration when, in his legal relations with it, he decides to appeal to the ordinary or the administrative courts, from which the administrative authorities may not withhold any data required for the solution of cases.

Access Reserved to Scholars
This matter is not governed by any provisions which either make access easier for scholars or exempt them from the systems of secrecy in force. Like any other inquirers, they must apply to the authorities or their agents, and the holders of information decide how to deal with the requests. In practice, Belgian scholars are not victimised when they seek information held by the public authorities. In addition to administrative secrecy being more theoretical than real, though without any scandals being created, both on the level of the authorities and of their officials, there are in the administration many public servants who conduct scientific research, often concurrently with teaching. They are able, quite ethically, to supply their outside colleagues with an abundance of useful news and documents.

RESTRICTIONS ON USE BY RECIPIENTS OF INFORMATION

In this respect, the participation of private persons in administrative action raises a difficulty that is worthy of attention. Some of them come under the same system of secrecy as public servants while others do not, such as the board members of certain public institutions who are appointed in a personal capacity or as representatives of interest groups. Since they are not bound by the duty of discretion, they can ventilate everything they know about the life of the institution they help to manage. This is obviously absurd, and is the source of fairly frequent leakages which occur and for which people tend, indiscriminately, to blame civil servants in general.

INFORMATION PROCEDURES

THE HOLDING OF INFORMATION

There are no specifically Belgian problems in this field. More particularly, the computer's threats to the independence and privacy of persons have been discerned as they have elsewhere. Likewise, measures have been adopted to parry those threats. (They have been described earlier on.) A private member's Bill was introduced in the House of Representatives on 24 April 1973 with a view to the establishment of a national commission for the co-ordination and control of informatics. Another such Bill, introduced in the Senate on 26 January 1972, concerning the protection of privacy and personality would provide punishment for 'any person who, except in the cases specifically authorised by the King, wittingly removes or causes or allows particulars relating to the privacy and personality of a person to be removed from the file of a data bank, a computer, or any machine based on cybernetics, informatics, or any other techniques'. As on 6 May 1975, neither Bill had been proceeded with.

THE TRANSMISSION OF INFORMATION

Belgium has no remarkable features from this point of view. Like everywhere else, many rules of procedure lay down the conditions governing questions and answers in the field of information. They cover the time allowed, whether oral or written (e.g., registered letter, official notification by law), contents of communications, cost (e.g., stamp duty, tax, fee), original and/or copies, number of copies, and legal form of communication (e.g., sale, loan, inspection).

It should be emphasised that the members of the Belgian press, in the wider sense, are no less eager and tenacious than their colleagues abroad in their pursuit of political and administrative information. Without worrying about any nice distinctions as to whether the time is suitable for requesting and obtaining news, they harass all the possible holders of information at every moment before and after, but also during, decision-making. Again, this pestering is not peculiar to Belgium which, so far, has invented no way of trying to stop it. The politicians and public administrators are, however, no less proficient than those of other countries in eluding ill-timed, indiscreet, and inquisitorial questions without being betrayed into a silence that would arouse the anger of the press and of public opinion.

CLASSIFICATION AND DECLASSIFICATION

The Act concerning national security in the field of nuclear energy offers an example of the detailed classification of documents into the top secret, secret and confidential categories. A classification of this kind and the control required for its efficient use have not been instituted as a general and fundamental system in the Belgian administration. The reason seems to be that the strict and complex system which has stood the test in the field of nuclear energy cannot be organised on such a large scale.

The declassification applied to ordinary administrative documents as a result of their transfer to the archives has already been dealt with.

THE REFUSAL AND RELEASE OF INFORMATION

The silence of the administrative authority can only give rise to proceedings before the Council or State if the authority has a duty to deal with or to decide a matter. Since refusal to give information does not fulfil that condition, any inquirer whose rights may be encroached upon has no remedy other than to claim damages under article 1382 of the Civil Code, if he can prove that the state is at fault. The same remedy is available if he has been given an inaccurate reply by the administration. But the success of either type of appeal is obviously very uncertain. In the event of premature release or of mistaken information being communicated, public authorities and servants may be punished according to the status and degree of responsibility of the persons involved. The sanction will be political in the case of a minister and disciplinary in the case of an official.

CONCLUSION

The openness-secrecy dichotomy in politics, which originates from the vital and contradictory needs of protection through secrecy and of openness, including publicity, towards the community has given rise in Belgium to a legal system of ably and carefully measured compromise which is, in short, typically Belgian.

An unwritten, but unquestionable, principle of openness, has been supplemented by a series of secrecy regulations in such fields as national defence and security, the administration of justice, and the protection of privacy, which even the countries considered to be most liberal in the matter are unable to escape. The administration, in the narrow sense of public servants in general, is admittedly bound to secrecy. But the obligation is only a reasonable and necessary one placed on subordinates, and the competent and responsible authorities have a duty to satisfy any legitimate request for information. The entire Belgian political system is based on the supremacy of the people. That would be meaningless if the 'sovereign people' were not provided with the necessary means for obtaining information. The foregoing report shows that such means have been organised on every level of the political machinery. A detailed study of the actual position would show that, in Belgium, the reason why there is no general movement of protest against the secrecy of the political leaders and of their administrative assistants is that, in the vast majority of cases, information legitimately requested is supplied. Other information is withheld on behalf of the general interest, not to mention the right of officials, as persons, to think and work under the protection of a modicum of independence, with dignity and responsibility.

This, in our opinion, explains how the Belgian system of publicity of information differs from the Swedish system of publicity of documents. In theory, the Swedish system is more reliable for the information-seeker, since he can himself examine a document. But the question will always be whether the documents established reflect the truth, the whole truth, and nothing but the truth. To go further into this comparison of the Belgian and Swedish systems would be to intrude on the editor's task and would obviously take up too much space. We cannot, however, refrain from suggesting that anyone interested ought to read, in addition to the essay on Sweden in this volume, the article on the subject by Professor Nils Herlitz (see note 3).These surveys have led us to believe that if, among other things, the many exceptions attached to the principle of publicity, the controversies raised by the interpretation of both the principle and its exceptions, and the adjustments to theory made necessary by practice in Sweden are taken into account, the actual positions of that country and our own are really very similar.

NOTES

1. Cf. O. Orban, *Le droit constitutionnel de la Belgique* (Liége-Paris: 1906), 118, No. 72, referring to the spirit of the National Congress of 1830:

The political programme of the Congress may be summed up briefly as: freedom in all things and for all, placed beyond the assaults of Power by strong safeguards . . . Moreover, as a rule of practical interpretation, the need must be recognised, in any controversy involving the rights of the authority and those of freedom, always to decide in favour of the latter and against Power.

2. Cf. P. Wigny, *Droit constitutionnel* (Brussels: Bruylant, 1952), 345–6:

The newspapers keep public opinion on the alert and immediately denounce any arbitrary intrusion of the authorities in the field of the individuals' freedoms and immunities . . . The free press criticises governmental management . . . The freedom of the press is therefore the most valuable of all.

3. 'Publicity of Official Documents in Sweden', *Public Law* (spring 1958), 50–9.
4. 'Some Essential Characteristics of an Effective Public Record Law: Sweden and the United States', *Administrative Law Review* 25, 3 (1973), 330.
5. See Act of 26 June 1955 published in the *Moniteur Belge* of 12 August 1955, and Royal Order of 12 December 1957 in the *Moniteur Belge* of 20 December 1957.
6. The Penal Code, book II, concerning Infractions and their Punishment, in particular, title I, Crimes and Offences against Public Security, contains a series of provisions which are so important for this study that they are worth quoting in full here, in spite of their length:

Article 116. Any person who wittingly delivers or communicates, in whole or in part, in the original or a reproduction thereof, to an enemy power or to any person acting in the interest of an enemy power, any things, plans, written or other documents, or information whose secrecy from the enemy affects national defence or security shall be punished by death.

The use of 'any person' (*quiconque*) shows that the secrecy is of general application to the authorities as well as their agents and/or other persons. But article 118, summarised below, punishes the holders of public office more heavily.

Article 118. 1. [Same wording as article 116, except that the words 'enemy power' are replaced by 'foreign power' and 'death' by 'ten to fifteen years' imprisonment'.]

2. Should the convicted person be vested with a commission or public office or be performing a duty or carrying out an assignment entrusted to him by the government, he shall be punished by imprisonment with labour.

In paragraph 2, the care taken by the legislature, in defining all the persons to whom the punishments provided may apply, to include persons entrusted with work by the government, is noteworthy.

Article 119. Any person who wittingly delivers or communicates, in whole or in part, in the original or a reproduction, any objects, plans, written or other documents or information referred to in article 118 to any person unqualified to take delivery or obtain knowledge thereof shall be punished by from six months to five years' imprisonment and a fine of from 500 to 5000 francs.

Any person who, without the authorisation of the competent authority, reproduces, publishes, or divulges, in whole or in part, in any way whatever, any things, plans, written or other documents, or information referred to in article 118 shall be punished by the same penalties.

Criminal lawyers are meticulous jurists and administrators, and the way in which the statement is qualified should again be observed.

7. The Act of 4 August 1955 and the Royal Order of 14 March 1956 concerning the security of the state in the field of nuclear energy (*Moniteur Belge* of 19 August 1955 and 17 March 1956, respectively).

These texts are specially interesting because they irrefutably prove that, to ensure absolute secrecy, the necessary precautions are as numerous as they are strict and precise. The purpose cannot be achieved by half-measures adopted to apply vague and diffident principles that seem to be aware of their own futility, as is the case, among others, of articles 9 and 13 of the State Officials (Regulations) Act.

The Act of 4 August 1955, mentioned above, may be summarised as follows. Article 1: the King may, for the sake of national defence and security, subject the following to any security measures he may specify: (1) research; (2) materials; and (3) methods of nuclear production followed or utilised by the establishments and legal or natural persons who have at their disposal any information, documents or materials they have obtained either directly from the government or with its authorisation.

The purposes of such security measures are: (1) the installation, protection and supervision of all and any premises assigned to such research or other work; (2) the care of documents or materials; (3) and the determination of the conditions required to be allowed to carry on an activity or to enter the premises in question.

Articles 2 to 5 of the same Act organise the system of sanctions by referring more particularly to the above-mentioned articles of the Penal Code concerning secrecy in connection with national defence and security.

The Royal Order of 14 March 1956 (*a*) states which authorities are entrusted, under the responsibility of the Ministers of Foreign Affairs and of Justice, with the enforcement of the security measures. They are the Director of Nuclear Security and the Security Officer who assists him. They superintend the officials, one of whom in each establishment is responsible for ensuring compliance with the legislation and regulations.

It also (*b*) implements the security measures outlined by the Act, as follows:

1. Information and materials calling for security measures are classified according to whether they are 'top secret', or 'confidential'.

2. Such classified information or materials may only be communicated or transmitted, subject to the authorisation of the authorities, to the qualified persons who belong to the agency in question or exercise their activity in co-operation with those persons.

3. A strict system of identification, classification and circulation of the documents and materials has been devised so as to ensure their constant supervision.

4. The materials and documents are kept in appropriate premises, safes, cabinets, etc.

5. *Article 13.* Except when they are actually in use, top secret or secret documents must be locked up in safes having secret combinations. Those that are confidential must be kept in strong files or cabinets provided with a safety lock.

Article 14. Top secret documents may only be sent by special messenger. Secret or confidential documents may be posted as registered letters.

Article 15. Top secret or secret documents may only be kept or used in places protected by a security system established in accordance with the instructions of the Director of Nuclear Security, in such a way as to prevent access by unauthorised persons.

6. The land and buildings assigned to protected research or production shall be appropriately guarded so that only the persons who fulfil the conditions laid down by the regulations issued for that purpose may have access to them.

7. The said regulations apply to any persons who may be called upon to be in possession of classified documents or materials, to to carry on any activity in the premises where such documents or materials are held, and to obtain knowledge concerning information in respect of such documents or materials.

Some of the qualifications laid down for such persons are as might be expected expected—Belgian nationality (with special exceptions), enjoyment of civil and political rights, and exemplary conduct. Others are exceptional, namely physio-psychological qualities, no anti-Belgian activities, and no membership of anti-Belgian groups.

Persons concerned are allowed entry on the decision of the Director of Nuclear Security, after inquiries by the Security Officer and signing a declaration of compliance with secrecy.

8. See Michel Herbiet, 'Le secret dans l'Administration', Belgian report presented to the Capitant Session, Beirut (May 1954).

9. The Constitution of Belgium:

Article 21. Every person has the right to address petitions signed by one or more persons to the public authorities.

The constituted authorities alone have the right to address collective petitions.

It may be noted that the communes fairly frequently make use of the petitions mentioned in the second sentence of this article.

Article 43. It is forbidden to present petitions to the Houses personally. Each House has the right to refer the petitions addressed to it to the ministers. The ministers must provide explanations regarding their contents whenever the House so requires.

6 France

J. C. BOULARD

Apart from the cases specified by statute or case law or by regulations, the French administration is at present under no obligation to release any documents in its possession to outside persons. Non-disclosure is the rule and release the exception. A distinction should, however, be made between purely informative documents and those with legal implications, which are normally public. Legislation and regulations are not applicable until they have been published. Likewise, persons must be notified of decisions affecting them. The principle of information also applies to the texts which organise legal relations between persons. As to non-legal documents, the prevailing principle of non-disclosure stems from the traditions of an administration which is convinced that secrecy is essential not only to its comfort but also to its effectiveness. Its authority is asserted by keeping its distance from the citizen. A change of attitude towards information nevertheless seems to have been taking shape in recent years, since Governments have made frequent statements about the need for getting rid of the craze for secrecy.

In practice, the amount of information issued by the administration certainly goes far beyond its mere obligations. Though the legal position may therefore readily be stated, it is more difficult to assess the facts. It is not easy to draw the lines between a secret area established by positive law, a confidential field that varies with the practice by which it is defined, and the province of public information. Besides, the boundaries appear to shift and vary in time and space. What was secret yesterday may today be only confidential and a newspaper headline tomorrow. Hence, the unstable and changeable nature of the question cannot be overemphasised.

It would also be a mistake to view the subject of access as if an administration withholding information were opposed to a public constantly eager to obtain it. In fact, certain groups are not at all keen for the administration to publish the information it holds. A conspiracy of silence often arises between the administration and those who would prefer their position to be kept comparatively quiet. The tensions which develop along the borders of secrecy reflect differences of interest between groups as well as between the administration and the groups.

In the absence of general provisions recognising the citizen's right of access to administrative information, it seems desirable in the case of France to deal first with the general rule, which is that of secrecy, and afterwards with openness, which is the exception.

SECRECY AS THE RULE

When the law as applied to secrecy in public administration is discussed, two principles, professional secrecy and professional discretion, which have different foundations and purposes, are often confused. The former is not peculiar to the administration but is essential in the citizen's interest, while the latter is specific to public law and is essential in the state's interest.

SECRECY IN THE CITIZEN'S INTEREST

The obligation of professional secrecy incumbent on public servants does not apply to them alone, since it is based on the general provisions of article 378 of the Penal Code by which all public servants and even the public service's occasional helpers are bound whenever they hold any secrets.

According to a Council of State opinion of 6 February 1961, 'particulars of a secret character are those related to facts which are confidential by nature or have been imparted under the seal of secrecy and which the public servants have known because of their functions.' This definition is similar to that given by the ordinary courts, since many judgments of the Criminal Division of the Court of Cassation clearly state that 'article 378 only refers to facts which have come to the knowledge of a person, either in the practice of a profession to whose work the law, in the general interest and for the sake of public order, has imparted confidential character, or in the event of those facts having been confided to him under the seal of secrecy by reason of such a profession' (Correctional Court, Arton, 15 March 1896). The definition therefore refers both to the nature of the information and to how it reached the holder.

Professional, even medical, secrecy is generally waived when dealing with the person actually concerned. This in no way means that interested parties are entitled to access to any document concerning them, but only that disclosure to them is not forbidden. We shall see, further on, under what conditions professional secrecy may be claimed between administrative agencies and before the judiciary. Professional secrecy manifestly applies with regard to natural and legal persons outside the administration, unless they are involved in carrying out a public service.

SECRECY IN THE ADMINISTRATION'S INTEREST

To protect its information, the administration may avail itself of a general statement which covers all its activities and of special provisions concerning national defence. The statement is in the Ordinance (Public Servants' General Regulations) of 4 February 1959, article 10:

> Irrespective of the rules laid down by the Penal Code as to professional secrecy, every public servant is bound by the obligation of professional discretion as regards everything concerning the data and information with which he becomes acquainted during or in connection with the performance of his duties.
>
> Any removal or communication, contrary to regulations, of service papers or documents to outside persons is strictly forbidden. Except in the cases expressly provided for by law, a public servant may only be released either from the obligation of discretion or from the prohibition enacted in the proceeding paragraph with the authorisation of the Minister to whom he is answerable.

Clearly, the field of application of the above Ordinance does not coincide with that of article 378 of the Penal Code. Secret information is not covered on account of its nature, but simply because it is contained in internal documents of the administration. Besides, the borderline may vary, since higher authority may relieve the public servant of the obligation of professional discretion. In practice, a document intended for publication may be protected by that obligation, so long as the authority has not decided to publish it. This is, indeed, a field in which the administrative authority may exercise full discretion in fixing the limits of confidentiality, which have never been defined and vary in extent from one ministry, service, and even official, to another. It is a vague and shifting notion that depends as much on temperament as on the needs of administrative action. Everything is liable to remain secret, just as everything may possibly be divulged.

As to national defence secrets, they are protected by articles 72–8 of the Penal Code, which have no particularly original features. Nevertheless, the existence of nuclear defence makes them delicate to handle, because a deterrent strategy implies openness rather than secrecy.

In short, we find that secrecy is afforded by two systems. One is professional secrecy, which is linked to the nature of certain information, which exists solely in the interest of private persons, and from which there is no exemption except by law. The other is service secrecy, which is linked to the position of the information in the service, exists in the interest of the administration, and varies according to the practices of the ministry concerned.

On the ground that, unless there were some express provision to that effect, the administration was not obliged to disclose the data on which it based its decisions, the supreme administrative court (Council of State, *Gauthier* 12 March 1954, and *Botton* 7 June 1935) has confirmed the citizen's lack of a right to information. There are, however, many exceptions provided for by the legislation, regulations, case law or practice.

EXCEPTIONS TO SECRECY

LEGAL EXCEPTIONS

A full list of the provisions which, in certain fields or for persons in given circumstances, establish a right of access to administrative information obviously cannot be made. We shall simply try to classify them according to their purposes, which may be to protect the administration against temptations, to offset its prerogatives, to strengthen control over it, to give full effect to civic rights, and to facilitate research work.

As to protection of the administration against temptations, secrecy favours frequent injustice and the growth of temptations to institutionalise pressures, whereas publicity better ensures the rectitude of the action taken. In positive law, the desire to protect the administration from itself has already been reflected in the regulation of the contracts of public authorities and in the public service competitive examinations. The contract procedure provides ample scope for publicity since, in the event of competitive bidding or invitation to tender, the specifications or specimen tenders must be disclosed to the public. Likewise, the administration must publish the programmes and registration formalities of its competitive examinations and the conditions under which they are conducted.

The idea of the right to information as a compensation for the administration's prerogatives has also already been included in legislation. A public servant who is liable to punishment thus has the right of access to his file.[1] Similarly, a foreigner under a deportation order is able to be informed of any complaints considered against him. Also, persons affected by expropriation measures are able to have access to the documents relating to the aim in view, the planning of the work, and the summary estimate of expenditure.[2] Furthermore, a taxpayer, should his return be corrected, is entitled to be informed of the grounds on which the administration intends to make any adjustments. Obviously, the purpose of such legislation is to increase the citizen's ability to defend himself against the administration's decision-making power. Moreover, on the basis of that idea and in the spirit of the Constitution, the Council of State has constructed a principle in its case law, that when an administrative decision is in the nature of a punishment and fairly seriously affects an individual's position, the person concerned must have been given an opportunity beforehand to discuss the reasons for the decision (Council of State, *demande veuve Tropier Gravier*, 5 May 1944). But the right to previous information is set aside in the event of a police penalty.

As far as strengthening control over the administration is

concerned, it need not be stressed that there is no effective administration without control and no real control without information. When dealing with an administration which influences every facet of a citizen's life, internal control no longer suffices to regulate what the public services do, while parliamentary control, though it might be reinforced, can only be exercised over major policies. Accordingly, control by the users of a service will increasingly develop. A number of provisions organise the users' systematic information in order to facilitate the exercise in their control. That is why the Legislative Decree of 2 May 1938, article 21, ordered the publication in the *Journal Officiel* of the yearly reports of the Court of Audit. Moreover, under the Decree of 22 February 1971, the Taxation Council prepares a report which is also published in the *Journal Officiel*.

With regard to giving full effect to civic rights, the Declaration of Rights of 1789, article 15, provides that: 'The community has the right to call upon any public officer to account for his administration.' This principle has not yet been put into practice, and might in future serve as a foundation for general legislation concerning administrative information. On the other hand, there are already some provisions in which the right to information has been inferred from status as a citizen. Article 34 of the Municipal Administration Code thus grants any resident or ratepayer 'the right to demand access, without removing them, to a municipal council's minutes and to the municipal accounts and by-laws'. On the local level, the citizen is also entitled to access to a municipal council's working papers, the budgets, the cadastral survey documents, the register of voters, and the lists of socially-aided persons. What the citizen is allowed in his relations with his municipality might be extended to his relations with the state.

As to research work, the French legislature acknowledges that the notion of secrecy varies in time and that after a certain period a document should be accessible to the public for scientific and particularly for academic research purposes. The right of free access to archives was proclaimed by the Decree of 7 Messidor, Year II, whose article 37 states that: 'Any citizen may demand access, on the days and during the hours to be appointed, to the records kept in any repository of archives. He shall have access to them free of charge under appropriate supervision and may not remove them.' Regarding the lapse of time previous to deposit in the archives and hence to release, the Decree of 14 May 1887 laid down a general fifty-year rule, except for personnel files and criminal records, which may only be disclosed one hundred years after the dates on which the persons concerned were, respectively, born or sentenced. The period is even extended to 120 years for civil and military personnel files in the Ministry of Defence.

The above maximum period for documents which do not affect private persons has since been reduced, however. The Decree of 19 November 1970, for instance, opened the archives up to 10 July 1940, cutting down the fifty-year period to thirty years. It also provided that certain categories of documents subsequent to that date might be declared accessible by joint orders of the Ministry of Cultural Affairs and of the ministry concerned. Orders of this kind have already been issued jointly with the Ministries of Justice, Industrial and Scientific Development, the Interior, National Education, Public Health, Agriculture, Veterans, Equipment, and Postal Services.

It should be noted, however, that these orders are not uniform. The orders concerning Justice and National Education refer to 'all printed or mimeographed documents except those marked confidential or secret'. Such documents are not mentioned in the other orders. All the orders prescribe free access to statistical documents, except for those containing confidential information. They also all apply to 'any document intended by nature to be brought to the notice of the public'. It is doubtless unfortunate that there should still be some uncertainty as to the public nature of certain documents. The order concerning the Ministry of Justice also provides for free access to the decisions, deeds of partnership, and memoranda of association placed on record by the commercial courts. As to the Ministry of the Interior, its order makes accessible the minutes of meetings of a public nature and their supporting papers, and the documents prepared in connection with actions about which administrative inquiries have been made. Generally, the rules prescribing periods of non-disclosure may be waived by a joint decision of the Ministry of Cultural Affairs and the minister concerned.

The rules concerning legal deposit should also be mentioned. They are not specially made for the administration but apply to it. Under an Act of 21 June 1943, 'all publications, whether printed or reproduced by any graphical method, which are publicly offered for sale, distribution, or loan or are disposed of for reproduction' must be legally deposited at the National Library. These provisions greatly affect the right of persons to information because a document may be freely consulted as soon as a duty copy is available. A circular of 4 November 1943 of the Head of the Government explains the conditions under which they apply to the administration, and mentions that all the works it issues or publishes, whether for public circulation or only for internal distribution, must be legally deposited. But the obligation does not apply to service instructions. In any case, the National Library's practice in dealing with internal administrative documents is to withhold general documents for ten years and documents involving persons for fifty years.

The rules concerning archives and legal deposit undoubtedly open up two important avenues to information about administrative documents. Admittedly, these rules are not equally well complied with by the various administrative agencies. Besides, documents deposited in the archives and the National Library only reach highly specialised circles.

EXCEPTIONS PROVIDED BY CASE LAW

Decisions in recent cases have tended to relax the principle that there is no unwritten right to information. The idea of linking the right to information with the seeker's status was formulated in a Council of State decision (*Rousselot*, 17 December 1971). In that case, a right not recognised by law to information was derived from membership of a householders' association. The reason stated is particularly clear on this point: 'Householders who have formed an authorised association are entitled on account of their status as members thereof to have full access to the documents which are held by the association, a knowledge of which may be useful to them for exercising their rights in that public establishment.'

The Council of State confirmed this ruling in another case (*Commune de Pointe à Pitre*, 9 November 1973), concerning deputy mayors and municipal councillors. It was considered in the decision that membership of an assembly called upon to discuss the affairs of the commune gave them special responsibilities to which appropriate prerogatives ought to be attached, including the right to be informed about everything connected with the matters within the municipal council's competence, without there being any need for that right to be recognised by written law.

It is still difficult to tell how far this trend will go. The principle might eventually be extended to the relations between the citizen and the state. A citizen's right of investigation with regard to the state would then be acknowledged, since it would be derived from his very status as a citizen.

EXCEPTIONS BASED ON PRACTICE

The individual's possibilities of obtaining information from the public authorities are not fully reflected by the law and the leading cases, since the practice of divulging administrative information has gone far beyond the legal obligations. The extent of this practice is difficult to evaluate exactly, because it varies according to the government in power and from one agency to another. For instance, the reports of major commissions are usually published. So are yearly summaries of the observations made in the course of duty by certain supervisory bodies and inspectorates, such as the General Inspectorate of Social Affairs. Similarly, a Ministry of Finance publication analyses the current Inspectorate of Finance Reports. There really seems to be a growing tendency to inform the public more widely. Increasingly, administrative agencies are providing information services, reception bureau or public relations units. It is still difficult to determine the effect of such measures, but the fact remains that there is a marked tendency to question the discrimination between two classes of citizens – those who sit behind, and those who stand before, a counter.

Beyond the right to information, the question of the right to particulars about the documents and legal provisions published appears to be very definitely arising. As mentioned earlier, the principle applied to all documents with legal implications is that of publicity. If ignorance of the law is no excuse, everyone ought to have means at his disposal to know the law. But since the provisions are complex, scattered and overlapping, their publication in the *Journal Officiel* certainly does not alone suffice to ensure that they are known to everyone.

At present the right to such particulars exists only when expressly provided for (Council of State, *Miara*, 21 July 1950), and it should be made clear that express provision is rather uncommon. One example is the Decree of 26 December 1934 consolidating customs legislation, which provides that customs tariffs must be kept at the public's disposal.[3] Likewise, the Town Planning Code recognises a right to particulars concerning the town planning rules which apply to a plot of land.[4] It appears certain that this right will arise with increasing frequency in addition to the right to information. Secrecy is less often an obstacle to the citizen's exercise of his rights than the difficulty he experiences in having access to the documents, however public, which define his legal circumstances. In practice, moreover, one of the obstacles to the divulging of information is the insufficient stocktaking by the administrative agencies themselves of the materials in their possession. It might even be said that the data available are more often wrapped in oblivion than in secrecy.

THE HOLDERS OF INFORMATION

The distinction suggested in our editor's outline for country studies between administrative authorities and political executives as holders of information is not easy to make as far as France is concerned, since a French minister is both an administrative authority and a political executive. The distinction will nevertheless be made here so that the various national reports may be more easily compared.

CENTRAL ADMINISTRATIVE AUTHORITIES

In principle the public's right to information does not vary according to the ministerial department. But some departments obviously have stronger traditions of secrecy than others. Certainly the Ministry of National Defence has a particularly extensive notion of secrecy.

Differences among the departments are especially evident as regards the collection of information. Certain administrative authorities, such as the National Institute of Statistics, the General Directorate of Taxation or the Social Security Services, play leading parts in the collection of economic and social data. The most frequent requests for information are therefore made to them.

No department or agency has a right to information held by another, since each is bound by professional secrecy as well as professional discretion towards the others. Professional secrecy applies between services and, in extreme cases, even between persons in the same agency. For instance, in a public health centre, a doctor may not divulge medical data to anybody except the centre's other doctors (Council of State, *Crochette*, 11 February 1972). Moreover, the public servants who in the course of duty obtain information covered by professional secrecy are normally also entitled to take cognisance of that information. The obligation of professional discretion – which, as pointed out above, does not cover the citizen's secrets but those of the administration – also applies among services. This was confirmed by the Government Commissioner in his statement on the *demoiselle Faucheux* case (6 March 1953): 'A public servant is bound by professional discretion towards all his colleagues except those who, on account of their official duties, need to take cognisance of the document containing information about the matter being dealt with.' These rules of secrecy which govern relations between services obstruct the flow of information within the administration itself, and form an additional obstacle to its openness toward the public.

LOCAL AUTHORITIES

As already mentioned, a tendency is becoming apparent, both in legislation and court decisions, for obligations to supply information, which are not prescribed for the central authorities, to be imposed on local communities. The tendency is based on a desire to ensure closer control over local authorities by the citizens. Decentralisation, in bringing the administration closer to the citizen, certainly facilitates the establishment of information relationships. It may therefore be maintained that any trend towards greater devolution of powers increases the opportunities for information.

POLITICAL EXECUTIVES

The secrecy which prevails in administrative circles predominates among the political executives. Cabinet proceedings, and also those of interdepartmental committees and commissions, are of a confidential nature. After each Cabinet meeting, a statement is usually made by the Government spokesman and no other information is normally given. Moreover, prime ministers have often had occasion to remind ministers that they should not give the press any details of cabinet discussions other than those in the official statement. The public therefore, as a rule, have no other means of knowing how ministerial decisions are reached. Though the preambles to legislation may be referred to, they are in most cases very short and do not suffice to reveal the full grounds for the action taken by the political authorities. The fact remains that practice is more liberal than theory. Well-restrained indiscretion and well-organised leakage provide important sources of information. They show that reticence can nowadays less and less be maintained, since its chief effect is to favour those able to establish privileged links with administrative circles.

THE RECIPIENTS OF INFORMATION

Under this heading it will be seen that, though there are no legal differences in access to information among particular segments of the public, the same does not apply to certain institutions, viz. Parliament, the Judiciary and the Mediator.

NO DIFFERENCES IN ACCESS

Legally at least, citizens are equally excluded from administrative information. But of course, in practice, certain persons or groups establish relations with the administration which enable them to obtain certain privileges in this respect. It would doubtless be rather delicate to establish legal variations in the rules of confidentiality according to categories of enquirer, since an inequality of access (which would be difficult to justify), would thus be introduced. Moreover, it would not be easy to make sure that information reserved to a segment of the public would not ultimately be more widely divulged. It should, however, be clearly realised that the information relationships between the administration and the public are more often than not indirect. That is why reference should be made now to the special relationships established with certain particular segments of the public, namely journalists, union representatives and scholars.

Journalists

The controversial discussion which arose when the News Delegation was set up in France early in 1974 shows what difficulties are involved in establishing a special reference organisation for journalists. The Delegation was initially defined as an instrument placed at the disposal of all journalists in order 'to provide them at all times with statistical and background documents about current problems and the activities of the various ministries'.

The effective performance of such a task will evidently mean that the practice of secrecy will be largely reduced, at least with regard to journalists. It is doubtless too early to express an opinion about the improvements which the Delegation may have introduced. However, it should be pointed out that, to be successful, the Delegation must remove the journalists' possible fear of being restricted and must avoid coming forward as a compulsory medium for any access to documents. Journalists are anxious to preserve their own right of investigation, so as to get information at its actual source and be able to consult first-hand documents. That being so, the Delegation should not seem to be a screen between the state and the press.

Union Representatives

The full consequences of the fact that employers' and employees' representatives sit on numerous advisory boards and committees ought to be reflected in the field of information. Such representatives should have an extensive right of access to the documents necessary for formulating their opinions. There is also a contradiction, which ought to be removed, between the secrecy that often marks the proceedings of advisory bodies and the idea of representation that implies an obligation of openness when reporting to the persons represented.

Scholars

Scholars are generally allowed facilities of access which the administration most frequently looks upon as favours in return for which adverse criticism should be abstained from or atleast moderated. Failure to observe this unwritten rule is liable quickly to dry up a scholar's sources of information. At present, French research workers and their administrative informants appear to hope that a code of ethics will be drawn up to clarify the relations between the administration and those engaged in its study.

The basic principles of such a code may already be outlined. First, as compensation for the right to criticise, on which the value of research depends, the administration should be entitled to have a reply included in the report concerned. It would, secondly, be normal for the administration, after having supplied information, to be able to see the text before publication so as to correct any mistakes, but without that right involving any claim to exercise censorship. Of course, should scholars be given a more extensive right of access to documentation, they ought to be reminded of the rules of secrecy concerning data whose release might be harmful to private persons or to the general interest. Thirdly, should a policy of greater openness towards research workers prevail, the question of checking their credentials would necessarily arise. The matter might be settled by a system for approving research centres which would not, however, result in the research workers being chosen by the administration.

PARLIAMENT

Though membership of Parliament confers legal rights to information that are much more substantial than those of the public, the Government nevertheless retains a discretionary power over access to documents whose distribution is not expressly prescribed.

Scope of the Legal Rights
In this connection, the rights of all members should be distinguished from the special rights of chairmen and members of parliamentary committees. Many statutes and regulations place the Government under an obligation to provide Parliament with reports, documents and particulars about a great number of subjects.[5] A large and even crushing amount of information is presented to Parliament in pursuance of statutes. The real difficulty is the lack of proportion between the amount of documents and the slender means granted for analysing them. An overwhelming mass of data eventually makes anyone who has inadequate tools for processing them feel even more powerless and uninformed.

The right to obtain information from the Government is further increased when a member is the chairman of a committee on a Bill. In the case of a Government Bill, the sponsoring minister will explain its purpose to the committee, answer questions and supply the chairman with any additional details he may require for drafting his report. This parliamentary procedure enables the chairman to have access to all the sources of information about the

Bill's subject-matter. The onus of using them with discrimination rests with him. Such powers of access to information become an unquestionable entitlement in the case of budget committee chairmen, since their competence is defined as follows in Ordinance No. 58.1374 of 30 December 1958 (Appropriation Bill for 1959). Article 64:

> Members of Parliament who are responsible, on behalf of the Finance Committee, for presenting a report on a ministerial department's budget shall permanently observe and check, against the documents there, the use made of the appropriations voted for that department. Except for matters of a secret nature concerning national defence, foreign affairs and the internal or external security of the State and subject to the principle of the separation of the judicial power from the other powers, they must be supplied with all and any information likely to assist them in their task. They shall be entitled to access to all service documents of any kind whatever.

Similar powers are entrusted to M.P.s appointed to observe and appraise, as part of the work of the Board of Audit for Public Enterprises (*Commission de vérification des comptes des entreprises publiques*), the management of national enterprises and mixed companies. The chairmen of *ad hoc* committees reporting to the Finance Committee or to the Board of Audit also have very wide statutory powers. They make ample use of them and, every year, the parliamentary clerks send the ministers detailed questionnaires on innumerable subjects related to the budget. The amount of accurate and varied information thus collected is considerable.

Discretionary Power to Refuse Access
The Government may still, at its discretion, refuse access to any documents whose communication is not officially provided for. Recent instances have shown that sometimes in practice it does deny M.P.s access to documents considered to be internal to the administration. Nevertheless, for some years it has gone far beyond its formal obligations. In a circular of 31 March 1955 to the heads of ministerial departments, the Prime Minister reminded them of the importance of keeping M.P.s as liberally informed as possible.

By and large, law and practice certainly make Parliament the ideal place for bringing together the information now dispersed in the various ministeries. In theory, except for certain data supplied to chairmen of standing or *ad hoc* committees, the documents issued to M.P.s in pursuance of legislation or regulations thereby assume a public character, however few copies are distributed. That being so, Parliament can obviously play a not inconsiderable part as an information relay from the administration to the public. This may best be illustrated by the system of written questions. From 1968 to 1972, M.P.s asked the various ministries 23,423 written questions and received 20,642 answers. A large amount of information is thus obtained from the ministers. Every kind of subject is dealt with, from the most general matters to individual cases – from, among other things, the choice of the channels for the country's nuclear energy policy to why a schoolmistress was not allowed to sit for a competitive examination. The M.P.'s possible role as an information relay between the citizen and the state depends essentially on the means of information processing that may be placed at his disposal. Much certainly remains to be done in this respect.

THE JUDICIARY

Members of the judiciary have more extensive rights of access to administrative information than have the public. For the sake of clarification, the powers of the ordinary courts should first be examined and then those of the administrative courts.

Ordinary Courts

As a rule professional secrecy may not be claimed before the courts in criminal cases. However, the Court of Cassation has tried, when setting precedents, to find a balance between the duty of secrecy provided for by article 378 of the Penal Code and the duty of disclosure instituted by article 109 of the Code of Penal Procedure. Broadly speaking, the Court's Criminal Division tends to make the obligation to give evidence prevail because a criminal court has a general right of full inquiry (Criminal Division, 5 November 1903). Two exceptions to that obligation are nevertheless allowed when public servants are involved. The first applies to police officers, who are not obliged to disclose their sources of information (Criminal Division, 6 July 1894), a ruling which the Court justifies by the need to protect the police's network of informers. The second concerns hospital administrators, for whom, in the Court's opinion, a patient's right to secrecy prevails over their own obligation to give evidence (Criminal Division, 16 March 1893). Nevertheless, medical secrecy does not prevent an examining magistrate from impounding medical records in a hospital centre (Criminal Division, 24 April 1969). As regards the other professions, the criminal courts, in the public interest, give precedence to the punishment of offenders over the keeping of secrecy.

Administrative Courts
Documents covered by professional secrecy should here be distinguished from those merely subject to the obligation of professional discretion. As to the former, the Council of State does not recognise that it has the right to order the administration to produce documents covered by professional secrecy (*Minister of Equipment and Housing v. Grongeon*, 24 October 1959). Nevertheless, while strictly observing that ruling, it begins, so as to avoid prejudice to any party, by inviting the administration to supply any desirable particulars (*Minister of State v. Coulon*, 11 March 1955), and then dismisses from consideration any data which could not be fully argued on both sides. Regarding data covered only by the obligation of professional discretion, an administrative court will consider itself entitled to access as part of the adversary procedure. Should the administration refuse access to documents or information having served as grounds for the contested decision, it will be assumed to have acted on irregular grounds and will therefore lose the case (*Barel*, 1955 and *Maison Genestal*, 1968).

THE MEDIATOR

Influenced, though only remotely, by the example of the Scandinavian Ombudsman, the French Parliament, on the Government's proposal, instituted the office of Mediator by an Act of 3 January 1973. The Mediator is appointed by a decree of the Council of Ministers, and cases may be referred to him by M.P.s only. He is responsible for examining the complaints of citizens concerning the administration of central and local government, public corporations and any other public services. When a complaint appears justified, he may make any recommendations he considers likely to solve the difficulty and, should the occasion arise, proposals for improving the operation of the agency concerned.

When the Mediator's powers were defined, the question arose of his rights to information in the light of the provisions governing professional secrecy and discretion. Under the Act, a compromise was adopted by which he may ask the responsible minister or the competent authority for access to any files or documents relating to a case into which he is inquiring. They may not be withheld from him on account of their secret or confidential nature, except in the event of secrecy concerning national defence, the security of the state or external policy. To ensure professional secrecy, the Mediator must take care that the documents published under his authority contain no clues to the identity of any persons whose names have thus been disclosed to him.

Since the Mediator may be refused access to defence, security and external policy secrets, the Act has obviously much curtailed his powers of investigation. The institution has been too recently established and practice too limited for any proper appraisal of his role in the development of information relationships between the administration and the citizen. Whatever the doubts about the effectiveness of such an institution, one cannot deny that it may lead to greater openness on the part of the administration.

INFORMATION PROCEDURES

HOLDING OF INFORMATION

Among the ways in which information is held, the conventional methods should be distinguished from the new information-processing systems.

Conventional Methods

It has long been maintained that the dispersal of data among different administrative units is one of the obstacles to ready public access to information. Though the criticism is partly justified, it should not lead to an unrealistic attempt to pool the information, but to the establishment of a proper information network.

Short of acting against each agency's desire to keep its own sources of information, the methods so far devised for pooling information can only be used within very precise limits. It is really only as regards archives that a degree of concentration of documentation has been effected in France. Even in that field and although the systematic transfer to the national archives of any documents which become accessible to the public is officially provided for, the various ministries have had to be allowed to develop their own records services. Admittedly, the system of attaching an archivist to a ministry has the great advantage of enabling its divisions better to classify and index their documents without having to part with them. Rather than to attempt to form collections which, except in specialised fields, may be doomed to failure, it appears far better to construct a genuine information network on the basis of the existing materials. For the purpose, each ministerial department ought to be responsible for periodically preparing a descriptive list, suitable for circulation to the other departments, of available documents. Finally, until administrative authorities have better examined and indexed the information at their disposal, only limited progress can be made on public access.

New Methods
The holding of information by means of computer-based files poses a number of new problems. At the collection stage, data processing provides possibilities of almost unlimited storage and preservation while, owing to its cost, implying a measure of data concentration. At the processing stage, it makes possible the simultaneous combination and knowledge of data concerning a given person. It is thus one of the best media for cross-checking. Moreover, at the utilisation stage, the fact that the points of access may be in widely decentralised terminals increases the number of potential users of the information stored. In any case, the development of informatics in public administration clearly leads both to decompartmentalisation and to the multi-purpose use of individual data. This places the citizen's right to both secrecy and information in a completely new context and points to the need for considering how the present rules should be adjusted. Changes ought to be made in the procedure for starting files and in their contents and conditions of access.

In France today, a file may be established through a mere order or circular. It is nevertheless significant that, before keeping a file of vehicle drivers under the Act of 24 June 1970, the Government applied to the legislature. But Parliament's intervention in such a matter can only be justified by assuming that, when a file includes personal data, its establishment, contents and conditions of access are connected with the fundamental guarantees granted for the exercise of public freedoms. Such a connection would place them in a field reserved to Parliament by the Constitution.

In so far as the vehicle drivers' file constitutes a precedent, it might be agreed that the establishment of a national personal data bank would have to be submitted to authorisation by Parliament. Though such a procedure is doubtless often liable to be rather laborious, the effort appears to be worth while in this case. The rules concerning the contents of a file ought to cover the nature of the data that may be stored, the erasing of obsolete data and the individual's right to check data concerning him. The freedoms of conscience and expression and the equality of all citizens are principles which appear to prevent the indexing of the political or religious opinions or racial groups of persons mentioned by name. Questions relating to the private lives of individuals should also be forbidden. The subject of medical particulars is more delicate, since a balance has to be struck between respect for medical secrecy and the consideration that medical progress largely depends on better information processing.

Private persons are not merely entitled to secrecy but also to oblivion, a right taken into account in the above Act of 24 June 1970. Subject to a few exceptions, the Act provides that a driver's personal record should not mention any judicial or administrative sanctions more than six years old unless a further offence has since been entered. Besides, under mandatory legal provisions, convictions are erased from the files when an offender is amnestied, pardoned or rehabilitated in his rights. The notion of statutory limitation may be used as an additional guide to the time that should elapse before erasure.

It also appears reasonable to recognise the right of individuals to check the accuracy and relevance of the data filed. The same Act of 1970 makes it possible for a driver to have access to the particulars concerning him and to ask for any corrections to be made. The burden of proving the information's accuracy lies on the official responsible for the file. This arrangement, though important for the protection of public freedoms, reduces the advantages of data processing by compelling the administration to keep manuscript archives as well, so as to be able to produce evidence if challenged.

The most difficult problems, however, arise when information is released. That is when the most thorough legal and technical precautions need to be taken. From the legal point of view, very precise rules about access to information have to be established concerning the release of an entire file as well as some of the data it contains. To deal with these matters, separate regulations are required for each type of file, specifying who may be given which data. This involves examining the rules of secrecy in general, particularly the complex problem of the communication of data among different administrative authorities. It is also desirable to draw up a special code of ethics for all persons engaged in handling the files, since they are not necessarily on the staff of the authority which keeps and deals with the data. For instance, in public services, employees of private firms may often help to operate and maintain the equipment. Considering the special responsibilities of such personnel and the temptations which may come their way, their obligations ought to be clearly stated. At any rate, their professional organisations seem to hope for this. From the technical point of view, moreover, it would be advisable to prescribe the use of computer security systems, which are by now tried and tested. If this is done, provided that good use is made of the techniques of storage protection, automated information processing will enable secret or confidential data to be much more effectively guarded, since it will be more difficult to break open a computerised file than one kept manually.

COMMUNICATION PROCEDURES

Organisational Structure
Communication may be effected either by means of central units specially for that pupose or of units dispersed among the various administrative agencies. In France there are two specialised central agencies, the Interdepartmental Information Centre and the News Delegation.

The Centre (Centre Interministériel de Renseignements Administratifs – CIRA) was started as an experiment as early as 1956 and, in view of its success, was permanently established by Decree No. 59.153 of 7 January 1959, article 2 of which states that its function is 'to ensure liaison between the public and the administrative services. For that purpose, it shall direct its enquirers to the competent official services or provide them by telephone with any information likely to facilitate the carrying out of formalities or making of applications of an administrative nature.' In practice, in nearly all cases the Centre itself supplies the information, either at once or, after enquiry, usually within twenty-four hours. This is so whenever the questions are solely concerned with the application of legislation or regulations and are not very complex. Besides, the Centre has correspondents in the various ministerial departments. Only occasionally does it refer an enquirer to the specialised official in the competent administrative agency, when the problem set is found too complex or technical or calls for legal interpretation.

The distribution of tasks appears fairly satisfactory. It allows the Centre to screen the enquiries as much as possible, so that the administrative agencies receive only those which they alone can answer. The function of thus informing the public about the administration is combined with the reverse function. The Centre, because of many daily contacts with citizens who speak unreservedly since their names will not be mentioned, is in a position to detect the precise responses of public opinion to administrative problems. Hence, it can tell administrative agencies in which respects the need might arise to improve public relations or to simplify formalities.

Though CIRA was originally entrusted with supplying information in taxation matters, the fact became obvious that, in such a vast and difficult field, only specialised units with sizeable means could fully satisfy the needs of the public. Accordingly, a Taxation Information Centre (Centre de Renseignements Fiscaux) was opened in Paris on 27 December 1957, followed by similar centres in the main provincial cities. They are responsible not only for answering questions asked by telephone but also for interviewing visitors – whose names are not taken – and explaining any difficulties which the application of taxation provisions may raise. They may also give simple factual information, such as a scale of charges or what procedure to follow, and may specify which regulations apply to a given, even complex, situation. Such centres, however, are not competent to deal with any questions whose solution involves the study of a particular file held by an administrative agency or which have not been definitely settled in administrative theory. Neither may the information agency consulted adopt any attitude with regard to litigation in progress between taxation authorities and taxpayers. It may, in such an event, only provide enquirers with the details necessary for them to understand their tax position and tell them what legal formalities are prescribed. In any case, so that information obtained by asking leading questions may not be used against the authorities, the centres are not allowed to reply in writing.

The News Delegation (Délégation à l'Information) is a more recent institution set up at the end of 1973 to improve relations between the administration and the press. It is a flexible agency comprising a staff trained in information and communication techniques. They keep sets of documents for each of the principal administrative fields and can thus give journalists the fullest and latest information about the questions of the moment. The Delegation was not welcomed with open arms by the journalists, who feared that its role would limit their scope and that there would be no alternative means of access to administrative documentation. It is obviously too early to say whether their misgivings were justified. So far, however, contrary to the founders' ambitions, the Delegation does not seem to have profoundly altered the forms of communication between the administration and the public by increasing the administration's openness to the essential medium of the press.

Parallel to the trend towards establishing a structure common to all administrative agencies for informing the public, each ministerial department is developing its own system of public relations. In this respect the advisory institutions, which have grown considerably in number during the last few years on the national as well as the local level, are becoming important for transmitting information between the administrative agencies and the social groups. Similarly, committees of users are being attached to the ministries in order to improve the exchange of information between the administration and the citizen.

Scale of Charges
The public's increased rights of access to administrative information clearly raise, with greater urgency, the problem of charging for access. There are two principal reasons for the French administration's various practices in making such charges. The first is to avoid waste by discouraging frivolous requests. The second is to obtain the necessary funds to cover costs for which there are no explicit appropriations and which have become increasingly heavier, particularly owing to the use of information processing such charges, though, offer serious risks. First, the least prosperous applicants may be penalised when efforts may appear necessary to keep all citizens, perhaps above all the least privileged among them,

better informed. In fact, however, the billing rates in public agencies were intended from the start to make the charges reasonable by scaling them. Students and research workers are thus often allowed to have certain processing operations performed at reduced rates. Second, charging for information may have negative effects by discouraging enquiries which it would be much more advisable to encourage.

If the above considerations are taken into account, it seems possible to apply the three following general principles when fixing the rates to be charged: the rates should be heavy enough to induce users to specify and select the enquiries, they should not be an obstacle to the equality of access for the various classes of user, and they should not impede a widespread release of information. These three principles may appear to be contradictory, but this can be overcome by a number of means. In the first place, only certain cost factors ought to be covered, e.g. the cost of the medium, all or a part of the computer time, all or a part of the personnel costs of the distribution, and all or a part of the overhead expenses. Besides, the effect of the users' unequal ability to afford the services can be remedied either by varying the rates according to the class of user or by having a single scale of charges combined with a policy of aid to users. A distinction shoud be made, moreover, between the core of information (for general distribution or being systematically processed), whose distribution is entirely chargeable to the community, and the data that are only available after special processing which justifies the existence of a scale of charges (covering all or a part of the costs of access, both processing and distribution). Finally, there is the special case of trade enquiries, since certain files or studies are of economic value. If so, the charge for supplying them ought to correspond to their commercial value.

Legality and Liability
When the administration is under a written obligation to supply information, its compliance is a condition of the regularity of its action. When a stage of issuing reports or other documents is provided for in a decision-making procedure, failure to observe that stage makes the decision liable, if appealed against, to be declared illegal by the courts. Admittedly, however, their interpretation of the scope of the administration's official obligations to provide information is not very strict. Their attitude may be illustrated by a Council of State decision in an expropriation case

(*Syndicat de défense des intérêts des propriétaires exploitants agricoles de Varennes et Mâcon*, 27 May 1966). Under a Decree of 6 June 1959 regulating the inquiry procedure previous to declarations of public purposes, the administration must submit certain documents to a public inquiry. In the case in point, the transaction was intended to involve the carrying out of construction and other works as well as the purchase of a plot of land. The Council determined that, at the inquiry, the administration needed to produce only the documents specified in connection with the purchase of land, since the works project was not in a sufficiently advanced stage of preparation. Decisions of this kind show that the administration's obligations to supply information are judged according to whether the information is at its convenient disposal.

Since information is a condition of the legality of administrative action, it may also lead to the administration's liability being involved. Though it might cause injury, information given may not, if accurate, lead to the award of compensation (Council of State, *Société A. Carrette*, 3 June 1953). Administrative information only gives rise to liability to the extent to which it is mistaken or incomplete. An error or omission may sometimes be entered in the service record of the official who has supplied the information. This is so, for instance, if he has acted with gross negligence or has deliberately misled the inquirer. More often than not, misinformation would simply appear to be a service-connected fault. It might involve the public authority's liability, but even then is subject to a series of fairly restrictive conditions. The injured partly will only obtain compensation in so far as he can establish that he received sufficiently definite official information, that the injury was directly ascribable to the information and that he in no way acted rashly or negligently.

The first requirement is that the information should be of an official nature, which means both that the administration was bound to provide it and that it was provided by the competent authority. Conversely, the administration is not responsible for information which it has no obligation to release. Only officials who are authorised to inform the persons concerned can involve the liability of the public authorities. The State cannot be held liable for the detrimental consequences of information given unofficially by a public servant who had no authority to deal with the matter in question. The disputed information involves the liability of a public authority only if its purport can be established and if it is sufficiently definite. That is a point of fact which the administrative courts determine in each case according to its nature and whether the information was given orally or in writing. Data or information in the nature of estimate may thus not involve the administration's liability in spite of any errors they may contain (Council of State, *Société du Crédit Industriel*, 18 February 1944). Furthermore, the injury must be a direct result of the erroneous information. The Council of State was accordingly of the opinion that there was no direct relation of cause and effect between a prisoner of war's suicide and the information he had been given about his wife's conduct (*dame veuve Picarle*, 8 July 1955).

Generally speaking, it is certainly inadvisable to be too strict regarding the administration's liability when it issues information. Too wide a view of that liability would obviously have a deterrent effect on the efforts made by the various administrative authorities to provide information.

CONCLUSION

To sum up this rapid survey, it is clearly apparent that great efforts are still required to be made in France to develop the citizen's rights to administrative information. Improvements should be sought in the fields of both law and practice.

Some years ago the Government appointed a Commission for the Co-ordination of Administrative Documentation, whose purposes included an improvement in the keeping and availability of the documents held by the administration. It reported in 1974, and its conclusions very definitely advocate a reversal of the present legal position, so that the right to information would become the rule and secrecy the exception. This was because it appeared to the Commission that the arguments put forward to justify the keeping of administrative secrets, which should always be distinguished from secrets concerning persons, were for the most part flimsy and questionable.

A first series of arguments defending the practice of secrecy is related to concern for effectiveness and independence. The administration points out that the confidential nature of its documents ensures its freedom of decision, that too much information would give rise to pressures which might cause certain projects to be abandoned, and that surprise is often a condition of effectiveness. It may be replied, in the first place, that giving up projected measures under pressure from certain groups detracts less from the state's authority than calling decisions in question after they have been taken. Secondly, surprise will be used less and less as a method of government. The administration of the future will have to act less by surprise than by persuasion. Information is certainly not a neutral asset and plays a part in groups' strategies toward the state. Obviously, too, the development of access to the sources of administrative information would be likely to increase the citizen's scope of control and criticism. Since a liberal state cannot avoid a system of opposition, one may also ask whether it is not to the state's advantage for conflicts to take place on clearer ground between better-informed interest groups early enough to avoid agonising reappraisals or fruitless decisions.

A second series of justification for non-disclosure is connected with safeguarding the independence of informants. It is argued that the public servants or experts consulted would speak with less freedom and independence if they knew that their opinions might be divulged. Conversely, doubts may be expressed as to the significance of an independence of mind or a freedom of speech confined to the four walls of an office. Moreover, an assurance that a statement will not be repeated means that it is more likely to be irresponsible.

While the practice of secrecy is defended on account of the greater freedom of action it allows, the fear that information released might be used to unfair advantage, and concern for preserving initiative, this defence may really reflect misgivings, or even repulsion, towards the increased opportunities for control generated by a policy of openness. It also appears reasonable to question the practice of administrative secrecy because the state puts private persons under increasing obligations to supply information about themselves as well as others – through, for instance, inquiries, opinion pools, questionnaires, statistics or the information which enterprises must give to consumers and shareholders. As the information process is fundamentally one of exchange, the public may, after having been very fully probed and questioned, legitimately demand information in return. In short, it appears only natural that legal persons at public law who are working towards the public interest should do so under control by the public.

NOTES

1. Act of 22 April 1905, art. 65.
2. Decree No. 59.701 of 6 June 1959:

Art. 1: The expropriating authority shall send the Prefect, for submission to the inquiry, a file which must comprise the following: (1) where the declaration of public purposes is requested for the carrying out of construction or other works, a note explaining among other matters the aim in view, the layout plan, the general plan of works, the principal features of the more important construction works, and a summary estimate of expenditure; (2) where the declaration of public purposes is requested for purchasing house property, an explanatory note, the layout plan, an outline of the area to be expropriated, and a summary estimate of the purchases to be made.

3. *Art. 44, para. 2.* In every customs house, the administration must keep all the tariffs for its collection of duties, and also the various laws enacted for their application, so that persons who wish to examine the tariffs and legislation may have access to them. It must, moreover, by notices displayed in every customs house, indicate which clearance formalities traders have to comply with in different cases.

4. *Art. L.410. 1.* According to the reason for the application, the town-planning certificate shall, taking into account the planning provisions and the administrative restrictions on property which will apply to the plot and land concerned and also the position with regard to the existing or contemplated public services, and subject to the application of the zoning statutes and regulations, if any, indicate whether the said plot is intended to be used (*a*) as building land or (*b*) for carrying out a given plan, such as a building scheme which defines a special arrangement of the proposed buildings and their outside floor-space dimensions.

5. The first series of basic provisions appeared in Ordinance No. 59–2, concerning the presentation of Appropriation Bills, of 2 January 1959, article 32. The second series is found in the amended Ordinance of 30 December 1958, where articles 163 and 164 contain lists of documents to be appended to Appropriation Bills. In addition to the obligations to inform Parliament imposed on the Government by these two Ordinances, which already involved a very considerable amount of data, since 1960 many legislative provisions have ordered various reports to be presented. An official list has been made of those adopted since 1960. It reveals that the mass of information which the Government is under a statutory obligation to supply to Parliament is therefore considerable and even overwhelming.

7 United Kingdom

RONALD E. WRAITH

It is particularly necessary in the context of the United Kingdom to distinguish between central and local government, and to emphasise that the latter is a considerable holder of 'administrative information'. Central government departments naturally hold information of greater national importance, affecting among other things the security of the state, foreign affairs and the health of the economy. On the other hand, the public services which most affect the ordinary citizen in his everyday life, including education, environmental health, town and country planning, housing and the social services, are administered by *local* authorities with a significant measure of independence. The relevant point in the context of this chapter is that public access to the information held by central and local authorities is governed by different laws and conventions.

CENTRAL GOVERNMENT

In principle the public have no right of access to administrative information; that is to say, there is no statute in which any such right or principle is enshrined. On the contrary, the effect of past legislation has been to encourage secrecy on the part of government departments and civil servants. Nevertheless, the combined effect of administrative discretion, of *ad hoc* legislation and of decisions of the courts has been to release to the public a great deal of information from which they were previously excluded. Furthermore, since the beginning of the 1960s there has been a change in the climate of opinion, which has given rise not only to more relaxed attitudes in general but to an official investigation into the whole question of openness and secrecy in government; and legislation is contemplated which, if implemented, would alter the *de jure*, as distinct from the existing *de facto*, situation. It follows that the present time is somewhat unpropitious for a survey of the subject, and this chapter must distinguish between the situation now and the situation as it could be in a few years' time.

INFLUENCE OF THE OFFICIAL SECRETS ACTS[1]

In 1968 an influential report on the future of the civil service[2] (that of the 'Fulton Committee') suggested that 'the administrative process was surrounded by too much secrecy' and that 'the public interest would be better served if there were a greater amount of openness'. The Report proposed that the Government should set up the investigation referred to above, and said among other things that 'the Official Secrets Act would need to be included in such a review'.

Official secrets ought properly to be a minor aspect of the general subject of administrative information, since only a small proportion of administrative information might reasonably be expected to be secret. However, the lack of openness in government which the Fulton Committee apprehended had been generated by the unfortunate Official Secrets Act of 1911. One says 'unfortunate' because an Act whose real purpose had been to deal with espionage was extended – in Section 2 – after somewhat cursory deliberation by Parliament, to include (if taken literally) any kind of information whatsoever; and since the power and pervasiveness of the state has increased beyond recognition since 1911 this has had some regrettable results. The unauthorised disclosure of the most trivial piece of information acquired by a civil servant in the course of his day's work could (again if the Act were taken literally) be a criminal offence, as indeed could the knowing receipt of such information. This section of the Act has never been taken literally, of course, since the position would have been farcical if it had. Not only has good sense restricted its application, but a prosecution under its provisions has only been possible with the approval of the Attorney-General. In the course of 62 years only 30 prosecutions have been authorised. Twenty-three of these have been since 1945, and have involved 34 defendants, of whom 27 were convicted and six acquitted; two-thirds were Crown servants or former Crown servants; two were journalists.

Accordingly, Section 2 has not been applied oppressively, even though it is archaic. It has done very little specific harm in persecuting the innocent, but it has been harmful in subtler ways. Firstly, it may have caused civil servants to be over-cautious in disclosing information, thus creating the climate of secrecy which the Fulton Committee deplored; secondly, it has at times made the news media apprehensive and uncertain as to whether they were risking criminal prosecution.

The point of what may seem to be a digression from the main subject of this essay is that the committee of investigation (commonly known as the Franks Committee),[3] which was established in April 1971, and which derived from the concern of the Fulton Committee for more open government, was required to focus its inquiries on Section 2, the negative effects of which were thought to inhibit a positive approach to the subject of open government in its wider sense.

LIBERALISING TRENDS

The inhibiting influence of the Act must not, however, be exaggerated. Although pervasive, it is indirect. It has resulted in an attitude of mind whereby the citizen in search of information is expected to prove that he ought to have it, rather than the official should prove that he ought *not* to have it. But this has not prevented a number of developments which have greatly extended public knowledge of matters which were previously confidential.

For example, a feature of planning law in the U.K. – which is of exceptional importance because of the large population of the country in relation to its small size – is the multiplicity of inquiries, usually held in public, into planning proposals, ranging from major development schemes to quite small ones, even including domestic dwellings. These inquiries are held by 'inspectors' whose reports and recommendations have a great – usually a determining – influence on the responsible minister's decision. Until 1962 inspectors' reports were not available to the parties to disputes, so that the loser of a case did not know why he had lost; but in that year, by *administrative decision*, they were made public.

In 1967 the creation by *statute* of the Parliamentary Commissioner for Administration (P.C.A. or Ombudsman) has meant that, provided the citizen could establish a *prima facie* grievance on grounds of maladministration, records and files would be disclosed that would previously have been inaccessible. Legislation in 1973 and 1974 extended comparable provision to the national health service and to local government.

In 1968 an important ruling by *the courts* modified the doctrine of Crown privilege, whereby, on the sole authority of a minister, official information could be withheld, on the ground that its disclosure would not be in the public interest, even though its discovery was important for the defence.[4] The House of Lords held that

> The court has jurisdiction to order the disclosure of documents for which Crown privilege is claimed, as it is the right and duty of the court to hold the balance between the interests of the public in ensuring the proper administration of justice and the public interest in the withholding of documents whose disclosure would be contrary to the national interest.

The Court went on to say, in effect, that due weight would be given to a minister's view, and that if the considerations were of a kind that judicial experience was not competent to weigh the minister's view would prevail; but that it would be for the courts to decide whether disclosure should be made. This was a judgment of great importance to the subject under discussion.

Thus, three specific developments, arising respectively from an administrative decision, an Act of Parliament and a court judgment have enlarged public access to administrative information. But the changing climate of opinion, and the trend towards more open government, is perhaps better exemplified by *political* decisions to publish government intentions, and to invite public comment on matters which the Government must shortly decide.

CONSULTATIVE DOCUMENTS

This trend has been especially discernible since about 1967, when the Government of the day introduced a novel kind of document known as a 'Green Paper'. 'White Papers' had long been a familiar type of government publication; in general, they summarise the

Government's conclusions on a particular matter, and their intentions about prospective legislation; although there is still a margin for amendment in the light of professional or parliamentary criticism, the main conclusions will stand. The Green Paper was novel in that it did not represent settled government policy, but was intended to set out the nature of a problem and the possible ways of dealing with it, and to invite public discussion which would be helpful to the Government when they came to bring the matter to a conclusion. Green Papers, and other kinds of consultative document, are now common. They vary a good deal in character; some represent the Government's earliest stage of thinking, all of which is open to revision in the light of public reaction; others are obviously addressed, because of their subject-matter, to small expert audiences rather than the public at large; and some are biased towards imparting information as much as inviting discussion. But they have in common that they are about matters on which the Government have as yet reached no firm conclusion and on which they seek public reaction. Some twenty Green Papers, on a very wide variety of topics, were published between 1967 and 1974. The first concerned a tentative proposal for a regional employment premium in development areas; among the most important which followed were two on the future of the national health service; others have been concerned with such disparate matters as the speed limit on the roads, value-added tax, the future shape of local government and the future of Northern Ireland.

'INFORMATION AND THE PUBLIC INTEREST'

In 1969 the Government brought together the threads of our subject in a White Paper entitled 'Information and the Public Interest',[5] which was in effect the report of an internal inquiry recommended by the Fulton Committee into ways of getting rid of unnecessary secrecy. The report confirmed and documented the trends towards the increasing publication both of factual information, especially by the Government Central Statistical Office, and of forecasts upon which government policy was being based, notably economic forecasts in relation to the budget. It also reported that civil servants were more and more emerging from anonymity, appearing on public occasions and giving interviews to the press, radio and television.

There were two pronouncements of a more general kind. First, the Government confirmed their belief in the value of secrecy at the actual policy-making stage, saying that civil servants and ministers alike should be able to discuss and disagree among themselves without feeling that their individual views could become a matter of public knowledge.

Second, they advanced the view, which was not well received in all quarters, that the Official Secrets Acts were 'not in any way a barrier to greater openness in government' since they related only to *unauthorised* disclosure, and the areas of authorisation could always be extended. The tone, as much as the content, of this pronouncement offended those who did not accept that the Government alone should be the arbiter of what it was good for people to know; and the statement paid too little heed to the indirect, and frustrating, effects of the legislation.

SUMMARY OF POSITION IN CENTRAL GOVERNMENT

The background to the subject, therefore, is that so far as central government is concerned there is no acceptance of a general principle that the public have the right of access to administrative information; but that by a series of pragmatic arrangements such information is in fact quite widely available for particular purposes.

'Open' systems of government start from the premise that the public have a right of access to all administrative information except that which may be prohibited for specific reasons, such as defence, foreign policy or the national finances; the British system starts from the premise that the public have no right of access to any information except when it is made available for a particular reason. The gap between the two systems may not *in practice* be very great. The gap between the mental attitudes is possibly a good deal wider. By training and tradition British civil servants are instinctively reticent. This reticence is reinforced by the influence of the Official Secrets Acts, though this can be exaggerated, especially in the higher ranks of the service. But in recent years much more information has been disclosed at all levels than was once customary; and the predilection for government to be regarded by its initiates as a mystery whose secrets it is their function to guard is far less pronounced than it was a decade ago.

LOCAL GOVERNMENT

The position in local government differs in two ways. First, the provisions of the Official Secrets Acts do not apply. Local authorities have a power, delegated to them by Parliament, of making what are known as Standing Orders, that is rules regulating the conduct of their business, the relations between a council and its committees and the performance of their duties by officers, and these rules would normally cover the disclosure of information. Second, local authorities – unlike government departments – have a statutory obligation to provide public access to certain specified kinds of information.

A *similarity* between central and local government is that of recent years local authorities have been equally encouraged – by their parent department, the Department of the Environment – to move towards more open forms of administration.

THE OBLIGATIONS OF PUBLIC AUTHORITIES

GOVERNMENT DEPARTMENTS

Since there is no general right of access to administrative information, we must concentrate on the obligations which rest on politicians or civil servants to give or to withhold information.

Ministers of Cabinet rank have a strict obligation to preserve complete secrecy in Cabinet matters, and indeed in departmental matters which require Cabinet consideration or decision. This apart, they have full freedom in their purely departmental capacities, as have the much larger number of ministers and junior ministers who are not in the Cabinet. Naturally their position compels them to be discreet – often secretive – but they are not required to sign the same declaration as civil servants regarding the Official Secrets Acts, and since they are the authorising authority within their own departments they can disclose, or authorise their civil servants to disclose, what they wish.

Civil servants, who effectively administer departments, are all bound by a general code of behaviour, which now encourages openness towards the public and the press, though the permitted limits of disclosure are naturally more restricted in some departments than in others; and all have to sign a declaration that they have taken note of the provisions of the Official Secrets Acts.

The general code, which is embodied in a document known as ESTACODE (the first two syllables indicating 'Establishments') is somewhat outside the scope of this essay, as it deals with such matters as a civil servant's permitted 'extramural' activities – publications, broadcasts, speeches and the like – in which the unauthorised disclosure of official information, or participation in political controversy, is for obvious reasons forbidden. What is of more significance is that the part of the code dealing with 'Official Information' opens with the following statement:

General Considerations: The need for greater openness in the work of Government is now widely accepted. Openness in this context means two things:

(*a*) The fullest possible exposition to Parliament and to the public of the reasons for Government policies and decisions when those policies and decisions are formulated and announced;

(*b*) Creating a better public understanding about the way in which the processes of Government work and about the factual or technical background to Government policies and decisions.

This may at first sight seem to conflict with the Official Secrets Act, which forbids the unauthorised disclosure of official information. But the concept of 'authorisation' is by no means a simple one, as was apparent from the evidence given by civil servants to the Franks Committee, this being one of the many matters in public administration which are as dependent on convention as on rule. In theory, a civil servant may be required to have written permission from his senior before disclosing information. In practice, most of them will know instinctively, and from experience, what they should communicate, and to whom; others will be doing work in which the need to communicate is implicit; others will rely on common sense, reinforced by the knowledge that disciplinary measures, or a black mark against their promotion prospects, may result from being too communicative.

Accordingly the Official Secrets Act, though a manifest absurdity in that it is continually breached, does not of itself prevent the flow of information to press and public. It is true that the retention of criminal sanctions for disclosures which do not affect the security of the state is repugnant to some; though it has been defended by others who are by no means illiberal on the ground that the safety of the state may be prejudiced by many activities other than espionage, and that a line becomes impossibly difficult to draw.

The code's general exhortation to openness is, needless to say, qualified in later passages – to the effect that what is made public should rest with 'the appropriate authorities in departments'. This would seem to bring us back to where we started and to justify the critics who say that authorisation by privileged and anonymous persons is precisely what they complain of. On the other hand, the statement of principle with which this code begins represents a shift to a far more open attitude than has been traditional in the service.

Moreover it is now possible, because of the voluminous evidence given the Franks Committee, to examine what information the various departments think ought not to be disclosed; and this does not appear to differ significantly from the categories of information which remain secret in more professedly open systems.

The question was examined in 1964 by a Working Party whose conclusions[6] may be considered the more significant by virtue of their independence of Government, a working party of 'JUSTICE', the British section of the International Commission of Jurists; it comprised three independent lawyers and three journalists chosen by the British Committee of the International Press Institute. Its analysis is perhaps worth quoting at this point:

> It appears that there are five main types of information that we have to consider:
> (1) Information prejudicial to the security of the State, e.g., defence and police;
> (2) Information prejudicial to the national interest, e.g., foreign relations, banking and currency, commodity reserves;
> (3) Information which through premature disclosure can provide opportunities for unfair financial gain by private interests;
> (4) Information which is confided to Government departments on promise of non-disclosure;
> (5) Information which is not prejudicial to the national interest or to legitimate private interests, and relates solely to the efficiency or integrity of a Government department or public authority.

It is not surprising that the JUSTICE Report should have thought it reasonable for the criminal sanctions of the Official Secrets Act to apply to the first two categories; it is universally accepted that these subjects should be on the secret list. Nor could the Report have done other than declare that it was against the interests of good government for the disclosure of information in the fifth category to continue to be treated as a criminal offence. It is more interesting that it should have thought it reasonable for categories (3) and (4) to remain within the provisions of the Act. This is said not because the matters comprehended by these categories are unimportant, or that a great deal of information within them ought not to remain confidential; but because *local* authorities are presented with similar problems, which they manage to solve without the aid of criminal sanctions, since the Official Secrets Acts do not apply to local government.

The third category – the use of official information for private gain – is of course almost limitless in its potential application at a time when governments are increasingly concerned with planning, development and investment. It is virtually impossible for many public servants not to acquire information that they could turn to private gain, and this extends to many bodies on the fringe of government, to government contractors and to private consultants. The law of corruption does not deal with these matters unless there is an element of bribery, and it may be argued that the sanction of internal disciplinary measures only applies to a limited number of those to whom information is available. Moreover the state has a paramount obligation – far exceeding that of any private interest – to ensure complete fairness and impartiality in its dealings with the citizen, and this may be held to warrant the power to invoke criminal sanctions, even in matters in which the security of the state is not in issue.

Much the same may be said of the fourth category – information confided to governments in confidence. It applies equally to great industries, small firms and countless ordinary individuals. The Ministry of Agriculture and the Department of Trade and Industry are dependent on a mass of technical, financial and statistical information supplied to them in confidence by industry and commerce; the Department of Education holds over a million personal files of teachers; the Department of Health and Social Security has information about the intimate personal circumstances of many millions; and the income tax authorities are familiar with the finances of every taxpayer in the country. The point is too obvious to need labouring. The modern state, especially in its 'welfare' aspects, and in the age of the computer, may abolish personal privacy, and may also abolish personal freedom, unless the sanctions against improper disclosure of personal information are severe.[7]

Considerations of this kind led the JUSTICE Committee to accept the retention of criminal sanctions in matters which did not 'threaten the security of the state' but would merely be 'prejudicial to the national interest' or involve a breach of trust with individuals.

The fifth category – by which criminal sanctions can in theory be extended to the communication or receipt of official information of any kind – was of course deplored by the Committee. The point is not pursued here since their view has now received fairly general acceptance. Current proposals, outlined in the concluding part of the essay, suggest the abolition of protection to this category.

Meanwhile the accessibility of administrative information to the public will continue to be discretionary, and there are certain areas in which informed public opinion is dissatisfied. One of the most important concerns the administration of prisons. It is common ground that information that would endanger prison security, or facilitate crime or escape, must be secret; but the Official Secrets Acts bind all who enter prisons, including chaplains, recognised prison visitors or probation officers, and restrain them from making any comment, public or private, on day-to-day prison administration or the rules and conditions under which prisoners live.

More recently there has been public concern over the secrecy surrounding several aspects of pollution, ranging from the building of nuclear power stations and the disposal of radioactive waste to the transport of dangerous chemicals and the emission of fumes from secret manufacturing processes. Of a quite different order, confidential personal files are kept by education authorities on schoolchildren, and while the information in them is doubtless kept primarily – or wholly – for educational purposes, it is not available to parents though it could if need arose become available to the police.

NON-GOVERNMENTAL PERSONS AND BODIES

For the sake of completeness it should be added that the obligations resting on civil servants are extended to various kinds of persons and bodies to whom the Government must give official information in confidence. They comprise on the one hand a variety of expert individuals outside government, such as members of advisory committees, consultants and researchers; and on the other, contractors and sub-contractors engaged in government work. Some are in possession of classified defence information, others of information of no security significance; but as matters stand no distinction is drawn between them.

PUBLIC CORPORATIONS AND NATIONALISED INDUSTRIES

These are in a somewhat different position. Their normal *raison d'être* is that they carry out commercial operations of a kind inappropriate to direct administration by government departments, and except in matters of broad policy affecting the public interest they have the independence associated with the private sector. Their day-to-day administration, in which one may include the giving or withholding of information, follows the practice of private firms, and is based on internal rules and discipline.

The *giving* of information to the public is an ordinary matter of commercial public relations though in the nationalised public utilities such as electricity and gas, and also in the case of the railways, statutory consumer councils give to representatives of the public, if not the right of access to administrative information, at least a statutory right to demand facts affecting themselves as consumers, to complain and to advocate.

In the *withholding* of information the position is a little more complicated. In the first place *members* of the boards (i.e. the governing bodies) hold office under the Crown and are subject to the Official Secrets Act, whereas *employees* of the boards are not, in general, so subject. On the other hand, by their very nature the boards are in closer contact with government departments than most ordinary commercial firms, since a minister is ultimately responsible for them to Parliament, and since classified information must constantly be made available to them by civil servants; accordingly the employees who handle information of this kind are required to acknowledge the Official Secrets Act in the form of a 'Declaration to be signed by non-civil servants having access to Government information'. Also, there are special cases, of which the

United Kingdom Atomic Energy Authority and some aspects of the Post Office are the most obvious, where the national interest or even national security is involved, and where the application of the Official Secrets Act may be the rule rather than the exception.

LOCAL GOVERNMENT

Here, by contrast, the public have a number of statutory rights, dealing with the audit of accounts, planning applications, access to certain documents and attendance at meetings. They are, in summary:

(1) Audit
The Local Government Act 1933 provides that, not less than seven clear days before the annual audit, the accounts and supporting documents must be open to inspection by ratepayers and electors. Anyone entitled to inspect them may, if he wishes, do so through an accountant, and when the audit takes place may lodge an objection.

(2) Planning applications
The Town and Country Planning Acts provide that these must be recorded in a register which is open to public inspection, and any member of the public affected by a particular application may see the relevant file, and is entitled to object to the application being granted.

(3) Access to documents
The Local Government Act 1972 (Section 228) gives any local elector the right to inspect and make copies of minutes, orders for payments and statements of account.

(4) Attendance at meetings
The Public Bodies (Admission to Meetings) Act 1960 provides that the public may attend meetings of local councils, and also of statutory water and health authorities. The Local Government Act 1972 extends this right to attendance at committee meetings of local councils.

These statutory requirements are backed up by administrative advice and exhortation.

In 1974 a committee was appointed by the Prime Minister to examine the general question of conduct in local government

(Cmnd 5636). It proposed a draft National Code of Conduct for Councillors, which stressed at the outset the importance of maximum openness as an essential safeguard for honesty and public confidence in local government. But for many years before this the Department had urged local authorities to exercise their maximum rather than their minimum powers in providing information on matters affecting the public. For example, the publicity given to planning applications can, with imagination, far exceed the statutory requirement; similarly, in planning matters of a different kind – i.e. the future development plans of the authority itself for a town or neighbourhood – publicity can be the minimum required by statute or it can involve public participation of an elaborate kind, with public meetings, exhibitions and invitations for suggestions. Again, the requirement to admit the public to committee meetings can be extended to sub-committees, and a circular issued early in 1975 by the Department urged that this should be done. The same circular exhorted local authorities to improve their lines of communication with the press, and to keep them supplied well in advance with the agenda of meetings and supporting documents.

The speed of advance indicated by the last sentence may be judged from the fact that it was previously common for local authorities to promulgate Standing Orders based on a Model Order suggested by the Department itself, which read as follows:

> All agenda, reports and other documents, and all proceedings of committees and sub-committees shall be treated as confidential unless and until they become public in the ordinary course of the council's business.

In a number of ways, therefore, the public have been offered considerable opportunities of access to information. It must be said frankly that they have not, on the whole, availed themselves of these opportunities to a very impressive extent. Their attendance at council and committee meetings is meagre, and invitations to participate in development plans or civic affairs generally draw no great response from individual citizens. On the other hand, organised pressure groups are frequently keen and active, and municipal affairs are normally very well reported in local newspapers.

There are, however, in local as in central government, certain matters which in the interest of fair dealing ought to be kept secret.

These are not of an order that could cause grave harm to the community at large if prematurely revealed (though like the nationalised industries local authorities are from time to time entrusted with classified information), but they have in common with some Government secrets the fact that their disclosure could result in unfair financial gain by individuals, or in a breach of confidence with individual citizens.

The first of these may be seen in the exercise of certain planning powers, in which the disclosure of policy could result in fore-knowledge that the price of land may rise; or it could result in undeserved loss, since if it is known that land may be developed for some new purpose, those who own property on it may find it unsaleable at the current market price. The second arises because intimate personal details are confided to local authorities, as they are to government departments; education, housing and social service departments all have information about family finances, physical or mental health or, at the bottom of the social scale, social inadequacy and poverty.

The possession of so much information of this latter kind raises an interesting question on which Standing Orders are not always sufficiently specific and on which the law, if called in aid, is by no means clear. This concerns the right not of the public but of an elected councillor to see 'administrative information' in the form of files. The Model Standing Order of the Department suggests that a councillor should be allowed to inspect documents *for the purpose of his duty but not otherwise*, but from time to time the point is raised as a matter of dispute.

In 1974 a county councillor was denied access to a file in the social services department on the ground that it contained confidential reports from medical officers, though subsequently he was permitted to see it. But should the Hippocratic oath have any less validity when the doctor concerned is a public employee whose opinion must go on a local authority file? In this particular instance, research into case law and common law appeared to give only a limited right of access, depending on his need to see the file in order to do his job, which is much in line with the Department's Model Order. But it is a debatable point whether election to representative office should entitle a man to see confidential personal information about those who elected him.

Yet, in spite of handling so much sensitive information, local authorities have managed to preserve a creditable record for discretion and trustworthiness without the criminal sanctions which apply in the civil service.

THE SANCTION OF INVESTIGATION

This chapter deals primarily with the release of official information to the public as a deliberate act, but the account would be incomplete if no reference were made to information that is made available as a result of investigation, which may take place either as a matter of common practice, as with certain 'Parliamentary Select Committees', or under pressure of complaint, as with the various kinds of Ombudsman.

Even taking into account the trends towards openness which we have discussed, the Government of a country in which there is no right of public access may be thought to be in a privileged position, since it is they who decide whether and if so to what extent to release information, and they do not have to show the need for secrecy. Governmental authorities in the U.K., however – the Cabinet apart – are by no means immune from scrutiny, but may be called upon to give an account of their stewardship in a way which could require them to disclose information involuntarily.

THE CABINET

The Cabinet is in a category apart, not only because it is the apex of the governmental system, carrying ultimate responsibility for the decisions of the Government of the day, but because it works within the doctrine of collective responsibility, which demands the strictest privacy for its deliberations. Accordingly, as soon as working papers become Cabinet documents they become secret, and even the Franks Committee, which in general would have preferred to minimise secrecy, and to shift the emphasis from criminal sanctions to internal discipline, did not suggest that the full rigour of the Official Secrets Acts should not be applicable to Cabinet papers.

GOVERNMENT DEPARTMENTS

But the ordinary processes of executive government, which involve ministers and civil servants alike, may on occasion be liable to investigation – indeed 'inquisition' would not be an inappropriate word.

Two permanent 'Select Committees' of the House of Commons have the power to investigate departmental administration, to examine witnesses and to call for documents – the Public Accounts Committee and the Expenditure Committee, which include members of all the main political parties. Both, as their names imply, are intended to be instruments of financial control, but both, as is inevitable, go far beyond their original function of scrutinising past expenditure or examining future estimates.

The Public Accounts Committee, whose history goes back over a hundred years, meets regularly throughout the year to examine how the money granted by Parliament has been spent, and it works in collaboration with the staff of the Comptroller and Auditor-General, an official who enjoys the independent standing of a judge. The Expenditure Committee, successor to the former 'Estimates Committee', works through six sub-committees, each dealing with a group of subjects, and has a free hand to select departmental estimates for examination with a view to seeing, *inter alia*, how the policy which shaped the estimates can be most effectively and economically implemented. Both committees, in the course of their investigations, become closely involved not only with administration but with policy – the dichotomy between the two being largely mythical – and both are entitled to examine ministers and officials alike.

The result is that administrative information, and information on which policy is based, is made available to the representatives of Parliament, and subsequently to the press and public through the publication annually of a full account, including minutes of evidence, of the committees' investigations.

There are other Select Committees of more recent creation, some of which, like that on Science and Technology, deal with a subject affecting many departments, and are principally concerned with 'informing the House' on current developments; others are concerned with a particular department, e.g., Overseas Development or Agriculture, their brief being to 'consider the activities' of the department concerned and to report to the House with minutes of evidence, thus giving them virtually unlimited power of scrutiny.

These Select Committees consider broad issues of policy, while the Parliamentary Commissioner for Administration, the British name for the Ombudsman, investigates alleged maladministration in matters without policy significance. In doing so he is given access to administrative information which may thereafter become public in his reports. There is a proviso that a minister may give notice in writing that disclosure would be prejudicial to the interest of the state or otherwise contrary to the public interest, but in the normal run of cases his published reports give 'full but anonymised texts of reports on individual cases'. The British Ombudsman works under a number of limitations compared with his counterpart in some other countries. He is empowered to investigate complaints of alleged maladministration in government departments, but may only receive complaints through the channel of a Member of Parliament; and he is excluded from investigating the armed forces, the police and prisons, the nationalised industries, local government and the national health service (though under later legislation the last two have acquired 'Ombudsmen' of their own). Nevertheless, in the year 1976 the P.C.A. received 815 complaints, of which 329 were thoroughly investigated and the results reported.

THE NATIONALISED INDUSTRIES

The administration of the nationalised industries is closely scrutinised by a third financial Select Committee. Once again the original terms of reference – 'to examine the Reports and Accounts . . . and to report to Parliament – have been extended in practice to a free-ranging examination of administration, including internal organisation, managerial efficiency and recruitment and training of staff, as well as the actual conduct of their operations and the financial outcome.

The Select Committee on the Nationalised Industries, which has the power to summon ministers, civil servants and the heads of the nationalised industries, has been both active and thorough. During the first seventeen years of its existence (1956–73), it has submitted twenty major reports to the House of Commons. Most of these have dealt with individual industries, the National Coal Board and the Airways Corporations having been the subject of two reports each, while most of the others have been before the Committee once, as have the Bank of England and the Independent Broadcasting Authority. The Committee have also dealt with 'across-the-board' subjects, namely Ministerial Control of the Nationalised Industries

(1968), Relations with the Public (1971), and Procedures Governing Capital Investment (1973). Their voluminous reports and minutes of evidence, which leave little unsaid about internal administration, policy and commercial results, are available to press and public.

LOCAL GOVERNMENT

In 1974 the Ombudsman principle was extended to local government and to the National Health Service. In the former, 'Local Commissioners' accept complaints from elected councillors, just as the P.C.A. accepts them from M.P.s, but they may also investigate complaints that councillors have not necessarily endorsed. They are barred from investigating complaints about the police, or about policy decisions of local authorities which affect everyone alike, such as a rise in the level of the local tax. Their main purpose is to protect individuals from maladministration arising from delay, neglect, incompetence or prejudice, though they may not consider the *merits* of a decision if it has been reached fairly. Reports are available to press and public. In 1976/77 the Local Commissioners received no fewer than 2277 complaints, but a high proportion were misdirected or withdrawn, and only 256 were investigated.

The National Health Service is neither a government department nor a local authority, being in fact somewhat difficult to define in analogous terms, since it is an *ad hoc* body designed to circumvent the difficulty of marrying a government department to a highly independent learned profession. The minister is wholly responsible for the health service in that he provides the money and may give directives of a general – i.e. non-professional – nature. Management, however, is in the hands of regional and area health authorities which, though nominally appointed by the minister, are representative in character – notably of the various branches of the medical, dental and allied professions with additional lay or 'consumer' representation – and which have an independent legal status. The National Health Service (Reorganisation) Act 1973, which established these arrangements, provided also for 'Health Service Commissioners' who are Ombudsmen in all but name, and some of whose powers and duties are in fact transposed from the Parliamentary Commissioner Act 1967.

The first Health Service Commissioner to be appointed under the

1973 Act was the Parliamentary Commissioner himself. Although this is not necessarily a permanent arrangement there is a school of thought that it ought to be, on the ground that the administration of the National Health Service and that of the Department of Health and Social Security may be so closely intertwined that any alleged maladministration ought to be investigated by the same agency.

Indeed, a complaint *could* simultaneously involve a government department, a health authority and a local authority and arrangements exist for 'composite' investigations. They are, however, extremely cumbersome, and opinion exists that all three types of Ombudsman ought somehow to be merged into one overall authority.

THE OBLIGATIONS OF THE PRESS AND PUBLIC

Throughout this chapter there are considerable areas where 'the public' really means 'the press', since few ordinary citizens have the knowledge, ability or time – or even the inclination – to go in pursuit of administrative information, whereas it is an important function of the press to do so. For the next few pages, therefore, we speak simply of the press. The information we are considering is of two kinds – that which is voluntarily given to the press by the Government, and that which the press discovers for itself, possibly by devious means and to the embarrassment of authority.

THE WESTMINSTER LOBBY CORRESPONDENTS

One of the main recognised channels of communication is the 'Press Lobby' of the House of Commons, the word 'Lobby' simply meaning the outer entrance to the Chamber where accredited press correspondents meet and talk to Members of Parliament. Rather more than a hundred journalists are accredited to the Lobby, the majority from daily newspapers, others from the Sunday newspapers, the press agencies and the broadcasting networks. The Lobby is a curious institution, difficult to describe in straightforward, unambiguous terms, as it is governed by convention, mutual trust and unspoken assumptions rather than by rules, though its members have devised a code of rules for themselves, designed principally to preserve the relationship of trust between themselves and the politicians and civil servants whom they meet, and on which the effective working of the Lobby mainly depends.

Twice-daily briefings are given by the Prime Minister's press staff, and there are other regular briefings by departmental ministers, by the Leader of the House of Commons and the Leader of the Opposition. Ministers, accompanied by their civil servants, also hold special meetings with the Lobby to discuss policy on forthcoming legislation. Lobby correspondents are also supplied with a vast amount of documentary material, often before it is available to the House of Commons itself. The Lobby, however, is not simply a passive recipient of whatever information those in authority choose to give it. Some meetings are arranged by invitation of the Lobby, or a minister might seek such an invitation, for ministers need the Lobby as much as the Lobby needs ministers.

Formalised briefings, however, are probably less important than the network of personal contacts, often of personal friendships, which develop between journalists and politicians. A feature of both the formal briefings and of the personal contacts is that a very high proportion of what is told to journalists is understood to be 'non-attributable' – it may be freely used but the source must not be named specifically.

These arrangements, unconventional and haphazard as they may seem, work to the satisfaction of both sides. They are, however, open to some fairly obvious criticism. A relatively small and elite corps of journalists are naturally content with an arrangement whereby they enjoy the confidence and friendship of important politicians and civil servants. But such an arrangement is only possible on the basis of strict confidence, and the press are very much in the hands of their hosts. It is indeed a host-guest relationship, with all that that implies. Having said this, it is not easy, within the existing legislative framework, to suggest how the arrangements could be improved.[8]

Outside the Westminster Lobby there are other important specialist groups of journalists who get privileged treatment, e.g., the industrial, educational or financial correspondents. Moreover, a vast amount of information in the form of press notices, press conferences and briefings is given out by departments to general reporters and news desks, and departments maintain well-staffed public relations departments and information offices. The press does not, however, have direct access to departmental officials or documents.

VOLUNTARY AGREEMENT OF THE PRESS TO KEEP SECRETS

This aspect of the relationship between Government and press concerns editors rather than reporters – there being certain matters which, from time to time, they are asked not to publish in the interest of national security. This is done through a form of voluntary censorship, exercised by a body representative of the press and broadcasting interests on the one hand and the Government and the armed forces on the other, and known as the *Services, Press and Broadcasting Committee*.

Its function is to warn the media that it would be against the interests of national security to publish certain information and to seek the media's own consent to non-disclosure. Such requests, which take the form of what are called 'D-notices', have no statutory force and are not provided for in the Official Secrets Acts, though to ignore them would of course bring an offending editor within the purview of the Acts. The arrangement goes back some sixty years in one form or another, and until comparatively recent times was not regarded by the press as a threat to their freedom or as a kind of non-statutory extension of the Official Secrets Acts. It was, on the contrary, a singularly harmonious arrangement, which gave satisfaction to both sides. During the 1960s, however, tensions came into the relationship, the press thinking that the Government were tending to depart from the strict use of D-notices to preserve essential secrets, and were permitting their use to suppress information inconvenient or embarrassing to themselves.

At first, the press's justification was that a number of D-notices had been issued on subjects which were currently being freely reported in foreign newspapers, though as late as 1965 the Committee of JUSTICE did not consider these incidents to be serious, and were able to speak of the D-notice system in commendatory terms. In 1967, however, two more serious episodes shattered the relationship of mutual trust, which has been slow to mend. One sought to place an embargo on the publication of information about the Foreign Office traitors, Philby, Burgess and Maclean, although the fullest information was obviously available to the country to which they had defected; in this case two newspapers took their courage in both hands and published, and were not prosecuted. The other case, which caused a much greater furore, and which brought a much-resented intervention by the Prime Minister, centred on a report by the *Daily Express* about the

'vetting' of overseas cables by the Ministry of Defence. So serious
did this become that a small committee of Privy Councillors was
appointed to examine the facts.[9] These proved to be extremely
tangled and to be shot through with misunderstandings and half-
truths. It would be out of place to attempt to summarise them here.
But the fact that this affair could happen at all illustrates the
delicacy of voluntary arrangements based on trust and common
sense, and the need for great sensitivity on the part of authority in a
free democracy.

The D-notice system continues, but the media are more sus-
picious of it than they used to be, believing that the incidents of the
1960s marked a turning away from security secrets, in whose
suppression they willingly co-operated, to the suppression of
information which did not prejudice national security, but which
the Government would prefer to hide.

STATUTORY OBLIGATION ON THE PRESS TO KEEP SECRETS

Naturally the press is not content to gather its news solely in the
Westminster Lobby or from Government public relations officers.
Reporters will inevitably go behind the scenes and sniff out,
if they can, the exciting, the controversial and if possible the
scandalous, and will on occasion take risks in order to publish
something they consider to be in the public interest, or simply to file
a good story. One of their complaints is that the risks are difficult to
calculate, owing to the uncertain, and potentially capricious,
operation of Section 2 of the Act of 1911. The Attorney-General's
power to authorise prosecution may be very rarely used but it can
never be completely ignored. There have in fact been very few
instances of the Act being harshly or unreasonably applied, but the
veiled hint or the actual threat has been the cause of some concern.

One particular risk, however, was removed by legislation in 1939.
Before that date a journalist would have had to reveal his sources of
information, or suffer the penalties for not doing so, if charged with
an offence under either Section 1 or Section 2 of the 1911 Act. An
Official Secrets Act of 1939 restricted this power of interrogation to
Section 1, i.e., to cases of alleged espionage and not to offences of a
lesser kind concerning the more general 'interests of the state'.

The most important case in recent years occurred in 1971,
commonly referred to as the *Sunday Telegraph* case. A journalist,

Jonathan Aitken, came into possession of a document which was a military appreciation by the Defence Adviser to the British High Commission in Lagos of the prospect of a successful termination of the Nigerian Civil War by the Federal Forces, and the *Sunday Telegraph* accepted it for publication. Three men were prosecuted under Section 2 – Colonel Cairns, who originally sent the document to the U.K. (though not to Mr Aitken personally), the editor of the newspaper and Mr Aitken himself–and were tried at the Central Criminal Court. The trial itself is described in detail in Mr Aitken's book, *Officially Secret*,[10] and its details are impossible to summarise briefly. It was a somewhat tangled tale of mixed motives, indiscretions, misunderstandings and wrestlings with conscience. The essential facts in the present context are that the communicating and receiving of the document did not affect national security, though they did affect friendly relations between the British and Nigerian Governments, and seriously embarrassed British ministers and civil servants. Secondly, the jury found Cairns not guilty of making an unauthorised communication, and Aitken and the newspaper not guilty of receiving and communicating the document 'knowing or having reasonable grounds to believe' that they were acting in contravention of the Act. Thirdly, the judge, whose summing up had been strongly favourable to the defendants, ended the case with some caustic observations about Section 2, saying, in a much quoted remark, that the Act was just approaching its sixtieth birthday and that it was time it was pensioned off.

It was shortly after this case that the Franks Committee started its work, though the case was not, as is often assumed, the *cause* of the Committee's appointment. This had been decided upon before the trial began, but it was thought proper to postpone the beginning of its work until the *Sunday Telegraph* case was over.

There was another notorious case in the following year, associated with the name of the *Railway Gazette*. This was of a different order, since it was clear that a document had been stolen from a government department and given to the editor, and a warrant for arrest was accordingly issued under the Theft Act and not, as would have been equally possible, under the Official Secrets Act. But in the event the case did not come to trial, since the evidence proved insufficient to proceed to a charge. The document which had come into the hands of the editor, and which was used as the basis for an article in a national newspaper, the *Sunday Times*, dealt with a plan to close down 40 per cent of the railway system of the country within the next ten years. It was in fact one of a number of confidential alternative contingency plans, and not a proposal for action, but none the less it was dealing with a matter of high public interest. The point in the context of this essay is that the police raided the offices of the *Railway Gazette* and detectives closely questioned the editor of the *Sunday Times*, warning him that *receipt* of the information had been in breach of the Official Secrets Act. Both editors, however, refused, as they were entitled, to disclose the source of their information, and the case petered out.

The view of the press, generally speaking, is that those who have secrets should be responsible for keeping them, and that it ought not to be an offence merely to receive them; and that the reform that is most urgently needed is the simple repeal of Section 2 and its replacement by nothing whatsoever. But Governments, and the Franks Committee, have considered this view to be over-simplified.

SCHOLARS AND RESEARCHERS

These constitute the other section of 'the public' who most need access to administrative information. Their lot has been a hard one, as the predilection of the civil service for secrecy has been projected to the records of past deeds. Until recently, to the vast irritation of authors and scholars, public documents were closed to inspection for a period of fifty years, and the rule was strictly enforced regardless of the quality of the material in question. It is said in defence of a long period of restriction that the doctrine of collective Cabinet responsibility demands that papers should remain strictly confidential during the lifetime of the participants. While this may be a plausible argument for restricting Cabinet papers, it hardly justified the withholding of departmental papers with no bearing on either national security or Cabinet secrecy. Most scholars who have tried to get access to official records can bear witness not only to the triviality of the information they were seeking in terms of national security, but to anomalies such as the information being freely available in libraries overseas, or by word of mouth from participants in the events.

In 1970 the fifty-year rule was relaxed to some extent and became a thirty-year rule, which makes comparatively little difference to those interested in recent or contemporary history. The relaxation was, however, accompanied by a statement of intent by the Head of the Civil Service that sympathetic consideration would be given to requests within the thirty-year period for the purposes of research which would assist in the training of administrators, and later for purposes of normal academic research. Exceptions would be the reasonable ones of Cabinet papers, topics still within the field of active political controversy, and those which bore on national security.

Here is another straw in the wind which is blowing in favour of more open government and greater public access to information. But the scholar still has more hurdles to surmount than seem reasonable, and thirty years is still a long time.

Meanwhile, dissatisfaction is increased by the fact that ministers and Members of Parliament, in their voluminous memoirs, seem able to breach the rules without much difficulty. Their drafts have in theory to be cleared by the Cabinet Office before publication, and amendments have in practice been made which have removed the quotation of actual Cabinet papers, though not revelations of personal differences in Cabinet. A good deal is published under eminent authorship of a kind that could result in criminal prosecution for the ordinary person.

INFORMATION PROCEDURES

In a system in which there is no specific right of access to administrative information there are naturally no published rules, as there are in countries with 'freedom of access' legislation, about the ways in which documents are held and communicated, or the stage at which they pass from the kind of status to another. These are matters of internal administration. All that is known publicly is the ways in which various kinds of information are classified for security purposes in government departments, or in public corporations such as the Post Office or the Atomic Energy Authority. There are four classifications,[11] as follows:

(1) *Top Secret*
Information and material the unauthorised disclosure of which would *cause exceptionally grave damage to the nation.*
Examples would be largely drawn from the field of higher defence strategy and policy, but could also include plans which might

endanger the stability of the currency or reserves, or major plans of a political character; plans for the direct rule of Northern Ireland are cited as an example of the last category.

(2) *Secret*

. . . *cause serious injury to the interests of the nation.*

Examples would be of the same general order, but would in the judgement of the person classifying them be somewhat less serious, being against the nation's interest rather than actual safety; they would include information whose disclosure would prejudice relations with friendly governments.

(3) *Confidential*

. . . *be prejudicial to the interests of the nation.*

For example, routine reports of a political, military or economic nature, economic forecasts on which future policy is based, planning and compulsory purchase, proposals to vary rates or duties.

(4) *Restricted*

. . . *be undesirable in the interests of the nation.*

For example, routine military documents, departmental intructions, draft Bills.

It should be emphasised that classification has no connection with the criminal law, i.e., a prosecution under the Official Secrets Act would be unrelated to the degree of classification of the information alleged to have been disclosed.

The examples, which are highly condensed, do not purport to do more than convey the flavour of the kinds of information thus graded. They are possibly sufficient, however, to make clear that one classification merges into another, and that sharp definitions are impossible. Since it follows that there is a fairly large subjective element in deciding the appropriate category, it should be mentioned that the person responsible for deciding the classification is the originator of the document. He is given elaborate guidelines ('Aids to correct Classification and Regrading') which lay particular stress on the undesirability of 'over-grading', for reasons both of principle – since over-grading 'debases the currency' – and of expense – since the cost of making Top Secret and Secret documents secure is considerable. Instructions are also given with regard to regular periodic reviews of classification, for the purpose of downgrading or destruction.

None of this classified information would normally be available to the public, even at discretion and under the more open practices which are currently being adopted.

Top Secret information apart, the test for classification is whether, in varying degrees, the 'interests of the nation' would be affected. But in this area of the subject, as in others, the Government must also have regard to the interests of those who have entrusted it with confidential information, whether they be commercial firms or private individuals. As we have seen, the departments dealing with income tax, customs and excise, industry and trade and the social services are notable recipients of such information. It is not classified, but is accorded a 'privacy marking', consisting of the phrase 'In Confidence', preceded by the subject matter, e.g., 'Commercial – In Confidence'.

LOCAL GOVERNMENT

The position in local government is ill-defined. Standing Orders have no legal force, and may depart considerably in the direction of openness on the one hand or secrecy on the other from the Order recommended by the Department. The matter is complicated by the fact that while members of a local authority staff are subject to internal discipline if they wilfully or indiscreetly disclose information which they know to be confidential, no such sanction can be applied to *members* of the authority (i.e., the elected councillors). The marking of documents 'Confidential' is a restraining influence but could hardly prevent a councillor from disclosing the contents if he were determined to do so, and he would suffer no penalty.

However, this has not emerged as a serious problem in local government, whose record, as we noted, has been excellent. It has been marred in recent years by the somewhat different phenomenon of *corruption*, whereby members or senior officers have profited financially from their knowledge or their position. But these have been *causes célèbres*, and are happily rare exceptions to the general rule.

CONCLUSION

In recent years the enlargement of public access to administrative information has been rapid by the standards of the United

Kingdom, though no doubt it would be considered modest by countries in which public rights of access are specified by law. The process has perhaps been characteristic of political evolution in a country which is conservative in temper and pragmatic in its ways, and which in moving forward always tends to carry something of the past into new situations. In this particular matter the part of the past that has been carried forward has been the Official Secrets Act.

Seen in perspective it is remarkable how much this has figured in recent debate, since it is largely an irrelevance. When one reads the evidence of those nearest to the processes of government, it is clear that neither ministers nor civil servants give much conscious thought to the Act. The former are reticent or informative according to the sheer pressures and disciplines of being a politician; the latter are motivated far more by the traditions of their service, and by thought for their own careers, than by fear of the Act. Yet discussion of the Act tends to dominate discussion of public access to information. The press, the most hostile of the critics, seem always to be conscious of its shadow, though the number of prosecutions they have suffered has been minimal. The fact that the Attorney-General, a politician and a member of the Government, rather than the Director of Public Prosecutions, an official, is the certifying authority for a prosecution has been the subject of criticism, though in fact Attorneys-General are, in their judicial capacity, wholly independent of the Government and responsible only to Parliament; and by strong tradition neither Prime Ministers nor other ministers may seek to influence them. Moreover, although the Director of Public Prosecutions may normally act independently of the Attorney-General, he is ultimately responsible to him and would invariably consult him over problematic cases.

Nevertheless, the recommendation of the Fulton Committee that a committee should consider how to make government more open resulted in a committee to examine Section 2 of the Official Secrets Act 1911; not, as might have been expected, to examine ways of making official information more accessible.

There can be no doubt that the Fulton Committee's animadversions, backed by the Report of the Franks Committee and fortified by the coincidental *cause celèbre* of the *Sunday Telegraph* case have brought interest in the subject to a high pitch. Both political parties have committed themselves in principle to new legislation, on which a great deal of preparatory work has been done, or is in progress. And it must be admitted that it is hardly satisfactory that the validity of an Act of Parliament should rest upon the fact that it is hardly ever used, even though it is breached every day of the year. It is an absurdity that happens to work reasonably well, like the House of Lords, but on such sensitive matters, and at a time of heightened political consciousness, this is perhaps hardly sufficient justification.

What, then, had the Franks Committee, entering the subject by this side door, to say that is relevant to the subject of this book?

Their purpose, as it emerged after taking massive written and oral evidence, was to put something in place of Section 2 of the Official Secrets Act that would be 'more limited' and 'more certain in operation'. The possibility of doing this has been strongly disputed, since it is manifestly impossible to foresee every circumstance that might injure the interests of the nation (leaving aside espionage, which is dealt with under Section 1). This, however, is a difficulty which must arise in reverse form in the open systems, where exceptions have to be stated to the general right of access. The Committee declined to be deterred by it.

They accepted without question that 'the present law is unsatisfactory and that it should be changed so that criminal sanctions are retained only to protect what is of real importance.'[12]

They did not go as far as some critics of the 1911 Act – especially the press – would have wished, and propose that Section 2 should simply be abolished and not replaced. To put something in its place that would be 'more limited' and 'more certain in operation', they recommended an entirely new statute, which they would call the 'Official Information Act', and which would apply only to four categories of information – first, the customary one relating to defence, foreign relations, currency and the reserves; second, information likely to assist criminal activities or to impede law enforcement; third, Cabinet documents; and fourth, information entrusted to the Government by private individuals. Crown servants, Government contractors and persons entrusted with official information in confidence would be guilty of an offence in disclosing information in these categories, as would any other person if he had reasonable ground to believe that it had reached him as a result of contravention of the Official Information Act.

Prosecutions would in general continue to require the consent of the Attorney-General, though that of the Director of Public Prosecutions would be sufficient in the case of information used to further criminal activities or private gain.

In effect, the Committee accepted the need to give precise definition to information which must be secret, and to do away with the theoretical possibility – however remote – that *any* official information was secret if the Attorney-General said it was. On the other hand, the Franks proposals would do nothing whatever to increase public access to administrative information. All they would do would be to relieve the public – and specifically the press – of the anxiety and uncertainty that has hung over them in the past, though the press is disappointed that a proposal frequently advanced on its behalf finds no mention, namely that it should be a defence in a prosecution that publication was in the public interest.

Even so, the Government of the day greeted the proposals with only moderate enthusiasm. They accepted the principle that Section 2 should be abolished and a new Act put in its place, but were apprehensive about the Franks Committee's proposed categorisation. The Report was debated in the House of Commons in June 1973,[13] and the Home Secretary warned the House that he would probably have to widen the proposed area of sanctions, on the familiar ground – roughly speaking – that one category of information merged imperceptibly into another, and that it was virtually impossible to legislate for every eventuality. He also foresaw serious complications in determining who should do the classifying on the fringe of the reserved subjects, and how such classification could be challenged, except by calling on the courts to decide matters which were not within their proper competence. Hence the Government's preference for a theoretical but liberally interpreted embargo on all official information. Because of a change of Government in 1974 the matter will have to be debated again from first principles, but this is not a matter on which the political parties – judging by the public evidence of their leaders – appear to differ very much.

The main obstacle to progress is not one of reconciling political differences but of finding parliamentary time for legislation. The Queen's Speech to the British Parliament[14] on 19 November 1975 was extremely cautious on the subject:

> Proposals will be prepared to amend the Official Secrets Act 1911 and to liberalize the practices relating to official information.

This did not mean that a Bill would be introduced or even that a White Paper would be published; it need not have meant anything very much at all.

However, in 1976, and more particularly in 1977, momentum gathered. A vigorous parliamentary pressure group, advocating a Freedom of Information Act, developed into a national 'Freedom of Information Campaign'. A Working Party of the National Executive of the Labour Party (not, however, to be confused with the Labour Government) drafted its own Access to Information Bill, which it pressed upon the Party in Parliament. In August 1977 the Head of the Civil Service, on Cabinet instructions, issued new and positive guidance to heads of government departments. Among other things they were required thenceforward to prepare all policy analyses in two sections, the first of which would disclose the options drawn up for ministers in the later stages of formulating policy, the factual basis of which would be made public once ministers had announced their conclusions to Parliament. At the same time the Prime Minister announced that more Green Papers would be published and that departments had been instructed to respond more readily to requests for information from Members of Parliament, the public, journalists and research scholars.

These good intentions were embodied in a more positive statement in the Queen's Speech on 3 November 1977:

> Legislative proposals will be brought forward for the reform of section 2 of the Official Secrets Act 1911.

This at least means that a White Paper will be published in the 1977–78 Session of Parliament.[15]

The continued cautious approach prompts the question why some countries seem to have no difficulty in implementing 'freedom of access' legislation while the British Government finds it so difficult to come to the point, even after admitting the principle. The Franks Committee did not shirk this question – indeed they visited both Sweden and the United States (as well as France and Canada) in order to study it at first hand, and they discuss their conclusions in Chapter 6 of their Report. Their principal argument rests on the constitutional difference between such countries as Sweden and America, with written constitutions and a clear-cut separation of legislative and executive powers, and Britain, with an unwritten constitution and parliamentary control of the executive. They argue further that the gap between the two systems – with exceptions to openness on the one hand and exceptions to secrecy on the other – is not as wide as is often supposed; and they hint at the possibility that public access to documents could increase the amount of oral decision-making and drive written administrative information into the background.

No doubt other chapters in this book will throw light on these matters. It was a recurring theme of the Franks Report that what was needed in the U.K. was not so much a change in law as a change in mental attitude – the attitude, that is to say, of the civil service towards the public. The Committee had in mind that much of what would be achieved by a change in law could equally well be achieved by a change in administrative discretion, and they were undoubtedly on firm ground in saying that discretion had been exercised over-cautiously in the past. This was very obvious, for example, at the time (in 1962) when it was decided to publish the inspectors' reports on planning appeals. The team of civil servants who gave evidence at the investigation (curiously enough, also conducted under the chairmanship of Lord Franks) was emphatic that publication would cause embarrassment, would be a hindrance to sound policy-making and would create administrative difficulties amounting almost to chaos.[16] In the event, none of these gloomy prophecies was fulfilled. Indeed the whole atmosphere surrounding planning appeals became much healthier. It is human nature to foresee disaster when settled habits are changed, and in the U.K. it is probable that much more official information could be disclosed with benefit to some and detriment to none.

NOTES

1. The first Official Secrets Act of 1889 has been three times amended – in 1911, 1920 and 1939 – but the legislation has not been consolidated. Hence the occasional use in this chapter of the phrase 'Official Secrets Acts' in the plural. The principal references, however, are to the Official Secrets Act 1911.

2. *Report of a Committee on the Future of the Civil Service* (Chairman: Lord Fulton), Cmnd 3638 of 1968.

3. *Departmental Committee on Section 2 of the Official Secrets Act 1911* (Chairman: Lord Franks) Cmnd 5104 of 1972: Report and three volumes of written and oral evidence. Much information in this essay which is not otherwise attributed is gathered from this Report. A useful book spanning the whole subject of executive secrecy is David Williams, *Not in the Public Interest* (London: Hutchinson, 1965).

4. The case is usually known as *Conway v. Rimmer,* and the final decision is reported in the first volume of the All England Law Reports for 1968, the normal from of reference being 1968 1 All E.R. at p. 874. It went on appeal to the House of Lords, which reversed a previous decision of the Appeal Court (1967 2 All E.R. at p. 1260).

5. White Paper Cmnd. 4089 of 1969.

6. Reported in *The Law and the Press* (London: Stevens, 1965, since reprinted).

7. Space does not permit the proper development of the subject of privacy, which has had a separate major investigation. *Report of the Committee on Privacy* (Chairman: Kenneth Younger), Cmnd 5012 of 1972.

8. For a full account of the Lobby see Jeremy Tunstall, *The Westminster Lobby Correspondents* (London: Routledge & Kegan Paul, 1970).

9. *Report of a Committee of Privy Councillors appointed to inquire into 'D' Notice matters.* Cmnd 3309 of 1967.

10. London: Weidenfeld & Nicolson, 1971.

11. Written evidence of the Civil Service Department to the Franks Committee on the classification of official information. *Report*, Vol. 2, pp. 15–23. The descriptions of the four categories (underlined) are quoted *verbatim*. The examples are taken from the same source, but are condensed for reasons of space.

12. *Report*, para. 275. Paras 276 and 277 go on to outline the Committee's proposals, which are then set out in detail in para 278.

13. House of Commons Debates 29 June 1973: *Hansard* (Commons), Vol. 858, Cols. 1885–1973.

14. The Queen's Speech is the occasion on which the Government presents to Parliament its proposals for the ensuing year.

15. The White Paper, issued 19 July 1978, mainly followed the Franks proposals, and revealed that the Government had not yet made up its mind regarding a general access law. *Ed.*

16. *Committee on Administrative Tribunals and Inquiries, Minutes of Evidence*, Day 3, 22 February 1956, p. 71 *et seq.* (HMSO, 1957).

8 Western Germany

MARTIN BULLINGER

In the Federal Republic of Germany it is not recognised, either in theory or in practice, that everybody should have access to administrative records. Access has to be granted only when the applicant's personal rights or interests are concerned. Otherwise it is left to the administrative authority's discretion whether to grant access, and the decision is likely to be negative. The right of newspapers to be informed by the administration does not include the right to examine administrative records. Government and administrative authorities are inclined to regard their records as internal documents and prefer to inform the press and the public either orally or in writing.

BACKGROUND FACTORS

Although the accessibility of administrative records has been improved by recent legislation, there has been no radical change. The exclusion of public access is deeply rooted in Germany. Several historical, political and legal factors have contributed to this situation.

Public access is essentially an element of *direct* democracy. It enables the general public to control the administration and to form a public opinion which can influence administrative decisions. Constitutional history in Germany has, however, led to a predominantly *representative* democracy. Parliament is supposed to impose by statutes its will on the administration and to control it politically, for example by means of questions addressed to the Government. Administration has thus remained, in theory, a monolithic instrument, first of the monarch, later of governments which are responsible to parliament. It has therefore not been linked to democracy except at the highest level.

Under the present constitution, there is some tendency toward the establishment of more direct democratic influence on public administration. This is mainly done, however, by creating more self-governing units directed by elected councils, by instituting committees dominated by interest group representatives, and by strengthening the personal link between public officials and the political parties or certain interest groups, rather than by opening administrative records to discussion or criticism by the public.

Indirectly, the general public have access to administrative records if Parliament is entitled to examine these records. Traditionally, access has been granted only to committees of inquiry. The principle of separation of powers is considered to reserve for government an independent sphere of information where Parliament is not to intervene. This principle has recently been invoked by the constitutional court of Hamburg[1] in order to interpret restrictively a constitutional amendment which gives a minority of Parliament and its committees the right to examine administrative files.

A court can normally order the administration to produce all the relevant records, which thus become open to the parties concerned. It is not intended, but not excluded, that recorded information might thus indirectly become known to the general public. The guiding principle is not democracy, but the rule of law. This is significant. After the Second World War, public and legal opinion was for a long time primarily concerned with re-establishing the rule of law and strengthening the legal protection of the individual rather than with strengthening democracy which, in its direct form, seemed to have been discredited.

When administrative information is not general but deals with individual persons and cases, protection of privacy and not publicity is the main concern. It would be not only politically unthinkable but constitutionally impossible to open, for example, tax files to everybody's inspection. Data banks are considered a great danger to privacy and have brought forward data protection laws and bills.

There is also a strong feeling that the effectiveness of administration would suffer from a general publicity of records.[2] Thus it is argued that records would no longer contain all the relevant information, and this could hamper continuity as well as control of public administration. If citizens' groups trying to hinder administrative projects, such as atomic power stations, had a right to inspect all relevant files, administration would be more difficult, all the more so since revolutionary organisations might use the information as a means of destruction. Secrecy, as well as careful doses of publicity for certain administrative information, are considered political instruments. Universal accessibility of records would mean sharing political power with the opposition and with other influential groups. It is also argued that the attempt to introduce public access would meet much resistance because such access could disclose illegal practices, thus provoking claims for damages and a decline of confidence in the public administration.

For these and other reasons, the idea of general public access to recorded administrative information is quite unfamiliar and has not really been adopted even by those who emphasise the democratic aspect of administrative publicity.

RECENT CHANGES AND PROPOSALS

Legislative and judicial events seem to indicate that administrative records will become more accessible, but only to those whose personal rights and interests are at stake, not to the general public. Whereas former Bills or laws affecting administrative procedure adhered to the notion of a discretionary power of the administration, art. 29 of the Federal Administrative Procedure Act of 1976[3] creates a legal obligation to grant access to administrative records:

An administrative authority has to allow those who are involved in an administrative procedure to examine the records relevant to the procedure, as far as their knowledge is necessary to them to assert or to defend their legal interests.

This legal obligation is subject to several exceptions (para. 2):

The administrative authority is not under a duty to grant access if it would be prejudicial to the orderly performing of the authority's functions or to the well-being of the federation or of a state to make known the record's content, or if events have to be kept secret according to a specific legal provision or according to their nature, namely because of legitimate interests of the parties or third persons.

The administrative courts will finally decide whether one of these exceptions is applicable and might so strengthen the position of private individuals who are involved in an administrative procedure. They cannot, however, extend the new legal rule beyond its limits. The rule does not apply to persons seeking information without being personally involved, like journalists. Therefore, the courts are not in a position to introduce the idea of public access. They could, however, recognise all persons who could possibly be affected in the slightest way by administrative measures as being personally affected and thus entitled to examine the records. This would, on the other hand, hamper the administration in cases where a great number of persons may possibly be affected, as in the case of a new atomic power station. Therefore, recent legislation authorises the administration to grant access only to representatives of persons involved in great number in an administrative procedure; in other cases, e.g. atomic power stations, it is left to the administrative authority's discretion whether to grant access.

Moreover, art. 13 of the federal act of 1977 for the protection of personal data against misuse (Federal Data Protection Act)[4] provides that anybody who applies will have to be informed of his personal data registered by the administration in data banks, with the exception of data recorded by the secret services, the police, the public prosecutor or tax authorities. Information is not to be given if certain exceptions apply which correspond almost entirely to those of art. 29 para. 2 of the Federal Administrative Procedure Act cited above. Until a few years ago, examination files were regarded as essentially secret.[5] Many of these files are now open to the candidate, because of new legislation or jurisprudence.[6] Since 1969, the constitutions of several states have been amended, so as to give to their parliamentary committees of petitions the right to require administrative files to be produced.[7] Federal constitutional law has been amended in the same way.[8]

On the other hand, the new legislation will restrain rather than further *public* access to administrative information. Thus art. 30 of the Procedure Act of 1976 emphasises that personal or trade secrets are not to be communicated by the administration without special power to do so. Art. 11 of the Personal Data Protection Act goes even further: personal data which are not secret shall not be revealed if this is not necessary to the lawful fulfilment of the public authority's functions, except to those who can show a legitimate interest and provided that legitimate interests of the person concerned are not prejudiced.

GENERAL RIGHTS OF PUBLIC ACCESS

GENERAL SITUATION

Legal provisions which allow everybody to examine certain administrative records, for example urban development plans, are exceptional. More numerous are laws which grant access to certain administrative records provided that the applicant can show a legal or legitimate interest, for example to a register of births, marriages and deaths. The Administrative Procedure Act of 1976 provides that generally those who are involved in an administrative procedure are entitled to examine the relevant records. Several legal provisions require administrative information of a certain kind to be kept secret, particularly to protect personal privacy, trade or other business secrets.

In the absence of such legal provisions, it is left to the discretion of the administrative authority whether to grant access. Discretion does not permit arbitrary decisions. The authority has to weigh carefully the private or public interests in having access to a record against the private or public interests which could be adversely affected if the record came to be known to the applicant. There must be a sufficient interest of the applicant to get the information he needs specifically by examining the record. This is not easily recognised even if the applicant depends for his scientific research on having access to files. There is, in general, almost no chance of access for a lobbyist or journalist and even less for a simple citizen who just wants to know whether public administration is functioning according to the law.

Freedom of information, which is guaranteed by art. 5 of the federal constitution, is only the right 'to inform oneself without restraint from all sources of information which are open to everybody'. Since administrative records are regarded as being kept for internal purposes, art. 5 does not apply. Democracy as one of the leading principles of the federal constitution requires, and this is also implied in art. 5, that the public and especially the press should be sufficiently informed by the administration. This, however, is not considered as requiring general public access to administrative records.

TYPES OF INFORMATION TO BE KEPT SECRET

Public access to administrative records is entirely excluded if the recorded information is to be kept secret. Two different categories of secrecy should be but are not always clearly distinguished: formal and material secrecy.

Formal secrecy applies to administrative information regardless of its content and nature. A minister or civil servant is bound by law[9] to keep secret all information which he has received in the course of his official duties and which is not totally unimportant or already publicly known, except of course to communicate with his superior or other authorised persons. Outsiders are under the same obligation if they have formally promised not to reveal certain information, or documents are marked 'secret' or 'confidential'.[10]

This could be misunderstood as sheltering administrative information from outside knowledge almost totally. However, it is only meant to prevent unauthorised persons from revealing administrative information. The minister or public official who is authorised to handle certain administrative affairs is generally also authorised to decide how far and in which way persons affected or the general public should be informed. In this decision he is guided not by the personal obligation of a civil servant to keep administrative information secret but by his official duty to examine carefully whether special statutory provisions, legal principles or prevailing public or private interests either authorise certain officials (for example the head of a public authority) to give information or require certain information to be kept secret because of its special content (and thus create *material* secrecy). Formal secrecy is designed to canalise and organise, not to prevent, communication of administrative information; in fact, however, this canalising makes it more difficult for the general public and for the press in particular to get official access to administrative information.

Due to the traditional way of legal thinking, *material* secrecy is mostly required or guaranteed not for specific types of administrative information but in general terms which have to be interpreted from case to case. A typical example is art. 99 of the administrative court procedure code which allows an administrative authority to refuse to produce before the court administrative records whose content has to be kept secret 'according to a statute or according to its nature'. Scattered and rather unco-ordinated special laws as well as court decisions indicate that certain types of administrative information are likely to be regarded as requiring a high degree of secrecy. Many statutes order that administrative information concerning private life or business, for example medical data, tax declarations or trade secrets, shall not be revealed. Secrecy of such information is generally recognised by the courts even if it is not expressly required by statute. A court will normally recognise that information concerning foreign policy, defence, the secret service, political and criminal police, central bank operations or similar economic measures needs much secrecy and might even constitute a 'state secret', thus being protected from being revealed by severe criminal sanctions.[11]

Administrative records which are classified 'top secret', 'secret', etc., are not automatically recognised by the courts as being secret by their nature. This administrative classification intensifies, by special security rules and criminal sanctions,[12] the obligation of civil servants and other holders of administrative information not to reveal it to others (formal secrecy). But it does not create material secrecy, which is binding on the courts. It seems, however, that the courts will usually take for granted that the record is classified 'secret' because of its very nature.

All this does not mean that certain types of administrative records or other information are absolutely secret. There might be a legitimate public or private interest in giving or receiving information which prevails over the interest in secrecy and entitles or compels the administration to give access to the information. The police, for example, are normally in a position to withhold even from the courts the names of informers because otherwise the informers would not give their information to the police. If, however, an informer is guilty of malicious slander, the police must, on request, reveal his name to the person affected.[13]

THE HOLDERS OF INFORMATION

ADMINISTRATIVE AUTHORITIES

There is no major legal difference in access to information held by federal, state or local public authorities. Practically, access of the public is easier if the administrative authority is governed or advised by a council of elected citizens, experts or interest representatives, provided that this council is given access to recorded information. In the state of Baden-Württemberg for example, one-fourth of a local council can require the mayor to produce records provided that these records are not affairs of state delegated to the local community, and covered by secrecy rules.[14] Though the members of a local council are legally bound not to reveal information which is to be kept secret because of its nature, according to legal provisions or according to special orders issued in the public or private interest, this leaves legal as well as actual channels through which information can be passed to the general public.

State-owned corporations or enterprises are no more obliged or willing to give information than private companies. The federal and state administrative procedure laws have not changed the situation because they do not apply to business activities which are governed by private law. A local electricity and gas company owned by the local community, for example, is under no legal obligation to lay open its calculations before raising its rates. A professor of public law who wants to get information for research reasons is met with suspicion. Business and not democratic or social considerations prevail and make it even more difficult to get information here than from the administration in general.

POLITICAL EXECUTIVES

Information held by a chancellor, prime minister or minister (in his governmental and not his administrative capacity) and proceedings of Cabinets are not accessible to the public. It is almost inconceivable that a court would order such information to be revealed; this would be regarded as contrary to the 'welfare of the state' and thus excluded by all relevant procedure codes.

This is best illustrated by a Hamburg case. As already mentioned the Hamburg constitution since 1971 gives a minority of Parliament or of a parliamentary committee the right to have administrative records produced as far as this would not be 'contrary to legal provisions or to the welfare of the state'. The opposition members of the budget committee asked the Government (Senat) to lay open to the committee the records concerning the budgetary planning for the years 1971 to 1975. The constitutional court of Hamburg held this to be contrary to the welfare of the state as far as records concerned the deliberations of the Government or were in preparation for them.[15] According to the principle of separation of powers, the court argued, a government must have the possibility to decide independently and therefore have a sphere of deliberation and decision which is shielded from outside knowledge.

On the other hand, governments and ministers are entitled and sometimes even obliged by statute to give to interest groups concerned the opportunity to render their opinion before a decision is taken. The joint standing order of the federal ministries states that, at the discretion of the minister, internal drafts may be made accessible to the press or to interest groups, provided that the Cabinet decision is not unduly hampered and as far as drafts for new laws are concerned, provided that normally Parliament is informed at the same time.[16] In practice, proposed legislation is often discussed with interest groups in order to come to a political understanding before Parliament is given official notice. Also, parliamentary members of the governing party or coalition may get information through party channels because of the minister having to secure political support before undertaking important measures.

THE RECIPIENTS OF INFORMATION

GENERAL ACCESS

It is only in certain clearly defined and restricted areas that everybody is entitled to inspect public records. For example, records of public sessions of Parliament, of local councils and similar assemblies are either published or laid open to everybody. Before dangerous installations like atomic power stations can be authorised, the application with all accompanying documents, trade secrets excepted, has to be made accessible to everybody. This is meant to give access to all those who could possibly be affected and therefore want to object. The effect is, however, to give access to the general public.

Otherwise, access of the general public to administrative records is left to the authority's discretion and is not likely to be granted. A member of a local council recently tried to inspect certain records concerning the sale of public land in order to prove irregular practices of the mayor. The superior administrative court of Baden-Württemberg stated that the claimant was no more entitled than any other citizen to investigate personally the local administration and claim access to the records.[17] Neither private curiosity nor political interest in revealing maladministration is a legitimate reason for claiming access to administrative records. 'Self-appointed public prosecutors' are, in the general mind, not necessary to control the public administration.

Direct democratic control of the administration is entrusted neither to the individual citizen nor to groups of citizens but to the press. Press laws of the states recognise that 'the press fulfils a public function when it, in matters of public interest, procures and diffuses news, takes its stand, criticizes or participates otherwise in the forming of public opinion.' Consequently, public authorities 'have to provide the representatives of the press with the information which enables them to fulfil their public function'. Information cannot be refused except for certain reasons stated expressly by the press laws – for example, if the law or a dominant public or private interest requires the information to be kept secret.[18]

The right and the duty to inform the press are reserved to the head of a public authority or to his delegate.[19] Important public authorities such as the ministries have special press officials. Information is given orally (press conferences, etc.) or by handing over well-prepared statements. The statutory provisions as well as the constitutional guarantees of the freedom of the press and of information are not interpreted as granting access to public records. In practice, journalists do not even apply for access.

However, journalists do not always want to rely on the information which is officially given by the relevant authority, and which is not necessarily complete and objective. They sometimes resort to the indiscretion of civil servants. If the informer is prosecuted criminally, the journalist can refuse to give testimony. Like a Member of Parliament, normally he does not have to reveal the source of his information before a criminal court.[20] The journalist himself may be punishable as having instigated or aided the indiscretion, or as having made public 'state secrets' or administrative documents classified 'secret' and thus having endangered important public interests.[21] Criminal prosecutions of this kind, however, do not happen very often.

ACCESS BY PARTICULAR BODIES AND GROUPS

Indirectly, the general public can get access to administrative records if Parliament and its organs, a court, a third public authority or the person affected have access and are not bound by law to keep the information secret.

Parliamentary committees of inquiry and some committees of petitions are entitled to have administrative files handed over to them. Committees of inquiry of the federal lower house (Bundestag), for example, have the same investigating powers as a criminal court and can, therefore, require an administrative document to be produced if the highest administrative authority does not object that it would harm the well-being of the federation or a state to make known the document's content.[22] The committee can also try to rely on the administrative authority's obligation to assist the committee;[23] such assistance of one public authority to another can be refused, however, if the document at stake is to be kept secret.[24] In practice, secret documents are sometimes made available to a parliamentary committee, for example to the (federal) defence committee, which has the powers of a committee of inquiry. Members of Parliament thus informed, however, are not allowed to disclose their knowledge to the public. The standing orders of the lower house impose restrictions on the use of secret information which are similar to those applicable to civil servants.[25] Secret documents may not, for example, be handed over to a committee except for the time of its meeting.

Wider powers of inspection are entrusted to the military Ombudsman, who acts as an organ of the federal lower house and its defence committee but is independent to a large extent. He has access to all defence records, provided that secrecy is not absolutely indispensable, an objection which has to be brought forward and justified before the defence committee by the Minister of Defence or his deputy personally. Though the Ombudsman is bound, like a civil servant, not to reveal secrets, he can inform the lower house, its defence committee and to some extent the general public as far as this is necessary to fulfil his function and as far as public or private interests do not require secrecy. In his published annual report to Parliament, individual cases and documents are mentioned, but in a way that individual soldiers or officers cannot be recognised. Real defence secrets are not revealed. By means of his report and press interviews, the military Ombudsman contributes to some extent to the forming of public opinion, which in turn might influence defence policy. This is, on the other hand, the origin of some political tension between the defence ministry and the Ombudsman.

Civil Ombudsmen exist only in the state of Rheinland-Pfalz and, for the purpose of preventing the misuse of data banks, in the federation, in the state of Hessen, and (in the form of an independent commission) in the state of Rheinland-Pfalz. The commission for constitutional reform, instituted by the federal lower house, has rejected the idea of creating one or several civil Ombudsmen on the ground that control over the administration could be sufficiently improved by other methods.[26]

A court can generally require all the relevant administrative documents to be made part of the court files. As the court is not allowed to reserve these documents for an inspection *in camera*, the documents may be inspected by the parties to the process, who are not bound to keep their content secret. For that reason, secret information is not made available to the courts. As to the details, the different procedure codes vary considerably. The most important is the administrative court procedure code, which permits administrative documents to be retained if the highest administrative authority makes it plausible that the documents must by law or by their nature be kept secret or that their disclosure would harm the well-being of the federation or of a state. There is some suspicion that an administrative authority could reorganise its files and remove sensitive documents before handing the files over to the court, alleging that it had to single out documents which were not relevant to the case.

Apart from court procedure, administrative authorities prefer giving oral or written information to opening their files to the citizen. As mentioned, however, the Federal Administrative Procedure Act of 1976 gives all persons involved in an administrative procedure the right to inspect the relevant administrative files, subject to the specified restrictions. Persons so informed are allowed to make the information publicly known.

In many cases, public authorities are governed or advised by councils which consist to some extent of representatives of trade unions, industrial organisations, professional associations, and other interest groups. To decide important matters concerning the federal railways is, for example, the task of an administrative council. Five of its twenty members are nominated by the trade unions, and five by top organisations of the industry and other branches of the economy. These interest group representatives are, as in other cases, under an express statutory duty to keep secret what they come to know, as if they were civil servants. It is, however, quite unlikely that this obligation is strictly kept. The representatives cannot really be expected to keep the leaders of their respective organisations uninformed. On the contrary, they are made members of the administrative body in order to let their organisations take part in the decision process and thus win their support. From this angle, secrecy requirements need to be reconsidered.

On the other hand, information is normally not likely to be passed by the interest group to the general public. Interest groups will use the information to their advantage but are not interested in sharing it with others. For this reason public access to administrative records might become necessary in order to counterbalance interest-group participation in the administration. Otherwise, segments of the public are given exclusive information and consequently exclusive influence, thus favouring oligarchic instead of democratic government and administration. Besides, economic competition and equal economic chances for all might be endangered if administrative information were reserved to some competitors only.

Historians and other scientists who depend for their research on access to administrative records cannot be satisfied with oral information. Freedom of research is guaranteed by art. 5 of the federal constitution. This excludes state interference but does not give the right to search without restrictions in public or private documents. Research interest has to be weighed against a legitimate public or private interest in keeping information secret.[27]

As long as files are kept by an administrative authority, access for research reasons is not easily granted. To gain access to files of a federal ministry, for example, permission of the minister or his state secretary is needed.[28] Access is easier after several years, especially when the documents have been transferred to archives. After 30 years, files of a federal ministry are normally open for research.[29] According to the regulations governing the state archives of Baden-Württemberg (1955, 1973), it is one of the aims of a state archive to make documents available to scientific research. An applicant has to show a legitimate interest. Authorisation is given only for a specific research topic and can be made subject to certain restrictions, for example to submit the proposed publication for approval by the archives administration. Such approval is required if, even after a long time, publication of certain public or private data could harm legitimate public or private interests. Not at all accessible are documents which are classified 'secret', etc., or declared inaccessible by law or by the administrative authority that transferred the documents to the archives. The extent to which even archives have to keep outdated administrative information secret suggests to what extent recorded information is shielded from outside knowledge.

INFORMATION PROCEDURES

HOLDING OF INFORMATION

For federal as well as for state administrations there are registry instructions concerning the keeping of files. According to the federal registry instructions, all information shall be placed in the relevant file; files of principal importance shall be classified 'A-files', others 'B-files'; and once a year, files shall be examined to decide whether they are still necessary for current administrative purposes, or whether they should be destroyed or transferred to the federal interim archives. Here they are kept at the administrative authority's disposition for a fixed period, after which they will be transferred to the federal archives if they are worth conserving.

Working documents, especially draft decisions, are not filed except under certain conditions, for example after all officials concerned have signed, and are not accessible to third persons until after the procedure has been concluded, or not even then.[30] The process of decision-making is considered to be an internal affair of the administration as far as provisional reflections of public officials are concerned.

If information is registered in computer data banks instead of being filed, it is technically possible to make this information instantaneously known to anybody – to the public authority concerned, to other public authorities, and to private organisations or persons. Privacy and individual liberty depend to a considerable extent, however, on the fact that personal data, even when made known to one administrative authority, are not, as a matter of course, accessible to other authorities and to outsiders. For that reason, the Federal Data Protection Act does not allow computerised personal data to be made known except to the extent that this is necessary to the lawful fulfilment of administrative functions or complies with a legitimate private information interest without doing harm to the legitimate interests of the person affected.[31] It is difficult to see how these rather vague limitations could effectively prevent computer information from becoming more easily available than information kept in files.

CLASSIFICATION AND DECLASSIFICATION OF INFORMATION

According to the degree of secrecy which seems necessary, administrative records are classified by the competent administrative authority as 'top secret', 'secret', 'confidential' or 'for internal use only'. As the federal instruction concerning this classification[32] is itself classified 'for internal use only', private persons like the author of this report have to prove a legitimate interest and promise to keep the instruction secret before they get access to this instruction.

Anyhow, some general outlines of the federal instruction may be revealed here without getting into conflict with the law of secrecy. There is no formal administrative procedure designed to control classification and declassification. It seems to be difficult if not impossible to persuade a criminal court or administrative court to intervene and to pass judgment directly on whether a particular classification is justified. Indirectly, an administrative court could exercise a certain control in ordering an administrative record to be made part of the court file in spite of its having been classified 'secret', etc. In practice, this possibility seems slight. Excessive classification and tardy declassification may have been avoided to some extent because of the considerable burden which the handling of classified records places on the administrative personnel. The natural desire to reduce this burden is perhaps more efficient than formal control procedures, but it cannot be denied that a formal control mechanism might be useful.

REFUSAL AND RELEASE OF INFORMATION

If an individual's request for having access to administrative records is refused, the individual can enforce access provided that he can show a personal legal interest in the information, by suing the administration before an administrative court. A general or group interest or simple curiosity in the information is not sufficient. General public access is therefore not directly within the range of judicial protection.

Someone not having a personal legal interest may address himself to the federal or state parliament's committee of petitions. These committees do not, however, have the power to redress grievances. They can only recommend a solution. A constitutional reform is about to give to the committees of petitions wider competence, for example the power to correspond directly with a public authority and to obtain access to its records. This reform has already been successful in the federation and in some states. This does not mean, however, that the committees will pass the information to the applicants. Besides, the committees' access must be subject to certain restrictions so that it will not conflict with the constitutional principle of separation of powers.[33]

Redress might be obtained by complaining to a higher administrative authority. This informal procedure is open to everybody. Since, however, the idea of public access to administrative records is not likely to be adopted by administrative authorities, the complaint will almost certainly be unsuccessful. Journalists and interest group representatives wisely prefer to make use of political or personal good relations instead of complaining formally or informally.

Public officials who, without being authorised, release recorded information which is secret and thus endanger important public interests risk punishment by a criminal court.[34] However, prosecution has to be authorised by a higher administrative authority or even by the minister. Whenever the well-being of the Federal Republic or of a state is at stake, the secret is called a 'state secret' and criminal sanctions are particularly severe.[35] Indiscretion in itself is, without any additional requirements, a breach of duty of the civil servant which may incur disciplinary measures. Neither criminal nor disciplinary liability apply if the civil servant reveals unconstitutional activities after having exhausted all other remedies, for example after he has informed in vain his superior and the Member of Parliament of his constituency.[36]

Criminal liability is also incurred by private individuals (journalists, etc.) who release state secrets or who participate in the criminal act of a civil servant who does so. It is also incurred if they release information classified as 'secret' or to be kept secret according to a special obligation they have undertaken (for example in order to get access to a certain document), always provided that the indiscretion has endangered important public interests.[37]

Generally, in practice criminal or disciplinary sanctions are not applied except in important cases. Prosecution of all cases of indiscretion would probably involve a large proportion of the administrative personnel.

CONCLUSIONS

The justifications for the state of law and administrative practice in the Federal Republic as compared with the legal situation in the Scandinavian countries and the United States are not entirely convincing. Public access to administrative records could perhaps be facilitated without neglecting the real need for secrecy, and it should perhaps be introduced to some extent in order to improve democratic control over the administration. If oral information is given, for example to the press, access to the relevant records should not be excluded. It would avoid much suspicion, assure objective information and strengthen independent control over the administration. The *practical* problems are:

How to separate secret and non-secret documents. Often, both are combined in the same files. Public access would make it necessary either to record separately secret and non-secret information or to remove secret information individually in each case where access is applied for.

How to ensure that records are not damaged or taken away. This would create organisational and personnel problems because each administrative authority or group of administrative authorities would have to install a reading room where supervision could be guaranteed.

How to enable interested persons to find out what records exist, so that they could demand access to the relevant records. A list of records would have to be made available.

How to enable non-experts to read and to understand administrative records. Advice on this would have to be given if public access is to have the effect of strengthening democratic control.

Generally, administration would become more difficult and more expensive. Since the idea of public access is still resented by the administration and not really adopted by the general public, financial and organisational difficulties are likely to hinder any general reform.

On the other hand, public access as a means of public control of the administration seems to be necessary, if not required by the constitution, as far as parliamentary, hierarchical and court control of the administration prove to be insufficient. This is particularly true where the administration is not strictly bound by the law but is given policy-making power, either by including in the statutes sweeping clauses such as 'in the public interest' or by openly granting a discretionary power to the administration. To the extent to which neither elected assemblies nor higher administrative authorities or administrative courts are able to supervise this policy-making, there is a real danger that administration may become autocratic. Public access to the relevant administrative records could, perhaps, establish a minimum of supplementary democratic control.[38]

Administrative secrecy is required to a greater extent than is really needed to protect public or private interests. This legal surplus of secrecy requirements could be removed. Law reform having this aim does not seem to be impossible but would be difficult to achieve. Administrative records are likely to continue to be considered as internal and mainly non-public documents of the administration, even if this is not justified by their content.

NOTES

1. Decision of July 7, 1973, published in 'Die Oeffentliche Verwaltung', 1973, p. 745.

2. See e.g. the federal government's official comment on art. 25 of the Federal Administrative Procedure Bill of 1973 (Bundestagsdrucksache 7/910), p. 53.

3. Bundesgesetzblatt 1976, part I, p. 1253; this statute came into force on 1 January, 1977. All the states have passed administrative procedure acts which correspond almost entirely to the Federal Act. For this reason, only the Federal Act will be cited. These Administrative Procedure Acts do not apply if statutes provide for different procedure rules.

4. Of January 27, 1977, Bundesgesetzblatt 1977, part I, p. 201, coming into force on January 1, 1978.

5. See e.g. decision of the federal administrative court of 23 February 1962 (vol. 14, p. 31).

6. Cf. the decision of the superior administrative court at Lüneburg of 28 February 1972, published in 'Neue Juristische Wochenschrift', 1973, p. 638.

7. Cf., e.g., the constitution of Hamburg, art. 25a, 32.

8. Art. 45c of the federal constitution in connection with the Act concerning the powers of the committee of petitions of the Bundestag of 19 July 1975.

9. Cf. the civil service codes of the federation and the states, e.g. art. 61 of the federal civil service code and the collective agreements concerning federal or state employees.

10. Art. 353c of the (federal) criminal code.

11. Ibid., art. 93–97b.

12. Ibid., art. 353c, para. 1.

13. Cf. the decision of the federal administrative court of 30 April 1965, published in 'Die Oeffentliche Verwaltung', 1965, p. 488.

14. Art. 24 paras 3 and 5 of the local government code of Baden-Württemberg.

15. See note 1 above.

16. Art. 25 of the joint standing order of the federal ministries, part II (Gemeinsame Geschaeftsordnung der Bundesministerien, Besonderer Teil – GGO II).

17. Decision of 17 December 1973, published in 'Baden-Württembergische Verwaltungspraxis', 1974, p. 81.

18. Art. 3 and 4 of the state press code of Baden-Württemberg; the other states have similar statutory provisions.

19. Art. 63 of the federal civil service code.

20. Art. 53 of the (federal) criminal procedure code, revised in July 1975. Similar statutory provisions of the states were declared unconstitutional by the federal constitutional court because the states did not have the power to legislate.

21. Art. 353c, 93–97b of the (federal) criminal code.

22. Art. 44 of the (federal) constitution; art. 96 of the (federal) criminal procedure code.

23. Art. 44, paras 3 and 35, of the (federal) constitution.

24. Art. 5 para. 2 of the (federal) Administrative Procedure Act of 1976.

25. Cf. art. 21, 21a, 73, para. 9, of the standing order of the lower house (Geschaeftsordnung des Deutschen Bundestages) and the protection of secrets order of the lower house (Geheimschutzordnung des Deutschen Bundestages) as of April 1975, published in 'Bundesgesetzblatt, part I', p. 992.

26. Bundestagsdrucksache VI/3829, pp. 33–5.

27. Decision of the federal administrative court of 25 February 1971 (vol. 37, p. 265).

28. Art. 80, para. 2, of the joint standing order of the federal ministries, part I (Gemeinsame Geschaeftsordnung der Bundesministerien, Allgemeiner Teil – GGO I).

29. Ibid. art. 80 para. 1.

30. See art. 29 para. 1, and art. 21 of the registry instruction (Registraturanweisung) of the federal ministries.

31. Art. 10, 11 of the Federal Data Protection Act.

32. Verschlußsachenanweisung fuer Bundesbehoerden.

33. See note 1 above.

34. Art. 353b, 353c of the (federal) criminal code.

35. Ibid., art. 93–97b.

36. Decision of the federal constitutional court of 28 April 1970 (vol. 28, p. 191).

37. Art. 353c of the (federal) criminal code.

38. Cf. Walter Schmidt: *Organisierte Einwirkungen auf die Verwaltung* (Organized pressures on the administration), in Veroeffentlichungen der Vereinigung der Deutschen Staatsrechtslehrer, vol. 33 (Berlin and New York: Walter de Gruyter & Co., Verlagsbuchhandlung, 1975), pp. 203–9, 211–13; Richard Bartlsperger: *Organisierte Einwirkungen auf die Verwaltung* (Organized pressures on the administration), in Veroeffentlichungen der Vereinigung der Deutschen Staatsrehtslehrer, vol. 33 (Berlin and New York: Walter de Gruyter & Co., Verlagsbuchhandlung, 1975), pp. 255–8.

III Eastern Europe

9 Hungary

SÁNDOR BERÉNYI AND
TIBOR GYULA NAGY

BACKGROUND FACTORS

Some knowledge of the nature and organisation of the Hungarian
state is necessary if one is to understand the operation of its system of
public administration and information.

A main characteristic of the Hungarian People's Republic is that
it is a socialist state. The socio-economic order is basically socialist
but, as the constitution itself declares, the socialist reconstruction of
society is not yet complete. State property has a dominant role in
economics; state enterprises provide the greater proportion of
national income. Co-operatives have a major role in agriculture and
petty trading as well as handicrafts. These are voluntary economic
associations based on co-operative group property.

Another main characteristic of Hungary is that it is a unitary
state. Neither historical nor geographical factors, nor the presence
of national minorities has warranted a federal system.

We will now enumerate and briefly describe the main state
organs in the Hungarian People's Republic, and then explain their
relationship to non-state organisations and to citizens, in order to
give a better understanding of the system of access to administrative
information.

1. *The highest organs of state power and popular representation.* These
are Parliament and the Presidium, a collective body which carries
out the functions of a head of state. They express the fullness of state
power and popular sovereignty, and they are made up of representatives chosen by universal and secret suffrage. Their power over
state organisations taken as a whole has no bounds.

2. *The organs of public administration.* As in other countries, these are the Government, ministries, central offices, administrative organs of local self-government (the executive committee and the subordinated administrative services), decentralised administrative organs, etc. The socialist public administration organisation is the largest administrative organisation of society that directs the socialist economic system: it realises the rights of the state as owner in the administration of state enterprises, ensures the elaboration of national economic development plans, and organises the implementation of plans accepted by representative organs of state power; it manages and maintains social, cultural and health institutions; it exercises state supervision and control over the co-operative system, ensuring the conditions of economic development of co-operatives; and it carries out the traditional law-and-order duties of the public administration, as well as other conventional duties – foreign affairs, home defence, etc.

3. *The courts.* The courts generally enjoy rights of access to administrative information as they do throughout the world, since such information serves as evidence in both civil and criminal suits. It should also be noted that acts by organs of public administration can be fought through the courts. In such suits, administrative information acts as the basis of the suit.

4. *The public prosecutor's organisation.* This is a special type of state organ which carries out not only the conventional prosecuting functions but also serves as the supreme guardian of legality. It is headed by the Chief Prosecutor who is elected by Parliament and is responsible only to Parliament. He is responsible for constitutionality and for the implementation of laws and decrees passed or issued in a constitutional way. This somewhat resembles the position of the Ombudsman, though there are essential differences. Since the public prosecutor's organisation also supervises the legislative and executive activity of public administration, its complete access to administrative information is ensured both by the constitution and by legislation.

5. *Territorial administrative units* (towns, villages, rural districts, counties). Elected representative and self-governing bodies (local councils) operate within these, and they also carry out local administrative functions. Each council elects an executive committee which directs and co-ordinates the subordinated local administrative services (administrative organs) and has a number of highly specialised duties. A few decentralised administrative ser-

vices are not subject to the local councils. Such exceptions are the police, organs of defence administration, and functions which cannot be adjusted to the above territorial structure, such as the railways, post, water supply and irrigation. These services are governed by decentralised local organs which are subjected only to the central administrative authorities.

The Parliament, the highest organ of state power and popular representation, has full legal access to administrative information. This is also true of local councils which govern local administrative organs. Their functions of direction and control demand that they must have full access to information connected with their own executive organs. The courts and the Chief prosecutor's local agents are entitled to access to certain administrative information because of their constitutional function.

It should also be noted that both the state enterprises and institutions and the non-state (i.e. social) institutions and enterprises are linked to the system of public administration. In the first case the enterprises and institutions are managed by the state as owner, while in the second case the administrative organisation exercises the state's right to control and supervise. But all these organisations must, as part of a uniform informational and statistical system, supply information and data to administrative organs, and the administrative organisation must also supply all of them with information necessary for efficient operation.

An important place within socialist society is held by organisations which citizens have established, thanks to the right of association guaranteed by the constitution, in order to represent their interests or for social, cultural or sporting purposes.

Several hundred kinds of associations like these exist. Such organisations may be classified into the following major groups: Communist Party, Patriotic People's Front; political mass organisations such as trade unions and the youth federation; other mass organisations, clubs and associations; co-operative associations; and other autonomous social organisations. The co-operatives deserve special mention since, after state enterprises, they are the second basic institution of the socio-economic system. The co-operatives are economically autonomous. The public administration supervises their operation, and is therefore assured access to all their information, but it is, in exchange, obliged to make information available to them which will enable them to operate successfully in markets at home and abroad. The constitution not only recognises the right of citizens to form associations but it also provides for the participation of such associations in the management of society, and in the social and democratic control and supervision of public administration.[1] These organisations act as the partners of public administration, in a manner assured by law. Certain administrative decisions can be taken only in conjunction or after consultation with them. The state entrusts such organisations with numerous public duties, and ensures that the costs are covered. These associations enjoy access to administrative information. Laws define precisely what kind of information they are entitled to demand.

Individual citizens also enjoy access to administrative information. This is derived from two basic rights, as enumerated and explained below.

1. *The constitutional right of citizens to take part in public and political activities.*[2] According to law citizens may submit proposals and reports to all state or public administrative organs and may demand information from them which does not intrude into areas demanding secrecy. Thus the right to individual and collective participation in political activities also includes access to information. This is achieved partly through the elected representatives to Parliament and local councils from whom they can demand information about administrative activities. These representatives have the right to obtain information from administrative organs and to pass it on to their constituents. Collective access to information is also achieved through the socio-political organisations mentioned above – trade unions, associations, etc. These have a right to defined areas of administrative information, to which they can secure access at the request of their members.

The mass media play a key role in supplying the public with up-to-date information on the activities of public administration. They are obliged to publish important new legislation and draft outlines of projected legislation. Also, since citizens' access to and social control of public administration are basic principles, the administration is obliged to keep the public directly informed on its more important activities by issuing publications of various kinds.

2. *The right to a fair procedure.* The second legal foundation for the citizen's right of access to administrative information rests on the fact that the administrative authorities issue decisions which directly affect him. In such cases the law on procedure regulates the rights of the authorities and citizens. Basic to this is the citizen's right of access to the documents on which a decision affecting him is

based, even if they contain classified information.[3] This applies not only to citizens but to organisations generally outside the administration.

SPECIAL PROBLEMS AND TRENDS

So far our approach to administrative information has been from the viewpoints of political science and of constitutional law. The system of administrative information must also be seen from the angle of systems analysis, since this is now being employed to ensure that the informational system conforms to the demands of scientific management. From this angle public administration must be recognised as that organisation which collects, processes and stores information relevant to society as a whole. Public administration is thus the most powerful mechanism in society concerned with information.

This system is structured to include numerous sub-systems. The following four are stressed since they already more or less conform to the requirements of a scientifically organised system in which administrative data are stored and passed on by means of computerised electronic equipment. These are: the statistical information sub-system, with the Central Bureau of Statistics as its centre; the financial data sub-system, with the Ministry of Finance as its centre but with a number of related agencies such as the Central Revenue Authority, the Hungarian National Bank, etc; the population register, with the National Population Registry as its centre; and the register of immobile property, with the National Land Registry as its centre.

The information system of public administration is undergoing changes. The essence of these is the establishment of a uniform system of public administration scientifically organised through the use of electronic computers, etc. This process is part of a long-term development plan of Hungarian public administration, recently approved by the Government.[4] The system has not yet been fully developed. Far too much information is still collected, creating extra work for administrative personnel. At the same time often not enough information is available when decisions are taken. Data processing may well be centralised if a uniform system of public administration is established. Simultaneously the distribution of information may be decentralised, in accord with a major decentralisation process taking place in the whole system of public administration. However, the low standard of data processing work at lower levels leads to decisions that are not well founded, and this handicaps the process of decentralisation.

In our view, the changes will ultimately allow the administrative authorities to supply diverse organisations with information of the appropriate quantity and quality – particularly as regards economics – to permit their optimum functioning.

GENERAL RIGHTS OF PUBLIC ACCESS

THE GENERAL SITUATION

The direction and control of public administration by representative bodies is decisive. One must differentiate between information presented at the plenary sessions of such bodies in the course of taking decisions, and that supplied to committees and self-government bodies which are primarily concerned with exercising control over public administration. The latter includes information which members are entitled to demand on behalf of their constituents, and to pass on to them, as well as institutionalised democratic publicity of public administration, such as the right to information of social organisations (the party, trade unions, etc.), of the mass media, and of individual citizens.

As already noted, state and non-state enterprises and institutions enjoy access to administrative data. If, for example, an enterprise wants to build a new plant, it is entitled to a wealth of administrative data. Information is provided on the market situation at home and abroad, on probable state financial support, and so on. A special government information centre advises enterprises on suitable locations for investment, preferences granted in a given locality, estimated costs, the available infrastructure of services, etc.

TYPES OF INFORMATION KEPT SECRET

Secrets are classified into three groups in law. In the first group are two types between which the law makes a distinction from the point of view of the interests of the state: state secrets and public service secrets.

State secrets are those data which, in the hands of an unauthorised person, endanger the security or other important interests of the Hungarian People's Republic.[5] The scope of state secrets is determined by law,[6] but it also empowers the ministers concerned to classify certain information as a state secret.

A public service secret consists of information relating to a state organ, a social organisation or co-operative which, in the hands of an unauthorised person, would endanger its smooth operation or the good order of public administration, defence, justice or economic activity.[7] The head of the administrative organ has the right to determine what kind of information should be classified as a public service secret.

The second group includes secrets which every employed person must keep. These are determined by the Labour Code, which uniformly regulates conditions of employment in the Hungarian People's Republic. According to it, an employed person is obliged to guard state, service and job secrets.[8] The relevant paragraph continues: 'Furthermore, no unauthorised person may be supplied with information obtained in connection with his duties, the passing on of which may produce disadvantages for the employer or any other person.' Since the staff of administrative organisations are also in employment, these provisions apply to them as well.

The third group of secrets concerns those that affect the personal rights of citizens, and are therefore classified as secret by either the Constitution or some other legal norm. Professional secrets of medical practitioners, legal advisers and others belong to this category. Such sectrets may also be found within an administrative authority, in which case it is obliged to keep them secret. Their scope is too wide to be elaborated on here.

THE HOLDERS OF ADMINISTRATIVE INFORMATION

Since the administrative organisation is extraordinarily complex, major groups of administrative and other organs must be distinguished for purposes of discussing the holders of administrative information.

CENTRAL ADMINISTRATIVE ORGANS

First we must consider the political sphere, the Government itself (the ministers and secretaries of state). Second are the central administrative organs, which can be differentiated as functional or sectional ones. The functional organs, such as the Ministry of Finances, the Ministry of Labour, the Central Planning Office, and the Central Bureau of Statistics, are at the same time the most important centres of information since data collecting, processing and storing are among their major duties. Sectional organs, such as the Ministry of Education, the Ministry of Health and the ministries administering this or that industry, act as information centres of various sections of social activity.

For our purposes some enterprises and public institutions which serve as an information basis for public administration must be classified with central administrative organs. An example is the Hungarian National Bank, one of the country's most important centres of financial information.

LOCAL ADMINISTRATIVE ORGANS

The local councils control well-structured and specialised administrative services. These collect local information to ensure the smooth and uniform development of towns and villages.

SOCIAL ORGANISATIONS

Social organisations that carry out state duties have the necessary access to administrative information, and thus become holders of administrative information themselves. Some state duties are exclusively handled by a social organisation, or by an administrative organ working under its supervision. Social insurance is an example of the latter. Its central administrative organ is supervised and controlled by the National Council of Trade Unions. In such cases social organisations can be considered administrative organs, and are treated as such in respect to the secrecy or openness of information.

CENTRES OF DOCUMENTATION

As early as 1949 specialised centres of documentation were beginning to be established as part of the system of administrative information. Four of these centres held, respectively, technical, agricultural, medical and economic information; the fifth was a library. Their staffs collect and classify specialised documents and prepare précis, extracts and translations. Many other information centres have since been established. Their services complement the information services of administrative centres.

THE RECIPIENTS OF INFORMATION

No sharp dividing line can be drawn between those who hold administrative information and those who receive it. For this reason we include at the beginning of this section a discussion of special recipients of information within the administrative structure.

SPECIAL RECIPIENTS OF INFORMATION WITHIN
PUBLIC ADMINISTRATION

The four information sub-systems previously mentioned – the statistical and financial sub-systems and the registers of population and property – store and use administrative information from other state sub-systems and from outside sources. They serve as links between the administrative organisation, state economic enterprises, work organisations and the citizens.

The financial and statistical sub-systems are the largest and most uniform. They are legally regulated, nation-wide, scientifically sound and largely mechanised.

The financial sub-system includes the Ministry of Finances' budgetary information, the Hungarian National Bank, the State Development Bank (information on investments), the Ministry of Finances' Revenue Directorate and its local agencies, the National Savings Bank and its network of branches, and the financial sections of local councils. This means in practice that every kind of financial operation is supervised by the state, and that this is assured by a uniform financial information system. The state agencies mentioned, and to some extent the banks, have legal rights and channels to obtain the information they need from the other parts of the administrative organisation.

The statistical sub-system headed by the Central Bureau of Statistics consists partly of state information which is required by law to be provided, and partly of information which is voluntarily supplied. The other organs receiving and supplying state statistical information include the ministries, the National Planning Office, the National Bank, the Local Government Councils Office of the Council of Ministers, the National Bureau of Prices and Commodities, the National Water Board, the Central Committee for People's Control, the councils of Budapest and the counties, the public prosecutor's organisation, and the Hungarian Academy of Sciences. Within this state sub-system the supply of data is ensured by law and state discipline. Also co-ordinating instrumentalities to harmonise the financial and statistical sub-systems have come into being.

The population and land registers are being brought up to date, and a new system for keeping the population register is being developed. The population register covers everyone living within the Hungarian People's Republic, and all state, co-operative and social organs that are obliged to provide information (such as registries of births, deaths and marriages) are entitled to make use of its data. The central organ is the National Population Registry, which comes under direct government control.

The newly developed land register, which records rights and legal interests concerned with real estate, unifies title deed registers kept by district courts and other state registries. It describes all land and buildings in the country, all rights attached to these, and all other legally relevant facts. The Minister of Agriculture and Food Production is responsible for the central management of the National Land Registry. The various land registries supply data to the state administration and to the courts.

ACCESS BY THE PUBLIC

How can outside organisations and persons obtain access to information held by the public administration? Here the peculiarly Hungarian type of regulation prompts a three-way discussion according to the type of situation.

The first type is where an administrative authority makes a legal decision directly affecting a party – a citizen, a state organ outside the hierarchical structure, or a social organisation. Here, the law[9] ensures a right of access to parties and their representatives, including the right to copy documents. Further access to documents is provided also to other persons or organisations when the legal decision does not directly affect them but they can prove that they need to know the contents of the documents to properly carry out their duties. This wide-open gate is somewhat narrowed by a regulation prohibiting an authority from giving access to minutes of deliberations or the record of the vote taken, or to drafts of decisions or documents containing state or public service secrets. One may not, however, use the notion of public service secrets as an excuse to withhold access to a document on which a decision is based.

The second type of situation is where citizens are seeking not information on an administrative decision but merely a path through the administrative maze. Here, the law declares that an administrative official must provide all necessary information to any citizen, within the limits set by state and public service secrets, etc.[10]

Beyond this general right of access legal provisions determine the citizen's right to information related to the major information sub-systems. Thus a citizen may obtain from the population register documents in which he has a legal interest, and may even obtain addresses without evidence of a legal interest. The land register is equally public. With certain exceptions defined by law, everyone has access to it, and may make notes regarding its contents, or ask for copies of title deeds. A citizen's access to financial information may be restricted by specific types of secrecy, such as the secrecy of savings accounts and of banking. When a citizen requests financial (e.g. tax) information from administrative organs, such as the finance offices of local councils, the general rules of access described above usually apply.

An official certificate is a special way to obtain information from a public authority. Issued at the request of a citizen, this certificate confirms a fact or situation affecting his legal position for a specific purpose. A public authority cannot as a rule deny the right to an official certificate.

The third type of situation is where citizens wish to obtain administrative information because the need for social control requires them to act in the public interest. Here, the right of access is complex, since it involves questions of political and legal theory.

Through it, certain political and social organisations obtain the information they need to play their role in the political process. Two such organisations, which take a major part in the direction and management of Hungarian society, are the Hungarian Socialist Workers' Party and the Patriotic People's Front. In this type of situation, as already mentioned, the right to obtain administrative information is based on the citizen's constitutional right to take part in public and political activities, and hence to the necessary information allowing them to do this.

ACCESS BY PARTICULAR BODIES AND GROUPS

Members of Parliament

The National Assembly, like every other parliament, elects committees, both permanent and *ad hoc*. The right of access to information by these committees and by individual members of the Assembly is general and essentially unlimited. The constitution declares with universal validity[11] that every public authority (and indeed every citizen of the state) is obliged to release any information requested by a parliamentary committee and if necessary to give evidence before the committee. The constitution also requires officials of state organs to answer all questions, proposals or criticisms made by members at a sitting of a committee, either at that sitting or later in writing. An individual Member of Parliament is carrying out his legal duties when he requests information from a public authority.[12] The latter must therefore give every assistance to Members of Parliament in this respect.

Members of Parliament may request various types of information: (1) social, economic, health or cultural data referring to their field of activity; (2) information on matters of public interest connected with their constituents; and (3) general information concerning the country as a whole. They may at the same time demand that the public be informed as well.

Ministers, their deputies, heads of national authorities, the chairmen of local councils and the secretaries of local executive committees must provide Members of Parliament with all the information they need to carry out their duties. A Member of Parliament may ask for facts which are classified as state secrets, or demand access to documents that contain them. Such secret information is released for the personal use of the Member alone. It can be passed on only if it is declassified, or if the Member concerned is relieved of the obligation to keep it secret. There is one limitation to this regulation: the head of the authority concerned does not have to give access to state secrets on demand, but must without delay ask for instructions from his superior authority and act accordingly. If the answer is negative, and this rarely happens in practice, the Member may ask to be supplied with the information containing the state secret at a sitting of a parliamentary committee. Then the information cannot be withheld.

A Member of Parliament is entitled to find out whether a public authority acted in accordance with the law in matters concerning his constituents, or, if it had power of discretion, whether its action accorded with the demands of socialist humanism, showing due regard to social, group and individual interests. The authority must give him a hearing, and is obliged to give him access to all documents concerned, and information on proceedings and reasons for the decision taken.

At the request of Members of Parliament, the appropriate minister, the head of a national authority or the head of the Central Bureau of Statistics must supply them with all data which they need to carry out their parliamentary duties.

It is the constitutional duty of Members of Parliament to render account of their activities to their constituents at regular intervals. These reports are public, and constituents may ask questions which members must answer. On such occasions citizens can obtain information which they cannot get by other means. However, the provisions concerning state and public service secrets must be obeyed in these circumstances. If a member considers that a legal regulation or other fact that affects wide sections of the public is insufficiently known, he may demand greater publicity for it. The appropriate minister or head of a national authority, if necessary with the co-operation of the Information Office attached to the Council of Ministers, must then see to it that the public is given this information through the press, a special publication or in some other appropriate way.

Local Councils

Similar regulations apply to local councils, their committees and members. A significant proportion of economic, educational, health and social policy is implemented through local councils, or with their co-operation. These councils therefore have the right to obtain from public administrative organs any information that they need to carry out their duties.

Two types of public administrative organs exist within a given administrative unit: those directly subject to the local council and its executive committee, and decentralised organs subject to ministries and national authorities. The right to information by local councils and their committees is appropriately different for each type.

The right is more complete regarding organs directly subject to local councils. Councils and their executive committees are of course legally required to inform each other as part of their working relationship. The law governing local government councils specifies that the council's committees must keep a close eye on their specialised executive organs, and must improve them if possible. The committees therefore have a right to full information from these organs.[13]

Council committees are also entitled to supervise the operation of administrative organs that are not part of their hierarchy, particularly concerning questions of services and supplies to the public, and development plans for communities within their area. Committees may demand that those in charge provide them with information orally or in writing, and the latter must comply. Where state and public service secrets are involved, council members are subject to the same rights and restrictions as are Members of Parliament.

The law assures council members a personal right to request information. A member may accordingly ask, during council meetings or on other occasions, members of the executive committee, office holders, heads of administrative departments, or other organs to supply information on business that falls within the scope of the council. The answer must be supplied at the council meeting, or, if asked for outside the council, within fifteen days.

Council members are required to act on legitimate complaints of citizens and they maintain regular contact with the public in several ways: they must report to their constituents at least once a year, both on the work of the council and on their own activities; they may convene meetings of constituents to inform them on matters of public interest; and they generally keep 'surgery' hours to receive constituents' requests. Through these organised channels the public is informed of matters of public interest connected with the operation of local public administrative organs, both those subject to local government councils and those that are not.

The Courts

Though a separation of powers would obviously run counter to the basic principles of the socialist state, one cannot ignore the differences between the public administrative system and the courts. Also, one must differentiate between an appeal to the courts from an administrative decision, and civil or criminal proceedings for which the courts must obtain administrative information to clarify the facts.

In an appeal against an administrative decision, the courts need the information on the basis of which the administrative agency made its own decision. The courts are therefore able to demand the relevant documents and a statement from the administrative agency on all the facts and circumstances on which the appellants based their suit. The administrative agency responsible for the decision in dispute is legally obliged to provide this information. Other administrative information supplied to the courts is governed by general rules of civil procedure.

In civil or criminal proceedings, administrative information can be submitted either in documentary form, or as evidence given by witnesses. In a civil suit the courts are entitled to obtain relevant documents from a public authority, unless they contain state, public service or job secrets, in which case the authority must take measures to secure release from the obligation to secrecy.

In a criminal proceeding, two kinds of documents may be involved: those which may have been an instrument or objective of the crime, and those which contain information that may help solve the crime. In both cases the authority taking criminal action has the right to obtain, and seize if necessary, all such documents certifying a fact or circumstance, and to have access to everything that helps to prove this fact. Here the obligations of a public authority are the same as those for a civil suit.

Oral evidence given by witnesses is central to both civil and criminal cases. In either, a staff member of a public authority can act as a witness; this is therefore a suitable way in which administrative information can be obtained. In both types of case giving evidence is a legal obligation. But there are some restrictions against revealing certain kinds of secret while giving evidence. One may not examine a witness on questions classified as state or public service secrets in both kinds of procedures, and as job secrets in civil procedures, unless exemption has been granted to the witness. Also, a witness may refuse to give evidence.[14]

The Public Prosecutor's Office

The Public Prosecutor's Office is a large hierarchical organisation of prosecutors headed by a Chief Public Prosecutor. Among its main functions are the so-called 'general supervision and control' which are to ensure that the law is observed. This control extends to all public administrative organs, to their individual decisions, and also to regulations of general application issued by local councils.[15] The scope is extremly wide, and prosecutors may obtain administrative information either directly from public authorities or indirectly through the lodging of complaints by citizens or outside organisations.

A prosecutor may examine regulations and decisions of administrative organs, in order to judge their legality. Alternatively, he may invite an organ with powers of supervision and control to examine them, and report on the results. He may also require the heads of these organs to supply documents, facts and explanatory information. An administrative organ may not use the argument that state or public service secrets are involved to withold information from him.

People's Control Commissions

People's Control, part of the general organisational system of the public administration, has special tasks and entitlements. Although it is not the only type of agency that supervises the activities of administrative organs, it is the only type, except for the control of legality by prosecutors, which has a general right to secure any kind of information needed to carry out its duties. Moreover, the law obliges all central state, social and co-operative organs to report the results of their examination to the Central People's Control Commission when needed, or when requested by the latter. Local organs must report to the appropriate territorial People's Control Commission.[16]

The Central People's Control Commission has powers of the widest scope. It may institute an inspection of any administrative organ. Territorial People's Control Commissions which are chosen by local councils, may similarly inspect local government administration and most decentralised organs in their area. Such inspections, besides indirectly aiding local councils in their work, arc an additional means by which citizens can obtain information, since wide sections of the population are co-opted to carry them out. Also, members of a People's Control Commission, in carrying out their duties, may have access to all documents, plans, accounts and correspondence they deem necessary. The organ inspected must supply all the information, documents and explanations required.

Administrative information is as accessible to People's Control as to prosecutors. The only exception is that in justified cases ministers and heads of central organs have the right to make available information containing state secrets only through the Chairman of the Central People's Control Commission. The Chief Public Prosecutor and the Chairman of the Central People's Control Commission are both entitled to attend government meetings, while a local prosecutor and the head of a local People's Control Commission may similarly attend meetings of a local council's executive committee.

Particular Groups

Scholars are guaranteed freedom of research by a constitutional provision.[17] If their subject is in harmony with the social interest and is part of the government-determined long-range research plan, administrative organs cannot and do not refuse to co-operate. Much useful search has been done on administrative questions. Regulations governing secrecy naturally apply to scholars as well. An administrative organ may well enter into a contract with research organisations to carry out a project, offering its co-operation to ensure success. Of course, in all such cases the administrative information has to be supplied.

The mass media have generally the same access as ordinary citizens, but their responsibility is greater and more specific. The fact that they are socialist media is reflected in their criticism and the information they provide. Sometimes they act as an intermediary between the administrative organisation and other socialist units, either by providing information on the operation of public administration for the general public, or by allowing citizens to express complaints or observations. The administrative organs concerned are compelled to answer any questions or complaints published in the media.

The situation slightly differs for historical research. Administrative organs have their own archives, passing documents on to specialised archives after a given time. The law ensures that all those holding archive material provide information on their stock, and copies of or extracts from documents, to interested scholars.[18]

However, material in archives is not automatically exempt from the provisions regarding state secrets.

INFORMATION PROCEDURES

THE HOLDING OF INFORMATION

Most information held by administrative organs is stored in registries. A documentary file is defined as written texts, accounts, maps, plans and designs produced by an administrative organ, or with its co-operation, in carrying out its functions, regardless of the methods employed, except for matter designed for publication. The results of mechanical data processing are included as well. The dating of the document is irrelevant in this respect. Placing documentary files in a registry is compulsory, to ensure proper handling and also the interests of administrative organs and of those who have business with them.

The Council of Ministers has issued general instructions to ensure a nation-wide, uniform system. These have created a legal basis for ministers, acting in conjunction with the Minister of Culture, to issue model regulations requiring uniform procedures for all administrative organs under their direction. Each organ formulates its own standards in keeping with the model provided. These must be approved by the immediate superiors. The object is to regulate safe-keeping, classification, access, culling and transfer to archives appropriate to the special nature of the organ concerned.

Hierarchical regulation and the obligation to follow directive principles ensures some uniformity, but sectional interests sometimes arise, not always with justification. The right to special supervision vested in the Minister of Culture is designed to solve this problem.

The regulations do not differentiate between working files and those that contain final decisions. Access to both kinds is provided, except that when an administrative decision is made, the concerned parties or their representatives do not have a right of access to minutes of proceedings, or to the draft decision.

Only documents containing state secrets must be stored with greater than average care. They are generally handled by the registry of classified documents. Documents concerning public service secrets are stored and handled within the framework of general administrative work. Usually only the head of an organ may permit access to documents containing state secrets. They may only be released by staff at a certain level, generally ministers, and as a rule only to organs directly connected with governmental organs.

Although destruction of files is generally prohibited, there are procedures for administrative organs to dispose of documents. Files are culled at least once every five years under the supervision of the appropriate state archives. Out-of-date material is then discarded. An organ must have permission from the archives to destroy culled documents. Those that are not culled must be stored by the organ for at least fifteen years, then passed on to archives. The archives are naturally obliged to make documents available to authorities for a defined time if they are likely to be needed for current business. These regulations also apply to secret documents. Only secret documents culled and marked for destruction are submitted to archives for examination.

Archives are complemented by data banks and registries for such things as births, deaths and marriages, population and land ownership. The first steps towards standardisation of these registries have been taken, involving an extension of electronic data processing. One of the tasks of the informational systems to be so created will be making information available.

TRANSMISSION OF INFORMATION

The position of those who submit a petition to an authority is most clearly regulated in law, mainly because this right applies both to oral and written communications. Generally, such submissions must be answered in writing, particularly in relation to a decision on a matter of substance. There are two exceptions: where the administrative agency carries out the request on the spot and according to the relevant regulations a note on a document or a record in a register suffices; and where the decision is given orally to the party, if he does not request the answer in writing and the nature of the matter allows it. In the latter case, the decision may simply be recorded, but the party must acknowledge by his signature that he has received the information.

Such general rules have been complemented and amended in particular fields, such as housing and the registering of births, deaths and marriages. Here unfortunately, attitudes and practices are far from uniform. There are still many bureaucractic procedures and superfluous formalities. There is some hope that the general revision of the law now in process will introduce more uniform procedures in this respect.

Ways and forms of transmitting requested information between various elements of the state mechanism are heterogeneous. But the requested documents must generally be supplied within fifteen days, while a personal or oral request for information, or questions by members of elective bodies must be answered immediately, or also within fifteen days.

Precise legal regulation is given only by Act IV of 1957, which regulates the administrative procedure of administrative organs when making individual decisions. This sets a limit of thirty days on answering requests for information.

CLASSIFICATION AND DECLASSIFICATION OF INFORMATION

The scope of state secrets is determined generally by the law dealing with secrets,[19] and specifically by the discretion of ministers. The head of an administrative organ also determines the scope of facts to be considered public service secrets. Regarding both state and service secrets, the head of an organ is responsible for their keeping, and also for ensuring that anyone employed or commissioned by the organ who is in possession of such secrets knows and obeys all the regulations designed to protect them. The legal responsibility to keep state or service secrets also applies outside the public administrative structure, and includes individual citizens who come into possession of such secrets.

Files containing state or public service secrets generally are classified, but there is some information enumerated in law which must be regarded as a state secret without any classification on files. Files containing state secrets are marked 'top secret', and those containing public service secrets, 'for service use only'. The head of an organ is the one who must classify files and documents 'top secret'; in exceptional cases he may delegate this authority. The person preparing a document may also classify it as 'for service use only'. This means that the classification can be assigned at a very low level in the administrative hierarchy.

Formal classification and declassification are part of the duties of an administrative organ. If a file or document no longer contains a state or service secret, the classification must be amended or cancelled. This may happen when preliminary work for a decision is complete and the decision – the approval of a new regulation, for example – has been made, or if the facts concerned have been published.

A state or public service secret may 'escape' an administrative organ through communication (information given, evidence given to a court, access to the documents by entitled organs, etc.), or through publication. The first case does not affect the character of the secret; only the person who originally classified it is entitled to declassify it. But anything that has been legally published is naturally no longer secret.

The ways in which state secrets and service secrets may be legally communicated or published differ. Regarding state secrets, the head of an administrative organ, or someone to whom he has delegated the authority, may communicate a state secret to a Hungarian organ or person. Ordinarily only a minister may communicate a state secret to a foreign agency or person. A regulation issued by the Government containing state secrets, as well as further decisions, proposals and drafts connected with this, may be communicated to a foreign agency or person only with the concurrence of the government.

A public service secret may be communicated, without higher permission, to a Hungarian organ or person by the head of the organ concerned, or by someone to whom he has delegated his authority, provided of course that the nature of the matter demands it. But only the responsible minister, or someone delegated by him, may grant permission to communicate it to a foreign agency or person, or to take it abroad.

Provisions on publication are somewhat different, since only a minister may give permission to publish state or service secrets.

A special problem arises when a member of the staff of an administrative organ is faced with the possibility of including a state secret in his evidence to a court in a criminal or civil action, or in proceedings being conducted by another authority. As mentioned, neither an administrative organ nor a court may examine a witness with respect to such information, and the witness may refuse to give evidence. If the authorities disobey this regulation, such information may not be used as valid evidence. In proceedings of this sort, one must obtain prior release from the obligation to keep the secret. This release can be obtained as follows: the chairman of the Council of Ministers, his deputies and members can obtain a release from the Presidential Council of the People's Republic; organs directly under the supervision of the council of ministers, from the council of ministers; the staff of ministers or national agencies, and the heads of organs within a ministry's hierarchy, from the minister; the staff of decentralised administrative organs, from the head of the organ concerned; the staff of local councils or services, from the council chairman; council chairmen, from the chairman of the council next higher in the hierarchy; and finally, the chairman of the Budapest Metropolitan Council and chairmen of county councils, from the Councils Office of the Council of Ministers.

REFUSAL AND RELEASE OF INFORMATION

Socialist legal theory takes an integral view of rights and duties. Accordingly, where a right of access to information exists, the administrative organ may not refuse to supply it. This is reflected in labour law by the rule that public servants must deal with the business of citizens in a conscientious and direct way, avoiding all unnecessary proceedings. They must supply citizens with all the necessary information, and draw attention to their rights and duties.

A number of problems arise, however, from one central fact: the head of an organ and his staff must withhold information in some cases and release it in others. On the one hand, they are bound by an oath to keep state and public service secrets. Moreover, they may not communicate to unauthorised persons any information obtained as part of their work, and which may produce disadvantages for the organ or some other person. On the other hand, wherever a legal norm declares that information must be given, the staff of the organ must supply it. The only guidance they get is the rule stating that they must carry out their duties in accordance with the appropriate rules and regulations and the instructions of superior officers.

The essence of the question is this: in all cases where supplying information containing state or public service secrets is not a duty compelled by law, but is part of the discretionary power of ministers or heads of organs, who can compel them to supply the information, and in what ways? An important part of the question is: in what type of case should administrative organs, in their relationship with each other or the courts, be compelled to release staff from the obligation to keep a secret, and to what extent?

One must emphasise that regulations creating state and public service secrets were specifically designed to give greater protection to the information concerned. It was therefore determined that the discretionary powers should be vested in a fairly senior official – in the case of state secrets, the minister himself. There is no doubt that the establishing of secrets, especially service secrets at a low level, makes the work of interested parties and persons very difficult. But the need for administrative unity, and the duties deriving from the administrative division of labour, mean that no administrative organ is entitled to hinder the work of other organs or to withhold information in pursuit of its own interests. It happens all the same that a member of the staff of an administrative organ, or its head, relying on the notion of state and public service secrets, denies information. What can one do?

If a staff member does not supply information when he is legally bound to supply it, one can appeal to the head of the organ or organisation. The general legal instrument used in such cases is called a complaint. It can be used also when there is no legal obligation to supply information but the authority without justified reasons withholds the information. In both cases the organ must reply to the complaint. In practice, state discipline ensures that the needed information is made available. If need be, however, one can complain to the Public Prosecutor's Office. As the guardian of legality, it takes action on such complaints and any reports of a possible breach of the law. The administrative organ, or its superior, must take the necessary action to remedy the matter (e.g. to release information) within a given time. The prosecutor's power is reinforced by the fact that he may, once a breach of law has been established, start criminal, disciplinary or damage-retrieving proceedings.

What kind of sanction can be used if an administrative organ does not carry out its legal duty to provide information? In Hungarian law, the usual solution is disciplinary punishment. In a more serious case, when an administrative organ obstructs the access of an authorised person to a state secret, criminal proceedings must be taken. If damage was done, the plaintiff may sue for damages.

At the same time, illegally publishing or releasing state or service secrets, or giving unauthorised persons access to them are also criminal offences. The sanction, in the case of service secrets, is penal servitude up to twelve months; in the case of state secrets, penal servitude between one and five years, though in certain cases these limits can be extended.[20] Moreover labour law and the criminal code both provide special sanctions for offences against private secrets. Anyone who because of his occupation or office has access to private secrets and reveals them without good reason may be fined or sentenced to corrective labour for a period of up to a year.

CONCLUSION

In general, access to administrative information in Hungary is regulated by a fairly differentiated system of legal norms, which vary according to the main branches of public administration. The existing system, with its sub-systems, has been formed step by step under changing social and political conditions, and in its details bears the marks of each period of social development. Basically, it has proved to be well founded for securing the interests of the Hungarian socialist society and those of the citizen as well. However, recent preliminary works aimed at revealing the essential phenomena of Hungarian public administration have already proved that the time has become ripe for a unified and simplified system of legal regulation designed to secure a more unambiguous determination of the rights of citizens and other donors and recipients of administrative information.[21] The outlines of the future regulation of access are now formulated. They must of course be in harmony with the other sub-systems of public administration now being developed in Hungary.

NOTES

1. Act I of 1972 on the modification of Act XX of 1949 and on the uniform text of the Constitution of the Hungarian People's Republic (hereinafter Constitution).

2. Constitution, para. 2, indent 5: 'The citizens take an active part in the administration of public matters, both at their workplace and residence.' Para. 68, indent 1: 'Each citizen has a right to participate in the administration of public matters; he is obliged to fulfil his public duty conscientiously.'

3. Act IV of 1957 on the general rules of procedure of state administration (hereinafter Law of Procedure):

Para. 36: '(1) The client or his representative may have access to and make copies of the documents originating from the case.

(2) The Organ of State Administration may allow representatives of certain bodies, or persons other than the client or his representative, to have access to the documents or to make copies of them, in the event they can prove that knowledge of their contents are indispensable to exercise their rights or perform their obligations.

(3) The Organ of State Administration may not reveal the protocol of the conference or the voting, draft of proposals and the documents containing official or state secrets. Access to or copymaking of the document, on which the principal decision depends, cannot be refused with the pretext of its being an official secret.'

4. Decision No. 1012/1972 /27. Apr./ of the Council of Ministers on the complex scientific planning of the development public administration.

5. Act V of 1961 on the Penal Code of the Hungarian People's Republic, para. 163, indent 1: 'State secrets are those data, which, in the hands of an unauthorised person endanger the security or other important interests of the Hungarian People's Republic' (hereinafter Penal Code).

6. Resolution No. 14/1971/IV.15 of the Hungarian Revolutionary Government of Workers and Peasants, on the protection of state and official secrets (hereinafter Secret-resolution).

7. Penal Code, para. 163, indent 3: 'Official secrets are those data which refer to state organs, social organisations or co-operatives, and their operation, and which, in the hands of unauthorised persons endanger the undistrubed operation of the state organs, social organisations or co-operatives, or the order of state administration, home defence, the administration of justice or the management of the economy.'

8. Act II of 1967 on the Labour Code of the Hungarian People's Republic, para. 34, indent 2: 'An employed person is obliged . . . to guard state, service and job secrets. Furthermore, no unauthorised person may be supplied with information obtained in connection with his duties, the passing on of which may produce disadvantages for the employer or any other person.'

9. See Law of Procedure, para. 36.

10. See Law of Procedure, para. 22, indent 3: 'The executive in charge is obliged to furnish his client with the necessary information and to call his attention to his rights and duties, prior to hearing him. In the course of the procedure the Organ of State Administration sees to it that for lack of knowledge of the legal rules the client should not be put to disadvantage.'

11. Constitution, para. 21, indent 3: 'The authorities, offices, institutions and the citizens of the state are obliged to make available all data requested by committees of Parliament, and to give evidence before such committees.'

12. Decision No. 1041/1972/X.20 of the Council of Ministers, on the duties of the Organs of State Administration in backing the activity of the Members of Parliament.

13. Act I of 1971 on the local councils.

14. Act III of 1952 on Civil Procedure, para. 169, indent 2, and Act I. of 1973 on Criminal Procedure, para. 65.

15. Act V of 1972 on the Prosecutor of the Hungarian People's Republic.

16. Act V of 1968 on the people's control.

17. Constitution, para. 60: 'The Hungarian People's Republic provides freedom of scientific . . . activity.'

18. Law decree No. 27 of 1969 on the protection of the archivalia, para. 12, indent 1: 'The archives and other scientific institutions keeping archivalia shall provide information on the materials in their care and allow research work in a particular sphere stipulated by the rules of management.'

Indent 2: 'The archives shall make certified copies, and summaries, of the material in their care and make the latter available for people and bodies stipulated by the rules of management.'

19. See Secret-resolution, para. 1, indent 2, giving a detailed list of the protected items, which – independently from their qualification – shall *always* be considered state secrets.

20. See Penal Code, para. 160.

21. Act I of 1977, on petitions and proposals of public interest and on the individual complaints of citizens, is an example of the recent development.

10 Yugoslavia

MIODRAG PETROVIĈ

The development of democracy in every modern society depends on the openness of its institutions. Consequently, the accessibility of information held by public administration is one of the most reliable indicators of the development of democratic relations in a society.

Yugoslavia has a self-managing society. The essential goal of this society is that a working man participates in all political and other decisions concerning his life and work. The realisation of such a goal involves the development of real democratic relations among working people, as free and equal producers and creators of all social values. Such a position of the working man involves radical changes of character and role in all social institutions, especially the ones wielding power. Such institutions must participate in the development of socialist self-managing relations and must be under the permanent political and social control of working people. Consequently, particular forms and methods of political, economic and other decision-making based on direct self-managing by working people are being created in Yugoslavia.

The 1974 Constitution of the Socialist Federal Republic of Yugoslavia introduced a delegational system of all forms of power and management. Speaking precisely, in Yugoslavia, with a population of around twenty million inhabitants, about one million citizens participate directly and actively in the process of political decision-making in representative bodies, and more than three million citizens participate in various other forms of management (workers' councils, the assemblies of self-managing associations, etc). This means that almost all active citizens perform a direct function of managing social affairs.

Of course, the working people in Yugoslavia cannot perform such a social role without information as a basis for deciding which and what kind of decisions ought to be made. The important part of this information is held by public administration. One of the basic functions of public administration is to collect, classify and prepare for use all relevant information needed as a basis for determining the whole policy of social development. Consequently, in the Constitution, particular care was taken regarding the system of information. Under Article 75 the system of information must ensure appropriate recording, collection, processing and presentation of data and facts needed for recording, planning and guiding social development, and must ensure the accessibility of such data. Moreover, the Constitution stipulates, as one of its essential principles, that all state and other public organs are to be open. This means that the work of all these organs is, as a rule, accessible to the public. Free access to data and other elements of information held by public administration is included. The exceptions to this rule must be prescribed in advance and are restricted to confidential matters.

A conclusion can be drawn that in Yugoslavia there are very broad rights of access to information held by public administration, guaranteed by the Constitution. Although most of these rights are realised in practice, the practice is not always in conformity with constitutional principles and the goals of social development, due to the absence of detailed regulations which should define the conditions and procedures for receiving particular information. However, there are such regulations regarding the rights of the representatives of the press, radio, TV and other media of communication. For this reason, the use of the right to information is the most complete in that domain. Another limiting factor is the insufficient development of the material and technical base for the system of information, but intensive measures have been taken lately to introduce a comprehensive information system based on computer techniques.

In a self-managing society, the problem of developing an adequate system of information is very difficult. Numerous significant meetings of supreme political organs are devoted to searching for the best methods of providing complete information to the citizens about all important matters and events in the society. A special role in this is given to the media of public information, and increased attention is devoted to the local media as well as to the media of information in public enterprises. In all political territorial units and public enterprises, particular committees or commissions have been set up to ensure the complete and timely informing of citizens about all questions of social life.

GENERAL RIGHTS OF PUBLIC ACCESS

THE GENERAL SITUATION

All information held by public administration, except for state, military or official secrets, is accessible to citizens. Article 168 of the Constitution of Yugoslavia provides this right:

> Citizens shall be guaranteed the right to be kept informed of developments in the country and in the world which are of concern for their life and work, and of questions of concern to the community.

The notion 'developments' represents all relevant happenings in the society (for instance, economic, political, cultural, health and other events). This means that the amount of information is practically unlimited. One limitation is that these events must be relevant to the life and work of the citizen and of the community. Another limitation is that the public administration must possess information about these events. One of the essential functions of public administration is to collect and process facts about all such events and to make them accessible to the public.

A citizen may request information concerning his personal or political status, his property, health, education, etc. A citizen may also request information about matters of a general character, for instance, about the economic situation in the country and abroad or about the political situation. The interest of citizens in particular events and information is continuous and massive. Consequently, in Yugoslavia there exists a system of public information sufficient for the common needs of the majority of citizens. The press, radio, television and other media are bound to inform the public truthfully, objectively, fully and in time about events in all domains of life in the country and abroad. The media are required to make public the information held by public administration. The right of a citizen to request and receive particular information from public authorities is not in this way eliminated. Such a right is provided by Art. 171 of the Law on Administrative Procedure: on demand from citizens or social organisations, public authorities are obliged to issue various certificates and other public documents about all facts which exist in official records.

The right of access by the representative bodies to information held by public administration is guaranteed by their position in the socio-political system. They are the highest organs of power in the federation, republic and commune and have a right to look into all information necessary for the performance of their legislative functions. Under constitutional provisions, administrative organs are obliged to hand over to the representative bodies and their collegiate executive organs all explanations of questions of their competence, all data, official statements and other documents necessary for their work. Information concerning state security and national defence, however, is subject to a special regime. A commission for matters of state security, composed of the members of the representative bodies, examines such information. Access to information held by public administration is also secured for the courts and similar public organs, when this information is necessary for the performance of legal functions.

TYPES OF INFORMATION KEPT SECRET

Yugoslavia, like any other country, has a need to declare some information secret and to prevent access to it by those who might use it against the social order or interest. This is certain information which is generally regarded as official secrets, concerning state security, national defence, economic policy, the private lives of individuals, and business transactions. No explanation is needed of the first two categories. However, it should be mentioned that restrictions on access to even this type of information are reduced to a minimum. Only under provisions of law may certain data which are of interest for state security be declared secret. Moreover, Yugoslavia has enabled access to a great deal of military information that is treated as secret in other countries by its system of general national defence in which practically every citizen is included.

With regard to the other categories of information treated as 'official secrets', the treatment of particular data is similar to that in other modern countries. Classification of this information is reduced to three categories. All data concerning economic and other policy measures (provisions, particular restrictions on turnover, monetary, measures, etc.), belong to the first category, but only in the phase of preparation of drafts of documents. When such documents are adopted, they become public and are published in the relevant official gazette. All information concerning private lives of citizens is included in the second category. All information concerning business transactions of economic and other organisations and public services, and especially the use of patents and other protected rights, belongs to the third category.

The head of an organ in charge of information declared as an official, state or military secret is responsible for its safe-keeping. In the case of violating this official duty, disciplinary and criminal sanctions are provided. Every organ which keeps such information is bound to define the limitations on its use in a special regulation, in order to avoid arbitrary decisions.

THE HOLDERS OF INFORMATION

ADMINISTRATIVE AUTHORITIES

Administrative authorities are the most significant holders of information. In all of Yugoslavia's political territorial units (federation, republics, autonomous provinces and communes), there are corresponding administrative authorities whose essential functions are to carry out laws and to implement defined policies. In order to perform these functions, they must collect, hold and use all necessary information. Communal administrative organs hold the most detailed information and data, while republican, provincial and especially federal administrative organs hold information of a more general character.

The scope of accessibility of different categories of information to individual citizens and the general public results from this. The greatest interest in the right of access to information, and the broadest use of this right, are at the level of the communal authorities. The cases when citizens directly use the information held by superior administrative organs are very rare. However, accessibility to information held by all organs of administration is always guaranteed to the media of public information (press, radio, TV, etc.). Practically, all information held by communal, provincial, republican or federal administrative organs, if it is not of a confidential nature, is equally accessible to the representatives of the media and can be published.

POLITICAL EXECUTIVES

In every political territorial unit there is a collegial executive organ of the representative body. The primary function of this organ is to take care of the implementation of laws and of the established policy, to propose to the assembly new laws or the amendment of present ones, and to control and co-ordinate the work of administrative authorities.

All information held by executive organs, except confidential information, is accessible both to the representative bodies and to the media. This also applies to preparatory documents. The representatives of the press, radio and TV are present at the sessions of executive organs and of their committees. However, the working documents can be published only with the permission of the executive organ concerned. Such limitations are very rare in practice. Only exceptionally, when the organ deals with information of a confidential nature, can the representatives of the media be excluded from the sessions.

THE RECIPIENTS OF INFORMATION

GENERAL ACCESS

The recipients of information held by administrative authorities are representative bodies and their executive organs, citizens and their social organisations, scientists and the media of public information. The rights of recipients of information are regulated by particular regulations. These define the obligation of administrative organs to make accessible to users the information they hold. For instance, Article 310 of the Rules of Procedure of the Assembly of the Socialist Republic of Serbia contains the following obligations of the republican administrative organs to the assembly and its committees: to give information about particular questions and problems, and to hand over data they collect and register, as well as documents and other material necessary for the work of the Assembly and its committees. Article 171 of the Law on Administrative Procedure, mentioned before, defines the obligations of administrative organs to issue certificates about facts they have on record at the request of citizens. Under the provisions of the Law on Public Information, the media of public information have a right to receive necessary data. The accessibility of data to scientists and other scholars is not regulated separately, but it has never been difficult for them to receive information of interest for their research.

In sum, there are no regulations governing all situations involving the use of information held by public administration. However, in accordance with the principle of open work by all state organs (organs of public administration included), there is a legal supposition that official information is accessible, under equal conditions, to all subjects that have a legal interest in it.

The exception is information declared as secret. Such information is reserved for the needs of particular political organs or functionaries. The method of using this information is not defined by regulations, but, in practice, the main restriction is the prohibition of its publication. In particular cases, an authorised organ can permit the publication of certain confidential information.

RESTRICTIONS ON USE BY RECIPIENTS

The right of use of received information is not specially limited as a rule. However, there are particular situations when the use of defined information is related to definite purposes. Thus, for example, citizens can use requested certificates and other documents exclusively for regulation of their position, property and other rights.

The most significant restrictions on the use of information are prescribed for the media of communication. Issued information must be published according to its actual contents, and its sense cannot be changed. Documents and data declared official or economic secrets cannot be published. Finally, the publication of information which aims at the destruction of the basis of the sociopolitical system as defined by the Constitution, which threatens the peace, the equal international co-operation or the independence of Yugoslavia, or which arouses national, racial or religious hatred or intolerance is forbidden.

A conclusion can be drawn that limitations concerning the use of information received from public authorities are reduced to a small number of cases which could be designated as misuse of information.

INFORMATION PROCEDURES

THE HOLDING OF INFORMATION

Four basic methods of holding information are used in Yugoslavia:

(1) Official Books. All information regarding the personal status of citizens is held in these books (e.g. birth data, citizenship, marital status). Such a system has existed for a long time, and information held in these books is of permanent value. Various registers or data files belong to this category.

(2) Dossiers. This method of holding information is used when it is necessary to unite several documents related to one subject or object (e.g. personal dossiers, property dossiers, dossiers on the performance of a particular profession).

(3) Statistical and Financial Documentation. This method of data holding is mainly used for statistical research and financial transactions, and also for geodetical matters, land registers, urban plans, etc.

(4) Information Systems – Data Banks. Information systems based on the principles of computerised techniques are in increased use lately. These systems exist only in the larger cities at the moment, but there is a trend to extend their application all over the country.

Not all methods of holding information are included in these categories. For instance, there are also various documentation notebooks, stenographic notes, records, etc.

From the standpoint of public access, there are differences between working and final documents. As a rule, a look into working documents (drafts, propositions, etc.) is allowed to the media of communication. The contents of working documents may be published but only after permission has been given by the organ which examines them. In practice many working documents are presented to the public especially if they are important, such as ones concerning the constitution, labour relations, transport security, or social or urban planning.

The filing of documents is prescribed by regulations on office duties. Documents which are of permanent historical or scientific value are kept in special files. Other documents, with the exception of documents of permanent value (geodetical plans, urban plans, land registers, etc.), are kept at the longest for ten years. From the standpoint of public access, these documents are accessible to all users.

THE TRANSMISSION OF INFORMATION

The usual form for the transmission of information is a written document. The authenticity and permanence of information is ensured in this way. Particular information may be communicated orally. For instance, the authorised officials hold press conferences to communicate information about facts and events which are of general social significance (international relations, internal policy, etc.).

There are no general rules on the method of requesting information from administrative officials. The requests are oral or written. Members of the press or of the representative body may request information orally. Citizens request information for personal purposes in written form. In such cases special fees must be paid. If information is used to regulate social security or employment, the citizens are exempt from payment of such fees.

A comprehensive regulation prescribing uniform secrecy does not exist in Yugoslavia. However, under particular federal laws, the principles and criteria of classification for various categories of secrecy are defined. For example, under the Law on National Defence, certain data can be declared as a state or official secret. Documents containing such data must bear the indication 'state secret' or 'official secret'. A difference between these two categories is in the grade of secrecy that must be provided. Moreover, other categories of secrecy are applied in practice: 'top secret', 'secret', 'official' and 'for internal use'.

Several provisions of the *Book of Regulations on the Keeping and*

Release of Official Secrets for Internal Matters can serve as an example of the types of matters kept secret. Under Article 2 of these regulations the following are treated as official secrets:

everything defined as officially secret by particular laws or regulations based on law;

all data and documents concerning working and other organisations which are defined as official secrets by general rules of these organisations;

data and documents designated as official secrets by other state organs, organisations of associated labour and other organisations;

measures, activities, data and sources of information when their release would have a damaging effect on individual interests, interests of organisations of associated labour and other organisations, or on the successful performance of official tasks; .

drafts of regulations, reports and other data which are prepared for assemblies of socio-political communities and their executive organs if secrecy is expressly ordered by the authorised organ.

The method of declassification of confidential information is not defined by particular regulations. However, the afore-mentioned book of regulations envisages a possibility of releasing an official secret if there are justified reasons, and if it does not prejudice fundamental interests of the service of public order and is not violating freedoms, rights and civil interests protected by law.

It is understandable that certain confidential information gradually loses the character of confidentiality. That is the case of information about international relations and certain economic and financial data. This information can become accessible to the public. However, the information regarding the freedoms, rights and private life of citizens cannot be released without the permission of the citizens concerned. The violation of such a responsibility is always a breach of official duties and, in particular cases, a criminal act.

THE REFUSAL AND RELEASE OF INFORMATION

The right to information is one of the constitutional rights of the citizens of Yugoslavia. The Constitution of Yugoslavia envisages the protection of that right. The methods of protecting the principal rights and freedoms of citizens, including their right to information, are prescribed by the Law on Administrative Disputes. Under the provisions of this law, if there has been a violation of constitutional rights and freedoms, the damaged party has a right to appeal to the District Court. Legal sanctions provided by this law include a fine and dismissal of the responsible person. Other instruments of legal protection are also provided, such as compensation for damage caused by the refusal of information, or because the information was wrongly released. In particular cases when a criminal act of abuse of official duty was committed, a sentence of imprisonment could be passed.

CONCLUSION

In Yugoslavia the problem of access to the information possessed by public administration is taken very seriously. This is, above all, a consequence of the opinion that citizens' rights, including their right to information, are considered as their inalienable rights without which they can be neither free nor active nor equal citizens. More than that, these rights are a constitutent element of the self-managing socialist democracy, which could not function without citizens who are conscious of their rights and obligations and informed about all matters vital to their life and activities. Because of this, almost all of the significant political conferences on all levels and in all political organisations are tackling the problem of further developing, expanding and improving the quality of the public information system.

It is certain that the way to the complete realisation of constitutional and political demands for free access to the information possessed by public administration will be exceptionally difficult and complex. Numerous obstacles originating from historical, cultural, economic and other sources must be surmounted. But in the foreseeable future all these obstacles will be finally overcome.

IV North America

11 Canada

DONALD C. ROWAT

BACKGROUND FACTORS

Among the developed countries of the world, Canada seems to rank about midway between those having the most administrative secrecy and those enjoying the least. The main reason for this is not difficult to find. Historically, Canada has come under the strong influence of both the United Kingdom and the United States, and its political system is a remarkable blend of British and American influences. For instance, the very basis of its constitutional system is a mixture of the two. It has inherited the British parliamentary system, with a strong executive responsible to Parliament, and has, like the Americans, adopted a federal structure, with a clear division of powers between the central government and independent provincial governments. Since the United Kingdom has had a tradition of administrative secrecy inherited from earlier centuries when its administration was under the control of a powerful monarchy, and the United States has developed in the direction of greater administrative openness, it is not surprising that Canada's practice is about half-way between the two.

During the last century, when the provinces of British North America won responsible government in 1848, and established the principle that the executive Government, or Cabinet, must at all times be supported by a majority in the legislature, it was easy for provincial Governments to maintain the previous practice of administrative secrecy for their own convenience, as Governments had done in Britain. This practice was strongly supported by the concurrent development of contending political parties and a parliamentary system of Government and Opposition, which virtually required a Government to conduct its proceedings in secret so as not to reveal its hand to the Opposition. It was also buttressed by the adoption of the British practice of civil service anonymity and later by the need to protect national security. As a result, the principle of administrative secrecy – the release of information at the discretion of the Government – has never been seriously challenged in Canada until very recent years.

Several additional factors support administrative secrecy in Canada. One of these is Canada's relatively competitive economy. An accepted practice of economic competition is for businesses to keep information secret from one another and from their unions of employees. Besides encouraging an atmosphere of secrecy in society, this had led the federal and provincial legislatures to pass laws which forbid the release of information that governments may hold on individual business firms. Also, Canada has a tradition of personal privacy, which is closely related to its democratic tradition of the freedom and dignity of the individual. Although the courts have not developed a right to personal privacy as they have in the United States, some federal and provincial laws forbid the release of administrative information held on individuals. Moreover, Canada's federal system of government is probably the most decentralised in the world. Each of the ten provinces has its own legislature and Government, and negotiations between the central and the provincial Governments tend to take on the character of secret international negotiations.

Despite these influences favouring administrative secrecy, there are also strong influences in the direction of openness. So as not to exaggerate the picture of administrative secrecy in Canada compared with other countries, one must keep these in mind. First of all, Canada enjoys a solid democratic tradition and is one of the most fully operating democracies in the world. It has inherited the British system of open courts, and at both the federal and provincial levels of government, the executive is responsible to an open legislature. The Government's majority party is always faced by one or more freely operating opposition parties, and there is a strong free press. This means that the opposition parties and the press are constantly prying into the administrative affairs of the federal and provincial Governments. These Governments also make a positive publicity effort to inform the public about administrative activities (though the difficulty is that the Governments themselves choose what information is to be released). Canada has also followed the long-term trend in most developed countries towards a higher level of democracy through greater participation by the public in governmental decision-making. This ultimately requires greater administrative openness. Another factor favouring openness is that, compared with the European powers, Canada has been relatively isolated from international events, and so has not felt the need for national security so intensely. Also, since Canada is one of the 'middle powers', its need for measures to protect national security is not so pressing as that of the great powers. On the other hand, since Canada has not been a neutral nation like Sweden, its need for the secrecy of security documents has been greater. And its close links with Britain and the United States have tended to increase this need.

As a result of these contrary influences toward secrecy and openness, Canada has experienced a kind of schizophrenic conflict between the two in recent years. On one hand, there has been the sweeping Official Secrets Act, based on the British Act of 1911, and the all-inclusive secrecy oath for civil servants, requiring them not to disclose any administrative matter without due authority. The long period of international tension following the Second World War resulted in a number of serious security cases. These made Canadians aware that there was a real need for administrative secrecy for security reasons. They also caused the Canadian Government to appoint a Royal Commission on Security, which issued a report in 1969 favouring stronger security measures and no relaxation of administrative secrecy. Moreover, the increasing use of computers has led to a concern over the ease with which they can store, transfer and release information on private individuals, and to the adoption of federal and provincial laws against the invasion of privacy.

On the other hand, Canadians have become increasingly aware that the rule of administrative secrecy is incompatible with the right of the public to information in a democracy. They now see that an Official Secrets Act and a civil service oath which imply that civil servants must keep all administrative matters secret are not consistent with the fact that government departments pour out a torrent of information in an attempt to make the public understand the complex operations of modern government.

The federal and provincial Governments themselves have become increasingly schizophrenic about this matter. They recognise that in a democracy the public have a right to be fully informed, but at the same time they preserve the principle that all administrative information is secret unless and until the Government chooses to release it. The incongruousness of the present situation has given rise in very recent years to a number of 'leaks' of reports and information by federal employees on subjects which many people felt should never have been kept secret in the first place. Since the action of these employees has been supported by a large segment of the press and the public, the federal Government has recently engaged in considerable soul-searching about its traditional principle of administrative secrecy. To date, however, no general right of public access to administrative documents or information has been established by the federal Parliament.

RECENT TREND TO OPENNESS

Nevertheless, in recent years the balance between secrecy and openness has been shifting in the direction of greater openness, especially at the federal level of government. The main reasons seem to have been the growing international *détente*, which has been accompanied by a decline in the need for national security measures, and the recent stress on 'participatory democracy', which implies a better-informed public with greater access to information.

The year 1969 probably marks the beginning of this trend. It is true that the conservative report of the Royal Commission on Security was published in 1969. But in the same year the Government's Task Force on Government Information issued a fat two-volume report on all aspects of government information. It recommended a much more positive information and publicity effort and the creation of a central information co-ordinating and publications agency, Information Canada. It also criticised the Government's traditional policy of administrative secrecy, and quoted at length my earlier article proposing Canada's adoption of the Swedish principle of openness.[1] In that year, too, Prime Minister Trudeau announced that the Government was adopting a policy of making automatically available to the public most official records more than 30 years old. The Government then announced its acceptance of the main recommendations of the Task Force, and in 1970 established Information Canada. In that year it also had Parliament approve a Federal Court Act, which enlarged the power of the courts to compel the production of official documents in courts, and in 1971 sponsored the Statutory Instruments Act, which ensured the publication of all Government regulations and many related statutory instruments.

In 1973 the Government issued guidelines for the release of documents requested by members of the House of Commons, and referred these guidelines for study to the Standing Joint Committee (of the Senate and the House of Commons) on Regulations and other Statutory Instruments, along with a Private Member's Bill providing for a public right of access to administrative documents. This Bill (C-225) had been introduced in the House of Commons by Mr Gerald Baldwin, House Leader of the Opposition. Variations of the Bill had been submitted in earlier years by Mr Baldwin and others, but as is usual with such Private Member's Bills, the Government had ignored them.

The Joint Committee did not actually begin its study of these documents until the end of 1974. Since then it has been calling witnesses before it, including ministers, senior public servants and others. An interesting document tabled before the Committee on 25 June 1975 and published as part of its proceedings, was the so-called Wall report, *The Provision of Government Information*[2] which had been completed in April 1974 by an officer of the Privy Council Office, Mr D. F. Wall, at the request of the Secretary of the Privy Council, Mr Gordon Robertson. This was a liberal and far-reaching report, which recommended a wide extension of the area of documents to be made public, as well as a much narrower and more precise definition of matters to be kept secret, and a marked change of attitude by the Government and the bureaucracy in the direction of greater openness. The fact that the Government allowed this report to be published was in itself an indication of the Government's changing attitude.

To date (July 1978), the Committee has not completed its work, and is not likely to issue its final report until late in 1978 or later. However, in December 1975 it tabled a report approving in principle the concept of legislation relating to freedom of information. This report was approved by the House of Commons in February 1976, and in June 1977 the Government committed itself to introducing legislation on the subject by issuing a 'Green Paper' which discussed alternative proposals.

PROVINCIAL AND LOCAL GOVERNMENTS

Each of the provincial governments has its own administrative structure, quite separate from the federal administration, and each controls public access to its own administration. Local governments are under the exclusive jurisdiction of the provincial legislatures, and hence the laws governing public access to local administration vary from province to province. Since it would require too much space to report in detail on the laws and practices of the provincial and local governments, the remainder of this report will refer mainly to the federal level of government. However, some general statements can be made here about the situation at the provincial and local levels.

Because the provinces have inherited and operate under basically the same parliamentary system as does the federal government, the tradition of administrative secrecy has been much the same, even though there has not been the same need to withhold information on grounds of national security. Despite the recent changes at the federal level, the principle of discretionary secrecy – meaning that the release of information is at the complete discretion of the Cabinet – still prevails in all provinces except Nova Scotia. There, a new (though rather weak) law on public access to government information went into effect in November 1977. Also, in March 1977 the Government of Ontario appointed a Commission on Freedom of Information and Individual Privacy, which will probably report in 1979.

At the local level of government there is more administrative openness. This is mainly because local government does not have the parliamentary system whereby a government supported by a majority party wishes to keep its affairs and proceedings secret from the opposition. Also, the provinces have laws requiring normal meetings of municipal councils and school boards to be open to the public. Frequently, however, a municipal council or school board or their committees will meet informally in secret to discuss a matter instead of debating it at a formal open meeting.

The recent changes at the federal level and in Nova Scotia will no doubt influence the other provincial and local governments to favour greater openness and public access, and will probably result in more new provincial legislation on the subject.

PROVISIONS FOR SECRECY AND ACCESS

MAIN PROVISIONS FOR SECRECY

At the federal level, as mentioned above, the most general provision for the secrecy of administrative information is the secrecy oath required of all civil servants by the Public Service Employment Act. Each civil servant swears that in his employment he 'will not, without due authority . . . , disclose or make known *any* matter that comes to [his] knowledge by reason of such employment.'[3] This means that, theoretically, a public servant may not release any document or information without permission from his political Minister, and that the Government enjoys almost complete discretion regarding what administrative information is to be released. Several laws also have provisions requiring secrecy for information held on individual corporations and persons, to protect their privacy. Notable examples are the Income Tax Act and the Statistics Act. The most important provisions for secrecy, however, are those designed for the protection of national security in the Official Secrets Act, as supplemented by certain sections of the Criminal Code which define related offences, such as treason, sabotage, sedition, breach of trust by a public officer, making use of official papers, and preparation to commit an offence under the Secrets Act.

Canada's Official Secrets Act has a long legislative history. Between 1911 and 1920 the British Official Secrets Act of 1911 was applied to Canada. But when a new British Act was passed in 1920, it was not made applicable to Canada. The 1911 Act continued in force as part of the law of Canada, until it was displaced by Canadian legislation: the Official Secrets Act of 1939. This Act, as amended, is much the same as the British legislation of 1911 as changed in 1920.

The British and Canadian Secrecy Acts are mainly designed to cover spying with the intent of passing on secret government information to a foreign agent or government. But as Professor Maxwell Cohen has pointed out, section 4 of the Canadian Act (and section 2 of the British Act) embrace almost any form of information obtained in the course of service or contract of employment with the government and then passed on without authority to any other person, 'whatever his status and whatever the purposes of the transfer of information may be, [and] however unclassified the information may be'.[4] In both the British and Canadian Acts the onus of proof is on the accused if a limited case on the facts has been made out by the Crown, and a court has power to order the proceedings held so that the public is excluded from the trial (though not from the passing of sentence). The Acts also allow a defendant's purpose in revealing information to be implied from his conduct or known character. Any evidence of communication or attempts at communication with a foreign agent are *prima facie* evidence of his purpose.

There are two important differences between the British and Canadian statutes. Section 2 of the British Act has been drafted and interpreted so as to mean that the unauthorised communication of any official information is illegal, while under section 4 of the Canadian Act the criminal illegality is confined to any 'secret' official document or information. The other difference is that the Canadian Act provides a greater penalty for the non-espionage crime of unauthorised communication: the maximum penalty in Britain is imprisonment for two years, while in Canada it is for thirteen years. Since the Second World War, however, prosecutions in Canada have been much fewer than in Britain.

The Royal Commission on Security, the Wall report and several scholars have criticised the Official Secrets Act as being outdated and too sweeping, and have proposed its complete revision.

TYPES OF INFORMATION TO BE KEPT SECRET

Until recent years there were no general specifications by the Government of Canada of the *types* of administrative information that were to be kept secret, even as a guide to ministers in authorising its release. Recent official statements and provisions, however, have attempted to clarify this matter. Drawing on the Prime Minister's statement and the subsequent directive on the transfer of public records to the Archives, and on the Federal Court Act of 1970, one could say that in general the types of information to be kept secret are those having to do with foreign relations, national security, federal-provincial relations, Cabinet proceedings and papers, and the protection of business competition and of personal privacy.

In 1973 the Government's Directive for the release of papers to Parliament made a much more detailed specification of types of documents to be kept secret.[5] First, it specified 16 categories:

1. Legal opinions or advice provided for the use of the Government.

2. Papers, the release of which would be detrimental to the security of the State.

3. Papers dealing with international relations, the release of which might be detrimental to the future conduct of Canada's foreign relations; (the release of papers received from other countries to be subject to the consent of the originating country).

4. Papers, the release of which might be detrimental to the future conduct of federal-provincial relations or the relations of provinces *inter se*; (the release of papers received from provinces to be subject to the consent of the originating province).

5. Papers containing information, the release of which could allow or result in direct personal financial gain or loss by a person or a group of persons.

6. Papers reflecting on the personal competence or character of an individual.

7. Papers of a voluminous character or which would require an inordinate cost or length of time to prepare.

8. Papers relating to the business of the Senate.

9. Papers, the release of which would be personally embarrassing to Her Majesty or the Royal Family or official representatives of Her Majesty.

10. Papers relating to negotiations leading up to a contract until the contract has been executed or the negotiations have been concluded.

11. Papers that are excluded from disclosure by statute.

12. Cabinet documents and those documents which include a Privy Council Confidence.

13. Any proceedings before a court of justice or a judicial inquiry of any sort.

14. Papers that are private or confidential and not of a public or official character.

15. Internal departmental memoranda.

16. Papers requested, submitted or received in confidence by the Government from sources outside the Government.

The Directive also provided that 'Ministers' correspondence of a personal nature, or dealing with constituency or general political matters, should not be identified with government papers and therefore should not be subject to production in the House.' And it concluded with criteria for the release of studies prepared for the Government by outside consultants.

It will be noted that exemption no. 11 is really superfluous because such papers would be prohibited from disclosure in any case by the relevant Act of Parliament. As mentioned, several Acts, such as the Official Secrets Act, the Income Tax Act and the Statistics Act, forbid the disclosure of specific kinds of information in particular areas of administrative activity. They already cover to some extent types of information exempted from disclosure in other categories on the list. For instance, the Secrecy Act already covers category no. 2, while the Income Tax and Statistics Acts partly cover nos 5 and 6. Before 1973, however, no general criteria had been laid down for the withholding of other types of administrative information. For the first time ministers and senior officials had a general guide to follow in deciding whether a particular paper or document, if requested, should be released to Parliament. Moreover, since no such guide existed for the release of documents and information generally to the public, the guidelines are now being used to some extent for this purpose as well.

The Wall report recommends that a list of exemptions such as this should be used as a guide for making available to the public all other administrative documents and information. It also proposes that the list should be reduced from sixteen to eight categories by consolidating some of them into more general criteria. For instance, it proposes as one category of exemption from immediate availability 'information, the release of which would constitute a breach of confidence or of the law or of the rules of parliament'. This would incorporate nos 8, 9, 11, 14 and 16 of the existing list. The report omits no. 7 from its proposed list, and would narrow the exemptions somewhat by substituting the word 'would' in cases where the existing list uses the word 'might' [be detrimental to the future conduct of Canada's foreign relations or federal-provincial relations], and by using somewhat more restrictive wording in other cases.[6] It is not known, however, whether these proposals will be adopted by the Government or the Joint Committee on Regulations.

RECENT PROVISIONS FOR ACCESS

The first recommendation of the Task Force on Government Information was that 'the right of Canadians to full, objective and timely information and the obligation of the State to provide such information about its programmes and policies be publicly declared and stand as a foundation for the development of new government policies in this field'. Following the Government's acceptance of this and the other Task Force recommendations early in 1970, it sponsored the provisions and legislation for greater public access that we have already mentioned. These will be explained in greater detail here (except for the extension of production powers by the courts in the Federal Court Act of 1970, which will be discussed with the courts as recipients of information).

Regarding the Statutory Instruments Act of 1971, which increased the assurance that delegated legislation would be made public, it should be mentioned that an earlier Regulations Act (1950) had already required all Government regulations to be published in the *Canada Gazette*. The difficulty was that executive instruments were issued in many different forms (Orders in Council, regulations, minutes, directives, etc.), and it was possible for the Government to refrain from publishing some of its delegated legislation simply by not defining it as a 'regulation'. The new law clarified the types of regulations that could remain unpublished, or published only in part, on such grounds as national security. It also provided a more systematic mechanism for parliamentary scrutiny, while the Federal Court Act provided a means of judicial review. In introducing the Statutory Instruments Bill, the Minister of Justice stated his opinion that it was 'a significant step toward a more open society in Canada'.[7] It is still possible, however, for subordinate legislation or executive decisions that are in the nature of regulations to be withheld from publication by not being defined as 'regulations'.

More significant than this measure from the viewpoint of access was the Prime Minister's announcement in 1969 that Canada would adopt the 30-year rule and would 'make available for research and other public use as large a proportion of the records of the Canadian Government prior to July 1, 1939, as would be consistent with the national interest'.[8] This would not include records 'whose release might adversely affect Canada's external relations, violate the right of privacy of individuals, or adversely affect the national security'.[9] All other departmental records over 30 years old would be transferred to the Public Archives. In addition, departments and agencies would be encouraged to transfer to the Archives records less than 30 years old, but these would remain under the control of the Ministers concerned and they would be made available to the public under terms to be established by the Minister in consultation with the Dominion Archivist. In no case would Cabinet documents be made available until they were 30 years old. An Advisory Council on Public Records, consisting of the Dominion Archivist and departmental representatives, worked on implementing this announcement, and in April 1972 the Prime Minister announced that the Minutes of the Cabinet and the Cabinet War Committee for the period from the start of 1942 to the end of the Second World War (i.e., documents more than 27 years old) had been turned over to the Dominion Archivist to be made available for public examination. Then, in June 1973, the Government issued to all departments Cabinet Directive No. 46 on the 'Transfer of Public Records to the Public Archives and Access to the Public Records Held by the Public Archives and by Departments'. This will be discussed in detail under 'Information Procedures'.

Meanwhile, the Privy Council Office had been working on the guidelines for the release of documents to Parliament, and these were issued as Cabinet Directive No. 45, 'Notices of Motion for the Production of Papers', before being tabled in the House of Commons, briefly debated, and referred to the Joint Committee on Regulations in March of 1973. The significance of this Directive is that for the first time it stated publicly as a general principle, and as a guide to departments and agencies, that they should make public as much information as possible. The actual wording of the General Principle is as follows:[10]

To enable Members of Parliament to secure factual information about the operations of government to carry out their parliamentary duties and to make public as much factual information as possible consistant [sic] with effective administration, the protection of the security of the state, rights to privacy and other such matters, government papers, documents and consultant reports should be produced on Notice of Motion for the Production of Papers [in Parliament] unless falling within the categories outlined below in which case an exemption is to be claimed from production.

Then follow the already-quoted sixteen categories and other criteria which are to be applied in determining if administrative documents are to be exempted from production. It should be noted that the General Principle states only that government papers 'should' (not 'shall') be produced, and that an exemption 'is to' (not 'should' or 'may') be claimed from production. Also, the wording and punctuation are so awkward that they seem to imply that it is not the Government but Members of Parliament who are to 'make public as much factual information as possible'.

THE HOLDERS OF INFORMATION

THE POLITICAL EXECUTIVE

Because the Cabinet, the body responsible for directing the whole administrative system, itself meets and makes its decisions in secret, there is a strong tendency for administrative secrecy to become the rule rather than the exception, particularly when this is combined with the tradition of civil service anonymity. The secrecy of Cabinet decision-making also means that Government Bills must be presented to Parliament without the benefit of the views of outside interest groups, and without the participation of the public in the making of decisions, since they have no chance to criticise and discuss proposals before decisions are made. Yet the Cabinet system operates in such a way that the Government rarely accepts significant amendments to a Bill after it has been made public by its introduction in Parliament. Hence the Government has no easy way of getting the advice of outside experts or testing public reaction to a measure before it is presented in almost final form to Parliament. In some parliamentary countries of Western Europe, draft Bills are made public and widely discussed with all interested groups before being presented to the legislature, while in the United States competing draft Bills are introduced by individual Congressmen, and are fully discussed and often significantly amended in committees before they are presented to Congress.

One of the traditional ways of meeting this difficulty under the

British type of parliamentary system has been to resort to a Royal Commission to help form and sound out public opinion and receive the advice and proposals of interest groups before the Government drafts and approves a Bill on a matter. Another device has been to issue a statement of Government policy in the form of a White Paper, so as to receive the benefit of public discussion before a Bill is drawn up. More recently the Government has experimented with the so-called Green Paper, in which alternative solutions to a problem are discussed and more tentative proposals are made, so that the Government is not forced to issue a firm statement of policy, as in a White Paper, before receiving the benefit of public discussion. It has also set up continuing bodies, such as the Economic Council of Canada, the Science Council of Canada and the Institute for Policy Research, to make recommendations in broad areas of government activity. They are somewhat like continuing Royal Commissions, in the sense that they are relatively independent of the Government and conduct studies and issue reports with recommendations which are sometimes critical of existing Government policy. In other words, because of the lack of prior public discussion before policy decisions are made, the Government has recognised the need to create special institutions to inform the public and receive their advice on important policy matters.

DIFFERENCES AMONG AUTHORITIES

Apart from the Cabinet itself, there is no significant difference among administrative authorities in the public's access to information, except that regulatory bodies and public corporations which are relatively independent from the Government, in comparison with the regular departments, are somewhat more secretive. This is mainly because ministers are not considered as directly responsible to Parliament for their activities, and therefore more frequently refuse to answer questions in Parliament concerning them. Moreover, the public corporations have tended to take on the management practices of the business world, which, as already mentioned, is reticent about releasing information to the public.

THE RECIPIENTS OF INFORMATION

From the viewpoint of the recipients of administrative information, an important distinction must be made between access by official bodies, such as the legislature and the courts, and by members of the outside public.

OFFICIAL BODIES

The Legislature
Under a parliamentary system of government with a tradition of secrecy, the legislature is of course the chief means of access to administrative documents and information. Because Canada has inherited the principle of representative government, it has been considered that the people's representatives should have special rights of access. For this reason federal Members of Parliament have at times criticised the Government for releasing documents publicly before they are tabled in Parliament, or for making policy announcements directly to the public through the media, instead of in the House of Commons.

If the legislature is to hold the Government to account, naturally it must have as much information as possible about the Government's administrative activities. In Canada, as in other parliamentary countries, the federal and provincial Parliaments acquire this information as part of their general procedures and devices for controlling the Government. One of their main sources of information is their review of the Government's budget, through a study of past and proposed expenditures. As in other parliamentary countries, too, they have reporting to them an auditor who has special powers of access to financial accounts and documents. They also have the usual Question Hour, a special period within which Members of Parliament may ask oral or written questions of ministers, as well as standing committees for the study and possible amendment of the Government's proposed legislation.

The ministers frequently appear before these committees to explain a Bill which they have presented to Parliament, and if the Bill is related to on-going administrative activities, this frequently requires the minister to answer questions about these activites. The tradition of civil service anonymity and the theory that a minister is responsible and must answer for all the activities in his department, were formerly interpreted to mean that senior officials were not called before these committees to answer questions about their department's activities. In recent years at the federal level, however, the Government has allowed them to give evidence, and has provided the committees with additional funds for research and for the publication of their proceedings. Thus the Joint Committee on Regulations, besides questioning the ministers responsible for the new guidelines on the production of papers, was allowed to call for questioning the former Secretary of the Privy Council, who helped to prepare the guidelines. It is significant that he was allowed to submit the Wall report, prepared by a civil servant, for publication in the Committee's proceedings.

There are also other devices and agencies of Parliament for securing information that are worth mentioning. One of these, which exists at both the federal and provincial levels, is the commission of inquiry. If a question is raised in Parliament which does not seem to have been answered satisfactorily, and it is suspected that the Government is refusing disclosure to avoid embarrassment, in serious cases the Opposition may demand the appointment of such a commission. The constitutional practice is that usually the Government will agree. Although the Government decides whether to appoint a commission, and names its members, such commissions have special powers to investigate publicly, and hence are a valuable additional vehicle for the disclosure of documents and information.

A special agency of the legislature that exists only at the provincial level in Canada is the office of Ombudsman, set up in recent years to receive and investigate complaints from individuals about the decisions, action or inaction of the administration. Under a system of discretionary secrecy, often an individual affected by a decision is given no reason for the decision, and does not even have enough information about how it was made to know whether he has any reasonable grounds for complaint, except in the case of administrative delay. Since he has no access to the documents in his case, one of the great values of an Ombudsman is that the latter is given the power of access to administrative documents and information on behalf of the complainant. Since 1967 the Ombudsman plan has been established in nine of the ten provinces (all except Prince Edward Island).[11]

No such office for complaints exists at the federal level, however.

The only similar office is that of the Commissioner of Official Languages, who has the power to receive and investigate complaints from the public, but only with respect to the use of English or French by the federal administration. Just before the federal election of October 1972, the Minister of Justice announced that the Government intended to create a commission for the protection of human rights, which would include the powers of a Parliamentary Ombudsman to investigate complaints against the administration. In July 1975 the Government introduced legislation to create such a commission, but it does not include the functions of an Ombudsman. It does, however, give citizens the right to inspect files the government may be holding on them, and to file a correction or counter-statement to any information on file. But a file may be withheld if its subject-matter concerns any one of a long list of exemptions (though there is provision for appeal to one of the commissioners). This legislation, the Canadian Human Rights Act, was passed in 1977 and went into effect in March 1978. Also, late in 1977 the Government announced that it would introduce a separate Ombudsman plan, based on a favourable report by senior officials, *The Report of the Committee on the Concept of the Ombudsman* (1977), but action is unlikely before the next election.

The Courts

Canada has inherited the British system of independent common law courts, which hold their proceedings in public. These courts have considerable power to require the production of administrative documents as evidence. However, Canada has also inherited the British doctrine of Crown privilege, or discretion to refuse a request for the production of documents before an open court. Canada's courts have been heavily influenced by British judicial decisions, which until recently were willing to accept without question a minister's statement that on grounds of public interest a government document or testimony should not be disclosed to litigants or given to a defendant.

Even before 1970, Canada's courts were beginning to demand more specific grounds, such as interests of national security, for a Government's refusal to produce documents. In 1970 the Federal Court Act, which created a new Federal Court to replace the old Exchequer Court, clarified and limited the extent of Crown privilege. It gave to a presiding judge the power to decide whether documents claimed by the Government to be privileged must be submitted as evidence, except when a minister certifies that the production of a document 'would be injurious to international relations, national defence or security, or to federal–provincial relations, or that it would disclose a confidence of the Queen's Privy Council for Canada.' As Professor Cohen has pointed out, 'both the new Federal Court Act of 1970 and the evolving Canadian common law even before 1970, are now likely to produce fairer disclosure standards in both civil and criminal litigation between the Crown and a subject.'[12]

THE PUBLIC

Among the potential recipients of administrative information in the outside public are categories of individuals or segments of the public having a special interest in freer access to documents. The most important of these are: interested persons, that is, individuals who are personally affected by administrative action; reporters and the news media; and scholars.

Interested Persons
In Canada there is no special right for individuals to have access to the documents in an administrative decision or case affecting them personally. Nor is there any right of access to personal information about them that has been collected by provincial governments. For instance, citizens are not allowed to see or correct personal information that may be held in police files, and may not even know that such information is being held. In recent years about half of the provinces have approved laws for the protection of personal privacy, but these laws are directed against the invasion of privacy by businesses, such as credit agencies or advertisers, and either do not include information held by government or specifically exclude such information.[13] Many people argue that there is no good reason why government information should be excluded.

The News Media
To reporters and the news media, the lack of a general right of access to administrative documents is not directly apparent as a serious problem because their concern is with immediate news of a policy nature, and because of the huge flow of publications and information released by the federal and provincial governments. Under

the pressure of time, reporters are glad to receive news releases prepared by public servants containing brief summaries of important documents, and to get further information orally from ministers or officials, often by telephone or by questioning ministers directly on radio or television.

At the federal level, nearly all government departments maintain information offices with a large staff, and departments prepare thousands of publications each year. Between 1970 and 1976 these were printed and distributed mainly by Information Canada, but this agency was abolished in 1976. Moreover, ministers issue many news releases and may hold press conferences. They or senior officials are often willing to grant interviews in which they give background information and views which are not for quotation or attribution. All of this creates the impression that there is a free flow of administrative information. Reporters tend to forget that they do not have access to the original information and documents, and that the Government releases to them only what it *chooses* to release.

Serious problems created by the discretionary release of information are what have been called 'managed news' and 'slanted information'. In the first place, the Government directly manipulates the release of news in its own favour and suppresses unfavourable news. In the words of an Opposition Member of Parliament, 'In Canada there is a tendency on the part of Governments to be partisan in the papers made public. If it's good news, the Government releases it when it's advantageous, but if it's bad news, the Government doesn't want it known.'[14] Moreover, all official publications are at least slightly slanted in favour of the Government and the bureaucracy, even if only by never containing anything critical of them. This creates the subtle difference between the transmission of information and the release of propaganda.

Under a system of discretionary release, departments and their information services naturally tend to emphasise what is favourable to their department, or at least do not publish anything unfavourable. The Royal Commission on Government Organization revealed that the Department of National Defence was a prime example of this. In 1962 the information services of the armed forces were manned by 190 officials, significantly called public relations rather than information officers, who spent hundreds of thousands of dollars painting the armed forces in a favourable light.[15] The Naval Service had an internal inspirational document for its ideal public relations officer which even went so far as to say that 'he must be utterly devoted to the Service, itself, because he often has to deal with criticism from outside and defend the Service with resolute intelligence, though the criticism may be partly or wholly valid.'[16] Even if information releases are not obviously slanted, sheer volume can turn them into propaganda, simply because they are never unfavourable. In this respect the Royal Commission was critical of the armed forces, when it found that in a single two-week period in 1961 their public relations men had distributed 75 news stories or releases, over 1300 radio, television and film productions, and more than 2500 photographic prints.[17]

Reporters naturally take the path of least resistance and use such administrative 'handouts', instead of investigating for themselves. But to be fair, it is difficult for them to investigate if they have no right of access to officials and official records. A public right of access to the original undoctored documents instead of ones specially prepared for release would help to ensure that the media were reporting information rather than propaganda.

Another problem created by discretionary release, coupled with the anonymous and faceless nature of the public service, is that officials give reporters information and opinions which are not for attribution. The theory of ministerial responsibility preserves the fiction that only a minister releases information and that he is personally the author of documents released by his department. Hence officials' names are not given as spokesmen and rarely as authors of documents. Even if an official's name is given as author of an article or document, one can be certain that its wording has been carefully reviewed by a higher authority to be sure that it is not too critical, before approval is given for its release. The result, as stated in my earlier article (p. 479), is that reporters and broadcasters 'must work in a crazy world of illicit purveyors of official information, who, like gossipers, give them a story but insist that they must not tell anybody, or that if they publish it, they must not give its source'. Even ministers take advantage of this situation by leaking ideas or proposals through their executive assistants or senior officials as 'trial balloons', without having to take personl responsibility for them if they turn out to be unpopular.

If an official gives a journalist information or a document not authorised for release, the question arises whether the journalist can be compelled by the courts to disclose its source. The tendency in Canada has been for the courts to compel disclosure of journalists' sources,[18] and this, in turn, has tended to inhibit the release of administrative information. In the United States the courts have tended more to emphasise the liberty of the press, and several states have laws that recognise the right of a journalist to withhold his source of information,[19] while in Sweden the Freedom of the Press Act provides that a journalist cannot be compelled to disclose his source, and is even prohibited from revealing his informant's name without the latter's consent.[20]

Another difficulty caused by discretionary release is that individual ministers and departments differ in their practices, and there is no uniformity from one department to another in the standards of access. Related to this is what one might call the problem of favouritism and dependency. Because ministers (and senior officials with the approval of their minister) have complete discretion regarding to whom they will release information or provide access to documents, it is easy for them to show discrimination in their treatment of reporters or others seeking information. They are likely to favour some over others, especially in return for a promise or practice of not being too critical of the Government. Such reporters then find themselves in a position of dependency on the Government for future information, and fear that their source will be cut off if they are too critical. In fact, this dependency relationship applies to some extent to all reporters who are members of the National Press Gallery, because the Government provides them with working facilities in the House of Commons and often free travel with the Prime Minister and his ministers.

Scholars
This syndrome of discrimination, favouritism and dependency affects historians, social scientists and other scholars who wish to gain access to documents or information less than 30 years old, while the classification of scientific information limits its free exchange among natural scientists and holds back the advancement of knowledge. Social scientists in particular feel the limiting pressure of discretionary release. They know that they will be unable to get desired information from the bureaucracy if they are too critical of its senior officers, the ministers or Government policies. Also, more and more social scientists in Canada are becoming dependent upon the Government for short-term contract research. Consequently, there is a real danger that solid academic criticism of the Government's policies will disappear and thus delay the solution of social problems. Though one of the main functions of academics is

to be critics of society and government, their independence of view is jeopardised by these factors.

INFORMATION PROCEDURES

THE HOLDING OF INFORMATION

As a practical matter, the way in which administrative information is held has a great deal to do with its accessibility. Thus records held in government departments are likely to be organised for the convenience of the department in using them, while if they are held by archives the emphasis is likely to be on convenience for researchers from the outside public.

From this point of view the Cabinet Directive on the transfer of documents to the Public Archives takes on additional importance, because it urges departments to transfer documents that are even less than 30 years old. Thus it states that 'to facilitate research all departments should transfer their public records to the Public Archives of Canada as soon as practicable.' However, it specifies that a public record shall not be transferred to the Public Archives if:

(*a*) it is an exempted record, the release of which would be contrary to law;

(*b*) it is a record of a department that, in the opinion of the Deputy Head of that department, is or may be necessary for the efficient operation of that department;

(*c*) it contains information the disclosure of which, in the opinion of the appropriate Minister, would be prejudicial to the public interest.

The Directive also specifies that access to even a transferred record which is less than 30 years old is to be given only with the permission of the appropriate Minister, in accordance with the terms and conditions established in consultation with the Dominion Archivist. Access to records retained in a department is to be given 'only with the permission of and in accordance with terms and conditions established by the appropriate Minister', and no department is to permit access to any record 'in respect of which the department or agency that originated the record would refuse access'.

Where the Deputy Head of a department is of the opinion that a transferred record is an 'exempted' record, he is to advise the Dominion Archivist of this. The implication of this provision is that the Dominion Archivist must not release records less than 30 years old which are exempted. An exempted record is defined in the Directive as a public record:

(a) that contains information the release of which
    (i) would be contrary to law,
    (ii) is restricted pursuant to an agreement made between the Government of Canada and any other government,
    (iii) might be considered by any government to be a breach of faith on the part of the Government of Canada,
    (iv) might embarrass the Government of Canada in its relations with any other Government, or
    (v) might violate the right of privacy of any individual,
(b) that relates to security and intelligence; or
(c) that is a personnel record, except that a personnel record ceases to be an exempted record on the expiration of the period of 90 years from the date of birth of the employee with respect to whom the record is made.

It will be noted that ministers and officials are given greater discretion by the more permissive word 'might' rather than 'would' in categories (iii), (iv) and (v) above, and by the vague words 'relates to' in (b).

The Directive defines 'public record' as meaning:

correspondence, memoranda or other papers, maps, plans, photographs, films, microfilms, sound recordings, tapes, computer cards or other documentary material
(a) made or received by any department or agency,
(b) preserved or appropriate for preservation by a department or agency, and
(c) containing information relating to the organization, functions, procedures, policies or activities of the department or agency or other information of past, present or potential value to the Government of Canada.

This does not include 'working papers, stocks of publications or printed documents or library or museum material made, or acquired or preserved, only for convenience of reference'.

The internal management of departmental records is also relevant to access. The great bulk of departmental papers are merely 'house-keeping' records. They are of no interest to the outside public or to posterity and are not worth keeping. Some way must be found of winnowing this chaff from the wheat so that records of real interest are easily accessible. From this viewpoint the Government of Canada has made great improvements in its records management procedures in recent years. Since the Second World War it has created a Records Centre under the supervision of the Dominion Archivist and has transferred to it most old departmental documents for sorting and preserving what is of historical interest. The Government also established a Public Records Committee. To avoid the high cost of storing a great mass of useless old files and of searching them to find the few of historical interest, this committee established categories of documents to be marked from the beginning either for automatic destruction at the end of specified periods or for indefinite preservation. It then applied the new system to a wide range of housekeeping records. In 1965 a minute of the Government's Treasury Board required that the system be extended to all other records by 1969.

In Canada the distinction between working documents and completed documents has not been important, because even completed ones are not released until a decision has been made to publish them or table them in Parliament and they have actually been published or tabled. As the Wall report has pointed out (pp. 56–7), a very wide category of other documents prepared in departments could be considered completed and made available for publication without harm or inconvenience. This category could be extended to many additional documents, such as those prepared by consultants, if it were made known before their preparation that the public would have access to them.

The storing of information in computer data banks and the ease with which they can either regurgitate or withhold it is posing a new set of problems regarding the holding and release of information, accessibility and the invasion of privacy. The Government of Canada, like that of most developed countries, has had a study made of these problems,[21] but to date has proposed no legislation to solve them. A Canadian legal scholar has recently argued that there is too much emphasis on the potential invasion of privacy by computers. A more serious problem, in his view, is that they will make accessibility to government information more difficult and the withholding of it easier.[22]

SECURITY CLASSIFICATION

Until the publication of the Report of the Royal Commission on Security[23] little was known about the procedures for the classification of security documents or for the clearance by the police of public employees who have access to such documents, because these procedures themselves were regarded as confidential. It was therefore impossible for the public to find out whether they were adequate or fair, although the secrecy of Canada's clearance procedures, compared with those in the United States, had the advantage of not ruining personal reputations. The Commission's Report itself was published in abridged form because, the Government stated, certain material had to be removed for security reasons.

The Report revealed that the Government had adopted the four security classifications that were being used widely in other western countries: Top Secret, Secret, Confidential and Restricted. Also published in the Report for the first time (pp. 69–71) were the Government's official definitions of these classifications, its examples of the types of document to be included in each, and its statement of general principles governing the classification of documents. In the definitions, the distinction between the top three categories lies in the strength of the wording used. Thus Top Secret documents, information and material are ones the unauthorised disclosure of which 'would cause exceptionally grave damage to the nation'. In the Secret category are ones the unauthorised disclosure of which 'would endanger national security, cause serious injury to the interests or prestige of the nation, or would be of substantial advantage to a foreign power'. The Confidential category includes ones the unauthorised disclosure of which 'would be prejudicial to the interests or prestige of the nation, would cause damage to an individual, and [sic] would be of advantage to a foreign power'.

The definition of Restricted is very vague. It simply specifies material which 'should not be published or communicated to anyone, except for official purposes'. Thus no guidelines are given for documents to be classified as Restricted. Indeed, this category is so broad that it could include any administration information. Both the Royal Commission (p. 115) and the Wall report (p. 69) have recommended that this classification should be abolished, as it was in the United States in 1963.

Although the emphasis in the definitions of the top three classifications is on national security, among the examples given of matters to be marked and kept Secret are all records of discussions of the Cabinet and Cabinet committees, and particulars of the national budget prior to its official release. Of the four examples of matters to be marked Confidential, only one (*c*) has to do with national security (political and economic reports which would be of advantage to a foreign power). The other three are:

(*a*) Information of a personal or disciplinary nature which should be protected for administrative reasons;
(*b*) Minutes or records of discussions of interdepartmental committees when the content of such minutes or records does not fall within a higher category;
(*d*) Private views of officials on public events which are not intended to be disclosed.

As the Wall report has pointed out (p.46), 'The regulations currently in force fail to delineate adequately information procedures used against espionage from procedures used to safeguard information which must be confidential for a myriad of other reasons.'

The Wall report has also noted that procedures used for the security clearance or screening of personnel have similarly failed to make this distinction. They are being applied to increasing numbers of public servants without discrimination, the only test being whether an employee has or is likely to have access to 'classified' information. The procedures in all cases involve fingerprinting, a detailed questionnaire and a search by the federal police of their records on criminals and subversives. In most cases where there is to be access to Secret information, the police (or other competent authorities) also make an investigation of the employee's (or prospective employee's) past and present associations and habits of life. On the basis of the police report, the employing department or agency then makes a judgement on whether clearance can be granted. Since these procedures were adopted during the period of the 'cold war' mainly for the clearance of persons who had access to security documents, they are too elaborate and in many cases unnecessary for the clearance of persons who have access to other types of secret and confidential information. The Wall report found that 'apart from the dubious relevance of these measures in many areas of government administration, and their inhibiting effect on the provision of information to the public, as well as on prompt staffing, there was a good deal of concern as to their cost' (p. 46).

Although the Government's general principles governing the classification of documents recognise that the 'classification appropriate to a document may alter with the passage of time', it has no general system for the downgrading and declassification of documents. Downgrading is left to the discretion of departments, which are merely enjoined by the principles to 'arrange to review classified documents as and when required', though at the same time 'it is strongly recommended that the originating departments indicate wherever possible, either at the time of issue or later, that a document may be downgraded after a given date or event'. The Royal Commission noted (p. 71) that there is an obvious tendency, especially on the part of more junior officials, to 'play safe' and to classify too much or to over-classify, and that over-classification 'was a general current problem'. Yet, because of the administrative difficulties involved, it recommended against the adoption of a general system of downgrading and declassification, even though it recognised a need to release classified records as soon as possible for purposes of public appraisal and historical research. One must agree that such a system is not worth the effort and cost involved, unless the records are to be fully declassified and made publicly available at an early date.

CONCLUSION

Although Canada must still be classed among the countries where there is no general right of access to official documents and information, in recent years the federal Government has taken a number of significant steps in the direction of greater openness. Perhaps the most important of these have been the issuing in 1973 of its Directive for the production of papers to Parliament, which formally states as a general principle that 'to make public as much factual information as possible . . . government papers, documents and consultant reports should be produced' unless falling within the defined categories, and the Government's attempt to apply this principle to the release of documents and information to the public generally.

Considering the pressing need for greater administrative openness in Canada, however, the Directive is far from being a giant step toward a general right of access. As I argued in my evidence before the Joint Committee on Regulations, it should instead be regarded as a weak-kneed and faltering step.[24] It lists so many exceptions in such sweeping terms that the exceptions almost swallow the rule or general principle. Also, it is basically intended as a guide to the production of papers in Parliament rather than the release of information generally. More serious, it is in the form of a Cabinet Directive rather than legislation, and therefore is not binding on the Government. Nor does it include any general statement providing for the public's right of access to administrative information. The judgement about whether a particular document can be withheld because it falls within one of the sixteen exemptions is still completely at the discretion of the Government. There is no right of appeal against such a decision to an independent arbiter such as the courts or an Ombudsman.

If the shift toward greater openness is to have its desired effect on the entrenched attitudes of civil servants, what is needed is a dramatic and legally enforceable reversal of the principle of discretionary secrecy in the form of new law or even a constitutional right. It should clearly state that freedom of access is the main principle and that secrecy is the exception. It should also clarify and specify narrowly the types of information that should be kept secret, and the penalties for its unauthorised release. Civil servants would then have a clearer idea of their responsibilities for keeping certain matters secret and for providing easy access to all other government information.

By issuing its Green Paper, *Legislation on Public Access to Government Documents*, in June 1977, the Government has committed itself to some kind of legislation on the subject.[25] But the tenor of the discussion in this policy document indicates that the Government is likely to introduce a weak law. For instance, the document favours an extensive list of exemptions and opposes a right of appeal to the courts, even though such a right is an integral part of the laws in the United States and Scandinavia. For this reason, the Green Paper has been strongly criticised, particularly by the Canadian Bar Association and by a research study prepared for it.[26]

The Government appears to be in no hurry to introduce a Bill on public access, and has referred its Green Paper to the Joint Committee on Regulations for study. In mid-1978 this Committee issued a report which was also critical of the Green Paper.[27] It favoured an initial appeal to an information commissioner whose opinion would be only advisory to the Government, but there would also be a right of further appeal to the Federal Court. Now it seems probable that the Joint Committee will recommend a strong law on the subject, and it is possible that the Government and Parliament will accept the recommendation. But this is not likely to happen unless the pressure of public opinion for a strong law becomes great enough to force the Government's hand.

NOTES

1. *Report: To Know and Be Known*, Vol. II: *Research Papers* (Ottawa, Queen's Printer, 1969), pp. 25–31. My earlier article on Canada was 'How Much Administrative Secrecy?', *Canadian Journal of Economics and Political Science* Vol. 31, No. 4 (November 1965), pp. 479–98, with a comment by K. M. Knight and my reply in Vol. 32, No. 1 (February 1966), pp. 77–87.

2. Canada, Parliament, First Session, Thirtieth Parliament, 1974–75, Standing Joint Committee on Regulations and other Statutory Instruments, *Minutes of Proceedings and Evidence*, Issue No. 32 (Ottawa: Queen's Printer, 1975), pp. 30–71. The Wall Report has also been made available as a separate document by the Privy Council Office.

3. Public Service Employment Act, 1967, Schedule C. My italics.

4. Thomas M. Franck and Edward Weisband, eds, *Secrecy and Foreign Policy* (New York: Oxford University Press, 1974), p. 357.

5. Printed in Standing Joint Committee, op. cit., Issue No. 13, as 'Notices of Motion for the Production of Papers', pp. 13:28–9. Also printed in House of Commons *Debates*, Vol. 117, No. 51, p. 2288 (15 March 1973).

6. Standing Joint Committee, op. cit., pp. 32:51–5.

7. House of Commons *Debates*, 25 January 1971.

8. As quoted in *Research Papers*, op. cit., p. 26.

9. Ibid.

10. Standing Joint Committee, op. cit., p. 13:28.

11. See Janice Tyrwhitt, 'The Ombudsman: Canada's Trouble Shooters of Last Resort', *Reader's Digest*, Canadian Edition, Vol. 107, No. 64 (August 1975), pp. 39–43, and my *The Ombudsman Plan* (Toronto: McClelland & Stewart, 1973), Ch. 12, pp. 97–105.

12. *Secrecy and Foreign Policy*, op. cit., p. 369

13. Daniel Mayo, 'Privacy and Social Control', M.A. essay (Ottawa: Carleton University, 1974), pp. 61–5.

14. Quoted in *Research Papers*, op. cit., p. 26.

15. Canada, Royal Commission on Government Organization, *Report* (Ottawa: Queen's Printer, 1962), Vol. 3, p. 71.

16. Quoted in T. Joseph Scanlon, 'Promoting the Government of Canada', M.A. thesis (Kingston: Queen's University, 1964), p. 100.

17. *Report*, ibid.

18. Task Force, *Report*, op. cit., p. 33.

19. Ibid., p. 33.

20. See Hilding Eek, 'Protection of News Sources by the Constitution', *Scandinavian Studies in Law, 1961* (Stockholm), pp. 11–25.

21. Department of Communications/Department of Justice Task Force, *Report: Privacy and Computers* (Ottawa: Information Canada, 1972), pp. 236.

22. Hugh Lawford, 'Privacy versus Freedom of Information', *Queen's Quarterly*, Vol. 78 (autumn 1971), pp. 365–71.

23. Royal Commission on Security, *Report (Abridged)* (Ottawa: Queen's Printer, 1969).

24. *Proceedings*, op. cit., Issue No. 15, p. 15:18.

25. Issued by Honourable John Roberts, Secretary of State (Ottawa: Supply and Services Canada, 1977), pp. 39.

26. T. Murray Rankin, *Freedom of Information in Canada: Will the Doors Stay Shut?* (Ottawa: Canadian Bar Association, August 1977), p. 155.

27. Op. cit., Issue No. 34 of Third Session, 1977–78 (27 June 1978), pp. 3–12, 'Fifth Report to Both Houses'.

12 United States

MICHAEL JAY SINGER

A noted American historian, Henry Steele Commager, has observed that '[t]he generation that made the nation thought secrecy in government one of the instruments of Old World tyranny and committed itself to the principle that a democracy cannot function unless the people are permitted to know what their government is up to.'[1] An oft-quoted statement by James Madison – one of this nation's founding fathers and its fourth President – bears witness to that observation:

> A popular Government, without popular information, or the means of acquiring it, is but a Prologue to a Farce or a Tragedy; or, perhaps both. Knowledge will forever govern ignorance: and a people who mean to be their own Governors, must arm themselves with the power which knowledge gives.[2]

This early commitment to government openness has remained a hallmark of American democracy for almost two centuries. That is not to say, however, that the Government of the United States has always lived up to its commitment, nor that it *should* always keep the public fully informed on *all* matters. Some governmental functions do legitimately require a degree of secrecy in order to be performed properly and in the best interests of the country. In such instances, the people's right to know what their Government is doing is outweighed by the Government's need to conduct its affairs wisely and effectively. The problem, of course, is how to be sure that the Government's need for secrecy is legitimate in any given case. Moreover, even if a degree of secrecy is justifiable, there remains the problem of striking an acceptable balance with the public's right of access to the government information in order to ensure that the shroud of confidentiality is not over-inclusive.

Despite its long-standing commitment to openness, the United States has had an ample share of problems with government secrecy[3] – particularly since the burgeoning of the bureaucracy in the period following the Second World War. These problems exist at both the state and federal levels, but this chapter will deal primarily with the latter because an extensive inquiry into the varying public information laws and practices of the individual states would require far more time and space than is available. Nevertheless, before proceeding with this inquiry into the situation at the federal level, a brief word about the state level is in order.

The United States is comprised of fifty separate states, each of which has the authority to establish its own policies on public access to information held by the state government and the local political subdivisions. Since the early 1950s, many state legislatures and courts have, in fact, addressed this matter in legislation and judicial opinion. Because each state controls its own destiny in this regard, it is difficult to generalise about the results. Still, a few broad observations can be made.

GENERAL RIGHTS OF PUBLIC ACCESS

The State of California led the way to the enactment of modern freedom of information laws by passing the Brown Act in 1952. This comprehensive enactment contained provisions fostering open governmental meetings as well as access to governmental records.[4] Many states followed suit over the years – some by enacting open meetings laws, some by enacting open records laws, with the majority enacting both kinds of statute. By the end of 1974, thirty-five states had comprehensive 'freedom of information' laws on the books. Four states – Kentucky, Missouri, Tennessee, and Wyoming – had only open record laws; seven states – Colorado, Delaware, Maryland, New Jersey, Texas, Vermont, and Washington – had only open meetings statutes; and three states – Mississippi, Rhode Island, and West Virginia – had no general statutes governing public access to government-held information.

These state information laws are by no means uniform in language or effect.[5] By and large, they have brought the goal of open government closer to reality, but many obstacles have been encountered along the way to this ideal. Although this essay will not further explore the issues surrounding administration of state information laws,[6] one can gain a good deal of insight into them by examining the problems confronted at the federal level. The objectives, competing intersts, and various difficulties are basically the same on both levels.

The remainder of this article will deal only with public access to recorded information held by the executive branch of the federal government, which will be defined to include the independent regulatory agencies as well as the executive departments. Secrecy in the legislative and judicial branches of government has not posed so much of a problem, probably because many of the proceedings are open to the public and – in any event – deliberations, decisions, and actions are usually fully explained to the people.

For the past several years, the legal issues surrounding public access to recorded information held by the executive branch of the federal government have been largely determined by reference to the Freedom of Information Act of 1966 (FOIA),[7] although that statute has by no means eliminated the difficult task of balancing the competing interests in disclosure and secrecy. On 7 October 1974 the Congress approved several important amendments to the FOIA, but President Ford vetoed this legislation on 17 October. The following month, on 21 November, the Congress overrode the President's veto, having mustered the necessary two-thirds majority in both the House of Representatives and the Senate. Thus, the amendments[8] were enacted into law in November 1974 and became effective on 19 February 1975. Because of the central role played by the 1966 Act and the significance of the 1974 amendments, they will be the main focus of this chapter.

Although the FOIA is at the core of the public's legal right of access to government information, it does not exclusively control this whole area of the law. One must refer to other statutes, an executive order, the constitutional doctrine of executive privilege, and other legal principles – such as the right to individual privacy – that are intertwined with this complex legislation. Moreover, one must consider the special roles played by the three branches of government – executive, legislative, and judicial – as well as by private organisations. Especially important is the constitutionally protected [9] role played by the press, which keeps the public posted daily on what the Government is doing and which – from time to time – investigates, uncovers, and reports government secrets. These topics will all be broached in the discussion below, but space limitations dictate that the examination be brief.

THE FREEDOM OF INFORMATION ACT

BACKGROUND AND OVERVIEW

The present FOIA was preceded by section three of the Administrative Procedure Act, as enacted in 1946. That section, which fell under the rubric of 'Public Information', represented Congress' first statutory attempt to require routine disclosure of government-held information. The attempt failed, however, because the statute's vague language and broad exceptions enabled recalcitrant government officials easily to find reasons for withholding information, notwithstanding the clear congressional intent to the contrary. For example, the statute exempted from disclosure records involving 'any function of the United States requiring secrecy in the public interest' as well as 'information held confidential for good cause found'. Furthermore, only 'persons properly and directly concerned' were entitled to procure certain public records, and there was no provision for judicial remedy. Thus, it was soon recognised that section three would require amendment, but many years passed before Congress was able to produce a bill that gained sufficient support for enactment.[10] The Bill finally enacted – known as the Freedom of Information Act – was signed into law on 4 July 1966 and became effective exactly one year later. Upon signing the measure, President Johnson made clear in an accompanying statement that the United States was still dedicated to the principle of open government:

> This legislation springs from one of our most essential principles: a democracy works best when the people have all the information that the security of the Nation permits. No one should be able to pull curtains of secrecy around decisions which can be revealed without injury to the public interest. . . .

> I signed this measure with a deep sense of pride that the United

States is an open society in which the people's right to know is cherished and guarded.[11]

The FOIA's main purpose was to rectify the blatant weaknesses of its predecessor statute in order to foster greater public access to government information. Thus, it (1) abandoned the 'properly and directly concerned' standard and provided instead that 'any person' could obtain the public records; (2) replaced the vague exceptions with nine more narrowly defined exemptions; and (3) expressly created a right to appeal against administrative refusals of information to a federal district court. Even a cursory reading of the Act – along with its legislative history – leaves no doubt that disclosure is a 'transcendent goal', that Congress sought to make 'the general rule, not the exception'.[12]

The 1966 FOIA may be broadly viewed in three parts. Subsection (a) sets forth the kinds of information that must be made available to the public, and indicates the effect of and remedy for a failure to comply with the statutory requirements. Subsection (b) lists nine relatively specific categories of recorded information not required to be disclosed. Finally, subsection (c) provides that the FOIA cannot be used as a basis for withholding information 'except as specifically stated' in the Act and, in any event, 'is not authority to withhold information from Congress'. The 1974 amendments add two new subsections to the Act. Subsection (d) requires each federal agency to submit an annual report to Congress detailing its experience with and disposition of requests for information under the FOIA. Additional reporting requirements are imposed on the Department of Justice. Subsection (e) expands the definition of the term 'agency' for purposes of the FOIA.

This last point – the definition of 'agency' – must be clarified before proceeding further. In the past, that term has been defined solely by reference to the appropriate provision in the Administrative Procedure Act.[13] Thus, the FOIA has applied to 'each authority of the Government of the United States', but not to the District of Columbia, territories, and possessions. Clearly, then, the Act properly encompassed all executive departments and independent agencies, but the outer limits of its reach were ill-defined. As one federal appellate court observed: 'The statutory definition of "agency" is not entirely clear, but the [Administrative Procedure Act] apparently confers agency status on any administrative unit with substantial independent authority in the exercise of specific functions.'[14] The court went on to conclude than an organisation within the Executive Office of the President can fall into this category, but declined to decide whether the President himself was included. To clear up the confusion in this area, subsection (e) of the amended FOIA expressly provides that, for purposes of that Act,

> the term 'agency' . . . includes any executive department, military department, Government corporation, Government controlled corporation, or other establishment in the executive branch of the Government (including the Executive Office of the President), or any independent regulatory agency.[15]

Thus, Congress has now plainly expressed its intent that the FOIA's coverage be broad.

This discussion will now turn to a more detailed analysis of the FOIA's provisions.

PROVISIONS FOSTERING DISCLOSURE

(1) Publication in the Federal Register
Subsection (a) (1) of the FOIA requires each agency to maintain and publish a considerable amount of descriptive and explanatory material in the Federal Register – a daily, widely circulated government gazette that is codified annually in the Code of Federal Regulations.[16] This material includes (1) the organisational structure of the agency, (2) methods for public procurement of its information and decisions, (3) its mode of operation, (4) its procedural rules, (5) description of its forms, reports, and examinations, (6) its substantive rules, (7) its general policy statements and interpretations, and (8) changes affecting any of the foregoing materials. Obviously, the publication of such a broad range of information greatly assists individuals and businesses in their dealings with the agency. It enables them to ascertain the agency's position on many substantive matters within its purview and facilitates the making of effective and intelligent requests for further information.

Some of these provisions, however, are less than fully self-defining, particularly the subdivision ((a) (1) (D)) requiring publication of 'substantive rules of general applicability adopted as authorized by law, and statements of general policy or interpretations of general applicability formulated and adopted by the agency'. There is considerable room for argument between the agency and information-seekers over which rules are 'of general applicability' and over which policies and interpretations have actually been 'adopted'. Restrictive agency positions in this area have been challenged in court, and the judiciary will no doubt continue to play an important role in refining the meaning of this and other provisions.

In addition to setting forth the materials that must be published in the Federal Register, subsection (a) (1) provides a penalty to the agency for failing to comply. Unless the person affected by the omission 'has actual and timely notice of the terms' of the undisclosed information, he 'may not in any manner be required to resort to, or be adversely affected by' the omitted materials. A recent decision of the United States Supreme Court demonstrates that this provision is to be taken quite seriously. In *Morton v. Ruiz*,[17] the Court construed certain general assistance eligibility requirements of the Bureau of Indian Affairs to be 'substantive rules of general applicability' under subdivision (a)(1)(D) of the FOIA. The Bureau's failure to publish these rules in the Federal Register was therefore advanced by the Court as one of the reasons that the claimant involved in that litigation could not be deemed ineligible for the general assistance benefits at issue; he could not be 'adversely affected' by the Bureau's unpublished substantive rules. In so deciding, the Court shed further light on the policy underlying this portion of the FOIA. These publication requirements not only facilitate the framing of meaningful requests for information to the agencies but also ensure 'that administrative policies affecting individual rights and obligations be promulgated pursuant to certain stated procedures so as to avoid the inherently arbitrary nature of unpublished *ad hoc* determinations.'[18]

(2) Making Available for Inspection and Copying

Subsection (a)(2) refers to materials that need not be published in the Federal Register but should nevertheless be made 'available for public inspection and copying'. This requirement applies to (1) concurring, dissenting, and majority opinions that are 'final', (2) adjudicatory orders, (3) policy and interpretive statements that do not fall under the command of subdivision (a)(1)(D), discussed above, and (4) administrative staff manuals and instructions affecting members of the public. If the agency promptly publishes and offers these materials for sale, however, it has discharged this duty. Moreover, in all categories but adjudicatory orders, the agency may delete identifying details '[t]o the extent required to prevent a clearly unwarranted invasion of personal privacy', provided it justifies such action in writing. Subsection (a)(2) further requires that indexes of all matters issued, adopted, or promulgated be maintained for public inspection and copying, and that such indexes be published and distributed at least quarterly–unless the agency officially determines that such dissemination would be 'unnecessary and impracticable'. Failure to comply with these provisions precludes the agency from relying on such materials unless the party against whom they are being used is (1) another agency, or (2) has had actual and timely notice of their contents.

Again, as in subsection (a)(1), the language of these provisions invites dispute over which agency documents fall within their purview. It is not always so clear which opinions may be characterised as 'final', which statements have been 'adopted', which manuals pertain more to administration than to law enforcement, what degree of invasion of privacy is 'clearly unwarranted', and so on. In time the agencies, the courts and perhaps the Congress will clarify these terms; indeed, the judiciary has already made some progress in this regard. The Supreme Court, for example, has recently handed down two decisions that, among other things, examine and define the meaning of 'final opinions', as used in subdivision (a) (2) (A). Discussion of these cases will be deferred to the portion of this chapter dealing with the exemption for inter- and intra-agency memoranda (Exemption Five), since the controversy involves the relationship between this exemption and the 'final opinions' provision.[19] However, the decision in *Tax Analysts and Advocates v. Internal Revenue Service* (IRS), [20] which will be examined now, also offers a significant and instructive illustration of the courts' efforts to define the terms employed in subsection (a) (2).

An issue in the *Tax Analysts* case was whether certain IRS letter-rulings and other memoranda[21] were available to the public as 'statements of policy and interpretations which have been adopted by the agency' within the meaning of subdivision (a) (2) (B). The IRS, of course, maintained that memoranda did not fit into that category, arguing that only statements invoked as precedent in subsequent proceedings may be deemed 'adopted' by an agency and that letter-rulings are never so invoked. The court, however, held:

It matters not that the interpretation is never again cited or relied upon by the agency or anyone else, for this cannot obliterate the fact that the interpretation was once adopted by the agency and thereby came within the express terms of the Freedom of Information Act.[22]

This holding is consistent with the liberal disclosure policies of the FOIA and makes available to the public an important source of information about IRS interpretations of the tax laws. This decision will also open the files of other agencies following similar practices.[23]

The courts have also clarified the language of subdivision (a) (2) (C) requiring disclosure of 'administrative staff manuals and instructions to staff that affect a member of the public.' The legislative history makes clear that the word 'administrative' was selected in order to exclude manuals and instructions relating to law enforcement, thereby protecting 'the traditional confidential nature of instructions to Government personnel prosecuting violations of law in court.'[24] In many cases, however, it is extremely difficult to characterise a manual as wholly falling into one category or the other. By and large, the courts have favoured disclosure under such circumstances,[25] and allow withholding of the materials only upon a compelling showing that law enforcement would be seriously impaired by public access.[26] Again, the Act's general policy of broad disclosure has been vindicated by the courts.

(3) Requests for Reasonably Described Records

Prior to enactment of the 1974 amendments, subsection (a) (3) of the FOIA required the agencies to make documents not covered under subsections (a)(1) and (a)(2) 'promptly available to any person' who properly submitted a 'request for identifiable records'. Unlike the subsections previously considered, this provision put the burden of initiating disclosure procedures upon the person seeking the information. This fact underscores the crucial importance of the publication and indexing requirements imposed upon the agencies under subsections (a)(1) and (a)(2). Without the information furnished pursuant to those provisions, the requester's task under subsection (a)(3) would have been exceedingly onerous – as it sometimes was even with the benefit of the published and indexed materials.

Under the 1966 Act, the threshold inquiry was into the meaning of 'identifiable records'. Generally, the courts accepted the following definition of 'identifiable', gleaned from the Act's legislative history: 'a reasonable description enabling the Government employee to locate the requested records.'[27] However, this definition, although helpful, did not address some of the problems that arose in its application, especially (1) the agency's duty with respect to overly broad and burdensome requests and (2) the extent to which the agency should engage in further research to transform an unclear request into one capable of being answered. With respect to the former issue, the decision in *Irons v. Schuyler*[28] suggested that an agency may properly deny a broad request for all records in a specified category, even though the documents were readily 'identifiable'. As to the latter issue, the opinion in *National Cable Television Association v. Federal Communications Commission*[29] indicated that an agency did have some duty to go beyond the information furnished in a request in order to locate the desired records.

To alleviate some of the confusion in this area and to clarify the purpose of the 'identifiable records' provision, the 1974 amendments changed the language of subsection (a)(3) to state that any properly submitted 'request for records which . . . reasonably describes such records' shall trigger the agency's duty to 'make the records promptly available to any person'. Although this new 'reasonably describes' standard signifies Congress' desire to ease the burden on information-seekers, it seems unlikely that this change in terminology will have much substantive impact. After all, as noted above, the courts had already recognised that 'a reasonable description' of the records is all that subsection (a)(3) required. Therefore, it is probable that the issues confronted by the courts under the 'identifiable records' test will be much the same under the 'reasonably describes' formula.

Because the problems raised in the *Irons* and *National Cable* cases remain relevant to a consideration of subsection (a)(3) as amended, an examination of a factor underlying both cases – monetary costs – will be instructive. In both cases the agencies were capable of identifying and locating the desired materials, but they balked partly because of the expense of doing so. Because staff and funds are needed for performing the agencies' assigned functions, this concern would perhaps justify the denial of some frivolous and burdensome requests. On the other hand, the agencies perform their functions on the public's behalf, and one of their most important functions is keeping the public informed on their activities and actions.

One way of shifting this balance of competing interests toward disclosure would be to charge information-seekers for the costs incurred in complying with burdensome requests, rather than to deny such requests entirely. The agencies do have authority to charge fees under section 483a of Title 31 of the United States Code (1970), but such fees are required to be deposited in the Treasury. If these funds could be rechannelled to the agencies incurring the expenditures, agencies would be better equipped to handle the requests without serious disruption. Some agencies in fact, have been charging for their services in complying with record requests, but there has been little uniformity in determining when a requester must pay such a charge and how much of the total costs he must bear.[30] Fee-charging practices have varied considerably – not only from agency to agency, but also within a single agency.[31]

Fortunately, however, the situation need not remain one of hopeless confusion. The Administrative Conference of the United States has studied this issue and has made a recommendation which, if implemented, would facilitate the disclosure of reasonably described records without imposing an inequitable burden upon those without means to pay.[32] And Congress has responded by incorporating part of that recommendation into its 1974 amendments to the FOIA. The new statutory language, contained in subdivision (a)(4)(A) of the amended Act, reads as follows:

[E]ach agency shall promulgate regulations . . . specifying a uniform schedule of fees applicable to all constituent units of such agency. Such fees shall be limited to reasonable standard charges for document search and duplication. Documents shall be furnished without charge or at a reduced charge where the agency determines that waiver or reduction of the fee is in the public interest because furnishing the information can be considered as primarily benefiting the general public.

In a statement explaining this provision, the congressmen primarily responsible for its drafting went on to emphasise their intention 'that fees should not be used for the purpose of discouraging requests for information or as obstacles to disclosure of information.'[33] Thus, as a consequence of the attention this issue has received and of the new legislation, there is now hope for a fee-charging policy that will foster – not hinder – compliance with requests for reasonably described records.

(4) Judicial Review

Prior to enactment of the 1974 amendments to the FOIA, subsection (a)(3) contained – in addition to the 'identifiable records' provision – provisions spelling out a person's right to judicial review of an agency's denial of his record request, and to judicial enforcement of his rights of access, if any. Such judicial remedies would probably have been available in any case,[34] but it is well that the Act expressly precluded argument to the contrary by recalcitrant record-holders. Despite these specific provisions in the Act, there remained numerous questions about their actual operation and the scope of their coverage. Consequently, a considerable number of FOIA cases dealt with issues arising under these provisions, and the Congress regarded them as prime candidates for revision by the 1974 amendments. The amendments have, in fact, made several changes in and additions to the provisions, which are now embodied in new subdivisions (a)(4)(B) through (a)(4)(G).

Under the review provisions in the 1966 Act, the court was obliged to hear the matter *de novo*, and the agency carried the burden of justifying its non-disclosure. Failure to comply with a court order to disclose the records following such a hearing authorised the court to punish the offending agency official for contempt of court. Finally, the subsection concluded with a provision encouraging expedited judicial action in such cases by requiring that they 'take precedence over all other causes' except 'as to causes the court considers of greater importance'. These provisions of old subsection (a)(3) have been carried over by the 1974 amendments into the new subdivisions on judicial review. In addition, the amendments authorise the court to (1) examine agency records *in camera, i.e.*, within closed chambers, to determine whether the Act's exemptions from disclosure properly apply, (2) assess attorney fees and other litigation costs against the Government when the complainant 'has substantially prevailed' in his FOIA claim, and (3) find 'that the circumstances surrounding the withholding raise questions whether agency personnel acted arbitrarily or capriciously', thereby triggering the Government's statutory duty to hold an administrative proceeding to determine whether disciplinary action against the responsible employee is warranted. Furthermore, one of the new subdivisions requires the Government to file an answer to any FOIA complaint within thirty days, rather than within the sixty-day period ordinarily permitted for the Government's responsive pleadings. The court, however, has discretion to direct otherwise 'for good cause shown'.

Although the 1974 amendments' more elaborate judicial review provisions definitively put to rest one of the most troublesome issues under the 1966 Act and shed some light on another prominent question, many of the old problems remain untouched. The issue expressly addressed by the new legislation concerns the manner in which 'the court shall determine the matter *de novo*'. The use of the term *de novo* suggested that the court could sit as the administrative decision-maker does, which, in turn, suggested that it could review the documents at issue in order to determine whether the basis for non-disclosure asserted by the agency was valid. Ordinarily, this task has been performed by the judge in an *in camera* review so that the documents – if properly withheld – would remain confidential. But even this cautious procedure did not appear to accommodate sufficiently the competing policy considerations where the documents had been 'classified' – that is, restricted against release as Top Secret, Secret or Confidential for national security reasons. A Supreme Court decision, *Environmental Protection Agency v. Mink*,[35] had cast a shadow on ready resort to this procedure. In deciding that the lower appellate court erred in remanding the case to the trial court with instructions to hold an *in camera* review of the documents in question, the Supreme Court held that the exemption for national security records (subsection (b)(1)) precluded any *in camera* inspection once it was established that the documents were classified under proper authority. As for the exemption for internal memoranda (subsection (b)(5)), the Court had the following to say:

> Plainly, in some situations, *in camera* inspection will be necessary and appropriate. But it need not be automatic. An agency should be given the opportunity, by means of detailed affidavits or oral testimony, to establish to the satisfaction of the District Court that the documents sought fall clearly beyond the range of material that [may be ordered disclosed]. The burden is, of course, on the agency resisting disclosure, and if it fails to meet its burden without *in camera* inspection, the District Court may order such inspection . . . A representative document of those sought may be selected for *in camera* inspection . . . In short, *in camera* inspection of all documents is not a necessary or inevitable tool in every case. Others are available.[36]

Fortunately, the lower courts did not take this language to mean that *in camera* review of documents should be employed only as a last resort; rather, they continued to treat that technique as a viable alternative to be used at the discretion of the trial judge[37] – except, of course, with respect to the national security exemption. Congress, in its 1974 legislation amending the FOIA, took a similar position in support of *in camera* inspection. In fact, new subdivision (a)(4)(B) specifically states that the court 'may examine the contents of . . . Agency records [challenged as improperly withheld] *in camera* to determine whether such records or any part thereof shall be withheld under any of the exemptions.' And by 'any' of the exemptions, the legislators intend to include the national security exemption, thus altering the result of the Supreme Court's decision on that point.

Another issue touched upon, though not expressly addressed, by the 1974 amendments is the question of whether the judicial review provisions may be invoked to redress alleged violations of the publication, indexing, and other requirements set forth in subsections (a)(1) and (a)(2). As noted above, the provisions for judicial review were formerly contained in subsection (a)(3), which also dealt with record requests. This structural juxtaposition, along with other factors, led many observers to assert that judicial review was available only for complaints arising under subsection (a)(3). The Attorney-General's analysis of the FOIA, for example, assumed that subsections (a)(1) and (a)(2) were to be self-executing, since they both state that any agency's failure to heed the statutory requirements precludes that agency from relying on its non-complying administrative rules, regulations, orders or statements, to the detriment of an uninformed member of the public. However, while such sanctions are helpful in some cases where an agency attempts to supply such a procedurally deficient rule directly against an individual, they fail to assure that the agencies will generally comply with the publication, indexing, and other requirements set forth in those subsections, and they afford no recourse to the public, which is thereby deprived of administrative information to which it is entitled. Clearly, some means of judicial review of the agencies' conduct and enforcement of the statutory commands is needed to make the Act's broad policy of disclosure become a reality. Thus, a noted scholar of administrative law convincingly argued – for these and other reasons – that the judicial review provisions contained in subsection (a)(3) of the 1966 Act were applicable to the other subsections as well, [38] and at least one court of appeal has observed that a judicial remedy would be available to enforce those subsections.[39]

The structural changes wrought by the 1974 amendments support this broad interpretation of the scope of judicial review under the FOIA. The applicable provisions have been extracted from subsection (a)(3) and now comprise – along with new provisions – most of the matter under subsections (a)(4). This new arrangement plainly recognises the judicial review provisions as independent from the subsection on record requests, and it will probably enable future FOIA discoverants to obtain judicial assistance in compelling agency compliance with subsections (a)(1) and (a)(2) as well as (a)(3).

An issue of judicial review unaffected by the 1974 amendments is whether the courts may exercise their discretion to permit withholding of records even though no provision of the Act expressly supports such withholding. Ordinarily, courts do have such powers of equitable discretion when working with broad and complex legislation, for they are traditionally envisioned as Congress' partners in clarifying the meaning and application of broad principles in specific factual contexts. Thus, for example, in interpreting a provision of the Emergency Price Control Act of 1942 unequivocally stating that injunctions 'shall be granted' against violations, the Supreme Court pointed to time-honoured principles of equitable jurisdiction and concluded that the courts – despite the express statutory language to the contrary – need not issue the requested injunctions 'under all circumstances'.[40] A similar problem is presented by the FOIA, which contains language pointing to a restrictive judicial role in interpreting the scope of the Act's exemptions. Subsection (c) expressly states that the Act 'does not authorize withholding of information or limit the availability of records to the public, *except as specifically stated in this* [*Act*]' (emphasis added). And most courts have taken this language – along with a reading of the legislative history – to mean that the exercise of equitable discretion in FOIA cases has been congressionally foreclosed, while a few courts have nevertheless adhered to the traditional view of their discretionary powers.[41] It is clear that Congress has the authority to limit judicial review in this fashion, but it is unlikely that the legislators actually intended such a result. Accordingly, it is probably true, as a leading commentator has concluded, that '[t]he court that has jurisdiction to enforce the

Information Act also has jurisdiction to refuse to enforce it whenever equity traditions so require.[42] The question remains unsettled in the courts, though there now seems to be a judicial consensus that equitable discretion has been foreclosed in FOIA cases.

The power and propriety of issuing a stay of an administrative proceeding pending adjudication of an FOIA claim is also an issue on which the lower courts are divided, and the Supreme Court's decision in *Renegotiation Board v. Bannercraft Clothing Company*[43] has done little to elucidate this troublesome area of the law. On the one hand, a person appearing in an administrative proceeding should have access to all the government-held information to which he is entitled under the FOIA. If his rights of access are not vindicated until after the proceeding has concluded, the information may no longer be of use to him even though it would have been germane to his presentation at the proceeding. On the other hand, the courts should not lightly interfere with the progress of such proceedings. If the agencies had to halt every time an interested party sought a judicial determination of his rights of access under the FOIA, the process of administrative decision-making would be seriously disrupted.

The Supreme Court's decision in *Bannercraft* addressed only a narrow issue confined to the context of that case. It decided – by a slim five-to-four majority – that a stay of the administrative proceeding at issue would be inappropriate, but it did not rule out the possibility that stays would be appropriate in other circumstances. Resolution of this question will have to await further litigation, but it is likely that the courts will ultimately fashion a balancing formula that takes into account the competing interests of the agencies and parties appearing before them. Moreover, it is reasonable to predict that stays will be granted only in rare cases where the party might otherwise suffer irreparable injury.

A related issue involves the doctrine of exhaustion of administrative remedies, which holds that an individual should ordinarily carry his grievance through all appropriate administrative channels before petitioning a court for a judicial determination. This doctrine has generally been followed with respect to FOIA claims,[44] but it is not always adhered to where it clearly appears that further administrative appeal of a denial of the claim would be futile.[45] Furthermore, it must be recognised that an administrative appeal can entail inordinate delay,[46] sometimes rendering a valid claim useless by the time access is finally obtained. Under such circumstances, a court should consider hearing the case before the administrative remedies have been exhausted.

The Administrative Conference of the United States has also addressed this problem of inordinate delay in making administrative decisions on FOIA claims. It recommended the imposition of time limitations which, if implemented, would substantially eliminate any unfairness resulting from exhaustion requirements.[47] These guidelines were partially incorporated into the 1974 amendments to (subsection (a)(6)) despite the President's objection to them as 'simply unrealistic in some cases' and his plea 'that additional latitude be provided.'[48] Thus, the agencies will now have to give FOIA claims their immediate attention and process administrative appeals in accordance with a fairly strict timetable.

(5) Miscellaneous Provisions

To round out this discussion of provisions fostering disclosure, two other subsections must be noted. Subsection (a)(5) – (Formerly subsection (a)(4) –)provides that every multi-member agency 'shall maintain and make available for public inspection a record of the final votes of each member in every agency proceeding.' Because this requirement is non-controversial and readily complied with, no further comment is necessary.

Almost as non-controversial is the portion of subsection (c) providing that the FOIA 'is not authority to withhold information from Congress.' This provision probably does no more than preserve Congress' fact-finding powers intact, allowing it to get all the information from the executive branch that it could prior to enactment of the FOIA. Congress has long played a special role in obtaining such information – a role that will be briefly examined later under a separate heading.

THE EXEMPTIONS

Subsection (b) of the FOIA lists nine categories of information to which the Act does not apply. The agencies may nevertheless choose to disclose most of this exempt material, and the Justice Department – from the outset – has encouraged such voluntary disclosure when the public interest would be better served thereby.[49] Some of the exemptions have stirred little controversy and litigation to date. The majority of the provisions, however, have served as battlegrounds for hard-fought contests over rights of public access to government-held information. While a detailed account of those battles is beyond the scope of this article, a brief examination of the contours of the major campaigns is in order. Each category will be discussed in turn.

First, however, a word must be said about a short provision added to subsection (b) by the 1974 amendments. The new provision states that '[a]ny reasonably segregable portion of a record shall be provided to any person requesting such record after deletion of the portions which are exempt under this subsection.' Many courts have already followed this practice when dealing with requests for partially exempt material. But now this procedure will no longer be a matter of judicial discretion; it will be a statutory right of the discoverant. There can be no doubt that this explicit statutory narrowing of the exemptions' coverage will foster even greater public access to documents under the FOIA.

(1) National Defence and Foreign Policy
Under the 1966 FOIA, subsection (b)(1) (Exemption One) authorised the withholding of records 'specifically required by Executive Order to be kept secret in the interest of the national defense or foreign policy'. Of course, under the constitutional doctrine of executive privilege, there were some matters that the President could keep secret even without the benefit of this provision.[50] But Exemption One went much further. Any matter that was properly classified pursuant to the relevant executive order fell within this exemption. And, as noted above, the Supreme Court's decision in *Environmental Protection Agency v. Mink*[51] further insulated such material by precluding *in camera* inspection of documents that were thus classified.

At the time of the *Mink* case, the executive classification system was governed by Executive Order 10501,[52] which conferred authority to classify documents as Top Secret, Secret and Confidential upon a large number of administrative officials in a host of federal agencies. During the course of that litigation, however, the President issued Executive Order 11652,[53] which superseded the former order and sought to eliminate some of the widespread abuses under the old system.[54] The statement introducing the new order explained that its purpose was '[t]o ensure that [national security] information and material is protected, but only to the extent and for such period as is necessary.' To carry out this purpose, the 'order identifies the information to be protected, prescribes classification, downgrading, declassification and safeguarding procedures to be followed, and establishes a monitoring system to ensure its effectiveness.'[55]

While Executive Order 11652 is definitely an improvement over its predecessor, it fails to correct many of the problems experienced under the old system. Although fewer government officials have authority to classify material, it is contended that there are still far too many individuals holding such power and insufficient controls over their use of that power. Clearly, overclassification will remain a serious problem under the new system unless some means is devised to assure that the classifiers rigorously adhere to the dictates of the executive order.

Congress, in its 1974 amendments to the FOIA, has partly addressed this problem by overriding *Mink*'s determination that Exemption One documents are not subject to *in camera* inspection and by altering the language of Exemption One so that it expressly authorises courts to make sure that the documents 'are in fact properly classified'. In response to the President's objections to these provisions prior to their enactment,[56] the legislators put the following language into their official explanation of the amendments:

[T]he conferees recognize that the Executive departments responsible for national defense and foreign policy matters have unique insights into what adverse affects [sic] might occur as a result of public disclosure of a particular classified record. Accordingly, the conferees expect that Federal courts, in making *de novo* determinations..., will accord substantial weight to any agency's affidavit concerning the details of the classified status of the disputed record.[57]

Even so, the President vetoed the amendments, relying partly on the ground that the legislation failed to meet his objections in this regard.[58] But Congress overrode the President's veto, and its view has become the law.

(2) Internal Personnel Rules and Practices
Subsection (b)(2) (Exemption Two) exempts from disclosure matters 'related solely to the internal personnel rules and practices

of an agency'. The Senate and House committee reports put substantially different interpretations on the scope of this exemption, the latter giving it far greater breadth. While the Senate report offered 'use of parking facilities or regulation of lunch hours, statements of policy as to sick leave, and the like' as example of material falling under Exemption Two,[59] the House report maintained that '[o]perating rules, guidelines, and manuals of procedure for Government investigators or examiners would be exempt from disclosure...'[60] The courts have generally held that the Senate report more accurately reflects the congressional intent and have, accordingly, narrowly circumscribed the applicability of Exemption Two[61] – a result consistent with the Act's liberal disclosure policy.

(3) Other Statutes

Subsection (b)(3) (Exemption Three) exempts from disclosure matters that are 'specifically exempted from disclosure by statute'. There are many statutes that clearly fall within the terms of this exemption, and the question raised usually is the factual one of whether the statute applies to the records being sought. A recent example of such a case is the court of appeals' decision in *Tax Analysts and Advocates v. Internal Revenue Service* (IRS).[62] The IRS conceded that the records being withheld were of the type that would ordinarily be available under the FOIA, but it argued that sections 6102(a)(1) and 7213(1) of the Internal Revenue Code – which protect the privacy of taxpayers and their tax returns – 'specifically exempted' the records at issue from disclosure. Consequently, said the IRS, they fall under Exemption Three of the FOIA and need not be disclosed. The court of appeals agreed with this analysis in so far as it applied to one type of document – the technical advice memorandum. It concluded, however, that the other kind of document – the letter-ruling – did not enjoy the special protection afforded by the Internal Revenue Code provisions invoked by the IRS and, therefore, must be disclosed.

A broader issue of greater significance is whether a statute conferring upon an agency general discretionary authority to withhold information falls within the meaning of Exemption Three. The appellate court in *Evans v. Department of Transportation*[63] addressed this question with respect to the Federal Aviation Administration and section 1504 of Title 49 of the United States Code (1970). In that case, the FOIA claimant sought to learn the identity of the person who sent letters to the agency questioning his competence as a pilot. The informant, however, had requested official assurance of anonymity as a condition precedent to naming the allegedly unfit pilot, and such assurance had been given. According to the court, agency officials were authorised to make this grant of confidentiality pursuant to section 1504, which empowered them to respond to objections to the release of certain kinds of information by withholding the material 'when, in their judgment, a disclosure of such information...is not required in the interest of the public.' Hence, section 1504 'specifically exempted' from disclosure certain matters withheld at the agency's discretion, such as the informant's name in this case, bringing that information within the protection of Exemption Three. If such judicial reasoning gains widespread acceptance, a good deal of additional material may escape public access.[64]

Finally, another important question concerns the relationship between Exemption Three and section 1905 of Title 18 of the United States Code (1970). Section 1905 is a criminal statute generally prohibiting disclosure by government employees of a broad range of confidential information 'in any manner or to any extent not authorized by law.' Litigants have on several occasions argued that this provision constitutes a specific statutory exemption within the meaning of Exemption Three. Very few courts have squarely addressed this issue,[65] but they all concluded – without much analysis – that the confidential data protected under section 1905 is not 'specifically exempted from disclosure' in the sense required by Exemption Three. Furthermore, these courts held that since section 1905 by its own terms applies only to disclosures 'not authorized by law', it has no effect on information made public as authorised by the freedom of information law.[66] Another decision, however, has demonstrated that the statute does retain some vitality. In *Charles River Park "A", Inc. v. Department of Housing and Urban Development*,[67] the district court issued a permanent injunction pursuant to section 1905 to enjoin the Department from disclosing confidential financial data that apparently would have been entitled to an exemption under the FOIA. Thus, even though the FOIA permits agencies voluntarily to disclose exempt material, they may not do so if that material also constitutes confidential information within the meaning of section 1905.

In sum, as the law now stands, section 1905 has not been incorporated into Exemption Three and cannot be invoked to prosecute a government employee for releasing information as required by the FOIA. However, where the information falls within the specific exemptions to the FOIA – so that its disclosure is merely permitted but is not required by that Act standing alone – section 1905 can be invoked to prevent or punish disclosures of information that fall within the categories enumerated in that section. As a practical matter, the kinds of confidential data protected by section 1905 will usually find refuge in one of the specific FOIA exemptions, such as the exemption for trade secrets and confidential commercial or financial information.

(4) Commercial and Financial Information

Subsection (b)(4) (Exemption Four) exempts from disclosure records that are 'trade secrets and commercial or financial information obtained from a person and privileged or confidential'. The actual scope and meaning of this provision remains unclear in many respects despite the plethora of cases in which its words and legislative history have been scrutinised. In the final analysis, the courts have largely defined the scope of the exemption in accordance with the plain meaning most apparent on the face of the statute. Thus, it does not apply to information that is merely privileged or confidential without being a trade secret or commercial or financial in character.[68] Granting that the statutory language does lend itself to this construction, it is nevertheless a fair question to ask why the legislators excluded non-commercial, non-financial privileged or confidential information from Exemption Four. Just as the agencies must be able to promise confidentiality in order to obtain voluntarily certain commercial and financial data, they need the same power with respect to other kinds of sensitive information. The FOIA, however, simply does not contain an express exemption for such material, although other statutes may explicitly ascribe confidential status to certain records or authorise the withholding of some information at the agency's discretion.

The legislative history of Exemption Four gives no clue to the policies underlying its neglect of non-commercial, non-financial information. One plausible explanation is that Congress feared that a broad exemption for all privileged or confidential information would be too easily subjected to abuse, since information could be insulated from public access merely by a promise of confidentiality. The legislators may have preferred to rely only on the confidentiality afforded by the other exemptions and separate statutes that 'specifically exempted' certain material from disclosure. There may remain, however, some privileged information that is unprotected by other exemptions and statutes but nevertheless of a character warranting non-disclosure. For example, if a person were to donate private papers to the National Archives under a promise that they would remain confidential during his lifetime, it appears that the Government would be unable to make good its promise.[69] But such situations are probably rare. In any event, Congress could always frame a new statute that specifically exempted from disclosure a category of confidential information, such as voluntarily donated private papers, thereby bringing that information under the protection of Exemption Three. Moreover, in a compelling case the courts could apply the doctrine of equitable discretion, discussed above, and order the sensitive material withheld.

In determining whether commercial or financial information is also privileged or confidential and therefore entitled to the protection of Exemption Four, the courts have generally employed an objective test, asking if the information in question is of the sort that 'would customarily not be released to the public by the person from whom it was obtained.'[70] Even if the information qualifies under that standard, the court may nevertheless order disclosure of the material after deleting identifying details in order to protect the source of the confidential data.[71] Finally, it should be noted that a majority of the courts have construed Exemption Four as applying only to information obtained from sources outside the Government.[72]

(5) Agency Memoranda

Subsection (b) (5) (Exemption Five) exempts from disclosure 'interagency or intra-agency memorandums or letters which would not be available by law to a party other than an agency in litigation with the agency.' The policies underlying this exemption are twofold: (1) the fostering of uninhibited debate within the Government of all sides to the issues under consideration; and (2) protection against premature disclosure of the agency's position and strategy. Because the agencies do not hesitate to invoke Exemption Five whenever it is plausibly applicable and because a good deal of the information habitually sought by the public arguably falls within this category, it has proved to be one of the most controversial provisions in the FOIA.

One area of controversy has revolved around the effect of subdivision (a)(2)(A) upon Exemption Five. That provision requires agencies to make their 'final opinions' available to the public, but in some situations it is unclear whether an agency's pronouncement is a 'final opinion' or really no more than an internal memorandum subject to further review by another decision-making authority within the agency.

As noted earlier in this chapter, the Supreme Court has recently grappled with this issue in two cases. *National Labour Relations Board (NLRB) v. Sears, Roebuck & Co.*[73] and *Renegotiation Board v. Grumman Aircraft Engineering Corporation.*[74] In the Sears case, the Court meticulously analysed the function and effect of two kinds of NLRB memoranda prepared by the General Council's Office for the benefit of the Regional Directors, who are in charge of the Board's local offices. This analysis led the Court to the unanimous conclusion that those memoranda instructing a Regional Director to terminate a case constitute 'final opinions' within the meaning of subdivision (a)(2)(A), while those directing the prosecution of a case qualify as intra-agency memoranda under Exemption Five. The reason for this differing treatment is that memoranda in the former category state the NLRB's final position with respect to the matter at hand, whereas those in the latter category merely serve as the basis for further administrative action by the agency. Consequently, the NLRB must disclose documents of the former variety, but may withhold documents of the latter type. Taking the same analytical approach to the problem presented in *Grumman Aircraft*, the Court concluded – under the particular facts of that case – that the memoranda at issue could properly be withheld under Exemption Five.

A related limitation on the scope of Exemption Five was announced by the appellate court opinion in *American Mail Line, Ltd. v. Gulick.*[75] In that case, individuals who suffered an adverse administrative determination sought access to an agency memorandum expressly relied upon in the agency's final decision. While there could be no doubt that the staff advisory memorandum in question originated as an intra-agency memorandum, the *Gulick* court concluded that it lost that status when adopted by the agency as its final position. Though such a result runs counter to Exemption Five's declared policy of fostering uninhibited debate, it also seems that the greater likelihood of public disclosure will encourage memorandum writers to do a more careful job.

The Supreme Court addressed this same question in the *Sears* case and held that,

> if an agency chooses *expressly* to adopt or incorporate by reference an intra-agency memorandum previously covered by Exemption 5 in what would otherwise be a final opinion, that memorandum may be withheld only on the ground that it falls within the coverage of some exemption other than Exemption 5.[76]

As the quoted passage reveals, the Court followed the *Gulick* limitation as far as it goes, but then went on to allow for the possible withholding of an adopted or incorporated agency document under one of the FOIA's other exemptions. Moreover, the Court ruled that the agency is neither required to supplement its final opinions with explanatory material nor obligated to identify relevant pre-existing material that would make such opinions more meaningful to the reader. Thus, as the law now stands, documents that are explicitly adopted in an agency's final opinion will lose their Exemption Five status and be subject to mandatory disclosure, unless they are covered by another exemption as well. On the other hand, documents not specifically identified in the final opinion need not necessarily be disclosed, even though such material would assist the public in the full understanding of the agency's position. The practical effect of this decision may be that agencies will no longer cite the internal memoranda on which their final opinions are based, thereby avoiding a duty to disclose such documents. In that event the courts – or perhaps the Congress – may seek to refine the *Sears* rule in a way that would allow access to some of the more essential, though unspecified, memoranda underlying an agency's final position.

Not all situations have resulted in a restrictive judicial reading of Exemption Five. Memoranda prepared by private consultants pursuant to a government contract have been deemed to fall within the exemption's coverage even though the consultants themselves are technically not within any agency.[77] The policies underlying Exemption Five reasonably dictate this result, although a plain-meaning interpretation of the statutory language certainly does not require it.

Reference to the rules of discovery embodied in Rule 26–37 of the Federal Rules of Civil Procedure is central to a detailed understanding of Exemption Five. Such reference is required by the provision excluding from its coverage memoranda and letters that would be made available to a private party in litigation with the agency. Thus, even if a person is not actually in litigation with the agency, he can gain access to the kinds of materials that would be discoverable under the federal rules.[78] Most notably, a person seeking information in this fashion can obtain the factual material contained in memoranda and letters, since under the Federal Rules only matters reflecting deliberation and policy-making may properly be withheld from a discovering party.[79]

(6)Personnel, Medical and Similar Files
Subsection (b)(6) (Exemption Six) authorises an agency to withhold 'personnel and medical files and similar files the disclosure of which would constitute a clearly unwarranted invasion of personal privacy.' This provision reflects Congress' recognition that the FOIA affects not only the Government and the public at large but also individual rights of privacy, and it offers a modest degree of protection to those vast numbers of persons about whom the Government holds detailed information. The Act's liberal policy of disclosure, however, has overshadowed considerations of personal privacy in the context of this exemption: the kinds of files included within its protection are few, and the invasion of privacy involved must not be simply unwarranted, but 'clearly' unwarranted.

To date, only one court has inquired into the meaning of 'similar files', and it has given the phrase a very narrow scope. To qualify, the file must truly contain the kind of highly personal data found in personnel and medical files.[80]

On the other hand, a few courts have interpreted the phrase 'clearly unwarranted invasion of personal privacy'. In *Getman v. National Labour Relations Board*,[81] the appellate court balanced the potential value to the public of a study being conducted by two law professors against the possible detriment to the individuals whose names and addresses were being sought in connection with the scholarly study. The court concluded – after thoroughly considering the equities on both sides – that the invasion of privacy was not so serious as to be 'clearly unwarranted'. In the second case, *Wine Hobby, USA, Inc. v. Bureau of Alcohol, Tobacco and Firearms*,[82] a distributor of wine-making machinery sought the names and addresses of amateur winemakers, and the district court ordered disclosure of this information despite the agency's strong argument for withholding the data under Exemption Six. Here, the information was being sought to further the plaintiff's commercial opportunities. This motive seems distinguishable from the one advanced by the law professors in *Getman* and arguably warranted a shift on the equitable scales towards protection of individual privacy.

In any event, these two cases make clear something that the language and legislative history of Exemption Six plainly suggest, namely, that the courts must weigh and balance the equities on both sides of the issue when handling a claim for access infringing upon individual privacy. Despite the FOIA's general command that 'any person' shall have standing to obtain reasonably described records, the courts will inquire into that person's motives in Exemption Six cases, and will assess the effects of disclosure upon the personal privacy of the individuals concerned.[83]

Congress has recently demonstrated, by passing the Privacy Act of 1974,[84] its dissatisfaction with the inadequate protection afforded individual privacy in the handling of governmental records. By expressly exempting from its purview any disclosures 'required' under the FOIA,[85] the Privacy Act pays due deference to the strong policy of liberal public access to government-held records fostered by the FOIA. However, with respect to records containing personal data that previously could have been disclosed at the Government's discretion, the Privacy Act constructs an elaborate system for safeguarding against unwarranted invasions of privacy. Basically, with some exceptions, the Privacy Act protects personal privacy by (1) enabling an individual to ascertain what governmental records pertaining to him are being held, (2) allowing an individual to prevent the use of such personal records for purposes other than those specified in the Act, (3) granting an individual access to such records and an opportunity to have them corrected, (4) requiring the agencies to handle such records carefully, with painstaking attention to the safeguarding of individual privacy, and (5) subjecting federal agencies to civil suits for personal damages resulting from wilful violations of the Act.

(7) Investigatory Records
Prior to enactment of the 1974 amendments to the FOIA, subsection (b)(7) (Exemption Seven) authorised the withholding of 'investigatory files compiled for law enforcement purposes except to the extent available by law to a party other than an agency'. This provision had at least three identifiable purposes: (1) preventing a

request that would compel the Government prematurely to disclose its case against a person under investigation, (2) safeguarding the secrecy of investigative techniques, and (3) protecting the identity of confidential informants. A review of the various judicial interpretations of this exemption generally reveals that the courts had narrowly confined its scope in keeping with the FOIA's broad policy favouring public access,[86] but such a review also reveals considerable disagreement on some issues.

The primary unsettled issue was whether an investigatory file could lose its exempt status when enforcement proceedings were no longer contemplated or when the file had lain dormant for a substantial period of time. Some courts held the view that the files need never be disclosed – even after an agency had wholly abandoned any attempt to prosecute the case – because the investigative techniques and confidential sources still warranted protection from public scrutiny.[87] Other courts, however, held that investigatory files became subject to disclosure once a case had been closed if (1) no law enforcement proceeding had ever been instituted pursuant to the investigation and (2) no such proceeding was imminent.[88] In a case where no further law enforcement proceedings were imminently contemplated but one had previously been instituted and prosecuted, a court held that the investigatory files remained exempt.[89] Because nothing in the 1974 amendment addresses this question, the courts will undoubtedly continue to see cases along this line, and future decisions are likely to bring further variations in these judicial applications of the exemption. Perhaps, for example, the courts will foster disclosure of some otherwise exempt investigatory files by deleting material which divulges secret techniques and identifies confidential informants.

The 1966 FOIA's proviso to Exemption Seven expressly opened access to investigatory files that would be 'available by law to a party other than an agency'. The courts sometimes ignored this provision, and those few that dealt with it seemed puzzled over its meaning. Apparently, however, they concluded that the proviso allowed 'any person' to obtain access to investigatory files to the same extent that a defendant in a criminal proceeding would have access pursuant to the Federal Rules of Criminal Procedure and relevant criminal statutes.[90]

In the 1974 amendments to the FOIA, Congress substituted the word 'records' for 'files' and replaced the confusing proviso with a series of six relatively specific grounds on which withholding of investigatory records could justifiably be based. The shift in terms to 'records' signifies a legislative intent that each document within a file be given individual attention when determining the public's right of access, thus eliminating the tendency to regard the contents of a file as either wholly exempt or wholly discoverable. The inclusion of the new provision specifying several bases for withholding records adds three policy considerations to those noted above. In addition to preventing interference with enforcement proceedings, safeguarding the secrecy of investigative techniques, and protecting confidential sources, Exemption Seven's purposes now include the following: (1) preserving an impartial adjudication, (2) safeguarding personal privacy, and (3) protecting the life or physical safety of law enforcement personnel. Any other basis for withholding such investigatory records would be unacceptable. As explained by the legislators primarily responsible for drafting this provision, its overall purpose is to 'clarify Congressional intent disapproving certain court interpretations which have tended to expand the scope of agency authority to withhold' records under Exemption Seven.[91] The President's veto message specifically objected to this provision because of the burden it would place on enforcement agencies; they would have to respond to voluminous requests from 'any person' for such materials and demonstrate that at least one of the specific justifications was applicable.[92] Nevertheless, this provision has now become the law. Congress has made it clear that Exemption Seven must play a carefully confined role.

(8) Reports on Financial Institutions
Subsection (b)(8) (Exemption Eight) authorises the withholding of information 'contained in or related to examination, operating, or condition reports prepared by, on behalf of, or for the use of an agency responsible for the regulation or supervision of financial institutions'. In the sole reported case concerning this exemption, the district court suggested that neither national securities exchanges nor broker-dealers under the Securities and Exchange Commission's jurisdiction properly fall under the rubric of 'financial institutions'.[93] Moreover, the court indicated that the Commission's study, along with the related transcripts and documents, did not qualify as the kinds of reports specified in Exemption Eight. Thus, this judicial interpretation reflected a desire to give this exemption a restrictive reading and thereby foster disclosure. Any possibility that such disclosure would have a detrimental effect upon the

institutions involved was alleviated, according to the court, by deletion of identifying details.

The underlying purpose of Exemption Eight – 'insuring the security of our financial institutions'[94] – is evident. Nevertheless, one may question whether the security of financial institutions really depends on this cloak of secrecy. A noted commentator has argued that other statutes sufficiently assure the integrity of these institutions and has lamented that this exemption will encourage the maintenance of 'systems of secret facts, secret law, and secret policy'.[95]

(9) Information Concerning Wells

Subsection (b)(9) (Exemption Nine) authorises the withholding of 'geological and geophysical information and data, including maps, concerning wells'. The House committee report reveals that this exemption was added in response to testimony that 'disclosure of the seismic reports and other exploratory findings of oil companies would give speculators an unfair advantage over the companies which spent millions of dollars in exploration.'[96] There has been little controversy over the interpretation of Exemption Nine,[97] and no reported judicial decisions.

THE RECIPIENTS OF INFORMATION

SPECIAL INTEREST GROUPS

Although equal access to government-held information was one of the FOIA's primary goals, there are indications that this policy has not been perfectly carried out by the agencies. Ralph Nader, a leading public interest advocate, had charged that 'most agencies have a two-pronged information policy – one toward citizens and one toward the special interest groups that form the agency's regulated constituency.'[98] The policy toward the former, according to Mr Nader, is one of delay, evasion, or outright non-compliance, whereas, with respect to the latter, 'a pattern has emerged over the years of preferential access and treatment.'[99] Although Mr Nader in his role of advocate may have exaggerated the degree of discriminatory treatment, an objective empirical study sponsored by the Administrative Conference of the United States has confirmed its existence to some extent.[100] Interestingly, this study has pointed to evidence that Mr Nader's 'public interest groups' also enjoy some preferential treatment as compared to individual citizens standing alone.[101]

Quite apart from any conscious but unspoken policy of more readily accommodating requests from special interest groups, the system inherently favours such groups' information needs. The agencies, in the natural course of performing their assigned duties, are likely to collect the kind of data useful to the industries that they regulate, and these industries are more likely than individuals to be familiar with the existence of such data and the procedures for obtaining them. Furthermore, even if their requests are denied, these organisations are likely to have the means for appealing the denial and litigating the issue in the courts. Not surprisingly, then, a review of the cases brought under the FOIA readily confirms that most of the successful requesters have been corporations or persons financially concerned with the outcome of the litigation. Ordinary private citizens and impoverished public interest groups usually cannot afford the time and expense required to pursue claims to the finish. One observer has stated the problem in this way.

> Short of eliminating existing social and economic inequalities, completely equal access to government information cannot be achieved as a practical matter. However, procedures and practices implementing the Act should seek to limit such disadvantages as far as possible.[102]

Congress, too, has recognised the problem of unequal access under the FOIA to government-held information and has incorporated a few corrective measures into the 1974 amendments. These new provisions have already been mentioned above in another context, but they bear repetition at this juncture. One such innovation is the relaxation of former subsection (a)(3)'s 'identifiable records' standard to require merely that a request for information 'reasonably describes' the desired material. While this change may not put an individual citizen on an equal footing with special interest groups which are 'in the know', it may at least make it easier for 'any person' – even a person without an intricate familiarity with the agency involved – to submit a request triggering the agency's duty under subsection (a)(3) to comply. Another example may be found in the new subdivision – (a)(4)(A) – aimed at reforming the agencies' fee schedules for conducting searches and copying records. Not only does this subdivision seek to ensure that fees be uniformly fair, but it also encourages the agencies to reduce or waive such charges when the release of the information primarily benefits the general public. Of course, this provision will only assist individual citizens on a limited scale, but it may prove an invaluable aid to the public interest groups. Finally, the amendments, in new subdivision (a)(4)(E), also give the courts discretion to award 'reasonable attorney fees and other litigation costs' to a party who 'has substantially prevailed' in proving his right to records under the FOIA. This provision will not only discourage agency officials from making questionable denials of access, but it will also encourage those claimants with limited financial resources to pursue their valid claims into the courts.

THE CONGRESS

Subsection (c) of the FOIA provides that the Act 'is not authority to withhold information from Congress'. There have been some suggestions that this provision confers upon congressmen greater rights of access under the FOIA,[103] but this interpretation has never been passed upon by an appellate court[104] and, in any event, is inconsistent with the view that 'any person' has equal rights of access under the Act's provisions. More likely, this subsection simply means to make clear that Congress' traditional investigatory powers remain intact despite any provision of the FOIA that might otherwise be invoked to curb a congressional inquiry. These investigatory powers are quite extensive and warrant further discussion.

A leading case is *Barenblatt v. United States*,[105] in which the Supreme Court outlined the broad principles governing Congress' investigatory powers as follows:

The power of inquiry has been employed by Congress throughout our history, over the whole range of the national interests concerning which Congress might legislate or decide upon due investigation not to legislate; it has similarly been utilized in determining what to appropriate from the national purse, or whether to appropriate. The scope of the power, in short, is as penetrating and far-reaching as the potential power to enact and appropriate under the Constitution.

Broad as it is, the power is not, however, without limitations. Since Congress may only investigate into those areas in which it may potentially legislate or appropriate, it cannot inquire into matters which are within the exclusive province of one of the other branches of the Government. . . . [I]t [cannot] supplant the Executive in what exclusively belongs to the Executive. . . .[106]

Thus, Congress can and does procure extensive information from the executive branch without reference to the FOIA, and it frequently obtains the kind of material that would be withheld from ordinary citizens under one of the FOIA's exemptions. Moreover, Congress often publishes the information that it gathers, thereby opening multitudinous volumes of data to the public.

Generally, the executive branch readily complies with Congress' incessant demand for information. As one observer has put it: 'Furnishing information to Congress has become a major industry in the executive branch.'[107] Department and agency heads frequently testify before various congressional committees, and numerous government employees devote most or all of their time responding to congressional inquiries. On some relatively rare occasions, however, the President, or a suitable delegate, will invoke the ill-defined doctrine of executive privilege and refuse to respond to the full extent requested. A report by the Library of Congress revealed that executive privilege had been asserted only forty-nine times between 1952 and March 1973, and President Nixon invoked the privilege a few times thereafter.[108] This article is not the place to explore the complex and sensitive issues involved in presidential assertions of executive privilege in order to block congressional investigations into certain areas. Suffice it to say that the privilege does exist to some extent, and the courts have jurisdiction to define its scope in a particular factual setting.[109]

THE JUDICIARY

The courts provide a forum for litigation under the FOIA and wield the power of contempt for those who fail to comply with orders to disclose records. Moreover, as noted above, Exemptions Five and Seven implicitly make reference to the federal courts' rules of discovery, which define the extent to which one party must disclose relevant information to the other. But the FOIA does not – indeed, cannot – incorporate these Federal Rules *in toto*, for the two bodies of law simply have too many differences to permit such a clean fusion. As explained by the Supreme Court with regard to Exemption Five:

> [A]t best, the discovery rules can only be applied. . . by way of rough analogies. For example, we do not know whether the Government is to be treated as though it were a prosecutor, a civil plaintiff, or a defendant [each of which would require a different application of the rules]. Nor does the Act, by its terms, permit inquiry into the particularized needs of the individual seeking the information, although such an inquiry would ordinarily be made of a private litigant. . ..[110]

Still, even rough analogy to the rules of discovery has served to limit the exemptions' scope and foster public access to government documents.

When an information-seeker is also a party in litigation with the agency, however, he may invoke the discovery rules to their full extent and thereby – in some situations – obtain even greater access to government records than possible under the FOIA. For example, trade secrets insulated from disclosure under Exemption Four can sometimes be reached by a party pursuant to Rule 26(c)(7) of the Federal Rules of Civil Procedure, and certain information specifically exempted from disclosure by statute and, therefore, protected by Exemption Three can sometimes be obtained under Rule 34.[111] Moreover, a party may even be able to enjoy the best of both worlds by simultaneously seeking discovery of some records under the Federal Rules while pursuing others under the FOIA, e.g. when the requisite need cannot be demonstrated under the former. However, the courts are still split on the propriety of allowing the pursuit of both courses at the same time, thus compelling a party in some courts to choose one or the other method of obtaining information at the outset of the litigation.[112]

Finally, mention should be made of the courts' delicate and crucial role in piercing the veil of executive privilege in appropriate circumstances. As recent developments in the United States make clear, a court can sometimes order the production of evidence withheld by the President himself under a claim of executive privilege.[113] Although the evidence thus obtained is not immediately opened to the public, much of the information eventually filters through when the admissible evidence is introduced in open court.

Although the news media were instrumental in persuading Congress to enact the FOIA, they have rarely made direct use of it in the news-gathering process.[114] This neglect probably stems from the nature of the business, which requires daily coverage of newsworthy events. Typically, there is insufficient time to pursue the formal procedures for access. Reporters can usually find knowledgeable sources who are willing to discuss the information, thereby enabling the story to come out quickly, albeit less accurately.[115] In any event, the news media play – quite apart from the FOIA – a significant and unique role in obtaining access for the public to government-held information. This role will now be briefly explored.

Freedom of the press in the United States is safeguarded by an explicit provision in the first amendment of the U.S. Constitution.[116] This constitutional protection has enabled the newspapers and journals to defeat in the courts (1) governmental attempts to impose prior restraints on publication,[117] (2) contempt citations for alleged interference with the administration of justice,[118] (3) libel suits for comments on public officials,[119] and (4) a right-to-reply statute requiring publication of a political candidate's response to a newspaper editorial about him.[120] The Supreme Court's opinions in these and other cases reveal that the constitutional protection is not absolute; it will not shield the press under all conceivable circumstances. Yet the constitutional shield is quite sturdy and fosters an environment in which the press can vigorously pry into governmental affairs and report its findings – no matter how much they may embarrass the Government – to the American public. Recent and startling examples of this crucial function served by the press may be found in the *New York Times'* and *Washington Post*'s publication of the classified Pentagon Papers and the *Washington Post*'s investigative reporting of the Watergate scandal. The Supreme Court's decision in the Pentagon Papers case, however, raises some interesting legal issues about the possibility of prosecuting the publishers of defence information pursuant to certain espionage statutes.[121] Such a prosecution has never yet taken place, though, and the complex issues that would be involved cannot be explored in this limited space.[122]

The constitutional battle over a newsman's privilege to decline to divulge the confidential sources of his information has not fared so well as his right to publish the information thus gathered. In a series of cases decided under the name *Branzburg v. Hayes*,[123] the Supreme Court divided five to four and concluded that a newsman could constitutionally be compelled to disclose his news sources before a grand jury. The newsmen argued that such compelled testimony would seriously impede their ability to gather news, for the confidential informants would no longer come forward with newsworthy information; and if such sources run dry, the press will be hampered in performing its constituionally protected role. Although the Court majority seriously weighed this contention, it determined that both precedent and policy demanded that the grand jury's inquiry into possible criminal conduct take priority over this limitation upon the newsman's investigative techniques.

In the end, despite its wide-ranging discussion of the issues, the Supreme Court narrowly circumscribed its holding. There can be little doubt that other cases involving different aspects of the newsman's privilege will reach that tribunal in the future. Furthermore, nothing in the Court's opinion would prevent state legislatures or the federal Congress from enacting statutes establishing a newsman's privilege. A number of states already have such statutes on the books, and Congress has had such legislation under consideration for over a decade.[124]

The effect of the Constitution on the role of the press is well summarised in the following words from an extra-judicial speech recently delivered by one of the Supreme Court's nine Justices:

> . . . So far as the Constitution goes, the autonomous press may publish what it knows, and may seek to learn what it can.
>
> But this autonomy cuts both ways. The press is free to do battle against secrecy and deception in government. But the press cannot expect from the Constitution any guarantee that it will succeed. There is no constitutional right to have access to particular government information, or to require openness from the bureaucracy. The public's interest in knowing about its government is protected by the guarantee of a free press, but the protection is indirect. The constitution itself is neither a Freedom of Information Act nor an Official Secrets Act.[125]

CONCLUSION

Because this chapter has focused on the public's legal rights of access to government records in the executive branch, it may have created the false impression that most information is withheld unless and until a member of the public successfully asserts those rights. Nothing could be further from the truth. It has already been noted that executive branch officials and employees regularly testify in Congress about their agencies' activities and respond to voluminous congressional inquiries. Beyond this, they also regularly respond to public inquiries, prepare and publish informational materials for public distribution, and issue press releases carried in many major newspapers and reported on the radio and television networks. Thus, to a large extent, the public is kept informed on governmental activities without having to do legal battle.

Even so, there is a good deal of information that does not so readily come to the surface – partly because the agencies do not always take affirmative action to report on matters that no one has asked about and partly because some information is viewed as too sensitive for public dissemination. Congress has demonstrated its concern about both kinds of information in legislation that has already been enacted as well as in Bills currently under consideration. One result of this concern, separate from the FOIA, is the Federal Advisory Committee Act,[126] enacted in 1972. This legislation seeks to ensure that 'the Congress and the public . . . be kept informed with respect to the number, purpose, membership, activities, and cost of advisory committees.'[127] If it were not for the various requirements for reporting and openness imposed by this Act, such committees – which furnish 'expert advice, ideas, and diverse opinions to the Federal Government'[128] – would be relatively unaccountable to the public, though they may play a crucial role in the Government's decision-making process.

Another example may be found in legislation now being considered in the Congress, the 'Government in the Sunshine' Bill.[129] This Bill seeks to open to the public – in so far as practicable – the meetings of congressional committees and government agencies. Transcripts of open meetings would be available for distribution, and those of closed meetings would be subject to public dissemination after necessary deletions are made. This proposed legislation reflects a policy 'that the public is entitled to the fullest practicable information regarding the decisionmaking processes of the Federal Government.'[130]

Thus, the United States has remained firm in its original commitment to open government. Perhaps the ideal balance between necessary secrecy and rights of public access has never been achieved, but the problem continues to be openly discussed and to command the serious attention of all branches of the Government as well as of the public. So long as new solutions are actively being demanded and sought, there is no danger that the people will become reconciled to unwarranted secrecy and lose sight of the lofty goal of government openness espoused by this nation's founding fathers almost two centuries ago.

ADDENDUM

Since the author completed the foregoing in February 1975, the laws and policies concerning public access to government-held information in the United States have been in a state of continual ferment. President Carter, for example, has made openness the cornerstone of his philosophy of government, and has fostered the preparation of a new executive order for the security classification system, which was issued on 28 June 1978 as E.O. 12065. Moreover, the Congress has remained intensely interested in this area and, in this connection, has passed the 'Government in the Sunshine' Act.[131] In addition, the courts – in numerous cases – have continued to grapple with the many issues which have arisen under the FOIA and related laws.

One purpose of the 'Government in the Sunshine' Act, which became effective on 12 March 1977, was to amend Exemption Three of the FOIA. The Supreme Court, in *Administrator, Federal Aviation Administration* v. *Robertson*,[132] had interpreted Exemption Three to include not only those narrowly circumscribed statutes which designate the confidentiality of specific kinds of documents e.g. individual income tax returns, but also those more general statutes which confer on some agency officials broad discretionary authority to maintain the confidentiality of information. Under this construction, which gave Exemption Three a much broader scope than many observers had anticipated, a good deal of information could have found refuge from the disclosure requirements of the FOIA.

The Congress, however, enacted legislation to overrule the Supreme Court's interpretation of Exemption Three by adding a proviso to the exemption for matters 'specifically exempted from disclosure by statute'. Exemption Three, as now amended, provides that the FOIA's disclosure requirements do not apply to matters that are

> specifically exempted from disclosure by statute . . . , provided that such statute (A) requires that the matters be withheld from the public in such a manner as to leave no discretion on the issue, or (B) establishes particular criteria for withholding or refers to types of matters to be withheld.

This amendment to Exemption Three has a direct bearing on a related issue discussed in the body of this essay – the relationship between Exemption Three and section 1905 of Title 18 of the United States Code. The amended text of Exemption Three bolstered the argument against regarding that statute as included within the scope of the exemption, and the Court of Appeals for the District of Columbia Circuit has plainly indicated its view, by way of dictum, that section 1905 is not the kind of statute contemplated by the amended exemption.[133] In a subsequent case, however, that same court expressly recognised that the issue remains open and may have to await a determination by the Supreme Court.[134]

The exemption which has generated the most litigation and which has commanded considerable congressional attention is Exemption Four – the exemption for 'trade secrets and commercial or financial information obtained from a person and privileged or confidential'. *National Parks and Conservation Association* v *Morton*[135] is now recognised as the leading case for providing guidance on whether a matter qualifies as 'confidential' within the meaning of this exemption. In this regard, the court deciding *National Parks* has explained that

> commercial or financial matter is 'confidential' for purposes of the exemption if disclosure of the information is likely to have either of the following effects: (1) to impair the Government's ability to obtain necessary information in the future; or (2) to cause substantial harm to the competitive position of the person from whom the information was obtained.

Unless the Government can demonstrate that one or the other of these results will be likely to occur as a result of disclosure, the courts will generally conclude that the information requested under the FOIA cannot be withheld under Exemption Four.

The reason for the extraordinary amount of attention accorded to Exemption Four is that it directly concerns an area of extreme importance and sensitivity. In order to regulate the business community intelligently and effectively, the Government must collect information relating to the regulated industries' commercial and financial dealings, but this kind of information is usually highly valued and closely guarded by the business community. Nevertheless, when such information is obtained by the Government, it becomes subject to FOIA requests by 'any person', including business competitors and public interest groups.

This untenable situation has resulted in the proliferation of 'reverse FOIA' suits, i.e. actions brought by those who have provided business information to the Government and who seek a court order preventing the Government from disclosing such information pursuant to an FOIA request. Some of these suits have been successfully maintained under a variety of legal theories.[136] Congress, too, has considered this problem, and it is likely that the matter will ultimately be resolved by further amendment to the FOIA.

Another area which has undergone significant development is the opening of government agency meetings to the public. This objective was the main purpose of the 'Government in the Sunshine' Act, mentioned above in connection with the discussion of Exemption Three. In short, the open meetings provisions[137] of this seminal Act require that the federal agencies headed by collegial bodies of decision-makers open their deliberations to the public to the fullest extent practicable. Like the FOIA, this general requirement of openness is subject to a number of specific exceptions, but this new law has nevertheless caused these agencies to provide advance notice of meetings, to allow public attendance at such meetings, and to prepare transcripts of closed meetings so that the non-exempt portions of those meetings can be disclosed.

NOTES

ABBREVIATIONS USED IN NOTES

Ad. L.2d	Administrative Law Decisions, Second Series (Pike & Fisher)
aff'd	affirmed on appeal
C.F.R.	Code of Federal Regulations
cert.	certiorari (writ for review by the Supreme Court)
Fed. Reg.	Federal Register
F.R.D.	Federal Rules Digest
F. 2d	Federal Reporter, Second Series
F. Supp.	Federal Supplement
H.R.	House of Representatives Bill
H.R. Rep. No.	House of Representatives Report Number
id.	idem (refer to the preceding citation)
L.J.	Law Journal
L. Rev.	Law Review
n.; n.n.	footnote; footnotes
Pub. L.	Public Law
rev'd	reversed on appeal
S.	Senate Bill
S. Ct.	Supreme Court Reporter
S. Rep. No.	Senate Report Number
Sess.	Session of Congress
Supp.	Supplemental Volume
supra	referred to above
U.S.	United States Reports
U.S.C.	United States Code
U.S.L.W.	United States Law Week

1. N. Dorsen and S. Gillers (eds), *None of Your Business: Government Secrecy in America* (New York: The Viking Press, 1974), vi (foreword) [hereinafter cited as 'Dorsen & Gillers'].

2. Letter from James Madison to W. T. Barry, 4 August 1822, 9 *The Writings of James Madison* 103 (Hunt ed., 1910), quoted in *Environmental Protection Agency v. Mink*, 410 U.S. 73, 110–11 (1973) (Douglas, J., dissenting).

3. See generally Katz, 'The Games Bureaucrats Play: Hide and Seek under the Freedom of Information Act', 48 *Texas L. Rev.* 1261 (1970); Nader, 'Freedom from Information: The Act and the Agencies', 5 *Harvard Civil Rights – Civil Liberties L. Rev.* 1 (1970).

4. See generally 'Comment, Access to Governmental Information in California', 54 *California L. Rev.* 1650 (1966).

5. See e.g., Wickham, 'Let the Sun Shine In: Open Meeting Legislation in State and Local Government', 68 *Northwestern L. Rev.* 480 (1973), for a discussion of the differences among the various state open meetings laws.

6. For an overview of the law in this area, see Stein, 'The Secrets of Local

Government', in Dorsen & Gillers, *supra* note 1, at 151–79. For a more detailed analysis of particular information laws fostering public access to recorded governmental information in specific states, see Marino, 'The New York Freedom of Information Law', 43 *Fordham L. Rev.* 83 (1974); 'Note, Iowa's Freedom of Information Act: Everything You've Always Wanted to Know About Public Records But Were Afraid to Ask', 57 *Iowa L. Rev.* 1163 (1972); 'Symposium, Public Access to Information', 68 *Northwestern L. Rev.* 177–432 (1973) (emphasis on the State of Illinois and the City of Chicago); 'Comment, The Right to Inspect Public Records in Oregon', 53 *Oregon L. Rev.* 354 (1974); 'Comment', *supra*, note 4, at 1665–79 (1966) (California).

7. Section 3 of the Administrative Procedure Act, 5 U.S.C. S552 (1970). All references to the 1966 FOIA will be to its codified form in Title V of the United States Code.

8. Pub. L. 93–502 (21 Nov. 1974). All references to the 1974 amendments to the FOIA will be to the form in which it is to be codified in Title V of the United States Code.

9. The first amendment of the United States Constitution expressly prohibits laws 'abridging the freedom of . . . the press'.

10. Congress did, however, enact a related measure in 1958 when it amended the 1789 federal 'housekeeping' statute by adding the following sentence: 'This section does not authorize withholding of information from the public or limiting the availability of records to the public' 5 U.S.C. §301 (1970). The section to which this amendment applies gives the heads of executive departments broad authority over, *inter alia*, 'the custody, use, and preservation of [the department's] records, papers, and property' (id.).

11. The full text of this statement appears in a manual prepared by the U.S. Department of Justice, namely, the 'Attorney General's Memorandum on the Public Information Section of the Administrative Procedure Act II' (1967) [hereinafter cited as 'Att'y Gen. Memo'].

12. Foreword of Attorney General Ramsay Clark, id. at III.

13. See 5 U.S.C. §551(1) (1970).

14. *Soucie v. David*, 448 F.2d 1057, 1073 (D. C. Cir. 1971).

15. The conference report accompanying H.R. 12471 – the Bill that was eventually enacted into law as Pub. L. 93–502 (21 Nov. 1974) – further clarified the statutory language by explaining that the term 'Executive Office of the President' did not include 'the President's immediate personal staff or units in the Executive Office whose sole function is to advise and assist the President'. H.R. Rep. No. 93-1380, 93rd Cong., 2d Sess. 15 (1974).

16. It should be noted that the Office of the Federal Register also prepares an annually revised volume known as the *United States Government Manual*, which contains a description of most federal agencies and other governmental authorities along with a statement of their multifarious programmes and purposes.

17. 94 S. Ct. 1055 (1974).

18. Id. at 1073. Moreover, the Supreme Court asserted that an agency's power to administer such legislatively created programmes 'necessarily requires the formulation of policy and the making of rules to fill any gap left, implicitly or explicitly, by Congress' (id. at 1072). This decision strengthens the practical sanctions attaching to subsections (a)(1) and (a)(2)'s policy against 'secret law'.

19 See *National Labor Relations Board v. Sears, Roebuck & Co.*, 43 U.S.L.W. 4491

(U.S. 29 April 1975). *Renegotiation Board v. Grumman Aircraft Engineering Corp.*, 43 U.S.L.W. 4502 (U.S. 29 April 1975).

20. 362 F. Supp. 1298 (D.D.C. 1973), *rev'd in part on other grounds*, 43 U.S.L.W. 2095 (D.C. Cir. Aug. 19, 1974).

21. A letter-ruling is issued by the IRS to a particular taxpayer requesting advice on the tax consequences of a contemplated transaction. Although the IRS statement is not binding on the agency, it is ordinarily applied without question to the transaction at issue, but no other taxpayer may rely upon it. *See* 26 C.F.R. §601.201 (1973). The other memoranda involved in this case are 'technical advice' memoranda and related communications. For further details, *see* 362 F. Supp. at 1300–02.

22. Id. at 1303.

23. The Securities and Exchange Commission (SEC), for example, follows such a practice. See generally Smith, 'The Freedom of Information Act and the Agencies: SEC No-Action Letters'. 23 *Administrative L. Rev.* 133 (1971).

24. See Sen. Rep. No. 813, 89th Cong., 1st Sess. 1–2 (1965).

25. See, e.g., *Hawkes v. IRS*, 467 F.2d 787 (6th Cir. 1972).

26. See, e.g., *Stokes v. Brennan*, 476 F.2d 699 (5th Cir. 1973).

27. Sen. Rep. No. 813, *supra* note 24, at 8.

28. 465 F.2d 608 (D.C. Cir.), *cert. denied*. 409 U.S. 1076 (1972).

29. 479 F.2d 183 (D.C. Cir. 1973).

30. The cited statute, 31 U.S.C. §483a (1970), has been challenged as an unconstitutional delegation of authority because of the extremely broad discretion conferred upon the agencies, but it has withstood such attack. See *Aeronautical Radio Inc. v. United States*, 335 F.2d 304 (7th Cir. 1964).

31. Some inequitable practices have been reported. See House Subcommittee on Foreign Operations and Government Information, 'Administration of the Freedom of Information Act' 53–59, H.R. Rep. No. 92–1419, 92d Cong., 2d Sess. (1972) [hereinafter cited as '1972 Hearings']; Giannella, 'Agency Procedures Implementing the Freedom of Information Act: A Proposal for Uniform Regulations', 2 *Recommendations and Reports of the Administrative Conference of the United States* 160–66 (1972).

32. Recommendation 71–2 (formerly 24), part c, adopted by the Conference on 8 May 1971. This recommendation appears in appendix A following Giannella, *supra* note 31, at 171–72.

33. H.R. Rep. No. 93–1380, *supra* note 15, at 8.

34. Professor Giannella suggests three statutory provisions, in addition to subsection (a)(3), which afford a basis for judicial review of an agency's denial of or inaction on a request for records, namely, 28 U.S.C. §1361 (1970), 5 U.S.C. §555(b) (1970) and 5 U.S.C. §706(1) (1970). Giannella, *supra* note 31, at 150.

35. 410 U.S. 73 (1973).

36. Id. at 93 (citation omitted).

37. See, e.g., *National Cable Television Association v. FCC*, 479 F.2d 183, 194–95 (D.C. Cir. 1973); *Kreindler v. Department of the Navy*, 363 F. Supp. 611, 613–13 (S.D.N.Y. 1973).

38. See K. Davis, *Administrative Law Treatise* §3A.10 (1970 Supp.); Davis, 'The Information Act: A Preliminary Analysis', 34 *University of Chicago L. Rev.* 761, 775–77 (1967).

39. *American Mail Line, Ltd. v. Gulick*, 411 F.2d 696, 701–02 (D.C. Cir. 1969).

40. *The Hecht Co. v. Bowles*, 321 U.S. 321, 328–30 (1944).

41. Compare *Soucie v. David*, 448 F.2d 1067, 1077 (D.C. Cir. 1971); *Wellford v. Hardin*, 444 F.2d 21, 24–25 (4th Cir. 1971), with *General Services Administration v. Benson*, 415 F.2d 878, 880 (9th Cir. 1969); *Long v. IRS*, 349 F. Supp. 871, 875 (W. D. Wash. 1972); *Consumers Union of United States, Inc. v Veterans Administration*, 301 F. Supp. 796, 806–808 (S.D.N.Y. 1969), appeal dismissed as moot, 436 F.2d 1363 (2d Cir. 1971). Of the decisions asserting power to authorise non-disclosure notwithstanding the FOIA, only *Consumers Union* actually permitted the withholding of otherwise discoverable data.

42. K. Davis, *supra* note 38, §3A.6. For an able, more comprehensive analysis of this issue, reaching the same conclusion, see 'Note, The Freedom of Information Act: A Seven-Year Assessment', 74 *Columbia L. Rev.* 895, 912–18 (1974).

43. 94 S. Ct. 1028 (1974).

44. See, e.g., *Benson v. United States*, 309 F. Supp. 1144, 1145 (D. Neb. 1970).

45. See, e.g., *Soucie v. David*, 448 F.2d 1067, 1070–71 n. 6 (D.C. Cir. 1971).

46. See 1972 Hearings, *supra* note 31 at 16; Giannella, *supra* note 31, at 145–54.

47. See Giannella, *supra* note 30, at 169.

48. Veto of Freedom of Information Act Amendments, 10 Weekly Compilation of Presidential Documents 1318 (1974) [hereinafter cited as 'Veto Message'].

49. See Att'y Gen. Memo., *supra* note 11, at 2–3.

50. See *United States v. Nixon*, 94 S. Ct. 3090, 3105–11 (1974); *United States v. Reynolds*, 345 U.S. 1, 7–12 (1953); Dorsen and Shattuck, 'Executive Privilege: The President Won't Tell', in Dorsen & Gillers, *supra* note 1, at 27–60.

51. 410 U.S. 73 (1973).

52. 18 Fed. Reg. 7049 (1953).

53. 37 Fed. Reg. 5207 (1972), codified at 3 C.F.R. 375 (1974).

54. For a detailed account and critique of the classification system, *see* Phillips, 'The Government's Classification System', and Futterman, 'What is the Real Problem with the Classification System?', in Dorsen & Gillers, *supra* note 1, at 61–104.

55. 3 C.F.R. at 375.

56. See Letter from President Ford to Senator Edward M. Kennedy, 20 August 1974, reprinted in 120 Cong. Rec. S17828, 93d Cong., 2d Sess. (1974).

57. H.R. Rep. No. 93–1380, *supra* note 15, at 12.

58. See Veto Message, *supra* note 48.

59. S. Rep. No. 813, *supra* note 24, at 8.

60. H.R. Rep. No. 1497, 89th Cong., 2d Sess. 10 (1966).

61. See, e.g., *Hawkes v. Internal Revenue Service*, 467 F.2d 787 (6th Cir. 1972); *Consumers Union of the United States, Inc. v. Veterans Administration*, 301 F. Supp. 796 (S.D.N.Y. 1969), appeal dismissed, 436 F.2d 1363 (2d Cir. 1971); *Benson v. General Services Administration*, 289 F. Supp. 590 (W.D. Wash. 1968), aff'd 415 F.2d 878 (9th Cir. 1969). *Contra, City of Concord v. Ambrose*, 333 F. Supp. 958 (N.D. Calif. 1971).

62. 43 U.S.L.W. 2095 (D.C. Cir. 19 August 1974).

63. 446 F.2d 821, 824 (5th Cir. 1971), cert. denied, 405 U.S. 918 (1972).

64. Professor Davis, after examining a similar provision in The Securities Exchange Act, 15 U.S.C. §78X (1970), also concluded that such statutes conferring broad discretionary authority to withhold information should fall within the

protection of Exemption Three. See K. Davis, *supra* note 38, §3A.18, at 146.

65. See, *Sears, Roebuck & Co. v. General Services Administration*, 35 Ad. L. 2d 986, 991–95 (D.D.C. 10 Sept. 1974), aff'd, 35 Ad. L. 2d 1042, 1044–45 (D.C. Cir. 9 Dec. 1974); *Hughes Aircraft Co. v. Schlesinger*, 35 Ad. L. 2d 1000, 1003 (C.D. Calif. 30 Oct. 1974); *M. A. Schapiro & Co. v. Securities and Exchange Commission*, 339 F. Supp. 467, 469–70 (D.D.C. 1972); *Frankel* v. *Securities and Exchange Commission*, 336 F. Supp. 675, 678–79 (S.D.N.Y. 1971), rev'd on other grounds, 460 F.2d 813 (2d Cir.), cert. denied, 409 U.S. 889 (1972). The first reported case in which this question was broached is *Consumers Union of United States, Inc. v. Veterans Administration*, 301 F. Supp. 796, 801–02 (S.D.N.Y. 1969), appeal dismissed, 436 F.2d 1363 (2d Cir. 1971), but the court determined that the information at issue was not protected by section 1905 and, therefore, no further inquiry was necessary.

66. These decisions are compatible with cases where analogous authority was held to fulfil section 1905's proviso permitting disclosure if 'authorized by law'. Thus, for example, the courts have read this proviso to permit access pursuant to the Federal Rules of Civil Procedure. See *Pleasant Hill Bank v. United States*, 58 F.R.D. 97n.1 (W.D. Mc. 1973); *Exchange National Bank of Chicago v. Abramson*, 295 F. Supp. 87, 92 (D. Minn. 1969). Moreover, several opinions of the Attorney General have concluded that section 1905 does not prohibit disclosures made pursuant to express or implied duties under other laws. See, e.g., 39 Op. Att'y Gen. 1 (1937); 31 Op. Att'y Gen. (1919) (both dealing with predecessor statutes of section 1905). One of the tax privacy statutes discussed in the *Tax Analysts* case, 26 U.S.C. §7213 (a)(1) (1970), would be open to the same interpretation if it stood alone, since it merely penalises disclosures of income tax returns – 'except as provided by law'. However, that provision must be read in conjunction with the other statute, 26 U.S.C. § 6103 (a)(1) (1970), which specifically exempts tax returns from disclosure except as provided in that section or 'upon order of the President and under rules and regulations prescribed by the Secretary or his delegate and approved by the President.' This language plainly distinguishes the tax privacy statutes from the broad provisions of section 1905. Still, there is room for argument, and it is likely that the courts will see more litigation on this issue.

67. 360 F. Supp. 212, 213 (D.D.C. 1973).

68. See, e.g., *Consumers Union of United States, Inc. v. Veterans Administration*, 301 F. Supp. 796, 802 (S.D.N.Y. 1969), appeal dismissed, 436 F.2d 1363 (2d Cir. 1971); *Getman v. NLRB*, 450 F.2d 670, 673 (D. C. Cir. 1971). Earlier interpretations, however, did not always take this approach. See, e.g., *Benson v. GSA*, 289 F. Supp. 590, 594 (W.D. Wash. 1968), aff'd, 415 F.2d 878, 881 (9th Cir. 1969); *Barceloneta Shoe Corp. v. Compton*, 271 F. Supp. 591, 594 (D.P.R. 1967).

69. Cf. *Nichols v. United States*, 460 F.2d 671 (10th Cir.), cert. denied, 409 U.S. 966 (1972). In Nichols, the *plaintiff* sought access to records donated by the estate of John F. Kennedy to the United States Archives with the understanding that the papers would remain confidential during the lifetimes of members of the assassinated President's family. The non-disclosure of these records was upheld under Exemption Three because of certain statutes relating to the confidentiality of presidential documents. Apparently, the court would have ordered disclosure if non-presidential papers had been at issue, despite the promise of confidentiality.

70. *Sterling Drug, Inc. v. Federal Trade Commission*, 450 F.2d 698, 709 (D.C. Cir. 1971), quoting Sen. Rep. No. 813, *supra* note 224, at 9.

71. See, e.g., *Grumman Aircraft Engineering Corp. v. Renegotiation Board*, 425 F.2d 578, 581 (D.C. Cir. 1970).

72. See, e.g., id. at 582; *Consumers Union of United States v. Veterans Administration*, 301 F. Supp. 796, 802–03 (S.D.N.Y. 1969), appeal dismissed, 436 F.2d 1363 (2d Cir. 1971). For a critique of this judicial approach, *see* Note, *supra* note 42, at 952–53.

73. 43 U.S.L.W. 4491 (U.S. 29 April 1975).

74. 43 U.S.L.W. 4502 (U.S. 29 April 1975).

75. 411 F.2d 696 (D.C. Cir. 1969).

76. 43 U.S.L.W. at 4500.

77. See *Wu v. National Endowment for Humanities*, 460 F.2d 1030 (5th Cir. 1973), cert. denied, 410 U.S. 926 (1973).

78. See *Sterling Drug, Inc. v. Federal Trade Commission*, 450 F.2d 698, 705 (D.C. Cir. 1971).

79. See *Machin v. Zuckert*, 316 F.2d 336, 340 (D. C. Cir.), cert. denied, 375 U.S. 896 (1963). Sifting through memoranda to extract the factual from the deliberative components can be a burdensome and difficult task. In some instances the factual materials are 'inextricably intertwined with policy-making processes', rendering meaningful separation and disclosure of facts impossible. *Soucie v. David*, 448 F.2d 1067, 1078 (D.C. Cir. 1971).

80. See *Robles v. Environmental Protection Agency*, 484 F.2d 843, 845 (4th Cir. 1973).

81. 450 F.2d 670 (D.C. Cir. 1971).

82. 363 F. Supp. 231 (E.D. Pa. 1973).

83. For another decision supporting this balancing approach, see *Rose v. Department of the Air Force*, 495 F.2d 266 (2d Cir. 1974).

84. Pub. L. 93–579 (31 Dec. 1974). A comprehensive, six-volume congressional study of the uses and abuses of both manual and computerised data systems had been prepared by a Senate subcommittee to assist the congressmen in their consideration of the legislation leading to the Privacy Act. See *Federal Data Banks and Constitutional Rights: A Study of Data Systems on Individuals Maintained by Agencies of the United States Government*, Subcommittee on Constitutional Rights of the Senate Committee on the Judiciary, 93d Cong., 2d Sess. (1974). For a discussion of the computerisation of data banks, see Westin, 'The Technology of Secrecy', in Dorsen & Gillers, *supra* note 1, at 288–323; 'Comment, Public Access to Government-Held Computerized Information', 68 *Northwestern L. Rev.* 433 (1973).

85. Pub. L. 93–579, §3 (31 Dec. 1974), to be codified at 5 U.S.C. §552a(b)(2).

86. See, e.g., *Wellford v. Hardin*, 444 F.2d 21 (4th Cir. 1971).

87. See, e.g., *Frankel v. Securities and Exchange Commission*, 460 F.2d 813 (2d Cir.), cert denied, 409 U.S. 889 (1972).

88. See, e.g., *Bristol-Meyers Co. v. Federal Trade Commission*, 424 F.2d 935 (D.C. Cir.), cert denied, 400 U.S. 824 (1970).

89. See *Aspin v. Department of Defense*, 491 F.2d 24 (D.C. Cir. 1973).

90. See *Barcelona Shoe Corp. v. Compton*, 271 F. Supp. 591, 593 (D.P.R. 1967). For the general rules of discovery in criminal proceedings, see *Federal Rule of Criminal Procedure* 16. *See also* 18 U.S.C. §3500 (1970) for the Jencks Act provisions authorising prompt disclosure of exculpatory material held by the Government.

91. See H.R. Rep. No. 93–1380, *supra* note 15, at 12.

92. See Veto Message, *supra* note 48.

93. See *M.A. Schapiro & Co. v. Securities and Exchange Commission*, 339 F. Supp. 467, 470 (D.D.C. 1972). In support of this view, the court cited the Commission's own statutory definition of such institutions as including only a 'bank, trust company, investment banker, or banking association or firm . . .' See 15 U.S.C. §79q(c) (1970).

94. S. Rep. No. 813, *supra* note 24, at 10.

95. K. Davis, *supra* note 38, §3A.24, at 166.

96. H.R. Rep. No. 1497, *supra* note 60, at 9.

97. The report of the 1972 House subcommittee hearings did include letters revealing a dispute between Ralph Nader and the Federal Power Commission (FPC) over the scope of Exemption Nine. Mr Nader sought access to the FPC's reports on natural gas reserves in the United States, but the FPC successfully denied him access by arguing that its estimates of gas reserves were based on seismic data and geological maps. See 1972 Hearings, *supra* note 31, at 1970–74.

98. Nader, *supra* note 3, at 2.

99. Id. at 2–3.

100. See Giannella, *supra* note 31, at 121–27.

101. Id. at 123.

102. Id. at 124.

103. See H. R. Rep. No. 1497, *supra* note 60, at 11–12; *Soucie v. David*, 448 F.2d 1067, 1070–71 n. 6 (1971).

104. The FOIA suit in *Environmental Protection Agency v. Mink*, 410 U.S. 73 (1973), was brought by thirty-three members of Congress in both their private and official capacities; but the district court dismissed the suit in so far as plaintiffs' official capacities were concerned, and the issue was not reached on appeal. Id. at 75 n. 2.

105. 360 U.S. 109 (1959).

106. Id. at 111–12.

107. Dorsen & Gillers, *supra* note 1, at 49.

108. Id. at 29.

109. *See* cases and authorities cited in note 50 *supra*.

110. *Environmental Protection Agency v. Mink*, 410 U.S. 73, 86 (1973) (footnote omitted).

111. See *Pleasant Hill Bank v. United States*, 58 F.R.D. 97, 99–100 (W.D. Mo. 1973).

112. Compare *Hawkes v. IRS*, 467 F.2d 787, 792–93 and n. 6 (6th Cir. 1972), *with* Williams v. IRS, 345 F. Supp. 591, 594 (D. Del. 1972), aff'd *per curiam*, 479 F.2d 317 (3d Cir. 1973).

113. See *United States v. Nixon*, 94 S. Ct. 3090 (1974).

114. This writer has found only one reported case in which a journalist sought access under the FOIA to records withheld by the Government. The suit was successful. See *Stern v. Richardson*, 367 F. Supp. 1316 (D.D.C. 1973). Of course, to the extent that the FOIA has generated an atmosphere in which government employees respond more freely and openly to informal requests for information, and to the extent that its publication requirements have actually caused agencies to furnish information that otherwise would have remained buried in the files, the news media – along with the general public – have benefited from its enactment.

115. See generally Kohlmeier, '*The Freedom of Information Act and the Agencies: The Journalist's Viewpoint*', 23 *Administrative L. Rev.* 143 (1971).

116. Radio and television broadcasters, however, do not enjoy the same degree of constitutional protection, although the first amendment does afford them some safeguards. See *Columbia Broadcasting System, Inc. v. Democratic National Committee*, 93 S. Ct. 2080 (1973); *Red Lion Broadcasting Co. v. FCC*, 395 U.S. 367 (1969). The electronic media will not be treated in this discussion.

117. See *New York Times Co. v. United States*, 403 U.S. 713 (1971); *Near v. Minnesota*, 283 U.S. 697 (1931).

118. See *Craig v. Harney*, 331 U.S. 367 (1947).

119. See *New York Times Co. v. Sullivan*, 376 U.S. 254 (1964).

120. See *Miami Herald Pub. Co. v. Tornillo*, 94 S. Ct. 2831 (1974).

121. See *New York Times Co. v. United States*, 403 U.S. 713 (1971).

122. For a comprehensive treatment of these legal issues, see Edgar and Schmidt, 'The Espionage Statutes and Publication of Defense Information', 73 *Columbia L. Rev.* 929 (1973). See also Wise, 'Pressures on the Press', in Dorsen & Gillers, *supra* note 1, at 223–32.

123. 408 U.S. 665 (1972).

124. See statutes and Bills cited id. at 689 n.n. 27–28.

125. Address by Associate Justice Potter Stewart, Yale Law School Sesquicentennial Convocation, 2 November 1974. Excerpts from this address appear in the *Washington Post*, 11 November 1974, at A20, columns 3–5.

126. Pub. L. 92–463 (6 October 1972). See 5 U.S.C. Appendix I, p. 69 (1972 Supp. II).

127. Id. at $2(b) (5).

128. Id. $2(a).

129. S.5, 94th Cong., 1st Sess. (1975).

130. Id. at $2.

131. Public Law No. 94–409, 94th Cong., 2d Sess. (1976).

132. 422 U.S. 256 (1975).

133. *National Parks and Conservation Association v. Kleppe*, 547 F.2d 673, 686–87 (D.C. Cir. 1976).

134. See *Sears, Roebuck & Co. v. General Services Administration*, 553 F.2d 1378, 1383–85 (D.C. Cir. 1977).

135. 498 F.2d 765 (D.C. Cir. 1974).

136. See, e.g., *Westinghouse Electric Corporation v. Schlesinger*, 542 F.2d 1190 (4th Cir. 1976), cert. denied, U.S. (1977); *Charles River Park 'A', Inc. v. Department of Housing and Urban Development*, 519 F.2d 935 (D.C. Cir. 1975).

137. These provisions are codified at 5 U.S.C. $ 552b.

Index